# PHILOSOPHY

## A Christian Introduction

James K. Dew Jr.
and Paul M. Gould

Baker Academic
*a division of Baker Publishing Group*
Grand Rapids, Michigan

Published by Baker Academic
a division of Baker Publishing Group
PO Box 6287, Grand Rapids, MI 49516-6287
www.bakeracademic.com

Printed in the United States of America



Library of Congress Cataloging-in-Publication Data
Names: Dew, James K., Jr., author. | Gould, Paul M., 1971– author.
Title: Philosophy : a Christian introduction / James K. Dew and Paul M. Gould.
Description: Grand Rapids, MI: Baker Publishing Group, 2019. | Includes bibliographical references and index.
Identifiers: LCCN 2018036420 | ISBN 9780801097997 (pbk. : alk. paper)
Subjects: LCSH: Christian philosophy.
Classification: LCC BR100 .D4565 2019 | DDC 100—dc23
LC record available at https://lccn.loc.gov/2018036420

ISBN: 978-1-5409-6155-6 (casebound)



Baker Publishing Group publications use paper produced from sustainable forestry practices and post-consumer waste whenever possible.

# Contents

# Acknowledgments

The book you hold in your hands started with a simple vision to produce a clear, up-to-date, and comprehensive resource for Christians new to philosophy. Both of us teach or have taught in Christian settings (Jamie at Southeastern Baptist Theological Seminary and Paul formerly at Southwestern Baptist Theological Seminary) and have a particular burden to help Christians think clearly about the things of God and the deep things of life. Like most professors, however, over the years we've watched our students struggle with the concepts covered in our introductory philosophy courses. Some students give up and never return, while others plod along, eventually finding their philosophical legs. There are two things that are discouraging about those who give up. First, we believe that philosophy is simply too important to give up on. Philosophy continues to play a vital role in our lives and in contemporary discussions on almost everything. As such, we need more students, not fewer, to engage in these philosophical discussions. And, since we inevitably philosophize about the important things of life, we may as well learn how to do it well. Second, we're not convinced that philosophy needs to be so difficult. Sure, there are a lot of philosophical issues that are difficult, but there are also a lot of issues that aren't that difficult. We suspect that a focus on clarity from those who write, speak, and teach about philosophy, coupled with a bit of persistence and grit from students, will help students advance in their philosophical abilities. This book is our best effort toward clarity in writing about philosophy.

Like any project of this nature, producing the manuscript has had its ups and downs. Sometimes writing is easy, but most of the time it is painfully difficult. Without the help and encouragement of the people who surround us, such a project would never come to fruition. So, needless to say, we are deeply grateful to those who have pitched in to help us produce the manuscript for this book. First, we want to thank our friends and colleagues who read our chapters and provided valuable feedback. To Ross Inman, Robert Garcia, and Tyler McNabb, thank you for letting us bounce ideas off you and for the dialogue, which brought so much clarity to our work. To Wesley Davey and Ashlee Evans, thank you for reading and rereading each chapter. You've helped us tremendously, and we are grateful. To Alex Oakley, thank you for helping with research, formatting, and the bibliography. Second, we would like to thank our students for the years of dialogue, discussion, and questions that have sharpened us and prepared us to write this book. Without you, we certainly wouldn't have tackled such a project. Third, we want to thank our incredible editor, Dave Nelson, and the entire Baker family. Your encouragement, support, wisdom, and patience have been tremendous. Working with you all has been a truly fantastic experience. Finally, we would like to thank our families for their support. To our kiddos—Natalie, Nathan, Samantha, Samuel, Austin, Madeleine, Travis, and Joshua—thanks for keeping us grounded and for taking pleasure in our work. And to our incredible wives, Tara and Ethel, thank you for letting us do what we do and for the kindness and encouragement you offer each day. We surely wouldn't have finished this without you!

# 1

# Introduction to Philosophy

This is a book on philosophy. It is reasonable to ask, in this introductory chapter, about philosophy's aim and subject matter. What is philosophy? There are two historically prominent starting points for answering this question. Some say philosophy begins with human beings' awareness of their mortality.[1] Human life is fleeting and finite. We come into being and then, after a brief time, pass away. Death cannot be avoided. We will die, and so will those we love. This realization, it can be argued, is a fitting starting point for philosophy. Our awareness of our mortality prompts us to ask questions about life's meaning and to seek solace, if not salvation, from the perils of death. Philosophy, as Plato (427–347 BC) claims in the *Phaedo*, trains us for death.[2] How exactly does philosophy train us for death? For Plato, philosophy prepares the soul, on release from its body, to be united with that which it most deeply longs for: knowledge and wisdom. Thus philosophy can free us from the fear of death and help us to live well.

Another historically prominent starting point for philosophy, also found in Plato, begins not with humans' awareness of their mortality but with their wonder at the surrounding world. By nature, humans want to know truth about the world and their place in it. This sense of wonder, Plato states in the *Theaetetus*, "is where philosophy begins and nowhere else."[3] Our innate

1. See, e.g., Luc Ferry, *A Brief History of Thought: A Philosophical Guide to Living* (New York: HarperCollins, 2011), 2.

2. Plato, *Phaedo* 67e, in *Plato: Complete Works*, ed. John M. Cooper (Indianapolis: Hackett, 1997).

3. Plato, *Theaetetus* 155d, in *Works*, 173.

curiosity leads us to ask questions of ultimate significance: What is the nature of reality? What is knowledge, and how can I find it? What sort of person ought I be? Does God exist? If God exists, what is God like? "Philosophy," as the etymology of the word suggests (*philein*, "to love," and *sophia*, "wisdom") is the love of wisdom. Better, and more provocative, the philosopher is wisdom's lover. Philosophers are those who "refuse to accept what is false, [they] hate it, and have a love for the truth."[4]

Taking both of these historically prominent starting points into account, we shall understand philosophy as *the pursuit of knowledge and wisdom for the sake of flourishing*. This construal of philosophy views knowledge and wisdom as goods valuable in themselves *and* for what they bring.[5] Against the contemporary impulse to value knowledge and wisdom only if it has some obvious noncognitive benefit (e.g., for building a boat, pulling a tooth, accessing the internet, etc.), our view is that they are intrinsically valuable, worthy pursuits in themselves. Against the contemporary impulse to shallowness and a lack of concern for personal character, our construal of philosophy highlights the goal of flourishing, or well-being, which includes the cultivation of intellectual and moral virtue. Moreover, it allows for the pursuit of flourishing for the individual as well as for others, including nonhuman animals. Thus understood, we think philosophy is intensely practical, contrary to popular perception (more below).

## What Is Philosophy's Relationship to Christianity?

Philosophy, according to Plato, is "a gift from the gods to the mortal race whose value neither has been nor ever will be surpassed."[6] High praise indeed! For Plato, there is ultimately no conflict between philosophy and belief in God (or the gods). Philosophy leads the truth seeker, inevitably, to its divine source. Today the relationship between faith and philosophy, revelation and reason, is not always viewed in such a positive light (as we shall see in chap. 5). Contrary to Plato, the contemporary French philosopher Luc Ferry thinks philosophy is inherently atheistic. According to Ferry, the salvation that philosophy prompts us to seek "must proceed not from an Other—from some Being supposedly transcendent (meaning 'exterior to and superior

4. Plato, *Republic* 485c, in *Works*, 1108.

5. In the *Republic*, Plato discusses three kinds of goods: things good in themselves, things good for what they bring, and things both good in themselves and good for what they bring. Plato argues that justice is good in the third sense. We argue that knowledge and wisdom are also good in this third sense (357b–358a).

6. Plato, *Timaeus* 47b, in *Works*, 1250.

to' ourselves)—but well and truly from within. Philosophy wants us to get ourselves out of trouble by utilizing our own resources, by means of reason alone, with boldness and assurance."[7]

Philosophy, according to Ferry, leads to atheism for two reasons. First, the religious claim that we can overcome our mortality and be with our loved ones for eternity is too good to be true. Second, the goodness of God (expressed in this hope for eternity with loved ones) is hard to reconcile with the amount, distribution, and horrific nature of evil we find in this world.[8] Thus we must find salvation from "within" by the use of unaided reason.

In reply, eternity with loved ones is indeed desirable. Its desirability, by itself, does not render it false, however. The relevant questions, then, have to do with whether the claims of religion are true. These, as we've seen, are philosophical questions. If, as we shall argue in this book, (1) there are good reasons to think that God exists (chap. 12), (2) evil is compatible with God's existence (chap. 13), and (3) the religion that God founded provides a means of eternal life (for this possibility, see chap. 15), then philosophy does not, contrary to Ferry's claim, lead to atheism. We follow a more ancient path in this book, a path well trodden by those who think there is no inherent conflict between the deliverances of philosophy and the deliverances of religion.

To be more specific, we think Christianity is both true and desirable. In other words, God does exist, and the religion God founded is Christianity. Moreover, in the Bible we learn that in Jesus Christ "are hidden all treasures of wisdom and knowledge" (Col. 2:3 NIV). All the truths discovered, all the good in good things, and all the beauty in beautiful things find their source in Jesus Christ. The pursuit of goodness, truth, and beauty, if faithfully followed, leads to Christ.

What then is the relationship between philosophy and Christianity? We reject "conflict" models such as Ferry's, which hold the truths of philosophy as incompatible with the truths of Christianity. We also reject "compartmental" models such that the truths of philosophy and the truths of Christianity never intersect. Christianity, as a religion, makes knowledge claims that intersect with the deliverances of philosophy. We endorse a "convergence" model such that Christianity and philosophy work in concert, converging on the truth. In other words, faith and reason work together to provide truth about God, the world, and ourselves (see chaps. 3 and 5 for more). It is in this way that we walk the well-traveled path of those such as Plato, Aristotle, Augustine of Hippo,

7. Ferry, *A Brief History of Thought*, 10.
8. Ferry, *A Brief History of Thought*, 11.

Boethius, Anselm, Aquinas, Descartes, Leibniz, and others who think that philosophy and religion converge on the single supreme reality that is God.[9]

## What Are the Main Areas of Philosophy?

We have specified the aim of philosophy, but what is its subject matter? For most disciplines the subject matter is fairly obvious. For example, the biologist studies living organisms; the historian, ancient events; the psychologist, the contours of the human mind; the mathematician, numbers; and the lawyer, laws. What does the philosopher study? Arriving at an answer to this question is complicated by the fact that philosophy has a subject matter of its own but also serves as a foundation for other disciplines. As a **first-order discipline**,[10] philosophy studies the nature of belief, justification, knowledge, and truth (epistemology), the nature and structure of reality (metaphysics), the nature of God and religious belief (philosophy of religion), and the nature of the moral life, including human character and conduct (ethics). As a **second-order discipline**, philosophy studies the foundations of every area of human inquiry. So for each of the areas mentioned above—science, history, psychology, mathematics, law, and so on—there is a second-order philosophy of the area (i.e., philosophy of science, philosophy of history, philosophy of psychology, philosophy of mathematics, philosophy of law). As a second-order discipline, philosophy helps to clarify and justify the concepts, assumptions, and principles that govern the particular domain of knowledge in question.

This book is primarily concerned with philosophy as a first-order discipline. In addition to epistemology, metaphysics, and ethics, we've included one second-order discipline, the philosophy of religion, in the mix. Our reason for including this second-order discipline is twofold. First, since God, understood as the supreme reality, is its primary subject matter, philosophy of religion is synoptic in vision, pulling together truths discovered in metaphysics, epistemology, and ethics that might appear as disparate threads when shorn from a theistic foundation. Second, philosophy is concerned with ultimate questions about meaning, purpose, truth, goodness, beauty, justice, love, eternity, and more. These questions, for many, find answers within a religious framework. Thus it is only fitting to include a section that explores the rationality and justification for religion and religious belief.

9. For more on the relationship between Christianity and philosophy, see Paul M. Gould and Richard Brian Davis, eds., *Four Views on Christianity and Philosophy* (Grand Rapids: Zondervan, 2016).

10. Terms shown in bold are included in the glossary at the back of this book.

In this introduction to philosophy, our aim is to provide an opinionated survey of each subarea of investigation and then point the reader in the direction of a distinctly Christian approach, without necessarily arguing for our own particular view on the topic at hand. In this way we hope to arm the reader with the necessary conceptual framework from which to continue to develop more fine-grained positions on key philosophical topics.

## What Are Philosophy's Chief Activities?

How does one do philosophy? What are its chief activities? The philosopher is one who seeks justification for beliefs, clarity for concepts, and unity of worldview. Let's consider each of these activities in greater detail.

Beliefs matter. As J. P. Moreland puts it, beliefs "are the rails upon which our lives run."[11] Given their importance, it makes sense that we want our beliefs to match reality. We want true beliefs. A good indicator of true belief is *justification*: if our beliefs are justified, then we have reason to think they correspond to reality. The philosopher seeks justification for his beliefs by using logic and arguments.[12] Logic is the study of how we *ought* to think, including the principles of thought that govern the relationship among sentences. Three foundational laws of logic that govern thought are as follows:

1. The law of identity: "Whatever is, is."
2. The law of noncontradiction: "Nothing can both be and not be."
3. The law of excluded middle: "Everything must either be or not be."[13]

Given these laws of logic, if Clark Kent is identical to Superman, then they are one and the same person (according to the law of identity); it is necessarily false that Jesus is and is not divine (law of noncontradiction); and either humans are mortal or humans are not mortal (law of excluded middle).

Logical laws help us to evaluate sentences as well as the relationships among sentences. Of particular interest are **arguments**: sets of sentences consisting of premises that lead, by one or more rules of inference, to a conclusion. Arguments can take various forms. Two basic kinds of arguments are

11. J. P. Moreland, *Love Your God with All Your Mind*, 2nd ed. (Colorado Springs: NavPress, 2012), 86.

12. Things are not quite so simple, as we shall discuss in chaps. 2 and 3. Some beliefs are basic, justified in virtue of the relevant experience.

13. Bertrand Russell, *The Problems of Philosophy* (1912; repr., New York: Oxford University Press, 1997), 72.

**deductive arguments**, where the truth of the premises guarantees the truth of the conclusion (e.g., *modus ponens*, *modus tollens*, disjunctive syllogism, etc.), and **inductive arguments**, where the truth of the premises renders the conclusion probably true (e.g., the argument from analogy, inference to the best explanation, inductive inference).[14] By submitting beliefs to the laws of thought as well as arguments and counterarguments, the philosopher seeks to root out false beliefs and justify true ones.

Next, analyzing concepts to determine their meaning is essential to good philosophical reasoning. Consider the concept "chair." What does this concept mean? One way to answer our question is to provide a definition of "chair." To offer a definition of a concept *F* is to specify what *F* is, so a definition of "chair" would specify what a chair is. Easy enough, right? As students quickly find out, providing an adequate definition of things, even ordinary things such as chairs, is not easy. Let's try. A chair, as a first pass, is "something people sit on." To assess our definition, it is helpful to see if we can provide counterexamples of things that satisfy our definition but don't count (or obviously count) as chairs. Counterexamples to our first definition of "chair" are easy to come by: stumps and toilets are things people sit on, yet we don't usually think of them as chairs. We could refine our definition of chair to rule out stumps and toilets ("things people sit on that are designed and don't have plumbing attached to them"), but it might turn out, as it does in this case, that the resultant definition is still too broad (e.g., this definition doesn't rule out stools and couches). Some things, such as chairs, might be best defined ostensively, by pointing at them and saying, "That, and things like that, are chairs." In any case, in order to avoid talking past one another or committing fallacies of equivocation, it is important to define our terms and concepts. Conceptual analysis leads to deeper understanding and greater precision in our language.

Finally, the philosopher's task is to engage in a kind of system building in order to find unity in diversity. When we seek understanding, we begin, as Aristotle puts it, "from the things which are more knowable and clear to us and proceed towards those which are clearer and more knowable by nature."[15] We want to know the objects of everyday experiences as they really are, not how they appear. We come to know a thing once "we are acquainted with its primary causes or first principles, and have carried our analysis as far as its elements."[16] Seeking this deeper knowledge of the world takes effort. We

14. For an excellent introduction to logic, see T. Ryan Byerly, *Introducing Logic and Critical Thinking* (Grand Rapids: Baker Academic, 2017).

15. Aristotle, *Physics* 184a16–18, in *The Complete Works of Aristotle*, ed. Jonathan Barnes (Princeton: Princeton University Press, 1984), 1:315.

16. Aristotle, *Physics* 184a12–14, in *Works*, 1:315.

need a synoptic view of reality, a worldview, in which to unify the things of the world and our place in it. Many in the internet age substitute information for knowledge and wisdom. This is a mistake. Philosophic contemplation can free us, as Bertrand Russell describes, "[by enlarging] our interests as to include the whole outer world."[17] Russell continues:

> In contemplation . . . we start from the not-Self [i.e., the World], and through its greatness the boundaries of Self are enlarged; through the infinity of the universe the mind which contemplates it achieves some share in infinity. . . . The mind which has become accustomed to the freedom and impartiality of philosophic contemplation will preserve something of the same freedom and impartiality in the world of action and emotion. It will view its purposes and desires as parts of the whole. . . . In this [enlargement of soul] consists man's true freedom, and his liberation from the thraldom of narrow hopes and fears.[18]

Philosophy helps us to find a story that is alive and true. It pulls us out of ourselves and into a grander story. We think that philosophy's system-building task can point the seeker to Jesus and the gospel. If, as we think, Christianity is true, this is to be expected, for in the Gospel of John we learn that Jesus is the "Logos" (John 1:1–3). Wisdom thus is personal, or better, found most fully in a person: Jesus Christ. In this way too, philosophy is understood as the handmaiden to theology.

## What Is the Value of Philosophy for the Christian?

Philosophy suffers from an image problem.[19] In our technologically driven, anti-intellectual culture, it is widely perceived that philosophy offers no this-worldly good and is therefore a waste of time. This pragmatic "I'm interested in learning only if I can see the benefit" mentality has made its way into the classroom too. Often, as philosophers teaching in a Christian context, we

17. Russell, *Problems of Philosophy*, 158.

18. Russell, *Problems of Philosophy*, 159, 160, 161.

19. This section was originally published as Paul M. Gould, "Three Reasons Why I Teach Philosophy at a Seminary," *Theological Matters* (blog), November 8, 2016, https://theologicalmatters.com/2016/11/08/three-reasons-why-i-teach-philosophy-at-a-seminary/. The essay was later expanded and published (with the same title) in *Christian Research Journal* 40, no. 6 (2017): 58–59. Special thanks to Southwestern Baptist Theological Seminary and the editors of *Christian Research Journal* for permission to reproduce the essay here. The three reasons offered in this section are not original to me; rather, they are nicely set forth by two of my philosophical mentors from graduate school, J. P. Moreland and William Lane Craig. For an expanded discussion of these themes, see the first chapter of Moreland and Craig's monumental work, *Philosophical Foundations for a Christian Worldview*, 2nd ed. (Downers Grove, IL: IVP Academic, 2017).

spend the first few classes trying to convince students, many of whom are future pastors, of the importance of philosophy.

As already stated, we think that learning philosophy, the pursuit of wisdom and knowledge for the sake of flourishing, is an intrinsic good; it is something valuable in and of itself. But (tipping our hat to the pragmatist) it also has other benefits. What are some of the benefits of philosophy for the Christian? Here are three reasons—kingdom benefits—for helping Christians learn a little philosophy (these three reasons can be understood as some of the many fine-grained aspects to the "for the sake of flourishing" part of our definition of philosophy).

First, *philosophy is strategic for evangelism.* As Christians we are called to be faithful witnesses for Christ. We want every person on the face of the earth to ask and answer the question, "What do you make of Jesus Christ?" Unfortunately, in our day and age it can be difficult to get people to consider this question seriously. This is because Christianity is often viewed as implausible, undesirable, or both. Today it is difficult for the gospel message to receive a fair hearing. Philosophy can help! Philosophy helps us to understand the collective mind-set, value system, and emotional response patterns of culture. Christian philosophy can help to expose the false ideas that keep people from considering Christianity as a genuine option. Consider the words of the great Princeton theologian J. Gresham Machen:

> God usually exerts [his regenerative] power in connection with certain prior conditions of the human mind, and it should be ours to create, so far as we can, with the help of God, those favourable conditions for the reception of the gospel. False ideas are the greatest obstacles to the reception of the gospel. We may preach with all the fervor of a reformer and yet succeed only in winning a straggler here and there, if we permit the whole collective thought of the nation or of the world to be controlled by ideas which, by the resistless force of logic, prevent Christianity from being regarded as anything more than a harmless delusion.[20]

God has given us minds, and he wants us to use them to help others see the truth, goodness, and beauty of Jesus and the gospel. He wants us to use philosophy (and theology and more besides) to show that Christianity is both true to the way the world is and true to the way the world ought to be.

Second, *philosophy prepares us for ministry.* I (Paul) cannot tell you the number of times I've had students—usually a future pastor or even a PhD

20. J. Gresham Machen, *What Is Christianity?* (Grand Rapids: Eerdmans, 1951), 162, quoted in Moreland and Craig, *Philosophical Foundations*, 4.

student in theology or some aspect of Christian ministry—ask me why they should take logic. How would logic help them be better preachers or church leaders or students of the Bible? At first, when I was asked this question, I was dumbfounded. It seemed obvious to me that God wants us to be good thinkers, and logic is one of the tools that will help in that area. Now, when I'm asked to justify the necessity of taking logic, I simply invite them to "come and see." Thankfully, I've found these same students become the most ardent defenders of the use and benefit of logic for preaching, ministry, and Bible study.

Contrast this posture of skepticism toward the value of philosophy in general, and logic in particular, with the posture of the preachers and pastors of an earlier age. Here is John Wesley, who in 1756 delivered a talk to first-year seminary students titled "An Address to Clergy":

> Am I a tolerable master of the sciences? Have I gone through the very gate of them, logic? If not, I am not likely to go much farther when I stumble at the threshold. . . . Rather, have not my stupid indolence and laziness made me very ready to believe, what the little wits and pretty gentlemen affirm, "that logic is good for nothing"? It is good for this at least, . . . to make people talk less; by showing them both what is, and what is not, to the point; and how extremely hard to prove anything. Do I understand metaphysics; if not the depths of the Schoolmen, the subtleties of Scotus or Aquinas, yet the first rudiments, the general principles, of that useful science? Have I conquered so much of it, as to clear my apprehension and range my ideas under proper heads; so much as enable me to read with ease and pleasure, as well as profit, Dr. Henry Moore's *Works*, Malbranche's "Search after Truth," and Dr. Clarke's "Demonstration of the Being and Attributes of God"?[21]

Our passion is to see God raise up a generation of pastor-scholars who take seriously God's call to train the saints to "guard the good deposit [i.e., the gospel] entrusted to you" (2 Tim. 1:14 ESV).

Third, *philosophy plays a key role in our spiritual formation unto Christ.* Modern humans are hollow at the core. As a culture, we are largely what psychologists call empty selves: people who are passive, sensate, busy, hurried, and incapable of developing an interior life.[22] But Christians are commanded to "be transformed by the renewing of your mind" (Rom. 12:2 NIV) and to love God with all our mind (Matt. 22:37–39). Part of this process is seeing

21. John Wesley, "An Address to Clergy," delivered Feb. 6, 1756, reprinted in *The Works of John Wesley*, 3rd ed. (Grand Rapids: Baker, 1996), 6:217–31, quoted in Moreland and Craig, *Philosophical Foundations*, 6.

22. Philip Cushman, "Why the Self Is Empty," *American Psychologist* 45 (May 1990): 599–611.

Jesus for who he is: the fount of all wisdom and knowledge (Col. 2:3). Jesus is beautiful, and we rightly worship him as such. But Jesus also is *brilliant*, the smartest person ever. As Dallas Willard presses, "Can we seriously imagine that Jesus could be *Lord* if he were not smart?"[23] The obvious answer is no! As followers of Jesus, we too are to cultivate moral *and* intellectual virtue.

God has given each of us a mind. He wants us to use it for his glory. He wants us to live life rightly related to reality and to God, to one another, ourselves, and our purpose. Philosophy can help in all these areas.

## Conclusion

Have we convinced you of the value of philosophy? Do you see the benefit to learning philosophy as a Christian? If not, then we invite you to simply "come and see." Walk the path of reason, meet fellow travelers along the way, and follow the path to its source: Christ, the Eternal Son, the Logos, the perfectly rational Creator and Sustainer of all.

23. Dallas Willard, *The Divine Conspiracy* (New York: HarperCollins, 1998), 94.

PART 1

# EPISTEMOLOGY

Epistemology is the branch of philosophy that deals with philosophical questions about our knowledge. More specifically, epistemology deals with our knowing, believing, and attempts to be human beings who are rational about the things we claim to know. It is a branch of philosophy that you actually think about far more than you might realize. Most people might not be professional philosophers, but they do think of themselves as being rational beings (and employ philosophical methods in their attempts to do so), even if they don't realize this is what they are doing.

To see this, consider the kinds of philosophical questions we deal with in epistemology. We know all kinds of things. But what does it mean to "know" something as opposed to merely believe something? What, exactly, is the nature of knowledge? A quick example will illustrate the difference. Imagine that two people wake up the day after the last presidential election. One knows that Donald Trump won the electoral college vote, and the other merely believes it. How is it that one person knows it and the other merely believes it? Perhaps this is because the one who knows it stayed up until very late in the night to watch all the results come in and saw that Trump got the votes. The other became bored or frustrated, or perhaps fell fast asleep, never seeing the final results, yet did have a sense that Trump would win. As such, this person woke up the next morning with a belief that Trump was the new president-elect. So what's the difference between "knowing" and "believing"? Perhaps we could say that the one who knows has evidence, and the one who believes merely has a hunch. But then there are a series of follow-up questions. Do "hunches" count for nothing? How much evidence is needed? What counts as evidence? Is evidence always required? And what about times when we have lots of evidence for an idea that still turns out to be wrong? Such are the philosophical questions about knowledge itself.

There are plenty of other important epistemological questions. If, for example, we can identify what it means to "know" something, we might still wonder how we know those things. Do we know simply by way of rational reflection, as some suggest, or does knowledge require us to see, taste, touch, smell, or hear something? The possibilities represent the way two very different schools of thought have accounted for knowledge over the past few centuries. According to rationalists, for example, knowledge is primarily rooted in reason itself; on this view, we know those things we can demonstrate by rational argument. By contrast, empiricists have traditionally argued the opposite, that knowledge is primarily grounded in the different kinds of experiences that we have. On this view, roughly, we know something if it is evident to the senses. I know because I can see it or hear it, or because I have access to it by way of other sensory inputs.

In addition to these questions, and in response to the kinds of answers that philosophers give, there are also questions about whether our perceptions of the world (e.g., from sight, sound, or smell) properly reflect the world as it really is. So imagine that I have just brushed my teeth one morning and walk into the kitchen to eat breakfast with the family. I pick up the glass of milk that my wife poured for me and take a gulp. I cringe at the taste of the milk and declare to the family, "The milk has gone bad!" Of course, everyone at the table thinks I'm crazy because it tastes just fine to them. Here's an example where our perception has gotten reality wrong. In this case it's easy to say that this is not much of a worry since it is not an example of what normally happens. There is clearly some kind of polluting factor that caused the milk to taste funny (the lingering taste of toothpaste in my mouth). But then again, how do we know that this case is an exception to the rule and not what is happening all the time? How do we know that there aren't always some polluting factors that cause us to mis-see or mis-taste the world we live in? What if those pollutants just aren't evident to us? In response to these possibilities, however obscure and unrealistic they may seem, we are left with major philosophical questions about our perceptions.

Epistemology also deals with the related questions about truth itself. What does it mean to say that some statement or proposition is true? What is it that makes the statement true? Consider a proposition like "Vitamins are beneficial to our bodies." Leaving aside the medical debates about the value of vitamins, for the sake of argument let's grant that this is a true statement.

The question here is why. Why is it a true statement? What is it about the statement that makes it true? Is it true because it corresponds to the way the world really is? Is it true because it helps us in some way? Is it true because it is compatible with other things we think are true? Or is there some other thing that makes it true? Philosophers have debated questions like these for millennia, but especially for the past hundred years or so.

Another major set of philosophical questions that epistemology deals with are issues of certainty (or what we might call epistemic confidence) and skepticism. On the one hand, it seems plausible to doubt and question the vast majority of what we think we know. These doubts come from all directions and attack all sorts of beliefs that we hold. Not surprisingly, therefore, some philosophers in history have argued for epistemic skepticism, the idea that we really can't, or at least don't, have knowledge. Of course, they feel rather certain about this. But most other philosophers throughout history have rejected skepticism. The questions most philosophers ask have to do with the way we know things and the extent to which we can have epistemic confidence about truth and truth claims.

One final set of epistemological questions worth mentioning, though there are plenty of other issues we could mention, deals with questions about science and God. Because they have had extraordinary successes over the past few centuries, do the natural sciences hold a special privileged epistemic status? In other words, are the sciences able to establish a greater degree of epistemic confidence for what they say than theology, history, or some other discipline within the social sciences? Is a statement true simply because a scientist says so? Or, despite the sciences' extraordinary successes over the past few years, are there limitations to what the sciences can say to us and limits to their epistemic authority? On the flip side of that, how about religious knowledge? Is it possible to know things about God, or is theology lowered to the level of mere belief? If it is possible to know something about God, how are we supposed to get that knowledge? Does the Bible (or some other holy book) count as a proper source of knowledge? And what about nature itself? Can we derive any theological truth from the natural realm? These are all vitally important questions in the field known as religious epistemology.

Such are the questions that epistemology deals with. In this section, we explore some of these questions and offer a quick survey of historical and contemporary discussion on these matters. We trust that you will find them helpful as we explore an extremely important field of philosophy.

# 2

# Truth and Knowledge

Philosophy deals with questions about reality, human nature, morality, religious matters, and knowledge, to name just a few examples. **Epistemology**, the subject matter of this section, is the branch of philosophy that deals with the philosophical questions about knowledge. Epistemology is concerned with questions about how we know, what the criteria for knowledge are, whether our perceptions of the world line up with the world outside our minds, and the proper way to formulate theories. Over the course of this discussion we will not deal with every epistemological question. But we will deal with most of the important issues within this field of philosophy. For example, we consider the relationship between faith and reason, faith and modern science, skepticism, intellectual virtues, the possibility of gaining knowledge of God through nature (natural revelation and natural theology), and questions about truth, knowledge, and justification.

In this particular chapter we deal with philosophical questions about truth, knowledge, and justification. To be more specific, we will explore different theories about the nature of truth. What does it mean to say that some statement is true? To answer this question, we will consider three different theories of truth. After this, we will consider the nature of knowledge and whether we have an adequate set of criteria to determine when a person has it. As we will see, this amounts to answering the question of what exactly "knowing" is.

## What Is Truth?

Discussions about truth arise within any number of disciplines. Scientists, for example, make claims about the world and develop theories that they hold to be true. Likewise, theologians set forth ideas and make truth claims. The same could be said for historians, psychologists, medical doctors, lawyers—just about everybody, for that matter. In short, we all make truth claims about the world around us. But what makes a statement true instead of false? How are we to adjudicate between truth and falsehood? In this section, we explore three major attempts to answer this question: correspondence theory, pragmatic theory, and coherence theory.

### *Correspondence Theory of Truth*

Historically speaking, philosophers have generally affirmed what we now call the **correspondence theory of truth**. That is, they agreed, at least until recent history, that true propositions are those that correspond to reality. For example, on this account of truth, the proposition "The United States is in North America" is true because it is a matter of geographical fact that the United States is indeed in North America. As a matter of geographical fact, this statement corresponds to the way things really are in our world. If the world turned out to be different than this, then such a statement would be false. But since the world is the way that the statement says it is, the statement is true. Plato, the ancient Greek philosopher, put it this way: "A false belief will be a matter of believing things that are contrary to those which are."[1] Or as Aristotle put it, "To say of what is that it is not, or of what is not that it is, is false, while to say of what is that it is, and what is not that it is not, is true; so that he says of anything that it is, or that it is not, will say either what is true or what is false; but neither what is nor what is not is said to be or not to be."[2] Because of its straightforward and simple account of truth, the correspondence theory of truth was held by the overwhelming majority of philosophers from Plato until the end of the modern era and the beginning of postmodernity. But according to many postmodern thinkers, the correspondence theory of truth naively assumes a superhuman ability to be perfectly objective in our perceptions of reality. Postmodern thinkers staunchly reject this possibility, arguing instead that we are creatures situated within cultures

1. Plato, *Sophist* 240d, in *Plato: Complete Works*, ed. John M. Cooper (Indianapolis: Hackett, 1997), 261.

2. Aristotle, *Metaphysics* 1011b.25, in *The Complete Works of Aristotle*, ed. Jonathan Barnes (Princeton: Princeton University Press, 1984), 2:1597.

and contexts that inevitably influence the way we see the world. Because of this, we have no basis for thinking that our ideas "match up" with the way the world really is. And as a consequence, "truth," for postmodern thinkers, simply cannot be a matter of correspondence.

### *Pragmatic Theory of Truth*

But if postmodern thinkers reject the correspondence theory of truth, what do they put in its place? Generally speaking, postmodern philosophers go in one of two possible directions. First, postmodern thinkers sometimes embrace a **pragmatic theory of truth**. Pragmatists reject correspondence theory and any sense of absolute truth shared by all people in all places. On pragmatic theory, a proposition or idea is true, in a lesser sense, if the proposition or idea works for us in some way. As Stewart Kelly puts it, "The ballpark idea is that truth is to be construed instrumentally, such that true beliefs always prove useful or expedient to those who believe them."[3] According to William James, often thought to be the central figure in pragmatic theory and a source of influence for later postmodern thinkers, "The true is the name of whatever proves itself to be good in the way of belief, and good, too, for definite assignable reasons."[4] James's rationale for grounding truth in utility is not arbitrary or without cause. After all, one feature of truth is that it does tend to be helpful in navigating the world. In this sense, truth is fruitful and productive for us. Because of this, we could rightly think of pragmatism as a legitimate test for truth claims. In other words, one thing we might expect of true propositions is that they are useful.

Nevertheless, despite whatever usefulness pragmatic concerns might have for us in testing truth claims, pragmatism seems to be lacking as a way to define truth, since it is always possible that an idea can be helpful in some way without also being true. Paul Horwich puts it this way: "True beliefs tend to foster success. But it happens regularly that actions based on true beliefs lead to disaster, while false assumptions, by pure chance, produce beneficial results."[5] Consider habits, such as the way children might close their eyes in a scary situation, believing that if they cannot see the bad guys, then the bad guys cannot see them. Such a belief may indeed help the child to cope with the situation, but nonetheless the belief is false. Furthermore, as Kelly points

3. Stewart Kelly, *Truth Considered and Applied: Examining Postmodernism, History, and Christian Faith* (Nashville: B&H, 2011), 281–82.

4. William James, *Pragmatism* (1907; Amherst, NY: Prometheus Books, 1991), 36.

5. Paul Horwich, "Theories of Truth," in *A Companion to Metaphysics*, ed. Jaegwon Kim and Ernest Sosa (Oxford: Blackwell Reference, 1995), 493.

out, pragmatism leads to relativism and logical absurdities, as each person's "truths" are shaped by different social and personal factors. "What is useful varies significantly from person to person. What is considered useful depends in part both on one's personality and on their outlook on life."[6] But if that is the case, absurdity seems to follow. "A wildlife biologist going to Antarctica believes it is true that various penguins inhabit the area. . . . But the average person could care less about the funny-looking birds that waddle thousands of miles away. Its usefulness to them is minimal at best."[7] And because of this, it "is true for the wildlife biologist but not for the average person" that "(P) Penguins live in Antarctica."[8]

### *Coherence Theory of Truth*

Another way that postmodern thinkers have defined truth is in terms of coherence. On the **coherence theory of truth**, a statement is considered to be true if it is consistent with other ideas or beliefs held within a system of beliefs. As Douglas Groothuis describes it, "Coherence theories of truth argue that what makes a statement or belief true is its coherence or consistency with one's other beliefs. If my 'web of belief' is large and internally consistent—that is, if none of my beliefs contradict each other—my beliefs are true. A belief is false if it fails to cohere with the rest of my beliefs. In other words, truth is simply defined as logical coherence."[9] As an example, consider the way postliberal theologians emphasize the internal consistency of Christian beliefs as a way to defend such beliefs. According to Alister McGrath, theologians like George Lindbeck de-emphasized "the intellectual content of a doctrinal statement in order to stress its formal function. It is not what a doctrine appears to say that matters, but its place and function within the overall fabric of the Christian faith."[10] In other words, in Lindbeck's approach to doctrine, what matters is not so much whether a doctrine reflects the way the world really is. Rather, what is most important is whether the doctrine is internally consistent with other doctrines held by Christian theism.

As with pragmatism, coherence theory can be helpful in testing truth claims. As minimal features of truth, logical consistency and internal coherence are necessary conditions. When we find conflicting or contradictory ideas

6. Stewart Kelly and James K. Dew Jr., *Understanding Postmodernism: A Christian Perspective* (Downers Grove, IL: IVP Academic, 2017), 210.

7. Kelly and Dew, *Understanding Postmodernism*, 210.

8. Kelly and Dew, *Understanding Postmodernism*, 210.

9. Douglas Groothuis, "Truth Defined and Defended," in *Reclaiming the Center*, ed. Millard J. Erickson, Paul Kjoss Helseth, and Justin Taylor (Wheaton: Crossway, 2004), 73.

10. Alister E. McGrath, *The Science of God* (Grand Rapids: Eerdmans, 2004), 102.

present within a belief system, we are rightly inclined to conclude that either (1) one of the beliefs is false, (2) several of the beliefs are false, or (3) the whole system of beliefs is false. But, given the law of noncontradiction, we cannot say that two mutually exclusive beliefs are true. As such, we might think of internal coherence as a necessary condition for truth—a minimal condition that must be met for a proposition to be true. If so, the test of coherence will always be important for us in assessing claims. But here again, despite whatever usefulness coherence theory may have in testing truth claims, it too is an insufficient way of defining just what truth actually is. Put another way, while coherence is a necessary condition for truth, it is not a sufficient condition. Coherence is a condition that must be met for something to be true, but this condition is not sufficient by itself to guarantee that a given belief is true. McGrath is again helpful in showing us why this is the case: "The coherentist position, taken on its own, is perfectly capable of validating an internally consistent world-view which makes no significant point of contact with the real world, or which evades such contact altogether. Coherency does not guarantee truth—merely logical consistency. A belief can be consistent with all other beliefs within a system, and yet have no independent supporting evidence."[11] McGrath's observation is important for us to note. It is entirely possible for a belief system to be internally consistent and free from self-contradiction, while also being completely fictitious. As such, coherence is an important test for truth claims, but an insufficient definition of truth itself.

### *Back to Correspondence Theory*

Despite the concerns that postmodern philosophers have raised about correspondence theory, it is far more resilient than its critics give it credit for and continues to be the most widely held account of truth by philosophers, scientists, and others. We offer two reasons for this. First, while both pragmatism and coherence theories are helpful tests for truth, neither provides an adequate understanding of the nature of truth. Second, and even more important, all of our thinking, planning, theorizing, and cognition about the world seem to require the correspondence account of truth. John Searle contends that this "view" is one of several default positions about knowledge and reality that we simply must take as a starting point for our thinking: "In our ordinary everyday lives, these views are so much taken for granted that I think it is misleading to describe them as 'views'—or hypotheses or opinions—at all."[12] David K. Clark seems to agree: "Since virtually all people,

11. Alister E. McGrath, *A Scientific Theology* (Grand Rapids: Eerdmans, 2002), 2:19.
12. John Searle, *Mind, Language, and Society* (New York: Basic Books, 1998), 10.

including those who have never studied epistemology, typically assume something like this notion of truth, it is a *pretheoretic* intuition regarding truth. . . . This is *pretheoretic* in that it is not an idea that *results from* complex theory building about the nature of truth but a belief that people *bring* to their theorizing about truth. It is a basic assumption, rooted in experience. It is something people philosophize *with*, not something they philosophize *to*."[13] Third, there are also theological reasons to embrace the correspondence theory of truth. Groothuis states that this account is especially important for grounding the claims of Christianity: "The correspondence view of truth is not simply one of many options for Christians. It is the only biblically and logically grounded view of truth available and allowable. We neglect or deny it to our peril and disgrace. Truth decay will not be dispelled without it."[14] To underscore Groothuis's point, imagine trying to square the apostle Paul's claim in 1 Corinthians 15:3–4 "that Christ died for our sins according to the Scriptures, and that He was buried, and that He rose again the third day according to the Scriptures" (NKJV). What did Paul mean by this? If the pragmatic theory of truth is correct, then perhaps Paul simply meant to say that the idea of Jesus crucified, buried, and raised is a useful concept for us. Or, if coherence theory is correct, then perhaps he simply meant to say that the idea of Jesus crucified, buried, and raised is consistent with other things that we believe. But surely neither of these is what Paul intends to say to us. Rather, what Paul means to say here is that, in fact, Jesus was crucified, he was buried, and he was raised from the dead on the third day. He wants us to know that this is what really happened and that this claim expresses real facts about the world. In short, such claims require a correspondence theory of truth. For reasons such as these, philosophers and theologians should continue to hold to a correspondence theory of truth, even if they allow for pragmatism and coherence as tests for truth.

## What Is Knowledge?

Now that we have considered the various ways of thinking about truth, we turn to the issue of knowledge. As human beings, we know a lot of things. We know people and have relationships with them. This kind of knowledge is typically referred to as relational and is not usually the sort of knowledge we are concerned with in epistemology. We also have knowledge about how

13. David K. Clark, *To Know and Love God* (Wheaton: Crossway, 2003), 354 (emphasis in original).

14. Groothuis, "Truth Defined and Defended," 110.

to do things like tie our shoes, bake cakes, or throw a football. This kind of knowledge is sometimes called ability knowledge, but again, this is not generally what we focus on in epistemological discussions. The kind of knowledge we are concerned about in epistemology is called propositional knowledge. **Propositions** are about things, states of affairs, places, or people. Consider some examples of propositions that we know. We know that (A) Barack Obama was the forty-fourth president of the United States of America, (B) the United States declared its independence on July 4, 1776, (C) Elvis Presley was a musician, (D) red and green are the colors of Christmas, and (E) Raleigh is the capital city of North Carolina. That we know such things is rather clear and uncontroversial. But *how* we know these things is less clear and much debated, at least for philosophers. Notice that we do not merely *believe* these things: we *know* them. In this case, knowing is a stronger kind of cognitive activity than simply believing. But if so, what does "knowing" have that "believing" lacks?

### *Justified, True, Belief*

Another way to ask this question is to ask what the criteria for knowledge are. In other words, what criteria must be met in order to actually know propositions (A–E) above as opposed to merely believing them? Traditionally speaking, philosophers have tended to offer three criteria for knowledge: justification, truth, and belief. Or we might simply say:

Knowledge = Justified, True, Belief (JTB)

On the JTB theory of knowledge, we know some proposition like (A)—Barack Obama was the forty-fourth president of the United States of America—when (1) we believe (A); (2) we have some kind of evidential or rational justification for believing (A); and (3) as it turns out, (A) is a fact of history.

Consider the way this account evolves from belief to knowledge. We begin with some ideas that we believe. Yet, as we have already noted, belief is a weaker epistemic cognition than knowledge. That is because we believe all sorts of things that turn out to be false. To get from believing to knowing, something more is required. To belief we might add the truth condition. That is, perhaps we simply need it to be the case that what we believe is actually true. For example, imagine a person named Bruce buys a lottery ticket and believes that his is the winning ticket. Further imagine that, as he will later find out when the lottery numbers are published, by pure coincidence and dumb luck, Bruce's belief that his ticket is the winning ticket is true. In this case, Bruce has a "true belief." Given that Bruce's belief is actually true, we might be tempted to think that this is enough of a basis to claim that Bruce "knows" he has a winning ticket. But we shouldn't be so quick to settle for "true belief" as a proper basis for knowing. After all, even though Bruce is right in believing that he will win the lottery, he still does not "know" that this is true. Since he does not actually have justification for believing that he will win, he really has no good reason for thinking that he is right. His belief is just lucky. Describing this kind of situation, Bertrand Russell declares, "Such instances can be multiplied indefinitely, and show that you cannot claim to have known merely because you turned out to be right."[15]

In his work *Meno*, Plato describes the key distinction between knowledge and true belief, or what he calls "true opinion." He says, "For true opinions, as long as they remain, are a fine thing and all they do is good, but they are not willing to remain long, and they escape from man's mind, so that they are not worth much until one ties them down by giving an account of the reason why. . . . After they are tied down, in the first place they become knowledge, and then they remain in place."[16] As Plato notes, "true opinions" are the kinds of ideas that do not remain long, because we hold them without rational support. But once "one ties them down by giving an account of the reason" for holding them, thus providing justification for them, we are then in a position of "knowing." In other words, by meeting all three criteria—justification, truth, and belief—we are said to have knowledge.

### *The Gettier Problem*

For the most part, JTB has been, and continues to be, the most common way to think about knowledge itself, though contemporary advocates offer various tweaks and revisions of this account. Such revisions and tweaks were prompted by a three-page article by a relatively unknown philosopher named Edmund Gettier; the article was published in 1963 and is now widely regarded as the greatest challenge to JTB. In short, Gettier offers two different scenarios where the criteria of JTB can be satisfied, but where we are still not confident that we have knowledge. In particular, his scenarios are designed to show problems with the justification criterion of JTB:

> Suppose that Smith and Jones have applied for a certain job. And suppose that Smith has strong evidence for the following conjunctive proposition:

15. Bertrand Russell, *Human Knowledge: Its Scope and Limits* (New York: Routledge, 2009), 140.

16. Plato, *Meno* 98a, in *Plato: Complete Works*, 896.

> (d) Jones is the man who will get the job, and Jones has ten coins in his pocket.
>
> Smith's evidence for (d) might be that the president of the company assured him that Jones would in the end be selected, and that he, Smith, had counted the coins in Jones's pocket ten minutes ago. Proposition (d) entails:
>
> (e) The man who will get the job has ten coins in his pocket.
>
> Let us suppose that Smith sees the entailment from (d) to (e), and accepts (e) on the grounds of (d), for which he has strong evidence. In this case, Smith is clearly justified in believing that (e) is true.
>
> But imagine, further, that unknown to Smith, he himself, not Jones, will get the job. And, also, unknown to Smith, he himself has ten coins in his pocket. Proposition (e) is then true, though proposition (d), from which Smith inferred (e), is false. In our example, then, all of the following are true: (i) (e) is true, (ii) Smith believes that (e) is true, and (iii) Smith is justified in believing that (e) is true. But it is equally clear that Smith does not *know* that (e) is true; for (e) is true in virtue of the number of coins in Smith's pocket, while Smith does not know how many coins are in Smith's pocket, and bases his belief in (e) on a count of coins in Jones's pocket, who he falsely believes to be the man who will get the job.[17]

What Gettier shows here is that there are some cases where our beliefs about certain things that turn out to be true also have a justification, but it is a justification that is based on a piece of false information or improper inference. Put more simply, there are times when we have justification for a true belief, but the justification is questionable.

There are other ways of illustrating this problem. As Russell (1948) noted prior to Gettier (1963), we might imagine being asked what time it is, looking at the stopped clock on the wall to see that it says 2:10 p.m., and answering back that it is 2:10 p.m. We can further imagine that at the moment we are asked about the time, it really is exactly 2:10 p.m.[18] If such were the case, we

17. Edmund L. Gettier, "Is Justified True Belief [the Same as] Knowledge?" *Analysis* 23, no. 6 (June 1963): 122.

18. This illustration is owed to Russell, who interestingly offered it in 1949 prior to Gettier's treatment. He said, "There is the man who looks at a clock which is not going, though he thinks it is, and who happens to look at it at the moment when it is right; this man acquires a true belief as to the time of day, but cannot be said to have knowledge." See Russell, *Human Knowledge*, 140. In fairness to Gettier, however, Russell offers this illustration not as a way to articulate the exact objection that Gettier sets forth. Rather, Russell offers this as a way to illustrate the inadequacy of "true belief" as a complete account of knowledge.

have satisfied JTB, but should not feel confident that we "know" it is 2:10 p.m., since our justification for saying so is complete luck or coincidence. Numerous other illustrations could be offered. The important thing to see in them is that in such cases, JTB has been satisfied, but despite this, we should not be confident that we have knowledge. As a result, JTB cannot be a sufficient condition for knowledge.

### *Responses to Gettier*

If Gettier showed that JTB has a serious problem, how might an advocate of JTB respond? As Noah Lemos has noted, one way the JTB advocate could respond is by adopting an additional criterion we might call the No False Grounds criterion. According to such an approach, the major problem that Gettier surfaces for JTB is that the justification in such cases is based on questionable or problematic premises. This proposed solution suggests that we address this problem by adding something to address the weak premises. That is, perhaps we could now just say something like "no false propositions can be a part of the justification." If so, then by adding the additional criterion to the JTB definition of knowledge, our new definition of knowledge would be something like this:

> *S* knows that *p* = Df. (1) *S* believes that *p* [is true], (2) *p* is true, (3) *p* is epistemically justified for *S*, and (4) *S*'s grounds for believing that *p* [is true] do not include any false propositions.[19]

But as Lemos points out, there are problems with this approach. Among other problems with this revision, he notes that this approach may be so strong that it rules out some things we clearly know. What if, for example, we form a belief about who won the football game on the basis of fifteen reports from friends who watched the game, and that only one of those friends lied about watching the game? In this case, we form a belief that the Patriots beat the Falcons on the basis of their collective fifteen testimonies. In this scenario, we are able to satisfy JTB, but we cannot satisfy the new criterion of No False Grounds, as one of the fifteen is a lie. Despite the lie of the one friend, it seems like we are still right in thinking that we know the Patriots won the game in light of the fourteen other true reports.[20]

Another popular response is to add what we might call a defeasibility condition to JTB. On this approach, we must require that there is justification of

19. Noah Lemos, *An Introduction to the Theory of Knowledge* (New York: Cambridge University Press, 2007), 28.

20. Lemos, *Theory of Knowledge*, 28.

the belief in question and that there be no defeating evidence for that belief. With this in mind, Keith Lehrer and Thomas Paxson offer the following formulation of knowledge:

> *S* has nonbasic knowledge that *h* if and only if (i) *h* is true, (ii) *S* believes that *h*, and (iii) there is some statement *p* that completely justifies *S* in believing that *h* and no other statement defeats this justification.[21]

So then, as long as there are no claims of evidence that defeat the belief in question, we are within our epistemic rights to think that we actually have knowledge. But once again, there is a problem with this solution. How are we to know if there is no defeating evidence? It may certainly be the case *that we may not know* of any defeating evidence for our knowledge claims, but it does not follow from that *that there is no* defeating evidence. Since our knowledge of the world is forever partial and extremely limited, it is entirely possible that we simply don't know about the evidence that defeats our knowledge claim.

There are other ways epistemologists have tried to salvage JTB, but questions linger about each attempt, and philosophers generally disagree about the best way to resolve the Gettier problem. For now, we might simply note that while Gettier shows the inadequacies of JTB as a full account of knowledge, it is not the case that JTB is useless for us. JTB may not be a sufficient condition for knowledge, but it does seem to be a necessary condition.

## Conclusion

In this chapter we have offered a brief overview of the major discussions surrounding the questions of truth, knowledge, and justification. Truth, we argued, has been variously understood, yet the correspondence theory of truth continues to be the most viable option for us moving forward. It seems to capture our basic intuitions concerning the way we think about truth claims, and it allows us to make sense of the world around us. Knowledge has traditionally been thought of as justified true belief (JTB), but JTB has challenges of its own. The Gettier problem seems to suggest that JTB might not be a sufficient condition for truth after all, and philosophers are still divided over the best way to move forward. In the next chapter, we will zero in on one specific criterion in the JTB formulation—namely, justification.

21. Keith Lehrer and Thomas Paxson Jr., "Knowledge: Undefeated Justified True Belief," in *Journal of Philosophy* 66, no. 8 (1969): 227.

# 3

# Justification and Reformed Epistemology

In the last chapter we explored the issues of truth and knowledge to see just what they are. There we discovered that knowledge has traditionally been defined as justified, true, belief, or JTB for short. One of the major criteria for knowledge, according to JTB, is the criterion of justification. It is justification, according to many epistemologists, that differentiates knowledge from mere true belief or opinion. But as we will see below, justification is a hotly disputed and debated question in modern epistemology: What is it? How does it work? Do we need to have it? All these are important discussions and call for attention.

In this chapter we will focus on justification and some variations of that concept. We will discuss and distinguish between internalism and externalism and provide some examples of each. After this, we will turn to the view known as Reformed epistemology in general and Alvin Plantinga's proper functionalist A/C models in particular. We will begin with the question of justification.

## What Is Justification?

Consider two true beliefs that a particular person named Benjamin may hold. Belief 1 is that it will rain next Thursday, and belief 2 is that he will meet his student Kevin next Thursday. Both of these beliefs are about events next Thursday, but more important, both of these beliefs are true beliefs. That is, as it turns out, it does rain next Thursday, and he does meet his student Kevin. But there is a sharp difference between Benjamin's two beliefs. While both of those beliefs are true, one of them is a "justified" belief and the other is not: the latter is simply a true belief. His second belief, that he will meet his student Kevin next Thursday, is a justified belief since it is based on the details found in Benjamin's calendar of future meetings. Because of this, we would typically think that Benjamin is rational in holding such a belief. But what about his belief that it will rain next Thursday? Even though this too turns out to be a true belief, it is nevertheless irrational since it is not based on anything other than a lucky guess. As we will see below, epistemologists are divided over whether this is the right way to think about justification. In fact, offering an exact definition of justification is quite difficult.[1] For now, let us just say that, roughly speaking, **justification** is about being rational in holding the beliefs that we hold. If we are rational about our beliefs, then perhaps we are more likely to be right about them.

So what does it mean to be "rational" about our beliefs? As simple as this question may be, there are at least two major schools of thought on how to answer it. Perhaps the most common school of thought since the Enlightenment is known as **internalism**. Generally speaking, internalists argue that what justifies a person in holding a particular belief depends on what is "internal" to their own mind. As Lemos puts it, "Let us take internalism, then, to hold that the epistemic justification of a subject's belief depends solely on factors internal to the subject's perspective, factors directly accessible to him through reflection."[2] But what does this mean? Dan O'Brien further elaborates: "For internalists, the justification for a thinker's beliefs must be cognitively accessible to her. She must be able to reflect upon what it is that suggests her beliefs are true."[3] In other words, according to internalists, a person is justified in holding a certain belief if she knows (has internal access to) the reasons or evidence supporting that belief and is able to offer such evidence and reasons as support for the belief in question.

By contrast, **externalism**, the second major school of thought regarding justification, rejects the internalist requirement that we must have internal access to the supporting reasons for our beliefs in order to be justified. Externalists contend, instead, that what justifies a belief for a person is something external

1. Duncan Pritchard, *What Is This Thing Called Knowledge?*, 2nd ed. (New York: Routledge, 2010), 31.

2. Noah Lemos, *An Introduction to the Theory of Knowledge* (New York: Cambridge University Press, 2007), 109.

3. Dan O'Brien, *An Introduction to the Theory of Knowledge* (Malden, MA: Polity Press, 2016), 87.

to their own perspective. Lemos is again helpful: "Externalists, however, deny that justification depends solely upon what is internal to the subject's perspective. Externalists hold that whether a belief is justified might also depend on whether it came about in the right way, through good intellectual procedure or on the basis of an intellectual virtue."[4] So, in other words, what matters for externalism is not what the person has internal access to but rather something external: the process by which, and the environment in which, the belief was formed. If a person is in the right circumstances for forming a belief about something, and if the belief came about by a reliable process, then the belief in question is justified. Internalism and externalism come in a variety of forms. In what follows, we outline two different forms of each while also noting some of the challenges that each approach faces.

### *Internalism: Classical Foundationalism and Coherentism*

One very popular—perhaps the most popular—way of construing an internalist approach to justification is called **classical foundationalism** (CF). Roughly, CF maintains that there are two general kinds of beliefs: basic and nonbasic. A nonbasic belief is one that is supported by, or justified by, some other belief. As such, we aren't rational in holding nonbasic beliefs unless we have some justification in holding them. A basic belief, however, is one that needs no further beliefs beneath it to justify it. It is a belief we just hold to be true yet that cannot, nor need not, be supported by argumentation. One might wonder just what kind of beliefs could qualify as basic. Classical foundationalists often offer beliefs that are either (1) self-evident or (2) incorrigible as examples of basic beliefs. A self-evident belief might be something like "2 + 2 = 4," "a bachelor is an unmarried male," or "I exist." An incorrigible belief would be one that cannot be defeated by anyone else because it can be held only by the one holding it. This would be something like "The ball *seems to me* to be red." People may dispute that the ball is red. But they cannot dispute how the ball "*seems to me.*"[5]

So how does this all fit together as a way to understand justification? Consider an analogy that illustrates the concept. Imagine that we are building a house. Like any good house, it will have floors, walls, doors, windows, and a roof. But most important, the house will have a foundation made of footings

4. Lemos, *Theory of Knowledge*, 113.

5. We should be careful to notice that there are other and more recent forms of foundationalism. Modest foundationalism, e.g., doesn't require self-evidence and incorrigibility but rather depends on defeasible experiential grounds from five or so sources: sense perception, memory, rational intuition, testimony, and introspection.

dug deep into the ground. Metaphorically, basic beliefs are like the foundation of the house, and nonbasic beliefs are like all the other components of the house. With this distinction, foundationalists argue that epistemic justification is a matter of supporting our beliefs by demonstrating that those beliefs are supported by basic beliefs that serve as a foundation for our nonbasic beliefs. W. Jay Wood puts it this way: "*Foundationalism* stands historically as one of the most significant efforts at showing what an ideal ordering of one's cognitive life should be like, if we have a maximally justified set of beliefs as our goal. The root idea suggests that each of us holds some beliefs 'basically' or 'immediately,' while we hold other beliefs 'nonbasically' or 'mediately.' Nonbasic or mediate beliefs receive their support from other beliefs we hold."[6] As such, CF is an example of an internalist approach to justification. People who are justified in their personal beliefs will, via reflection on those beliefs, be able to see which beliefs support their belief system.

But if it is true that "one must know which beliefs are basic, which are non-basic, and how the basic beliefs support the nonbasic beliefs," then, as Alvin Plantinga has pointed out, CF has a big problem. He says, "If you believe a proposition for which there isn't any evidence from self-evident or incorrigible propositions, then you are unjustified and violating your epistemic duty. But here's the problem: there don't seem to be any incorrigible or self-evident propositions that support CF itself."[7] In other words, the statement "One must know which beliefs are basic, which are non-basic, and how the basic beliefs support the nonbasic beliefs" itself is neither (1) self-evident nor (2) incorrigible. Therefore, it seems that the basic premise of CF is unjustified. Another objection suggests that there really aren't any beliefs that could be basic. On this objection, each supposed basic belief needs a justification. And once we start down this path, we end up in an infinite regress that is never satisfied. Indeed, as the Pyrrhonians argued (we deal with this matter in chap. 4), this could lead us into total skepticism.

Earlier in the book we were introduced to coherentism as a way that some postmodern thinkers have attempted to define truth. Not surprisingly, then, coherentism has also been offered as a way to provide justification for our beliefs. The main idea here is that a belief has justification if it is consistent, or coheres, with other beliefs that we hold to be true in our system of belief. As O'Brien notes: "A particular belief is justified if it increases the coherence of your belief system. Linear justification involves local relations: beliefs are

6. W. Jay Wood, *Epistemology: Becoming Intellectually Virtuous*, Contours of Christian Philosophy (Downers Grove, IL: IVP Academic, 1998), 78.

7. Alvin Plantinga, *Knowledge and Christian Belief* (Grand Rapids: Eerdmans, 2015), 15.

justified by their inferential relations with a small number of related beliefs. Belief A's justification is wholly provided by beliefs B and C. Holistic justification, however, involves global relations: a particular belief is justified if it fits in well—or 'coheres'—with the whole of your belief system."[8]

O'Brien goes on to explain further, just as foundationalism uses the analogy of a house and its foundations, coherentism uses the analogy of a boat. He says, "They see a belief system as more akin to a raft floating at sea. The structure remains afloat, not through the action of certain key foundational planks, but as a result of the way that all the planks are meshed together."[9] But as we saw with the concerns surrounding coherentism as a way to understand the nature of truth, it seems that we have a problem. As a minimal condition for truth, belief systems must be internally consistent and coherent. But just because it does cohere, it does not follow that the system is actually true. We can imagine and articulate very complex stories that are perfectly consistent and cohere within themselves. But it is also possible that such stories are make-believe. Countless stories from fiction illustrate the point.

#### *Externalism: Causal Theory and Reliabilism*

Other examples of internalism could be considered, but foundationalism and coherentism are enough for now. What about externalism? Again, there are a variety of views we could consider here, but we will focus on causal theory and reliabilism. According to **causal theory**, justification for a belief is grounded in the causal connection between the objects, or events, outside a person's mind and the corresponding ideas that form as a result. As Alvin Goldman explains, "*S* knows that *p* if and only if the fact *p* is causally connected in an 'appropriate' way with *S*'s believing *p*."[10] So, for example, we might say that I am justified in believing that the ball hit me in the head if in fact the ball hit me in the head. Or perhaps we might say that I am justified in believing that the sun is setting over the mountain in front of me if in fact the sun is setting over the mountain in front of me. In both of these cases, my beliefs are caused by objects and events outside of my mind. As such, causal theory is an externalist account of justification. As straightforward as the causal account of justification may be, it too seems to have a problem. How do we know the events and objects outside our minds are actually what give rise to the corresponding (or at least seemingly corresponding) beliefs in

8. O'Brien, *Theory of Knowledge*, 77.
9. O'Brien, *Theory of Knowledge*, 77.
10. Alvin Goldman, "A Causal Theory of Knowing," in *Knowledge: Readings in Contemporary Epistemology*, ed. Sven Bernecker and Fred Dretske (Oxford: Blackwell, 2000), 28.

our minds? It may very well be that the belief that a ball hit me in the head occurred in my mind simultaneously with the ball actually hitting me in the head. But how do I know the event caused the belief? What if, as it turns out, years ago I was in a terrible deep-sea fishing accident and damaged all the nerves in my head such that I can no longer feel anything that touches my head? If that were the case, then the ball hitting me in the head could not be what caused the belief to form in my mind. I have no feeling in my head. What if also, due to brain damage from an old drug habit, my brain is predisposed to form random beliefs about balls hitting me in the head? If such were the case, then I would hardly have confidence that the event of the ball hitting me in the head is what caused the belief of a ball hitting me in the head to form.

Another externalist variation of epistemic justification is called **reliabilism**. According to reliabilism, a belief is justified if that belief was formed in the appropriate environment and the cognitive faculties of the mind were functioning in a reliable fashion. Lemos notes, "Reliabilism is taken to be an externalist view because it holds that the epistemic justification of a belief depends at least in part on its being the product of a reliable cognitive process. . . . What matters, according to the reliabilist, is whether one's belief is reliably produced, not whether the reliability of the process is available through reflection. Reliabilism does not limit the factors relevant to justification to those internal to the subject's perspective."[11] So, for example, consider a group of persons who believe that the sun has just set in front of them over the mountain range. What justifies this belief is not that they are able to introspectively reflect (as internalism would require of them) on a set of basic beliefs that support the newly formed belief that the sun has just set in front of them. Rather, their belief that the sun has just set in front of them is justified from the facts that (1) they are in the right environment to witness a sunset (they are outside looking across the horizon as the sun is actually setting, with no environmental factors that hinder a proper view) and (2) the perception results from a "reliable cognitive process" (they are not crazy and have not been taking hallucinogenic drugs).

Reliabilism is a relatively popular externalist approach to justification, and for good reason. Advocates have found it to be faithful to our commonsense intuitions about the way we actually form our beliefs. Moreover, this view doesn't seem to place unrealistic epistemic requirements on our beliefs the way foundationalism seems to do. At the same time, this approach is rigid enough to prevent us from being fast and loose with our belief. On this account, justification is not open to any and all beliefs. But like the other approaches,

11. Lemos, *Theory of Knowledge*, 110.

reliabilism also has its challenges. How are we to know that our cognitive processes have been reliable? And how are we to know that our environment is not some illusion?

## What Is Reformed Epistemology?

Thus far we have focused on the difference between internalism and externalism broadly construed. Over the past few decades, and within the context of the internalism/externalism debate, a very particular epistemic movement known as **Reformed epistemology** has been established. Andrew Moon notes that, simply put, Reformed epistemology is the "thesis that religious belief can be rational without argument."[12] So, for example, Reformed epistemologists typically hold that a person can be perfectly rational about one's belief in God without the kind of evidential or argumentative support that is required by internalism. Defined as such, the temptation here would be to understand Reformed epistemology as nothing more than an externalist variation of justification described above. But as we will see, Reformed epistemology is far more nuanced and detailed than this initial assessment would reflect, and there are also internalist versions of justification that are compatible with the Reformed epistemology thesis. In what follows, we outline three unique strategies for epistemic justification that are expressions of, or at least compatible with, Reformed epistemology.

### *Plantinga's A/C and Extended A/C Account*

Any discussion about Reformed epistemology must center on the work and contribution of Alvin Plantinga, who adopts and develops what he calls the A/C model (A and C refer to Aquinas and Calvin respectively). Starting in 1967 with the publication of *God and Other Minds*, Plantinga began setting forth some of his principal concerns with internalist (specifically evidentialism)[13] requirements of justification.[14] In 1993 he published the first two volumes of his *Warrant* trilogy,[15] and in 2000 completed the series with the most influential

12. Andrew Moon, "Recent Work on Reformed Epistemology," *Philosophy Compass* 11 (2016): 879.

13. In short, evidentialism is the idea that to be justified in our beliefs, we are obligated to have evidential support for them.

14. Alvin Plantinga, *God and Other Minds: A Study of the Rational Justification of Belief in God* (Ithaca, NY: Cornell University Press, 1990).

15. Alvin Plantinga, *Warrant: The Current Debate* (New York: Oxford University Press, 1993); Plantinga, *Warrant and Proper Function* (New York: Oxford University Press, 1993).

work, *Warranted Christian Belief*.[16] More recently he published a shorter overview of his account, titled *Knowledge and Christian Belief*.[17] Throughout these works, Plantinga has championed the idea that we can be perfectly rational in many of our beliefs, including religious beliefs about God and Christian faith, without having the kind of epistemic justification that most evidentialists demand. He says,

> In any event, it is perfectly plain that someone could be justified in accepting the whole Christian story; that is, it is plain that someone could accept that story without going contrary to duty. It isn't at all difficult for a Christian—even a sophisticated and knowledgeable contemporary believer aware of all the criticisms and contrary currents of opinion—to be justified, in this sense, in her belief; and this whether or not she believes in God (or in more specific Christian doctrines) on the basis of propositional evidence.[18]

So while evidentialists argue that religious belief is unjustified—such that a person is irrational for holding such beliefs—without evidential support for them, Reformed epistemologists disagree. Plantinga has been the leading force in making this case. But how does he make his case?

To understand Plantinga's account, we must begin with the distinction between two different objections to Christian faith. First, as Plantinga notes, are the de facto objections, which are "objections to the *truth* of Christian belief."[19] In other words, de facto objections are the kind of objections that attempt to show us that, in fact, Christianity is just false. As Plantinga makes clear, this is not the sort of objection that is in his central focus. Rather, his focus is on a second kind of objection, what he calls de jure objections. As he explains, de jure objections are the sort of objections aimed at showing that Christian faith, "whether or not true, is at any rate unjustifiable, or rationally unjustified, or irrational, or not intellectually respectable, or contrary to sound morality, or without sufficient evidence, or in some other way rationally unacceptable, not up to snuff from an intellectual point of view."[20] One way to describe de jure objections is to say that they seek to show that Christian faith is not the kind of thing we are rational to believe since it does not have the same kind of evidential support that some scientific or philosophical beliefs might enjoy. Consider the following argument:

16. Alvin Plantinga, *Warranted Christian Belief* (New York: Oxford University Press, 2000).
17. Alvin Plantinga, *Knowledge and Christian Belief* (Grand Rapids: Eerdmans, 2015).
18. Plantinga, *Warranted Christian Belief*, 100.
19. Plantinga, *Warranted Christian Belief*, vii.
20. Plantinga, *Warranted Christian Belief*, ix.

1. It is rational to believe in theism only on the basis of a good argument.
2. There is no good argument for theism.
3. Therefore, it is not rational to believe in theism.[21]

As Moon explains, evidentialists are of the persuasion that the best way to respond is by attacking premise 2, "There is no good argument for theism." In response, evidentialists typically offer any number of arguments for God's existence. But Plantinga and those in the Reformed epistemology camp believe that attacking 2 is the wrong way to reply. Instead, they contend that it is better to attack premise 1, "It is rational to believe in theism only on the basis of a good argument." As Plantinga will argue, theistic belief can be not just "basic" (held without argument or evidential support) but also "properly basic." The distinction between "basic" and "properly basic" is important to note. A person can have a basic belief that is irrational. Moon illustrates this point by saying, "My friend Gambler has no good argument for his belief that his next gamble will win; he believes because of wishful thinking. This belief, though basic, is not properly basic."[22] In this case, Gambler's belief is basic because it isn't held on the basis of an argument. But it is not "properly" basic because it is an irrational belief. Why is it irrational? It is irrational because it is held on the basis of wishful thinking. So then, a belief is "basic" when it is held without argument. It is "properly" basic when (1) it is held without argument and at the same time (2) it is rational to believe such a thing. Moon adds, "On the other hand, when I stub my toe and believe that I feel pain, this belief is both basic and properly basic."[23]

But in the case of our belief in God, how could we say that such a belief is "properly basic"? In other words, how could we (1) hold to the belief that God exists without argumentation and (2) be rational in so doing? In response to these questions, Plantinga offers his account of warrant and proper function, which turn out to be of central importance to his A/C and Extended A/C accounts of Christian belief. Let's begin with his concept of warrant. Whereas most epistemologists have emphasized the concept of justification in their epistemic models, Plantinga offers the concept of warrant. According to Joseph Kim, "Warrant for Plantinga is that quality and quantity that distinguishes knowledge from mere true belief. It is not merely a quality but a quantity since warrant also comes in degrees."[24] Three things are important to

21. Moon, "Reformed Epistemology," 880.
22. Moon, "Reformed Epistemology," 880.
23. Moon, "Reformed Epistemology," 880.
24. Joseph Kim, *Reformed Epistemology and the Problem of Religious Diversity* (Eugene, OR: Wipf & Stock, 2011), 18.

note about Kim's observation. First, as Kim indicates, for Plantinga warrant serves a similar role to what other epistemologists have attributed to justification. As Plantinga sees it, warrant is what differentiates knowledge from mere true opinion. Second, warrant is similar to justification in that it is a quality that a belief may have, but it is different from justification in that it is *also* a quantity: it comes in degrees. Finally, as critics and advocates of Plantinga's concept of warrant have noted, warrant and justification are also focused on different epistemic values. On the one hand, justification is focused more on the issue of epistemic duty (what should one believe?), and on the other hand, warrant seems to be focused more on the value of rationality.[25]

What is it then that renders a belief warranted? As Plantinga makes clear, it is not the case that just any idea will qualify as warranted. According to Plantinga, "A belief has warrant if it is produced by cognitive faculties (subject to no malfunctioning) in a cognitive environment congenial for those faculties, according to a design plan successfully aimed at truth."[26] This definition of warrant is highly important to Plantinga's system, and we must unpack it to see the details. Plantinga elaborates on this definition in any number of his works, but most concisely in *Knowledge and Christian Belief*, offering four general conditions of this idea of warrant.

First, he notes the emphasis on "proper function" within this account. He says, "My suggestion begins with the idea that a belief has warrant only if it is produced by cognitive faculties that are functioning properly, subject to no disorder or dysfunction."[27] This condition is rather straightforward. If our cognitive faculties are malfunctioning, then we simply are not warranted in holding the beliefs that they form. But there is more.

Second, Plantinga contends that those cognitive faculties must also be functioning *in the proper environment*. He insists that our cognitive faculties "will achieve their purpose only if functioning in an environment much like the one for which they were designed."[28] What Plantinga recognizes here is that a person's faculties may themselves be functioning properly yet may be doing so in an environment that is not conducive to producing proper beliefs. For example, if you form a belief that your body is only two inches wide while looking at a funny mirror at the circus, we would not think that you are warranted in believing that you actually are just two inches wide. Your faculties

25. See Kim, *Reformed Epistemology*, 18; and James Beilby, "Plantinga's Model of Warranted Christian Belief," in *Alvin Plantinga*, ed. Deane-Peter Baker (New York: Cambridge University Press, 2007), 127.

26. Plantinga, *Warrant and Proper Function*, viii.

27. Plantinga, *Knowledge and Christian Belief*, 26.

28. Plantinga, *Knowledge and Christian Belief*, 27.

may be functioning properly, but they are doing so in an environment that prohibits a belief from forming properly.

Third, Plantinga argues that our belief-forming mechanisms must be aimed at true beliefs. In his account, the first two conditions are not enough. He notes that, per Freud's and Marx's specific de jure objections to Christian faith, it is always possible that our belief in God is formed as a survival mechanism to help us deal with the cold, hard realities of the world in which we find ourselves living. If so, then it would be possible for such a "survival" belief to satisfy the first two criteria: proper cognitive function and proper function in the correct environment. And if so, then something more must be added. For this, Plantinga adds "aimed at true belief" as a third criterion to warrant. Kim explains the importance of the third condition:

> Proper function and the right sort of environment for a cognitive faculty, though necessary, are still not sufficient for warrant. The fact that a cognitive faculty is to be successfully aimed at truth is something distinct from merely providing us a survival advantage. Consider a rabbit whose faculties give off a warning that there is a predator nearby whenever the rabbit hears any sudden noise. It may be that 99.9 percent of these noises are false alarms, but the fact that the rabbit acts on all of them and runs away ensures its survival. Still, this is not a faculty that is aimed at true beliefs.[29]

What Kim's rabbit illustration shows is that warrant requires more than simply proper function of faculties in the appropriate environment. There are cases, such as the rabbit example, that satisfy the first two conditions but still don't produce warrant. The rabbit's belief that a predator is coming each time it hears a noise may have formed with properly functioning cognitive faculties and in the right environment, but such a belief is nevertheless nothing more than a survival mechanism that fails to produce truth 99.9 percent of the time. In this case, the belief is intended only to help the rabbit survive. It is not intended to inform the rabbit of what is taking place around him in each case. As such, Plantinga's third condition of being "aimed at true belief" is intended to address this issue.

Fourth, and finally, Plantinga recognizes that even the first three conditions by themselves are not enough to ensure warrant. As a fourth condition, he argues that our faculties must not only be (1) functioning properly, (2) in the right environment, and (3) aimed at true belief, but they must also be (4) *successfully* aimed at true belief. Realizing that our faculties can function properly in the right environment and be aimed at forming true beliefs, Plantinga

29. Kim, *Reformed Epistemology*, 22.

observes that it is still possible that our true beliefs about the world are still nothing more than a lucky guess. As a final condition, therefore, "what must be added is that the design plan in question is a good one, one that is successfully aimed at truth, one such that there is a high probability that a belief produced according to that plan will be true (or nearly true)."[30]

So what does all this mean for belief in God? In short, what Plantinga has done is offer an account of knowledge that bypasses the internalist/evidentialist account of justification by developing an account of proper basicality, warrant, and therefore knowledge. A belief is properly basic (rational) if it is warranted, and it is warranted if it satisfies the conditions of (1) proper function, (2) right environment, (3) aimed a true belief, and (4) successfully aimed at true belief. With all this in place, Plantinga argues in favor of his famous A/C and Extended A/C model for Christian belief. The A and the C in his account, as noted above, are references to Thomas Aquinas and John Calvin, two theologians on whose work he models his account.

What Plantinga argues in the A/C model, from Calvin in particular, is that God has designed us in such a way that we have a natural capacity to form theological beliefs, what Calvin called the *sensus divinitatis* (sense of divinity). More specifically, given the *sensus divinitatis*, Plantinga argues that our cognitive faculties are designed in such a way that when in the right environment (such as looking at the stars or pondering beauty) they will naturally form beliefs in God. He says, "The purpose of the *sensus divinitatis* is to enable us to have true beliefs about God; and when it functions properly, it ordinarily does produce true beliefs about God. These beliefs therefore can meet the conditions for warrant; when they do, if they are strong enough, then they constitute knowledge."[31] Beyond this claim, Plantinga offers the Extended A/C, which moves beyond the generic beliefs that God exists to the more "full-blooded Christian belief in sin, atonement, and salvation."[32] Here, Plantinga argues that such "full-blooded" Christian beliefs can be warranted within his account.

### *Alternative Reformed Epistemologies*

There is, of course, much more that could be said about Plantinga's approach to Reformed epistemology, but this at least provides an overview of his system. Before concluding, it is worth noting that there are indeed other forms of Reformed epistemology that could be explored. For instance, John

30. Plantinga, *Knowledge and Christian Belief*, 28.
31. Plantinga, *Knowledge and Christian Belief*, 36–37.
32. Plantinga, *Knowledge and Christian Belief*, 45.

Greco and Anthony Bolos have formulated an account that is also externalist in nature.[33] In contrast to Plantinga, their account builds on the notion of epistemic virtue, suggesting that intellectual ability or achievement (as opposed to luck) is what warrants our beliefs. Moon illustrates the key concept. "Suppose I am up to bat, get distracted by an annoying fly, try to hit the fly and, in the process, happen to hit a speeding baseball and score a home run. This is success through accident, not success through ability; it is not an achievement. A true belief is warranted, on Greco's theory, when one attains a true belief because of one's intellectual ability."[34] While this virtue approach differs from Plantinga's in that its focus is on intellectual ability and achievement, it is still an example of Reformed epistemology, since it contends that we can be rational without argument, and it is externalist, since it does not say that we must have epistemic access to the evidence or processes that support our beliefs.

Alternatively, some internalist accounts are, surprisingly, compatible with Reformed epistemology. Consider, as an example, Michael Huemer's account, known as **phenomenal conservatism**.[35] In his account, the notions of "seeming" and "defeat" are of central importance to our knowing. He says, "Phenomenal conservatism holds that undefeated appearances are a source of justification (perhaps the *only* source of justification) for belief."[36] By "appearances," Huemer is referencing the way things seem to us. If, for example, it seems to me that there is a tree in front of me, then I have at least prima facie reason—that is, initial reason—to think that there is a tree in front of me. But this is not all that it takes to have justification in his system. It must also be the case that there are no defeaters for that "appearing" or "seeming." And what does it mean for a belief to not have a defeater? Simply put, Huemer says, "An appearance is 'undefeated' when there are no positive grounds for doubting it."[37] This account of justification is interesting for two reasons. First, it is an internalist account, because it requires the person holding the belief to be aware of the fact that there are no defeaters. Second, and most interesting, despite being an internalist account of justification, it is nevertheless compatible with Reformed epistemology, since it allows a person to hold the belief without argumentation.

33. See John Greco, "The Nature of Ability and Purpose of Knowledge," *Philosophical Issues* 17, *The Metaphysics of Epistemology*, special issue of *Nous* (2007): 57–69; Greco, "A (Different) Virtue Epistemology," *Philosophy and Phenomenological Research* 85, no. 1 (2012): 1–26; and Anthony Bolos, "Is Knowledge of God a Cognitive Achievement?," *Ratio* 59, no. 2 (2016): 186–201.

34. Moon, "Reformed Epistemology," 886.

35. Michael Huemer, *Approaching Infinity* (New York: Palgrave, 2016).

36. Huemer, *Approaching Infinity*, 96.

37. Huemer, *Approaching Infinity*, 96.

## Conclusion

Far more could be said on each of the issues covered in this chapter: questions about justification are complex and endlessly debated. We hope our short survey is helpful for the student to get a sense of the questions epistemologists ask and the kinds of answers that are given. Internalism and externalism come in a variety of forms, and there are several epistemic values at play in the discussions.

# 4

# Skepticism, Certainty, and Virtue Epistemology

Epistemology deals with the philosophical questions that pertain to knowledge, truth, justification, and the relationship between faith, philosophy, and science. But in addition to these important discussions, epistemology also deals with the opposing tendencies that human beings have to be skeptical about certain kinds of knowledge claims while being extremely confident in other such claims. For some ideas, our confidence seems to rise to the level of absolute certainty. But for other ideas, we are never settled, always questioning and debating the truth. As such, we tend to wonder whether our beliefs are accurate. We wonder if we can be certain about things or if we should be forever skeptical.

The issues of skepticism and certainty represent two perspectival poles that require some attention. On the one hand, we do succeed in knowing things and have great confidence in what we know. In light of this, skepticism seems a bit absurd and counterintuitive. And yet, on the other hand, when we pause to reflect on how we know certain things, we begin to see where epistemic error may have come into play, rendering what once seemed so sure to be much less certain. Once these possible errors are in view, skepticism seems to be more intuitive after all. So who is right? Is it the person who claims to have absolute certainty, whom we can call the certaintist, or is it the skeptic?

In some ways, setting the discussion between the two poles of certainty and skepticism is a bit odd. One might note, for example, that when we talk about certainty, we are talking about an epistemic property that we either have or do not have. But by contrast, when we talk about **skepticism** we are talking about a philosophical movement that can be traced back into the ancient world to Pyrrho of Elis and up through many modern-day philosophers. Nevertheless, it seems that any discussion about one must be pursued with the other clearly in view, even if one is an epistemic property that a person claims to have and the other is a philosophical tradition that spans philosophical history. Those who claim to have certainty are generally pushing back against those who endorse skepticism. And those who are skeptics are typically pushing back against those who claim to have absolute certainty.

In this chapter we explore certainty and skepticism. We offer an overview of each and delineate the various forms that skepticism, in particular, may take. After this we consider the epistemic factors that give rise to skeptical dispositions, but also give attention to the counterfactors that increase our epistemic confidence. In the later part of the chapter we discuss the concept of intellectual virtues, along with virtue epistemology itself, and how they may be used to bolster our epistemic endeavors in such a way that we achieve greater epistemic success.

## Skepticism: Global, Local, and Methodological

What is skepticism? In short, it is the view that rejects all or some kinds of knowledge claims. For many people, the word "skepticism" carries with it a very negative connotation about the person who affirms it. Perhaps, one might think, skepticism in all forms is a pesky disposition bent toward doubting everything and everyone. While there are certainly some who fit this definition, the description is not entirely accurate, since most people are inclined toward skepticism about some, but not all, things. For example, we often employ what we might call commonsense skepticism about the promises of a politician's speech or the value of a product pushed on us by the salesperson. In these cases, skepticism serves us well. But this is not the kind of matter we are dealing with when it comes to philosophical considerations regarding skepticism. In philosophy, skepticism has taken a variety of different forms, which we will describe here. Generally speaking, skeptics come in global/Pyrrhonian, local/metaphysical, and methodological forms.

### *Global/Pyrrhonian Skepticism*

**Global skepticism** is often thought to be the most radical form of skepticism and is often associated with the Pyrrhonian skeptics, whom we will describe in the next section. This version is described as "global" because these skeptics have tended to be skeptical about any and all knowledge claims. In other words, their skepticism is applied globally to knowledge itself.

*Local/Metaphysical Skepticism*

In contrast to global skepticism, metaphysical skepticism is less radical in nature. Unlike methodological skepticism, **local/metaphysical skepticism** is concerned with particular kinds of knowledge claims. Specifically, it involves claims related to metaphysical matters. So this kind of skeptic might not be troubled with knowledge claims about the physical world, yet would be deeply troubled by knowledge claims regarding God, souls, moral values, or other metaphysical entities. This approach to skepticism is described as local because of its rejection of global skepticism. Recall that the global skeptic rejects all knowledge claims, whether empirical or metaphysical. But the local skeptic is skeptical only about certain kinds of claims, specifically, metaphysical claims.

*Methodological Skepticism*

**Methodological skepticism** is an even less radical form of skepticism. It makes use of skepticism for the process of gaining knowledge but is not skeptical of knowledge claims in general. As we will see below, this is the kind of skepticism found in the work of René Descartes in his quest for absolute certainty. In this approach, one employs skepticism about the claims that legitimately should, or even could, be doubted for the purposes of exposing an idea or set of ideas that is undoubtable. Once such ideas are found, a system of knowledge is built on them. In this case, the skeptic is skeptical for methodological reasons only. Here it is important to recognize that this version of skepticism is related to, if not a form of, global skepticism due to its universal application. Yet it is not exactly the same thing as global skepticism, as we will explain shortly.

---

But why would one be a skeptic in the first place? To some, such positions seem deeply problematic. Most of us hold to particular ideas with such confidence that skepticism seems counterintuitive and obviously false. Throughout history, philosophers have raised a variety of problems for knowledge that help us to understand why a person might be so inclined toward skepticism. In what follows we will consider the issues of epistemic regress, the possibility of deception, limitations with induction, and several other less theoretical factors that give rise to doubt and uncertainty.

## Skepticism: Historical Roots and Rationale

Questions relating to knowledge, certainty, and skepticism are as old as philosophy itself. In the fifth century BC, for example, Protagoras (485–410 BC) and the Sophist philosophers railed against the boisterous knowledge claims of the pre-Socratic philosophers. In particular, they were skeptical of the knowledge claims regarding moral and religious matters. Against the idea that there was some kind of objective standard for morality and other related truths, the Sophists argued that "man was the measure of all things." From the fourth century onward, however, skepticism began to take a more serious form and receive support from a variety of thinkers.

### *Pyrrhonians, Skepticism, and the Problem of Epistemic Regress*

Pyrrho of Elis (ca. 360–ca. 270 BC) and his followers put forth a rather radical form of skepticism, sometimes referred to as global. It is a "global" form of skepticism in that it applies skepticism globally to all knowledge claims. Diogenes Laertius (third century AD) summarizes Pyrrho's teachings: "The sceptics [Pyrrhonians], then, spent their time overturning all the dogmas of the schools, whereas they themselves make no dogmatic pronouncements, and while they presented and set out in detail the views of others, they themselves expressed no determinate opinions, not even this itself [that they had no determinate opinion]. Thus, they even abolished the position of holding no determinate opinion, saying, for example, 'we determine nothing' since otherwise they would be determining something."[1]

Roughly five hundred years after Pyrrho, Sextus Empiricus (AD 160–210) championed this position and further developed it. In his view, knowledge claims give rise to conflict, disagreement, and social disturbances. As such, he argues that skepticism is a way forward that would relieve society of such conflict: "The sceptical ability is the ability to set in opposition appearances and ideas in any manner whatsoever, the result of which is first that, because of the equal force of the opposed objects and arguments, final suspension of judgment is achieved, and then freedom from disturbance."[2] He then adds, "We say most definitely that the goal of the sceptic is the freedom from disturbance with respect to matters of belief and also moderate states with respect to things that are matters of compulsion."[3]

1. Diogenes Laertius, *Life of Pyrrho*, in *Hellenistic Philosophy*, trans. Brad Inwood and L. P. Gerson (Indianapolis: Hackett, 1997), 288.

2. Sextus Empiricus, *General Principles* [*Outlines of Pyrrhonism*], in Inwood and Gerson, *Hellenistic Philosophy*, 303.

3. Sextus Empiricus, *General Principles*, 307.

In addition to these kinds of concerns, the Pyrrhonians were troubled by what we might call the problem of epistemic regress. The concern here stems from the need for beliefs to have some kind of justification. That is, a person who believes *A* should then have reasons for believing *A*.[4] Linda Zagzebski explains the Pyrrhonians' basis for concern: "The standards for knowledge presupposed by the Pyrrhonists are quite ordinary. They argued that all a person needs for a justified belief is that the evidence for some proposition believed exceeds the evidence against it."[5] And yet, even with such a minimal requirement, she reports how the Pyrrhonians thought that skepticism would always follow. They maintained that the evidence in favor of any proposition would never exceed the evidence against it. Zagzebski offers the following argument as a way to express the point.

1. For any proposition *p*, I know *p* only if I am justified in believing *p*.
2. I am justified in believing *p* only if I have evidence E that justifies *p*.
3. No evidence E can justify a proposition unless E is justified.
4. So E is justified only if there is evidence E1 that justifies E.
5. E1 is justified only if there is evidence E2 that justifies E1.
6. E2 is justified only if there is evidence E3 that justifies E2 . . . ad infinitum.

Since the process of justification is never ending, it follows that

7. I am never justified in believing any proposition.

Hence by statement 1 it follows,

8. I do not know anything.[6]

What the Pyrrhonians contend in the regress problem is that justification is an ongoing and never-ending endeavor that is never complete, and thus we never have, in their view, the ability to know anything at all.

In chapter 3 we addressed the issue of justification and saw that the various approaches to it are in many ways attempts to avoid skeptical concerns like the regress problem. For different reasons, foundationalists, coherentists, and Reformed epistemologists all reject the above argument from epistemic regress.[7]

4. As we saw in chap. 2, not all philosophers agree that this requirement is legitimate. Some argue that such a standard is too high.

5. Linda Zagzebski, *On Epistemology* (Belmont, CA: Wadsworth, 2009), 29.

6. Zagzebski, *On Epistemology*, 30.

7. For reasons why, refer back to the section on justification in chap. 3.

Likewise, arguments like those expressed in the regress problem also failed to persuade philosophers in Pyrrho's own day. These arguments do, however, provide a glimpse into the kinds of reasons why some have been inclined toward skepticism.

### *René Descartes and the Problem of Deception*

Despite the skeptical dispositions of these early philosophers, most Western intellectuals, as well as nonintellectuals, were disinclined toward skepticism. They thought it was possible to know things and to develop accurate theories about reality. But in the seventeenth century the issues of skepticism and certainty took center stage in the thinking of René Descartes (1596–1650). Whereas most philosophy before Descartes was done with primary emphasis on ontology (the study of being), with Descartes philosophy took an epistemic turn. That is, with Descartes epistemic questions received primary attention and emphasis. Underwhelmed and unimpressed by the progress in knowledge of the generations before him, and bothered by the fact that our senses can mislead us in the way they represent the external world, Descartes was deeply concerned to set the foundations of our knowledge. Specifically, Descartes noticed the possibility that our senses could be deceiving us in every perception we have of the world outside our minds. Or what if, Descartes wondered, there is "an evil genius, supremely powerful and clever, who has directed his entire effort at deceiving me"?[8] If such is possible, then it seems as though our deception is widespread, and we must therefore be suspicious of all our knowledge.

What could one do to overcome such radical skepticism? Reflecting on that question, Descartes came to believe that perhaps doubt itself could be a vehicle for finding a sure and certain foundation for knowledge. But to get there one must employ systematic doubt. That is, one must embrace the possibility of being deceived in every belief. Descartes says, "[I would] reject as absolutely false everything in which I could imagine the slightest doubt and to see, as a result, if anything remained among my beliefs that was completely indubitable. Thus, because our senses sometimes deceive us, I decided to assume that nothing was the way the senses made us imagine it."[9] Descartes thought, that is, that doubt allows us to strip away all the things that are actually questionable. But when doubt has done its work and certain ideas remain firm and undoubtable, perhaps then we have stumbled onto the kinds of ideas that can serve as the foundation for our knowledge.

8. René Descartes, *Meditations on First Philosophy*, trans. Donald A. Cress, 4th ed. (Indianapolis: Hackett, 1993), 16.

9. René Descartes, *Discourse on Method*, trans. Desmond M. Clarke (London: Penguin, 1999), 24.

Using this method of systematic doubt, Descartes quickly discovered the kind of idea he was looking for: the idea that he himself must exist. He says, "But I noticed, immediately afterwards, that while I thus wished to think that everything was false, it was necessarily the case that I, who was thinking, was something. When I noticed that this truth 'I think, therefore I am' was so firm and certain that all the most extravagant assumptions of the sceptics were unable to shake it, I judged that I could accept it without scruple as the first principle of the philosophy for which I was searching."[10] In other words, Descartes recognized that doubting was a kind of thinking that he was having, and that in order to have it, he must actually exist to have it. This was sure and certain. And on this basis, Descartes sought to build a system of knowledge that leads to absolute certainty.

While building on the certainty of his own existence, he noticed that his thinking was marked by the imperfection of doubt. And yet the very presence of imperfection implies the idea of perfection and suggests that this concept could not have arisen from within himself. Thus it must come from something, a perfect something, outside himself. This, he thought, is at least part of the basis to believe in God. He says, "This idea was put in me by a nature that was really more perfect than I was, one that even had in itself all the perfection of which I could have some idea, that is—to express myself in a single word—by God."[11] And now with God in the picture, Descartes concludes that such a being would not allow us to stray into uncertainty and epistemic error.

Historically speaking, Descartes's starting point—"I think, therefore I am"—enjoys far more agreement than does the rest of his argument. And as such, many philosophers tend to think that Descartes underscores the problem of doubt without actually solving it. While Descartes was convinced that doubt itself could lead us out of such awful epistemic states of affairs, numerous philosophers throughout history have been less inclined to agree with him. In their minds, the problem Descartes raises is bigger than the solution that he provides. Maybe systematic doubt will yield the certain conclusion that Descartes himself must exist, but it is less clear that his next steps are a sufficient ground on which to build an epistemic system.

### *David Hume and the Problem of Induction*

We must say something about at least one other figure, David Hume (1711–76), before leaving our brief background of the issues of skepticism

10. Descartes, *Discourse on Method*, 25.
11. Descartes, *Discourse on Method*, 26.

and certainty. Hume, a Scottish philosopher known for his skepticism, raised objections with induction. With the inductive method, one gains knowledge incrementally as evidence mounts and probability rises. Contrary to deduction, however, certainty is never achieved. So, for example, we may know that the sun will rise tomorrow based on the vast number of previous events of history where the sun has risen. With every additional instance where the sun rises, our confidence in tomorrow's sunrise is strengthened. We have come to "know" that the sun will rise by the accumulation of evidence from past experience. As Duncan Pritchard has noted, Hume raised a serious question about the epistemic legitimacy of this by asking "how we could be sure that regularities that are observed within a representative sample . . . should increase the likelihood that the unrestricted generalization . . . is true."[12] In other words, in the case of a sunrise, induction claims require that the regularities within the laws of nature in the past will automatically work the same way as they did in the past. But how do we know that is the case? In Hume's mind, one could only assume this to be the case and could never prove it. Hence Hume thought that induction as a whole was suspect and an unsure guide to knowledge.

Hume himself expressed this concern regarding a widely assumed belief in the nature of cause and effect. Consider the movement of an eight ball on a billiards table and the question of why it moved. According to almost anyone assessing the situation, the likely answer to the question of the eight ball's movement will be something like the following: the eight ball moved because the cue ball hit it, causing it to move across the table. In this case, (1) there is clearly pairing of movements: the cue ball moves and the eight ball moves; (2) there is a sequence in which the movements happen: the cue ball moved first and then the eight ball moves; and (3) there is a physical connection between the movements: the cue ball touches the eight ball. According to Hume, that is all we can observe or say. We do not observe (4) a causation between the cue ball and the eight ball. Since we do not observe the causation, we therefore cannot say anything about causation itself. Do we observe in our experience causation itself? "No!" proclaims Hume. On the basis of (1–3), we assume causation. He famously says: "Thus not only our reason fails us in the discovery of the ultimate connexion of causes and effects, but even after experience has inform'd us of their constant conjunction, 'tis impossible for us to satisfy ourselves by our reason, why we shou'd extend that experience beyond those particular instances, which have fallen under our observation.

12. Duncan Pritchard, *What Is This Thing Called Knowledge?*, 2nd ed. (New York: Routledge, 2006), 102.

We suppose, but are never able to prove, that there must be a resemblance betwixt those objects, of which we have had experience, and those which lie beyond the reach of our discovery."[13]

In other words, reason itself does not and cannot establish the assumption that because things have worked a certain way in the past, we have assurance that they will work that way in the present or in the future. Such assurance is based on the inductive basis of probability and nothing more. It never yields absolute certainty.

Philosophers agree about the nature of induction on which Hume's "problem" is based. Generally speaking, however, they are far less concerned with this as a problem since most see probability as an adequate basis for epistemic assurance and confidence. It may not offer absolute certainty, but it does yield a sufficient basis for trusting the data produced by induction. So then, if certainty is not required, there doesn't appear to be much of a problem.

### *Other Epistemic Factors That Cause Doubt*

There are plenty of other figures that we might consider regarding the background of skepticism and certainty. The brief overview above, however, should be sufficient to help us see that skepticism has had a variety of philosophical contributors. And yet, before moving forward, we might also highlight some other, perhaps less theoretical, factors that contribute to epistemic doubt and skepticism. First, we should recognize the impact our finitude has on our epistemic confidence. In short, we are finite creatures and thus lack the ability to perceive, much less process or understand, all the relevant aspects of reality. We have little minds that struggle to grasp all the data and handle it accordingly. Hence our finitude can at times hinder our epistemic abilities and keep us from seeing the world perfectly. Second, we are also fallen creatures whose minds have been tainted by our sin. Our minds are often clouded by biases, prejudices, and other kinds of hindrances, which make knowing difficult. Third, as knowers we must face the reality that we are epistemically situated within contexts that shape our view of things. An Anglo-American Southerner in the nineteenth and early twentieth centuries might, for example, have a view of racial matters shaped by the cultural and economic specifics of the Southern context. The same would be the case, of course, for an African American Southerner during those same periods of time. As has been demonstrated well by critics of modernity, situatedness is a genuine factor in our

13. David Hume, *A Treatise of Human Nature* (Oxford: Oxford University Press, 1987), 91–92.

knowing, sometimes hindering and sometimes helping us as we go about the process of gaining knowledge.

Plenty of other things could be mentioned about the rationale behind skepticism and epistemic doubt, but this quick survey is sufficient to show that skeptics have their reasons for holding the views that they do. We now turn to consider why it is that we, despite our causes for doubt, have epistemic confidence.

## Why We, Nevertheless, Have Epistemic Confidence

Thus far we have encountered various rationales for skepticism, and we've been exposed to the thinkers behind those ideas. Now we turn our attention to the various reasons for why we have confidence in the things we claim to know. Why is it, despite the factors considered in favor of skepticism, that most people aren't epistemological skeptics? One reason for this is that skepticism has its own problems. To begin with, some versions of skepticism are self-defeating or impractical. If, for example, a skeptic were to claim that no one knows anything at all, this would be a self-defeating claim since it is itself a knowledge claim. Ideas like these just can't be held with consistency, no matter how big a fuss someone makes about it. Moreover, even in cases where inconsistency is not involved, it is still often the case that skepticism is unlivable or impractical. Skeptics might claim to know nothing at all, but this is surely not the way they live their lives. They operate in the day-to-day matters of life and plan their affairs in response to information they gather from their senses, the testimony of others, and their own sense of right and wrong. No matter what they claim about knowing, they live as one who does know a host of things about the world in which they live. And in doing so, they demonstrate the impractical and unlivable nature of skepticism. But there are, of course, more positive reasons for us to have epistemic confidence. We now turn our attention to those considerations.

### *A Priori Knowledge*

We know things in different ways. For some things, like the desk in front of me, I know about it by looking at it, feeling it, and so forth. Knowledge of such things requires empirical data—data gathered by experience, observation, and the senses. But this is not the only way of knowing. For other things, it is possible to know without any reference to experience, observation, or the senses. In these cases, we are able to grasp some truths simply by analyzing concepts. These truths, often referred to as analytic truths, are considered

**a priori knowledge**: without or apart from experience. Take, for example, our knowledge of certain mathematical truths like $5 + 7 = 12$; $10 - 4 = 6$; or $18 \div 3 = 6$. It's safe to say that you know these things as opposed to merely believing them. But how is it that you know them, and how did you get that information? Did you survey the world around to discover that this was the case? Did you perform some experiment in a laboratory to find this out? No, you didn't. Rather, you simply thought about the numbers and functions in question, and the answer was obvious and certain. It just is the case that $5 + 7 = 12$, and you know that without some kind of empirical experience.

But are there other truths, beyond mathematical truths, that can be known in this way? Philosophers throughout history have agreed that indeed there are. A classic example is the idea that a "bachelor is an unmarried male." Again, it is safe to say that you know this is true. But again, how did you arrive at such a conclusion? Did you interview all the bachelors in the world to see if they were unmarried? Did you perform an experiment in a laboratory to gather evidence for this conclusion? Again, no, you didn't. Instead, you simply reflected on the concept of a bachelor, which just is an unmarried male. Nothing beyond your reflection on the concept was required for the conclusion.

One final example, from someone we have already considered in this chapter, may help to make the point. Recall that Descartes worried that all that he believed could be based on deception and illusion. It seemed, at least for a moment, that it was possible to doubt everything. And so, in an effort to find a foundation for all of his beliefs that was sure and certain, that is exactly what he set out to do: doubt everything. As he undertook this project of systematic doubt, he considered his own physical body and concluded the same thing about it that he did about all other physical objects. His body, like a tree or a table, was something that he could doubt. But when he considered himself, he quickly realized that this was something he couldn't doubt, for to doubt himself required that he must actually exist. This was the truth that Descartes believed was sure and certain. And yet it was not a truth he arrived at by way of experience, empirical observation, or from his senses. He knew this a priori. All this to say that there are some things we know a priori. But there are still other reasons for thinking that knowledge is possible.

### *Common Sense*

Other philosophers have pushed back against skepticism by appealing to common sense. Sure, they may admit, it is possible that we are deceived in some of the things we think we know. But the fact is, they argue, there are some things that we just know. In response to Hume's brand of skepticism, the

Scottish philosopher Thomas Reid (1710–96) argued that common sense is the basis on which to build all philosophical knowledge. In his famous *Inquiry*, he makes note of the way philosophers like Descartes, Nicolas Malebranche (1638–1715), and even John Locke (1632–1704) set up the skepticism that would eventually result in Humean skepticism. Mocking those who have "employed their genius and skill to prove the existence of a material world," Reid thought such efforts had been met "with very bad success."[14] Instead of refusing to hold beliefs about the external world unless he had good philosophical reasons for doing so, Reid contended that such beliefs should be held on the basis of common sense. He says, "Let scholastic sophisters entangle themselves in their own cobwebs; I am resolved to take my own existence, and the existence of other things, upon trust; and to believe that snow is cold, and honey sweet, whatever they may say to the contrary. He must be a fool, or want to make a fool of me, that would reason me out of my reason and senses."[15]

In other words, Reid thought it a terrible mistake to go down the path of his contemporary philosophers by trying to justify basic beliefs about our own existence and the information given to us by the senses. He argued that such beliefs should be held on the basis of common sense. Furthermore, not only should common sense be the basis for such beliefs; common sense should also be the foundation of philosophy and philosophizing itself. He says, "Common Sense holds nothing of Philosophy, nor needs her aid. But, on the other hand, Philosophy (if I may be permitted to change the metaphor) has no other root but the principles of Common Sense; it grows out of them, and draws its nourishment from them. Severed from this root, its honours wither, its sap is dried up, it dies and rots."[16]

At the turn of the twentieth century, G. E. Moore (1873–1958) argued for a similar view regarding the information we gain from the senses. In a short article titled "Proof of an External World,"[17] Moore offers the following argument in favor of our confidence in common sense and the ability of our senses to give us accurate information about the world around us:

1. Here is one hand.
2. Here is another.

14. Thomas Reid, "An Inquiry into the Human Mind on the Principles of Common Sense," in *Inquiry and Essays*, ed. Ronald E. Beanblossom and Keith Lehrer (Indianapolis: Hackett, 1983), 5.

15. Reid, "An Inquiry," 11.

16. Reid, "An Inquiry," 7.

17. G. E. Moore, "Proof of an External World," in *Philosophical Papers* (New York: Macmillan, 1959), 127–50.

3. There are at least two things outside of us.
4. Therefore, an external world exists.[18]

Moore's point here is fairly obvious and simple to grasp. Despite the possibilities of deception that were raised by Descartes and others, and despite the other reasons skeptics might have for questioning the senses or any other sources of knowledge, there are some things we just know. This truth about Moore, "I have two hands," is obvious and shouldn't be doubted. In many ways, Moore's argument is intended to mock and scoff at skepticism, showing that no matter what skeptics insist, we succeed in knowing things about the world, and it is foolish not to take as basic the information given to us by the senses.

Another specific example of this kind of view comes from the philosophers known as particularists. In the twentieth century, American philosopher Roderick Chisholm (1916–99) was largely responsible for establishing this as a respected school of thought. Understanding both Reid and Moore as advocates of this view, he distinguished his particularist view from a view called methodism. The debate between these two camps revolves around two epistemic questions:

Question A: *What* do we know?
Question B: *How* do we know what we know?

Let us call question A the content question, as it pertains to the content of what we know, and let us call question B the method question, as it deals with the "how" of our knowing. Methodists are the group of philosophers who believe we must start with B, the method question: How do we know what we know? In this approach, what one is trying to figure out is what it means to know something and what the proper way is for us to go about gaining knowledge. Exemplified by philosophers like Descartes, Locke, or even Francis Bacon (1561–1626), these thinkers developed philosophical systems that gave primary attention to the methods of knowing. Particularists disagree with the methodist approach of making the method question primary. For them, the proper starting point for epistemology is A, the content question: What do we know? Following in the wake of philosophers like Reid and Moore, Chisholm believed that methodism was fundamentally mistaken and would likely lead to skepticism. He noted three distinct possibilities: "There is skepticism (you cannot answer either question without presupposing an answer to the other,

18. Moore, "Proof of an External World," 166.

and therefore, the questions cannot be answered at all); there is 'methodism' (you begin with an answer to B); and there is 'particularism' (you begin with an answer to A). I suggest that the third possibility is the most reasonable."[19]

And so, instead of trying to identify the proper methods for knowing, perhaps, Chisholm argued, we should simply start with something that we do know and use that example of epistemic success as a case study of sorts that could then be used to figure the proper methods for knowing. All this is to say that Chisholm, with Reid and Moore before him, thought that we are within our epistemic rights to believe basic things about the world based on our senses. They did not deny that we can and do make epistemic errors or that deception is a real possibility. But they did insist that common sense forces us to trust our sense data and that our senses are largely successful in helping to give us knowledge of the world.

### *Science and Epistemic Success*

In addition to the arguments from a priori knowledge and common sense, philosophers have provided another significant reason for why it is that we have epistemic confidence. In the estimation of many, the success of modern science to make progress in the areas of technology, medicine, and computer science is enough for us to reject skepticism. As Alister McGrath has put it, "It seems to many that the success of the natural sciences shows that they have somehow managed to uncover the way things really are, or to lock into something which is fundamental to the structure of the universe."[20] In other words, the discoveries made by modern science, and the opportunities that arise from them, are strongly suggestive that we have been successful in coming to understand the way the world is. Knowledge is being attained step-by-step and with steady progress. But how is such a thing possible if skepticism were true? It would seem that the kind of progress we describe here would be forever off-limits and impossible for us to have. But that is not how things really are. Instead, we have been successful in attaining knowledge of the world.

Thus far we have explored two topics in this chapter. First, we've considered skepticism and the various reasons why some have held this position throughout history. Second, we've considered why it is that, despite the concerns of the skeptics, we nevertheless have epistemic confidence in the things we claim to know. In short, epistemic error is possible, yet we are nevertheless largely

19. Roderick M. Chisholm, *The Foundations of Knowing* (Minneapolis: University of Minnesota Press, 1982), 69.

20. Alister E. McGrath, *The Science of God* (Grand Rapids: Eerdmans, 2004), 126.

successful in knowing things about our world. As we ponder such questions, a new question should be considered: How can we be most successful in attaining knowledge? To answer this question, we now turn to explore intellectual virtues and virtue epistemology.

## Virtue Epistemology

Numerous philosophers have contended for something called **virtue epistemology** as an approach to knowledge acquisition that builds on the concept of intellectual virtues.[21] To begin with, we need to set forward what we mean by "virtue." Simply put, a virtue, like a vice, is a particular kind of characteristic or quality that a person may have. Vices are qualities that are negative in nature and that hinder, hurt, destroy, or make something very difficult. When we say that someone has a vice, we are saying that they have a particular kind of quality or characteristic that causes trouble and difficulty both for them and for those around them. For example, if someone has the vice of having a quick temper, it typically causes problems in some way. By contrast, virtues are positive qualities or characteristics that a person may have that help, bless, create life, or give a particular kind of advantage. As a result of having a virtue, the person who has it is helped in some way. Plato summarized the difference well, declaring that virtue is "a kind of health, fine condition, and well-being of the soul," while its opposite, vice, can be understood as "disease, shameful condition, and weakness."[22]

Today, discussions about virtue typically arise within the context of ethical considerations. This is fitting, but it is certainly not the only application of the concept of virtue. In the ancient world, philosophers like Aristotle seem to have given equal attention to something we might call intellectual virtues. At the beginning of his discussion about virtue, for example, Aristotle distinguished two kinds: "Virtue, then, is of two sorts, virtue of thought and virtue of character."[23] Virtue epistemology is an approach to knowledge that

21. See Ernest Sosa, *A Virtue Epistemology: Apt Belief and Reflective Knowledge* (New York: Oxford University Press, 2009), vol. 1; Zagzebski, *On Epistemology*; Linda Zagzebski, *Virtues of the Mind: An Inquiry into the Nature of Virtue and the Ethical Foundations of Knowledge* (Cambridge: Cambridge University Press, 1996); Robert C. Roberts and W. Jay Wood, *Intellectual Virtues: An Essay in Regulative Epistemology* (New York: Oxford University Press, 2007); W. Jay Wood, *Epistemology: Becoming Intellectually Virtuous*, Contours of Christian Philosophy (Downers Grove, IL: IVP Academic, 1998).

22. Plato, *Republic* 444e, in *Plato: Complete Works*, ed. by John M. Cooper (Indianapolis: Hackett, 1997), 1076.

23. Aristotle, *Nicomachean Ethics*, trans. Terrence Irwin, 2nd ed. (Indianapolis: Hackett, 1999), 2.1.

builds on the notion of intellectual virtues. Like a moral virtue, an intellectual virtue is a cognitive characteristic or quality that allows a person to think well, acquire knowledge, and avoid epistemological error. Or, as Pritchard has put it, an intellectual virtue "is a character trait which makes you better suited to gaining the truth."[24]

There are numerous examples of the kind of characteristics that might be thought of as intellectual virtues, including such things as humility, studiousness, honesty, courage, or even carefulness. These concepts clearly have moral connotations to them, but according to virtue epistemologists, they are equally clear examples of intellectual virtues. Take humility and honesty as two quick examples. In the case of humility, we can think of two opposing characteristics that would be vices and would also be opposites of humility. Persons who are arrogant or prideful would be overconfident in their intellectual abilities or in their understanding of a particular topic. As a result of that arrogance and pride, therefore, they may be prone to overlook, ignore, and dismiss important details that need to be considered in evaluating a theory. Or it could also be the case that their pride and arrogance predispose them to intellectual laziness. In either case, a person marked by the vice of arrogance has a significant intellectual liability. Additionally, we can also think of another vice that stands in contrast to intellectual humility—namely, despair. In this case, persons have absolutely no confidence in their intellectual abilities and either give up too early or never set out to gain knowledge and understanding. As such, both arrogance and despair are intellectual vices that sit in contrast to the intellectual virtue of humility.

Persons who have the virtue of humility are not hindered by the liabilities of arrogance or the defeat of despair. Instead, they will approach a topic with earnestness, paying attention to all the relevant details. By having the virtue of humility, they are better suited to gain knowledge. We might also consider the intellectual virtue of honesty. Again, consider how someone with an opposing vice of dishonesty will be hindered in grasping the truth. Because dishonest persons are unwilling to tell the truth about the facts of the matter, it is also safe to say that their account of a particular thing is suspect. But the person who is honest enough to tell the truth about the facts of a matter is far more suited to gain knowledge about the way the world actually is. Many other examples could be mentioned, but these two are sufficient to help us see how intellectual virtues make us better suited to know and understand.

24. Pritchard, *What Is This Thing Called Knowledge?*, 58.

## Conclusion

We have covered a lot of terrain in this chapter. First, we looked at skepticism, its history, and the kinds of concerns that have caused some to be skeptics. As we saw, skeptics have been concerned with the issue of epistemic regress, the possibility of deception, the uncertainty involved in induction, and several other factors. But second, we also considered the reasons why, despite the concerns of skepticism, we can still have epistemic confidence. There we gave consideration to a priori knowledge, common sense, and the epistemic success of modern science. Finally, we also gave a quick survey of virtue epistemology as a way to navigate through the concerns of skepticism and as a way to increase epistemic success.

For Christians, virtue epistemology is a promising pathway forward. If nothing else, it provides a way to deal with doubt that sometimes arises with faith. And what is more, the pathway provided by virtue epistemology allows us to deal with doubt without committing the sins of intellectual hubris or intellectual laziness. The intellectual virtues are designed to produce the proper balance between humility and confidence.

# 5

# Faith, Reason, and Modern Science

How should Christians, or religious people more generally, think about and relate to philosophy? Is it OK to do philosophy or even use philosophy in relationship to the things we believe about God? For example, if philosophy or science provides a new discovery or insight that has bearing on an item of faith, can the believer make use of that information and incorporate it into the fabric of a rationale for God? Or is this the kind of thing that should be avoided at all costs because philosophy and science are "of the world" and bring with them the possibility of polluting the way we think about God?

Questions like these have been around since the beginning of the Christian era, and Christians have taken a wide variety of views. In the early church, believers like Tertullian (AD 160–220) famously quipped, "What indeed has Athens to do with Jerusalem?"[1] In Tertullian's mind, philosophy, associated with the Greeks and the city of Athens, was concerned with very different things than was Christian theology and, even worse, was utterly pagan. As such, he felt that the use of philosophy by Christians in the defense and formulation of Christian doctrine was problematic.[2] Origen (AD 184–253), a younger contemporary of Tertullian, took a much different approach, making significant use of Plato's philosophy to account for the doctrines of anthropology,

1. Tertullian, *Prescription against Heretics* 7, in *Ante-Nicene Fathers*, ed. Alexander Roberts and James Donaldson (Peabody, MA: Hendrickson, 2004), 3:246.

2. This is at least the textbook account of Tertullian regarding faith and reason. But we should notice that this slight caricature of Tertullian isn't completely accurate. As it turns out, Tertullian actually made use of Stoic philosophy to work through the doctrine of the Trinity.

Christology, and some aspects of his doctrine of God. We will say more on this history in a moment. For now, Tertullian and Origen demonstrate the history of the debate.

In this chapter we address the relationship of faith and reason and a related question about the relationship of theology and modern science. We start by setting out just what we mean by the terms "faith" and "reason," then end with a quick survey of various models for understanding these relationships.

## The Nature of Faith, Reason, and Science

Before we begin our survey of the different approaches to the relationship between faith and reason, we need to first set out what we understand by each of the terms involved in the discussion. And we must also say something about where these debates arise. The conversation about this relationship comes up in two areas: (1) the relationship between theology and philosophy and (2) the relationship between theology and science. What we will see below is that, throughout history, there have been numerous models for thinking about the relationship of theology to both philosophy and science. As such, the question about the relationship between "faith and reason" is general enough to include faith's relationship to both philosophy and science. But before we get to those models, we first consider the terminology involved.

So what exactly is this thing called "faith"? The term gets used in a variety of ways and needs some clarification before we begin exploring its relationship to reason. In popular usage, faith might refer to any number of things. For instance, faith is sometimes spoken of as a sort of optimism or positive thinking. A person may face a difficult circumstance and think of faith as a way forward, hoping for the best and wishing to avoid the worst. This is not the kind of thing we are speaking of in this chapter as we think about faith. A second popular way of thinking about faith must also be noted and rejected. In modern Western culture, faith is also thought of metaphorically as a blind leap one makes in affirming an idea in the absence of supporting data or facts. In this case, a person may hold to a religious or nonreligious idea that they hope to be true but that faces serious intellectual problems. Once again, this is not what we are talking about when we speak of faith in this chapter. We are not denying that the term "faith" is sometimes thought of in these ways; rather, we are simply suggesting that neither of these conceptions capture what needs to be in view as we think of the relationship of faith and reason. In fact, it should be recognized here that the "blind leap" construal of faith (1) does not do justice to the way Christians throughout history have understood faith and (2) immediately prejudices the case against a relationship between faith and reason. If faith just is a blind leap, then we should want nothing to do with the actual facts of the matter. But this is decidedly not the way Christians have thought about faith, so we can and should set this construal aside.

With these clarifications out of the way, we now consider the ways the term "faith" is employed in our current discussion. Interestingly, the term "faith" has had, and continues to have, a double meaning within Christian thought. It can be used as both a noun and as a verb, and both have importance for the way we think about the relationship of faith and reason. Consider faith as a noun. As a noun, the term "faith" simply refers to what it is that a person believes, or to a set of beliefs that are held by a particular group. When a person asks what your faith says about a particular topic, they are asking what your belief system says about an issue.

Faith can also be understood somewhat differently when we think of it as a verb. In this case, faith is a sort of act we perform. In particular, it is an act of ventured trusting in someone or something in response to information that may be given. This seems to be what is involved when the Bible calls us to have faith in God and Jesus Christ. In Romans 1:17, for example, the Bible says, "The just shall live by faith" (NKJV). When the Bible speaks this way, it is making clear that our salvation comes to us via our trust response to the person Jesus Christ. As with what we saw above when we considered faith as a noun, there is likewise nothing in the verbal concept of faith that should prejudice us one way or the other for the relationship of faith and reason. The Bible also sometimes uses the word "believe" to convey this idea. In Acts 16:31, for instance, Paul tells the Philippian jailor to "believe on the Lord Jesus Christ, and you will be saved" (NKJV). In these cases, and many others like them, faith is an act of ventured trust. Persons who have faith are those who have placed their faith in Christ to save them from sin. Or in other aspects of Christian life, they may be placing their faith in Christ for provision or guidance in some particular situation. Thus faith should be thought of as a kind of trust act of the person who has it.

But what about the terms "reason" and "science"? Defining "reason" is a bit more difficult, since it is something that takes place with so many disciplines. As a tentative starting point for the discussion, we might just think of reason as a cognitive activity that involves comparing, analyzing, and investigating data to formulate judgments regarding beliefs or theories. And as just indicated, reason is employed in a host of disciplines like philosophy, science, history, mathematics, theology, psychology, and any number of other intellectual fields. In each field we use reason to compare one idea with another, analyze the coherence of that idea, and test whether that idea holds up against the data we receive from the empirical sciences. By using reason we can think critically, analyze data, consider probabilities, or provide appropriate evidence in favor of a view. What we mean by "science," however, is much more straightforward and simple to grasp. By "science" we are simply referring to the exploration and explanation of the physical world typically found in the disciplines of physics, chemistry, biology, geology, and the like.

It is important to note that there is nothing in the concepts considered so far that should prejudice us one way or the other regarding the relationship of faith and reason, or faith and science. There may be important discoveries in either discipline that cause problems or give favor for these relationships, but those should be thought of as separate matters. For now, we simply want to notice that there is no prima facie conceptual reason to say that faith is incompatible with science or philosophy. With that in mind, we now consider the most prominent views throughout history.

## Models for the Relationship of Faith and Reason

Throughout history, philosophers, theologians, and scientists have thought about the relationship between faith and reason in different ways. We will not list all of these approaches but will offer a quick overview of the most common perspectives that have been put forward. We have already mentioned some of the preliminary debates between Tertullian and Origen in the early centuries of Christian theological development. This debate sets the stage for what would become an ongoing debate in Western history. We begin with the medieval thinkers.

### *Faith Seeking Understanding*

One major view is commonly associated with Anselm of Canterbury (1033–1109). In his *Proslogion*, Anselm sets forth his famous argument for God's existence, what we now call the ontological argument. The details of that argument are not what we will focus on here. Rather, we will instead focus on the way he understood faith and reason. Because this is the work in which he sets forth the ontological argument, most readers who are new to Anselm expect him to begin by establishing some universally agreed-on premises and then move on to show that God must exist. But this is actually not the way Anselm proceeds at all. Instead, he starts with the belief in God and simply tries to show how this belief makes sense. He prays, "I do not try, Lord, to attain Your lofty heights, because my understanding is in no way equal to it. But I do desire to understand Your truth a little, that truth that my heart believes and loves. For I do not seek to understand so that I may believe; but I believe so that I may understand. For I believe this also, that unless I believe, I shall not understand."[3]

In other words, Anselm is decidedly not starting on neutral ground as he considers God's existence. Instead, he starts by admitting that he must begin with God's existence if he is going to be able to understand God. But this does not mean that he was opposed to using reason. Rather, in this approach, he starts with faith and then seeks to better understand that faith by way of rational reflection. What is interesting about the *Proslogion* is that the entire work is actually written as a prayer to God, where Anselm repeatedly asks God for help to better understand who God is and what God is like. In that posture of prayerful dependence on God, Anselm then uses reason to understand what he already believes and to love what he finds to be true of God. This approach recognizes two important things about understanding God. First, sin, pride, and finitude can limit us in such a way that God must help us to see clearly. Second, it holds reason in high regard as a God-given faculty that guides us in truth. But reason by itself cannot bring us to a proper view of God. Anselm says that the awareness of God in us is "so effaced and worn away by vice, so darkened by the smoke of sin, that it cannot do what it was made to do unless [God] renew it."[4] Hence the relationship of faith and reason in this tradition is one of *faith seeking understanding*, where disciplines like philosophy and science are valuable resources deriving from our faith.

Anselm is not the only one to think about the relationship of faith and reason in this way. In fact, Anselm understood himself to be operating in the same tradition started by Augustine of Hippo (354–430), who in a sermon on John's Gospel exhorts, "Believe that thou mayest understand."[5] Likewise, Boethius (477–524) is another example of someone in the medieval tradition who approached faith and reason in this way. In *The Consolation of Philosophy*, he personifies the subject as "Lady Philosophy," who, by reminding him who God is, brings comfort to Boethius as he awaits his martyrdom. In this work, Boethius establishes and defends what we could call classical theism by using reason alone.[6] The same could be said for Thomas Aquinas (1224–74), who came after Anselm. He says that theology "can in a sense depend upon the philosophical sciences, not as though it stood in need of them, but only

3. Anselm, *Proslogion*, in *Anselm of Canterbury: The Major Works* (New York: Oxford University Press, 2008), 87.

4. Anselm, *Proslogion*, 87.

5. Augustine, *On the Gospel of St. John* 29.6, in *Nicene and Post-Nicene Fathers*, ed. Philip Schaff, Series 1 (Peabody, MA: Hendrickson, 2004), 7:184.

6. Boethius, *The Consolation of Philosophy* (New York: Oxford University Press, 2000).

in order to make its teaching clearer. . . . Therefore it does not depend upon other sciences as upon the higher, but makes use of them as of the lesser, and as handmaidens. . . . That it thus uses them is not due to its own defect or insufficiency, but to the defect of our intelligence, which is more easily led by what is known through natural reason."[7]

Here Aquinas is clear that the doctrines of the church do not depend on reason as a foundation but that the church nevertheless is served well by philosophy since its teachings can be demonstrated by reason. Because of this, philosophy is a helpful handmaiden to theology. All of these thinkers approach the relationship between faith and reason as one of faith seeking understanding, where reason serves faith.

Critics of this view have come from inside and outside the faith. Some within the faith have shared the same kinds of concerns that Tertullian once had in the patristic era, being greatly anxious that using philosophy for theological purposes could only corrupt doctrine. Critics from the outside have considered this approach to be guilty of question begging. Nevertheless, the view still enjoys considerable support by Christian apologists and philosophers.

### *Reason as Magistrate*

Enlightenment philosophers took a much different view on the matter. They saw the Enlightenment as stripping away all the myths, biases, spiritual prejudices, and folk beliefs of the past and letting reason and science guide the way into truth. As has been well noted, the Enlightenment world rejected the Judeo-Christian metanarrative that offered God as an explanation of all things and replaced God with modern philosophy and modern science. Where religion once explained things, science and philosophy were now preferred. In this new age, reason ruled over all matters of thinking. This did not necessarily mean the end of religious thinking or believing. Rather, it simply meant that religious beliefs were held to be epistemically inferior to the natural sciences. And as such, religious belief was judged by philosophy and science. One was still free to believe in God and exercise faith, but only insofar as such belief was not at odds with rational argument. Put another way, unless a religious idea could be established by way of rational argument, then such beliefs were deemed to be problematic.

One example of this way of thinking was Immanuel Kant (1724–1804). This is seen in the way Kant sought a completely objective basis for knowledge. He thought we could identify universal methods of thinking that could be applied

7. Thomas Aquinas, *Summa Theologica*, trans. Fathers of the English Dominican Province (Notre Dame, IN: Christian Classics, 1947), 1.1.5.

to all people in all places. As Alister McGrath explains, "Kant had argued, in what now seems a somewhat optimistic manner, for a transcendental criteria of judgment, valid for all minds and across all cultures and traditions at all time[s]."[8] The Enlightenment took "the view that human reason elevated the intelligent and the enlightened individual above the shadows and clouds of tradition, and allowed the 'big picture' to be seen with unprecedented clarity. In the light of this comprehensive overview of the totality of things, reliable judgments could be made concerning religions, traditions and other such outmoded ways of thinking and behaving."[9] Indeed, in his *What Is Enlightenment?* Kant argues that the scholar is finally able, and even obligated, to strip away the biases of religion and superstition. "Likewise the clergyman is obliged to teach his pupils and his congregation according to the creed of the church which he serves, for he has been accepted on that condition. But as a scholar, he has full freedom, in fact even the obligation, to communicate to the public all his diligently examined and well-intentioned thoughts concerning erroneous points in that doctrine and concerning proposals regarding the better institution of religious and ecclesiastical matters."[10]

As popular as this view was during the Enlightenment, and even with some today, it is not without its problems. To begin with, the kind of objectivity Kant seeks is not so easy to attain. Human beings are situated within contexts that shape the way we look at the world and think about important issues. Therefore, a universal rationality has not been found. Furthermore, the Enlightenment thinkers' opinions about the "biases" and "religious ideas" have turned out to be just that: opinions. While the Enlightenment popularized the idea that religious ideas are based on mere hopes, opinions, and speculations, it turns out that many of the central ideas that support Christian thought are far more resilient than depicted by these thinkers. As the past hundred years of science and philosophy have shown, Christian thought enjoys a significant amount of support from these disciplines.

### *Warfare Thesis*

Another dominant view throughout the past few hundred years has been called the warfare thesis, which sees the relationship between faith and reason as being hostile and unfriendly. According to advocates of this view, religion and science (and even religion and philosophy) are natural enemies to each

8. Alister E. McGrath, *A Scientific Theology* (Grand Rapids: Eerdmans, 2002), 2:57.

9. McGrath, *A Scientific Theology*, 2:58.

10. Immanuel Kant, *What Is Enlightenment?*, in *Basic Writings of Kant*, ed. Allen W. Wood (New York: Modern Library, 2001), 137.

other. In his essay titled "The Conflict of Science and Religion," Colin Russell notes the tendency to think this way: "The history of science has often been regarded as a series of conflicts between science and religion (usually Christianity), of which the cases of Galileo Galilei (1564–1642) and Charles Darwin (1809–82) are merely the most celebrated examples."[11] Russell reports, "Such a view of the relations between science and religion has been variously described as a 'conflict thesis,' a 'military metaphor,' or simply a 'warfare model.'"[12]

One example of this view is Andrew Dickson White in his famous book titled *A History of the Warfare of Science with Theology*. In his introduction, he is careful to state that he believes the conflict is not between science and religion but between science and dogmatic theology that is based on biblical texts and ancient modes of thinking. He says, "In all modern history, interference with science in the supposed interest of religion, no matter how conscientious such interference may have been, has resulted in the direst evils both to religion and to science."[13] Thus, for White, the relationship between science and theology is one of conflict and harm.

It seems, however, that maintaining such a thesis is difficult. First, the relationship between the two disciplines is actually far more complex than this view suggests.[14] Second, this view is a rather recent phenomenon, popularized by those with clear ideological agendas.[15] Perhaps the greatest reason for rejecting the conflict thesis, however, is that there is sufficient evidence to suggest that religion has played an important role in the development of modern science.[16]

### *Fideism*

The word "**fideism**" comes from the Latin word *fides*, which means "faith." In this approach, one does not base belief in God on rational argument or scientific evidence. Rather, one simply has faith, and this is what is pleasing

11. Colin A. Russell, "The Conflict of Science and Religion," in *Science and Religion*, ed. Gary B. Ferngren (Baltimore: Johns Hopkins University Press, 2002), 3.

12. Russell, "Conflict of Science and Religion," 3.

13. Andrew Dickson White, *A History of the Warfare of Science with Theology*, 2nd ed. (New York: Dover Publications, 1896), 1:viii. For another example of those who hold this position, see John William Draper, *History of the Conflict between Religion and Science* (London: Pioneer, 1874).

14. Russell, "Conflict of Science and Religion," 7–9.

15. Nancy R. Pearcey and Charles B. Thaxton, *The Soul of Science: Christian Faith and Natural Philosophy* (Wheaton: Crossway, 1994), 19.

16. Vincent Carroll and David Shiflett, *Christianity on Trial* (San Francisco: Encounter Books, 2002), 57.

to God. As Chad Meister puts it, "Using reason to demonstrate or evaluate religions or religious beliefs is always inappropriate [for the fideist]. Faith is not the kind of thing which needs rational justification, fideists maintain, and attempting to prove one's religious faith may even be an indication of a lack of faith."[17]

One clear example of this approach to the relationship between faith and reason is the nineteenth-century Danish philosopher Søren Kierkegaard (1813–55). In Kierkegaard's mind, the quest for objectivity associated with Kant and Georg Hegel is a form of intellectual idolatry, an attempt to have the kind of perspective that only God can have. To seek such objectivity, therefore, is an attempt to be like God. In particular, Kierkegaard thought that such an approach stripped religious ideas and questions of all their existential concerns and treated the question of God's existence as a matter of mere intellectual wonder, like what we find in mathematics. God, for Kierkegaard, is not the kind of subject matter that can be thought of this way. Rather, to think of God requires doing so with emotion, passion, and most important, the will.

Kierkegaard was deeply skeptical of those who seek to establish faith by way of reason and historical support for biblical claims. In his mind, such an approach sterilizes faith and as a result kills it. He says: "Thus everything is assumed to be in order with regard to the Holy Scriptures—what then? Has the person who did not believe come a single step closer to faith? No, not a single step. Faith does not result from straightforward scholarly deliberation, nor does it come directly; on the contrary, in this objectivity one loses that infinite, personal, impassioned interestedness, which is the condition of faith."[18] He also asserts, "In order, however, to avoid confusion, it should immediately be borne in mind that the issue is not . . . about the indifferent individual's systematic eagerness to arrange the truths of Christianity in paragraphs but rather about the concern of the infinitely interested individual with regard to his own relation to such a doctrine."[19] Ed Miller explains that for Kierkegaard "Truth, at least the kind that ought to concern us most, is not a matter of objectivity but subjectivity. This truth cannot be grasped through philosophical, scientific, or historical methods, but only when through the passion of infinite concern the existing individual abandons himself to the Teacher in a 'leap of faith.'"[20] Meister seems to agree, adding that "for Kierkegaard, true religion is not cold and calculating, regurgitating the right answers to logical,

17. Chad Meister, *Introducing Philosophy of Religion* (New York: Routledge, 2009), 154.

18. Søren Kierkegaard, *Concluding Unscientific Postscript*, trans. Howard Hong and Edna Hong (Princeton: Princeton University Press, 1992), 29.

19. Kierkegaard, *Concluding Unscientific Postscript*, 15.

20. Ed. L. Miller, *God and Reason* (New York: Macmillan, 1972), 126.

formulaic issues in systematic, impersonal fashion. Rather, it is passionate and obsessive, more akin to an intimate relationship between two lovers."[21] The person of faith, therefore, is not one who is concerned with reason. In this view, faith is what pleases God.

Fideists offer a helpful reminder that considerations about God cannot, or at least should not, be passionless or indifferent. But it should be noted that having an interest in God does not require us to jettison reason, science, or historical considerations the way fideism suggests we must. Why not instead think that the two can go hand in hand? Furthermore, there is also legitimate concern that the fideist's approach to reason and evidence leads to relativism and absurdity. If one is to just believe and ignore reason, science, and history, then wouldn't just about any religious idea be acceptable? If the Christian is to operate this way, then couldn't a person of any other faith? In the end, this approach leaves us with no way to adjudicate between mutually exclusive belief systems.

### *Evidentialism*

In chapter 3 we explored the debate between internalism and externalism. **Evidentialism**, a very popular view in recent philosophical history regarding the relationship of faith and reason, is an example of an internalist approach to justification. Evidentialism was deeply influenced by the Enlightenment demands for rationality and intellectual support for belief. W. K. Clifford (1845–79) is often associated with this perspective. He famously said, "It is wrong always, everywhere, and for anyone, to believe anything upon insufficient evidence."[22] In other words, epistemologically speaking, Clifford felt that it was deeply problematic, to the point of becoming a moral issue, for a person to hold beliefs without rational or evidential support. He adds, "If a man, holding a belief which he was taught in childhood or persuaded of afterwards, keeps down and pushes away any doubts which could arise about it in his mind, purposely avoids the reading of books and the company of men that call in question or discuss it, and regards as impious those questions which cannot easily be asked without disturbing it—the life of that man is one long sin against mankind."[23]

In some ways, this view is similar to the "Reason as Magistrate" view mentioned above in that it requires our beliefs to have rational support. But

21. Meister, *Introducing Philosophy of Religion*, 154.

22. W. K. Clifford, "The Ethics of Belief," reprinted in *Gateway to the Great Books*, ed. Robert M. Hutchins and Mortimer Adler (Chicago: Encyclopedia Britannica, 1963), 10:21. Clifford's essay has been widely read and reprinted since 1879, when it first appeared in his work *Lectures and Essays* (London: MacMillan).

23. Clifford, "Ethics of Belief," 21–22.

interestingly, Christians have been willing to accept and work within this perspective. For these believers, the "idea was essentially to fight fire with fire—to show that a scientific approach to the Christian truth claims would vindicate their rationality."[24] This approach differs from the magisterial view in that it seems to lack the bias of the magisterial view that considers religious beliefs to be inferior to philosophical or scientific beliefs. That is, evidentialism, unlike the magisterial view, maintains that religious beliefs can enjoy as much support as any other kind of belief.

Evidentialism has helped us to avoid the relativism we expressed concern about in the section above on fideism. But not all Christian philosophers have found this approach appealing. As we saw in chapter 3, some have wondered why a Christian would accept the evidentialist's demands for evidence in the first place. For example, Alvin Plantinga asks, "Why should we think a theist must have evidence, or reason to think there is evidence, if he is not to be irrational? Why not suppose, instead, that he is entirely within his epistemic rights in believing in God's existence even if he has no argument or evidence at all?"[25] Ronald Nash wonders the same thing: "There are countless things that we believe (and believe properly, justifiably, and rationally) without proof or evidence. We believe in the existence of other minds; we believe that the world continues to exist even when we are not perceiving it. There are countless things that we not only believe but have a right to believe even though we lack proof or evidence."[26] Nash also observes that the very demands of evidentialism fail to satisfy its own standards: "For Clifford, it is immoral to believe anything without proof. But where is the proof for Clifford's claim? What evidence does Clifford provide for his belief that it is immoral to believe anything in the absence of evidence? First, Clifford warns his reader against acting immorally with respect to his epistemic activities. But then he turns around and acts 'immorally' by advancing a thesis for which he provides no proof or evidence."[27]

### *Pragmatism*

As we saw in chapter 2, pragmatism is an epistemological approach that grounds truth claims in their utility. In other words, truth is what works. In this approach we should not be concerned with whether a claim corresponds

24. Kenneth Boa and Robert Bowman, *Faith Has Its Reasons: An Integrative Approach to Defending Christianity* (Milton Keynes, UK: Paternoster, 2005), 140.

25. Alvin Plantinga, "Reason and Belief in God," in *Faith and Rationality: Reason and Belief in God*, ed. Alvin Plantinga and Nicholas Wolterstorff (Notre Dame, IN: University of Notre Dame Press, 1983), 30.

26. Ronald Nash, *Faith and Reason* (Grand Rapids: Zondervan, 1988), 73.

27. Nash, *Faith and Reason*, 73.

to reality or is internally consistent with other things we think to be true. Rather, on this account we are concerned only with whether an idea or belief is somehow useful for us. If it is useful, it is "true." If it is not useful, then it should be discarded. William James (1842–1910), often thought to be the father of pragmatism, writes that pragmatism was "the attitude of looking away from first things, principles, 'categories,' supposed necessities; and looking toward last things, fruits, consequences, facts."[28] By "looking away" from things like first things, principles, categories, and necessities, James is referring to foundations or rational supports for our beliefs that have typically been the focal point in epistemology. By "looking toward" last things, fruits, and consequences, James is referring to the results that come from our beliefs. Again, the concern for pragmatists is the utility of belief. He then adds, "The true is the name of whatever proves itself to be good in the way of belief, and good, too, for definite, assignable reasons."[29]

Within the context of the relationship of faith and reason, pragmatism is a unique approach. First, it seeks to dissolve any conflict between religious beliefs and the theories of science and philosophy. If truth is just what works, then beliefs of all kinds have their place in our lives. Second, pragmatism is a way to provide a degree of justification for our beliefs. One who holds a particular belief is always able to claim that that belief works for oneself. If pragmatism is true, then we are no longer forced to side with either religion or philosophy and science.

Like the other views we've considered thus far, there are some concerns with this view. First, pragmatism just doesn't seem to be a proper view of the nature of truth. In pragmatism, there is no such thing as Truth (with a capital *T*) in an ultimate sense. So, for example, when we say, "It is wrong to steal," we typically mean that this is true for me, for you, for us, for them, for everyone, for all time. We typically think that this is just true. But for pragmatism, there is no such thing as truth in this sense. The best a pragmatist can say is that "It is wrong to steal" is true (lowercase *t*) in a lesser sense. That is, "It is wrong to steal" is simply an idea that we find useful and that works for us in some way. Pragmatism doesn't square up with our basic intuitions about truth. Second, pragmatism, like other approaches we have considered in this chapter, leads to relativism. If truth is just what works for us, then what do we do when other persons find conflicting ideas and practices to be useful? We will again find ourselves in situations where mutually exclusive, and potentially dangerous, ideas are held up as being "true."

28. William James, *Pragmatism* (New York: Longmans, Green, 1907), 54.
29. James, *Pragmatism*, 57.

### *Dialogical Views*

One final view is also worth our consideration. Recently a number of theologians have advocated for what we might call a dialogical view of the relationship between faith and reason, where theology and science, as well as theology and philosophy, are set up to be natural dialogue partners. As McGrath puts it, "The natural sciences seem to offer to contemporary Christian theology the same intellectual opportunities that earlier generations discerned within Aristotelianism or Cartesianism—the possibility of a dialogue partner with genuine insights to offer, which might be accommodated and exploited within the theological enterprise."[30] Elsewhere McGrath adds that this should be thought of as a "natural dialogue, grounded in the fundamental belief that the God about whom Christian theology speaks is the same God who created the world that the natural sciences investigate."[31] David Clark has argued for a similar approach. For example, Clark says, "We place a particular scientific idea or theory into conversation with a particular theological tradition, model, or doctrine. That is, we bring *interpretations of Scripture*—theology—into conversation with *interpretations of nature*—science."[32] And he is clear that "we do not allow science to supersede the Bible itself,"[33] but we do allow it to override problematic interpretations of the Bible. One example of the kind of problematic interpretation would be the view that the earth is flat, does not move, or even that it is the center of the universe. He says, "No particular scientific theory, model, or idea possesses authority over Scripture, but there could be a scenario where a scientific claim trumps the deliverances of theology."[34]

A number of positives that these theologians believe come from such a partnership. First, they believe that this approach is simply fitting, given what Christians believe about creation. As McGrath notes, if in fact creation and Scripture originate from God, then perhaps they should be considered alongside each other as theories are developed. Second, the notion of "dialogue" is helpful. Dialogue partners often sharpen each other. Sometimes they agree

30. Alister E. McGrath, *A Scientific Theology* (Grand Rapids: Eerdmans, 2001), 1:18–19. See also Kees van Kooten Niekerk, "A Critical Realist Perspective on the Dialogue between Theology and Science," in *Rethinking Theology and Science*, ed. Niels Henrik Gregersen and J. Wentzel van Huyssteen (Grand Rapids: Eerdmans, 1998), 51–86; J. Wentzel van Huyssteen, *The Shaping of Rationality* (Grand Rapids: Eerdmans, 1999); Arthur Peacocke, *Theology for a Scientific Age* (Oxford: Basil Blackwell, 1990).

31. Alister E. McGrath, *The Science of God* (Grand Rapids: Eerdmans, 2004), 21.

32. David K. Clark, *To Know and Love God* (Wheaton: Crossway, 2003), 286 (emphasis in original).

33. Clark, *To Know and Love God*, 288.

34. Clark, *To Know and Love God*, 288.

with each other, sometimes they disagree. But in every case, both partners in a dialogue receive the benefit of clarification, further investigating, and a broader grasp of the important issues. These are benefits well worth the investment in dialogue. Third, both disciplines can actually help each other by filling in gaps of explanation or by providing some perspective that the other lacks. For theology, as Clark has mentioned, science can provide insights about the world that help us to avoid problematic interpretations of Scripture. For science, theology can provide a theoretical background for the work of science that explains why science works in the first place. For example, science assumes a rationality of the natural order that it actually has no way of explaining. As John Polkinghorne says, "We are so familiar with the fact that we can understand the world that most of the time we take it for granted. It is what makes science possible. Yet it could have been otherwise. The universe might have been a disorderly chaos rather than an orderly cosmos. Or it might have had a rationality which was inaccessible to us."[35] And as James F. Keating observes, this is precisely where theology is able to offer aid to science: "It is at this point that a Christian conception of nature as creation reveals its illuminative power for science. If one views nature as created by a deity who also created human beings in the divine image, an 'intrinsic resonance' between their mental constructs and the intelligible structure of nature is to be expected."[36]

Not everyone will be convinced of the virtues of the dialogical approach to faith and reason. As we have seen with thinkers throughout history, dating back as far as Tertullian, some are generally concerned anytime something other than Scripture, especially philosophy or science, is allowed to speak into theology. Some from the sciences will reciprocate, feeling the same way about theology. In their view, "letting religion in" is seen as a step backward, as something that will hurt rather than help science. Perhaps these concerns are legitimate. But then again, perhaps they are overstated.

## Conclusion

In this chapter we have explored the relationship between faith and reason by first setting forth what we mean by those terms and what those disciplines are about. We have also considered a variety of views, including faith seeking

35. John C. Polkinghorne, *Science and Creation: The Search for Understanding* (Philadelphia: Templeton Foundation, 2006), 29.

36. James F. Keating, "The Natural Sciences as an *Ancilla Theologiae Nova*: Alister E. McGrath's *A Scientific Theology*," *The Thomist* 69 (2005): 131.

understanding, the magisterial view, the warfare thesis, fideism, evidentialism, pragmatism, and what we have called the dialogical view. Each has had worthy defenders and champions. But what should we make of all this, and where should we land? While some may prefer different views, we are inclined to identify with Anselm and the tradition of faith seeking understanding. This tradition honestly acknowledges the fact that, as believers, we already have faith commitments. At the same time, with its pursuit of understanding, argumentation, and investigation into the world, this tradition avoids the worrisome concerns associated with fideism. Thus we suggest that this approach offers an appropriate balance between rationality and humility. Yet, in addition to this, we also suggest that there is great merit in the dialogical approaches described above. Indeed, it seems as though a commitment to the Anselmian faith-seeking-understanding approach to faith and reason will also require us to engage in dialogue with history, science, and philosophy.

# 6

# Natural Revelation and Natural Theology

As human beings, we know all kinds of things. We know that gravity causes things to fall when they are let go. We know that certain laws of aerodynamics cause airplanes to fly when air moves across the foil of a wing at a particular speed. These are examples of things we know about the natural world. We also have certain kinds of sociological knowledge. For example, I (Jamie) know that social difficulty will follow if I walk into a room full of people and proclaim that they are all fools. Epistemologists would identify these as very different kinds of knowledge, but they are examples of knowledge nonetheless. What is interesting about both of these examples of knowledge, however, is that I have learned them all by some kind of experience or observation. I watched the rock (and many other objects) fall from my hand repeatedly. I saw and felt the plane rise into the sky as we moved speedily down the runway. I observed what happened when my uncle walked into the room and proclaimed that we are all fools and idiots. Experience and observation teach us much. In fact, most of what we learn as human beings comes this way. We see, we feel, we hear, we smell, we taste, we observe, and we experiment.

So how do we come to know about God? Fortunately, we have a biblical testimony that reveals God to us, and we are not left to ourselves to wonder what God is like. But what if we didn't have the Bible? What if we had nothing from sacred theology or Holy Scripture? What if we had to start from scratch, with only what we find in nature to guide us? Could we—would we—know anything about God? Could we learn about God in the same way we learn about the laws of aerodynamics, gravity, or sociology? Could we learn about God and come to have knowledge about God from what we see, feel, hear, smell, taste, observe, or find in experiments?

At first blush it does not look as though it would be possible to know anything about God like this. Who among us, for example, has had the chance to observe God directly with one of the five senses? Under normal circumstances we do not see, touch, taste, smell, or hear God directly in the same way that we see things in the physical world. So, not surprisingly, modern philosophers have been skeptical of our ability to gain knowledge of God via the natural world. But perhaps this skepticism is misguided. Even if we do not have direct epistemic access to God via our five senses, perhaps we can still know something about God from what we find in nature. Perhaps, that is, we can discern things about God from particular aspects of the world as they point in his direction.

Considerations like these lead us to an exploration of natural revelation and natural theology. In what follows, we will define natural revelation and natural theology, showing how they are distinct and yet linked to each other. This chapter will focus primarily on the possibility of doing natural theology by evaluating the prospects of deriving knowledge of God from nature (specific natural theology arguments with be put forward in chapter 12). We will then give an account of natural revelation, identifying biblical data that supports it and how and where we find it in nature. We will then comment briefly on the history of natural theology and how it is envisioned by modern practitioners. After this, we will outline the common objections against natural theology and offer a response.

## Defining Natural Revelation and Natural Theology

The terms "natural revelation" and "natural theology" are often used interchangeably. In general, both deal with the knowledge of God that we obtain from nature, and it is therefore understandable that people use them synonymously. But there is a key difference between them that needs to be noticed and understood. To see this, it will be helpful to drop the word "natural" from them, at least for the moment, and see the difference between "revelation" and "theology" more generally. Revelation, as understood by the Christian tradition, refers to what God has done or said or given. Revelation is God's self-disclosure of himself that allows human beings to know and understand who he is. As such, revelation is something that God does and/or something that God gives. Theology, by contrast, is a derivative of revelation. It refers to what human beings do with revelation, as a human response to God's self-disclosure. It seeks to organize a body of teachings in light of God's self-disclosure that makes sense of God, human life, and the world itself. And because it is derivative in nature, unlike revelation, theology is something that can err. It is fallible and in many cases is open to revision, adaptation, rearticulation, or rejection. Because of this, theology evolves and develops over time and from one group to the next. It manifests various schools of thought about particular topics and allows for sharp disagreement and conflicting perspectives among theologians. These theological differences arise not because of differing revelation to which they have access; rather, their perspectives differ because their contexts are different and because they face different kinds of problems and questions. Either way, in theology one often finds diverse perspectives on particular issues.

So then, revelation is something that God gives to us. Theology, however, is a derivative response to revelation. It has the possibility of error and can express different perspectives from one group of theologians to the next. But how does this affect our discussion about natural revelation and natural theology? By seeing the general difference between revelation and theology, we can also see that natural revelation and natural theology are not the same thing. Here the same kinds of points apply. **Natural revelation**—also called general revelation—is still a kind of divine self-disclosure by God. But in this case it refers to God's self-disclosure of himself in the natural world of created things as opposed to a selected set of texts or writings like the Bible. It is what can be understood about God from creation, both physical and existential. It is the instinctual awareness of God that most people have, the awe we feel in our hearts as we gaze up at the stars and feel that there must be a God, or the sense of God we feel when we behave immorally and feel guilt or shame. Both physically and existentially, this world points us to God and reinforces belief in him. By contrast, natural theology—like theology in general—is derivative in nature. It is what we do with natural revelation by reflecting on it and formalizing what we say about God in light of that revelation. **Natural theology** is our attempt to draw theological conclusions from nature and to see what can be said about God by considering what we find in the universe. Though not always true, natural theology often takes the form of an argument that tries to prove, or at least provide warrant for, God's existence.

Examples of natural theology are numerous, dating from well before the time of Christ, with Plato and Aristotle, and onward to contemporary Christian philosophers who put forth various kinds of arguments. As we will discuss in chapter 12, some of the most popular and influential examples can be classified as cosmological, teleological, moral, and ontological arguments. Cosmological arguments, for example, start with the existence of the universe and argue that God is the best, or only, explanation for the universe. Teleological arguments are similar to cosmological arguments but tend to focus on particular details of the universe that have purpose or seem to be designed in a particular way to perform some function. In this case, teleological arguments argue for God's existence on the basis of purpose and design. Likewise, moral arguments do the same thing but focus on the existence of moral law and our sense of morality, arguing again that God is the best, or only, explanation for morality. And though ontological arguments are considerably different from cosmological, teleological, and moral arguments, they nonetheless are good examples of natural theology. These arguments start with the very concept and definition of God and then argue that it is necessary for this God to exist. Again, these arguments are given attention in chapter 12. For now, let's consider the case for natural revelation and the possibility of doing natural theology. For those who are interested in religious knowledge, natural revelation may give us what we need to pursue the important epistemic enterprise of natural theology.

## Natural Revelation

Some, even in Christian circles, argue that God has not revealed himself in nature. So we must consider whether they are right or wrong. Do we have natural revelation? Has God really disclosed himself in the natural world such that we can know something about him? Numerous texts in the Bible suggest that he has. In fact, the Bible seems to suggest that God has revealed himself in nature, the human heart, and the flow of history.[1] Three particular texts are most important for us at this point: Romans 2:14–15; Psalm 19:1–4; and Romans 1:18–21. Consider, for example, Romans 2:14–15, where Paul says, "When Gentiles, who do not have the law, by nature do the things in the law, these, although not having the law, are a law to themselves, who show the work of the law written in their hearts, their conscience also bearing witness, and between themselves their thoughts accusing or else excusing them" (NKJV).

This is a very interesting passage. Here Paul declares that even gentiles who lack access to the written law of God know what is right and wrong,

1. Passages such as Job 12:23; Pss. 47:7–8; 66:7; Isa. 10:5–13; Dan. 2:21; and Acts 17:26 suggest that God reveals himself through the flow of history.

based on what they have found dwelling within their own consciences. This is because the law is "written in their hearts, their conscience also bearing witness." Like Psalm 19 and Romans 1, this passage affirms that God reveals himself in creation. But in this case, it points specifically to the human being and what God has put within each person.

So why is this important? Even if the Bible does say that God has revealed his character to us through our sense of morality, does that make it true? One way to answer that question is to take a look at what we find in the world to see if it corresponds to the claims of the Bible. And interestingly, we find what Paul describes in Romans 2 to be exactly what we find in the human inclination toward morality. Human beings sense, no matter what worldview they might come from, that there is a right and a wrong way to live. We protest when things go "wrong" and argue for a "right" way that things should be. Atheists are no different. They may reject the Christian vision and understanding of the world, yet they continue with the same kinds of protests for "right" and "wrong" that we find in people everywhere throughout history. As C. Stephen Evans explains, "It thus appears to us that we are responsible and accountable for our actions. It is natural to wonder: To whom are we responsible? To whom are we accountable? The obvious and natural answer is that we are responsible to God. I believe our sense of obligation is a natural sign that points us to the one who has created us and has authority to demand from us what is right and good."[2]

Along related lines, consider the more general sense of God that is present within us. By nature, human beings are religious. No matter where you look, and no matter when you look, people are naturally inclined toward belief in something transcendent. People all over the world and at every point throughout human history have sought for and directed their lives after some kind of theological belief. Simply put, we are naturally disposed to believe in God, as if God has implanted this knowledge of himself in our hearts and minds. In the *Institutes of the Christian Religion*, John Calvin famously comments on this: "There is within the human mind, and indeed by natural instinct, an awareness of divinity. This we take to be beyond controversy."[3] He adds, "Yet there is, as the eminent pagan [Cicero] says, no nation so barbarous, no people so savage, that they have not a deep-seated conviction that there is a God."[4] As a result of this deep-seated knowledge, Calvin states, "Therefore,

2. C. Stephen Evans, *Why Christian Faith Still Makes Sense* (Grand Rapids: Baker Academic, 2015), 47.

3. John Calvin, *Institutes of the Christian Religion*, ed. John T. McNeill, trans. Ford Lewis Battles (Philadelphia: Westminster, 1960), 1.3.1.

4. Calvin, *Institutes* 1.3.1.

since from the beginning of the world there has been no region, no city, in short, no household, that could do without religion, there lies in this a tacit confession of a sense of deity inscribed in the hearts of all."[5] Calvin is right. Something deep within the human mind and heart directs us to believe in God. We are drawn to believe in something beyond ourselves and beyond the physical world.

In addition to the traces of God that we find in the human sense of morality and the general sense of God's existence within the human heart, the Bible also speaks about the knowledge of God that is evident within the physical world. Consider, for example, Psalm 19. The psalmist says,

> The heavens declare the glory of God;
> And the firmament shows His handiwork.
> Day unto day utters speech,
> And night unto night reveals knowledge.
> *There is* no speech nor language
> *Where* their voice is not heard.
> Their line has gone out through all the earth,
> And their words to the end of the world. (vv. 1–4 NKJV)

Notice the opening statement of this passage. We are told that the "heavens declare the glory of God" and that the "firmament shows His handiwork." That is, nature reveals something about God to us—namely, that God exists and is glorious. In the firmament—the sky and the atmosphere—we see God's work of wisdom and knowledge on display. But the psalmist goes on to say, "Day unto day utters speech, / And night unto night reveals knowledge," meaning that the regular flow of nature from day to night reveals God to us in a way that is unmistakable. And as he goes on to say, this revelation is given to all people everywhere: "*There is* no speech nor language / *Where* their voice is not heard. / Their line has gone out through all the earth, / And their words to the end of the world." In other words, the voice of this revelation is spread so widely that people of every language receive it, and it goes to every corner of the earth. As Psalm 19 makes clear, God's self-disclosure is found in nature itself so that people everywhere are moved by creation to ponder the existence and nature of divinity.

The apostle Paul adds to this in Romans 1:18–21. Here he declares that the knowledge of God is found in nature, within the human heart itself, and in the rest of creation.

5. Calvin, *Institutes* 1.3.1.

> The wrath of God is revealed from heaven against all ungodliness and unrighteousness of men, who suppress the truth in unrighteousness, because what may be known of God is manifest in them, for God has shown *it* to them. For since the creation of the world His invisible *attributes* are clearly seen, being understood by the things that are made, *even* His eternal power and Godhead, so that they are without excuse, because, although they knew God, they did not glorify *Him* as God, nor were thankful, but became futile in their thoughts, and their foolish hearts were darkened. (NKJV)

Several affirmations in this passage should be highlighted. First, Paul affirms that God has placed knowledge of himself within human beings. For example, Paul says this knowledge is "manifest in them." That is, humans have a knowledge of God that is innate, within. Humans naturally believe in God. But we will say more on this later. Second, this passage affirms that some knowledge of God comes through the things that are created. Paul says, "For since the creation of the world His invisible *attributes* are clearly seen, being understood by the things that are made, *even* His eternal power and Godhead." In other words, from the natural order of creation, humans can discern both that God exists (his Godhead) and that God is powerful (his eternal power). Third, this passage affirms that such knowledge leaves humanity "without excuse." Since God has revealed this to all people everywhere through nature, no one is able to say that they never knew anything about God.

There is good reason to believe that the details of the physical universe also point us to belief in God. In fact, as we will see below, although advances in the natural sciences once led scientists and philosophers to reject the idea that nature pointed toward God, more recent discoveries in the natural sciences have reversed that trend and reinvigorated interest in the idea of nature as revelation. These considerations will be examined in some detail below and revisited again in chapter 12.

For now, the important takeaway from all of this is that we find the world doing precisely what the Bible claims that it does—namely, pointing toward God or offering a form of revelation. This correspondence between Word and world suggests something important and significant to us about the reality of natural revelation. It is one thing for the Bible to tell us that God has revealed himself in nature, but it is another thing to find nature actually revealing God. With that in mind, it is now important to consider how Christian philosophers and theologians have taken the next step of moving from natural revelation to the doing of natural theology.

## Natural Theology: Problems and Prospects

Natural theology is as old as the Christian theological tradition, dating back to the earliest theologians of the church and extending into the present day. In his *Proofs of God*,[6] Matthew Levering charts the history of this discipline from Tertullian to Karl Barth. During the patristic and medieval periods, for example, natural theology was advocated and defended by theologians and philosophers like Augustine, Anselm, and Aquinas. Yet by most accounts and despite its long history, natural theology was considered to be obsolete by the middle of the twentieth century.[7] As Alister McGrath puts it, "If my personal conversations with theologians, philosophers, and natural scientists over the last decade are in any way representative, natural theology is generally seen as being like a dead whale, left stranded on a beach by a receding tide, gracelessly rotting under the heat of a philosophical and scientific sun."[8]

The specific challenges to the New Testament have come from developments in natural science, philosophy, and theology during and since the Enlightenment; by the end of the nineteenth century, natural theology was considered to be a futile enterprise. Nevertheless, despite the challenges and objections that natural theology faced in the Enlightenment, it has made a significant comeback in recent years. James Sennett and Douglas Groothuis suggest that this is because proponents of natural theology are "using many new developments in science, theology and philosophy to make new and intriguing cases for the justification of theistic and Christian concepts and beliefs."[9] In what follows, we briefly trace what the challenges have been to natural theology in philosophy, science, and theology and note what has taken place to enable a revival in its practice.

### *Philosophical Objections*

Philosophically speaking, natural theology has had its fair share of critics. For example, Paul Moser has registered a variety of concerns with natural

6. Matthew Levering, *Proofs of God: Classical Arguments from Tertullian to Barth* (Grand Rapids: Baker Academic, 2016).

7. See C. Stephen Evans, "Apologetics in a New Key: Relieving Protestant Anxieties over Natural Theology," in *The Logic of Rational Theism*, ed. William Lane Craig and Mark S. McLeod (Lewiston, NY: Edwin Mellen, 1990), 65–75; Gordon J. Spykman, *Reformational Theology* (Grand Rapids: Eerdmans, 1992), 168–70; Ned Wisnefske, *Preparing to Hear the Gospel: A Proposal for Natural Theology* (Lanham, MD: University Press of America, 1998), 7–8.

8. Alister E. McGrath, *A Fine-Tuned Universe: The Quest for God in Science and Theology* (Louisville: Westminster John Knox, 2009), 5.

9. James F. Sennett and Douglas Groothuis, "Introduction," in *In Defense of Natural Theology: A Post-Humean Assessment*, ed. Sennett and Groothuis (Downers Grove, IL: InterVarsity, 2005), 11.

theology. In his view, natural theology is largely ineffective because it tends to accept a somewhat naturalistic notion that empirical evidence is all that counts as evidence. This is problematic for Moser since he does not think such evidence is often successful in producing belief in the God of the Bible. Moreover, he thinks that the most powerful and perhaps the only sort of evidence for God is the evidence of a transformed life.[10] While many contemporary Christian philosophers would agree with Moser about the evidential value of a transformed life, not all are convinced that natural theology is as problematic as he contends. Nevertheless, Moser has at least raised some important questions for consideration.

Historically, however, natural theology finds one of its greatest philosophical challenges in the criticism of David Hume. As James D. Madden puts it, "Indeed, Hume's influence can still be seen among many contemporary philosophers of religion. J. J. C. Smart, Michael Martin, J. L. Mackie and a number of other prominent nontheists all employ criticisms whose historical origin can be found in Humean insights."[11] Hume's famous critique of the design argument was published in his book *Dialogues Concerning Natural Religion.*[12] Here, the reader finds a debate between three friends named Cleanthes, Demea, and Philo. The argument that Hume critiques is defended by the character Cleanthes, who says,

> Look round the world: Contemplate the whole and every part of it: You will find it to be nothing but one great machine, subdivided into an infinite number of lesser machines, which again admit of subdivisions, to a degree beyond what human senses and faculties can trace and explain. All these various machines, and even their most minute parts, are adjusted to each other with an accuracy, which ravishes into admiration all men, who have ever contemplated them. The curious adapting of means to ends, throughout all nature, resembles exactly, though it much exceeds, the productions of human contrivance; of human design, thought, wisdom, and intelligence. Since therefore the effects resemble each other, we are led to infer, by all the rules of analogy, that the causes also resemble; and that the author of nature is somewhat similar to the mind of man; though possessed of much larger faculties, proportioned to the grandeur of the work, which he has executed. By this argument *a posteriori* and by this

10. See Paul Moser, *Evidence for God: Religious Knowledge Reexamined* (New York: Cambridge University Press, 2010).

11. James D. Madden, "Giving the Devil His Due: Teleological Arguments after Hume," in Sennett and Groothuis, *In Defense of Natural Theology*, 150.

12. David Hume, *Dialogues Concerning Natural Religion* (1779; repr., London: Penguin, 1990).

> argument alone, do we prove at once the existence of a deity, and his similarity to human mind and intelligence.[13]

Later he says, "Consider, anatomize the eye: Survey its structure and contrivance; and tell me, from your own feeling, if the idea of a contriver does not immediately flow in upon you with a force like that of sensation. The most obvious conclusion surely is in favor of design; and it requires time, reflection and study to summon up those frivolous though abstruse objections, which can support infidelity."[14]

In response to this argument, Hume's work presents a variety of objections. Though Hume's objections are not presented in chronological fashion, Stephen Davis distinguishes at least five criticisms leveled at Cleanthes's design argument, including objections regarding (1) who designed God, (2) a coherent universe, (3) insufficient evidence, (4) the problem of evil, and (5) weak analogy.[15] Each of these criticisms is presented by Philo and appears to represent the thinking of Hume himself.

### The Who Designed God Objection

The first objection contends that if the universe needs a cause, then God must need one too. This appears to be one of Hume's great questions for Cleanthes when he suggests a cause for the universe. Davis summarizes Hume's question by asking, "Why can't we ask who or what caused that mind? What licenses design arguers to stop the regress once they get to the designer? Doesn't the order exhibited in minds require explanation as much as the order that we see in the universe?"[16] Hume argues that any attempt to end the search for a cause with deity is arbitrary. If this is so, then Hume believes he is also justified in either stopping his search with nature itself or continuing to press the issue back into an infinite regress. That is, unless Cleanthes can show why it is justifiable to stop with God, then his approach is arbitrary and no better than Hume's suggestion.

But how convincing is this objection? Is it really arbitrary to stop the search for a cause with God? It seems as if we have three choices regarding the cause of the universe: either (1) the universe is caused by nature itself; (2) the universe is caused by God, or deity; or (3) the universe has an infinite regress of causes. We have good reason to reject option 1. Nature itself cannot

13. Hume, *Dialogues*, 53.

14. Hume, *Dialogues*, 65.

15. Stephen Davis, *God, Reason and Theistic Proofs* (Edinburgh: Edinburgh University Press, 1997), 101–6. We have worded these objections differently than Davis.

16. Davis, *God, Reason and Theistic Proofs*, 101.

be the cause of the universe since nature did not exist to bring the universe into existence. Likewise, option 3 also has its difficulties. As William Lane Craig argues in multiple places, infinite regresses of this nature seem to be logically impossible.[17] Thus option 2 appears to be the best choice. As J. P. Moreland states, "Explanation cannot keep going on forever. One has to stop somewhere with an explanatory ultimate. And when it comes to examples of design as order or purpose, we normally accept an explanation in terms of a rational agent as a proper stopping point and do not so regard an explanation in terms of physical causes."[18] Although Hume's objection regarding who designed God causes theologians to think more carefully about positing God as the cause of the universe, it is not clear that this objection is a defeater for design arguments.

### The Coherent-Universe Objection

Hume also suggests that the structure and orderliness of the universe should not be taken as evidence of a designer, since this is something that would be expected of any universe where life can be found. In his view, life can exist only in an orderly environment, so anywhere life is found, orderliness will be present. He says,

> It is in vain, therefore, to insist upon the uses of the parts in animals or vegetables and their curious adjustment to each other. I would fain know how an animal could subsist, unless its parts were so adjusted? Do we not find, that it immediately perishes whenever this adjustment ceases, and that its matter corrupting tries some new form? It happens, indeed, that the pans of the world are so well adjusted, that some regular form immediately lays claim to this corrupted matter: And if it were not so, could the world subsist?[19]

Moreland explains, "From the time of Hume to the present, opponents of the design argument have pointed out that we should not be surprised at this data. If the world had been one in which intelligent life could not evolve, then we should not be here to discuss the matter. These factors are necessary for people to be around to puzzle over them."[20]

17. William Lane Craig, "Philosophical and Scientific Pointers to *Creation ex Nihilo*," in *Contemporary Perspectives on Religious Epistemology*, ed. R. Douglas Geivett and Brendan Sweetman (New York: Oxford University Press, 1992).

18. J. P. Moreland, *Scaling the Secular City: A Defense of Christianity* (Grand Rapids: Baker, 1987), 64.

19. Hume, *Dialogues*, 95.

20. Moreland, *Scaling the Secular City*, 54.

This objection seems to miss the point altogether. What design arguments point out is not that a human can observe the orderliness but rather that (1) the orderliness is there in the first place and (2) the orderliness is itself a strong suggestion of something—or someone—beyond the universe. Davis says that "the very fact being noted by the design arguer is the existence of a world of sufficient stability and order to produce such organisms in the first place. . . . We can easily imagine worlds far less regular and law-like than ours. And so it is a significant fact that our world is so regular as to produce intelligent organisms who can notice that fact."[21]

### The Insufficient-Evidence Objection

Hume's third objection simply states that the evidence drawn from nature may be enough to establish some kind of creator, but it is not sufficient to prove the God of Christian theism. He says, "For as the cause ought only to be proportioned to the effect, and the effect, so far as it falls under our cognizance, is not infinite; what pretensions have we, upon your suppositions, to ascribe that attribute to the divine being?"[22] If this principle is true, then Hume believes that the evidence is not sufficient for Cleanthes to establish theism. Based on the evidence, Hume contends that there are several other possibilities for the designer. For one thing, this creator could be a finite being. Likewise, Hume suggests, polytheism could be justified by the evidence. He says, "A great number of men join in building a house or ship, in rearing a city, in framing a commonwealth: Why may not several deities combine in contriving and framing a world?"[23] Because of these possibilities, Hume believed the evidence was not sufficient to justify theism as the clear explanation for the data.

There are at least three things that can be said here. First, Hume raises a fair critique of many versions of divine arguments. In the history of natural theology, there have been times when the arguments overextended themselves, and this needs to be corrected. At the same time, however, this has not always been the case. Second, the advocate of design arguments should point out that, although such an argument does not fully demonstrate Christian theism, it is still enough to disprove naturalism. Third, this objection seems to lose much of its force if all divine arguments are considered in conjunction with one another. That is, when the design argument is used as part of a cumulative case for Christian theism, then it seems that it can be quite helpful.

21. Davis, *God, Reason and Theistic Proofs*, 102.
22. Hume, *Dialogues*, 76.
23. Hume, *Dialogues*, 77.

### The Problem-of-Evil Objection

Hume also suggested that the evidence of imperfection should be given equal weight in determining what kind of thing caused the universe. Thus, given cases of imperfection and evil within the world, one could not conclude that the cause of the universe is the morally good agent suggested by theism. According to the evidence, Hume says there is no reason "for ascribing perfection to the deity, even in his finite capacity; or for supposing him free from every error, mistake, or incoherence, in his undertakings."[24] He adds, "This world, for aught he knows, is very faulty and imperfect, compared to a superior standard; and was only the first rude essay of some infant deity, who afterwards abandoned it, ashamed of his lame performance: It is the work only of some dependent, inferior deity; and is the object of derision to his superiors."[25] In Hume's writings, the presence of evil and imperfections in nature suggests an imperfect deity at best.

While this chapter is not intended to focus on the problem of evil, at least one thing can be said about Hume's objection here. Up until this point in his critique of the design argument, the focus has been on the evidence of design alone, and Hume seems to prefer this limitation. In raising the problem of evil, however, Hume brings counterevidence into the discussion, which should open up the question's discussion for all relevant evidence. Hence, now that Hume has introduced other evidences, the theist may do the same. Davis seems to agree with this idea: "Suffice it to say that nothing prevents a successful design arguer from trying to argue, on other grounds, that the designer of the world is both all-powerful and perfectly good."[26] With this in mind, the believer is free to develop a theodicy—a positive account of why God might allow evil to be in the world—that answers the objection.[27]

### The Weak-Analogy Objection

Finally, Hume argued that the analogy in Cleanthes's argument is itself weak because of the dissimilarities of design in the objects in question—nature and human-made things. Hume says, "But surely you will not affirm, that the universe bears such a resemblance to a house, that we can with the same certainty infer a similar cause, or that the analogy is here entire

24. Hume, *Dialogues*, 77.
25. Hume, *Dialogues*, 79.
26. Davis, *God, Reason and Theistic Proofs*, 104.
27. For examples of how this has been done recently, see Chad V. Meister and James K. Dew Jr., eds., *God and Evil: The Case for God in a World Filled with Pain* (Downers Grove, IL: IVP Books, 2013); Chad V. Meister and James K. Dew Jr., eds., *God and the Problem of Evil: Five Views* (Downers Grove, IL: IVP Academic, 2017).

and perfect. The dissimilitude is so striking, that the utmost you can here pretend to is a guess, a conjecture, a presumption concerning a similar cause; and how that pretension will be received in the world, I leave you to consider."[28] According to Hume, it is this dissimilarity that weakens Cleanthes's analogy. He says, "Wherever you depart, in the least, from the similarity of the cases, you diminish proportionably the evidence; and may at last bring it to a very weak analogy, which is confessedly liable to error and uncertainty."[29]

What should we make of this objection? It must be acknowledged that arguments from analogy can be weak, depending on the kinds of differences we find in the objects. But is Hume right that analogies are of no value whatsoever? We suggest that although arguments from analogy never render complete certainty, they may be helpful in identifying the best explanation of the data. In Davis's mind, "The question is whether there is any other, more plausible explanation of the similar effects. Arguments from analogy are at their strongest where there is some reason to think that this is the case, some reason to think that alternative explanations will not wash."[30]

### *Scientific Objections*

The scientific objections to natural theology are far easier to grasp. When Paley published his *Natural Theology* in 1802, his work became incredibly popular in the major universities of Britain and the United States. Nevertheless, it—and natural theology more generally—received a formidable challenge in the work of Charles Darwin (1809–82). In 1859 Darwin published his famous work titled *On the Origin of Species* and radically changed the trajectory of science from his day forward. John Polkinghorne explains the significance of Darwinism for natural theology as follows:

> The collapse of . . . natural theology was not brought about by philosophical criticism . . . but by a scientific discovery. In 1859, Charles Darwin published *The Origin of Species*. It became apparent that there was the possibility of the appearance of design without the need for appeal to the direct action of a Designer. The evolutionary sifting of small differences through natural selection, acting competitively over many generations, was perceived to be capable of producing the observed aptness of living creatures for survival in their environments.[31]

28. Hume, *Dialogues*, 55.
29. Hume, *Dialogues*, 54.
30. Davis, *God, Reason and Theistic Proofs*, 99–100.
31. John Polkinghorne, *Science and Theology* (London: SPCK, 1998), 70.

Neal Gillespie agrees, saying it "has been generally agreed (then and since) that Darwin's doctrine of natural selection effectively demolished William Paley's classical design argument for the existence of God."[32] He elaborates: "By showing how blind and gradual adaptation could counterfeit the apparently purposeful design, . . . Darwin deprived their argument of the analogical inference that the evident purpose to be seen in the contrivances by which means and ends were related in nature was necessarily a function of mind."[33] With Darwin, natural theology thus faced a serious scientific objection that seemed to make design arguments and other forms of natural theology obsolete. In the end, theologians were left with no way to empirically validate their claims, and they abandoned the practice of natural theology.

Since Darwin, scientists and philosophers have generally thought that evolution is a defeater for natural theology. Yet scientific discoveries of the past few decades have led to some significant doubt about this. This new doubt about evolution as a defeater for natural theology has come in two general groups of philosophers and scientists. One is the Intelligent Design (ID) movement in the 1990s and early 2000s. Led by scientists like Michael Behe and Michael Denton, ID advocates argued that naturalistic evolutionary accounts fail to explain the development of certain life structures and thus compel us to posit an intelligent designer behind the life structures found within organisms. As Jay Wesley Richards puts it, "For more than a century we have heard that scientific progress has made Christian belief obsolete. Given the cultural prestige of science, this claim has prevented many from considering the Christian faith. If Intelligent Design theory exposes the inadequacy of materialistic explanations in the natural sciences, it will deflate this assertion, and could contribute to a renewal of Christian belief in the twenty-first century."[34] In short, the ID movement directly challenges the explanatory adequacy of Darwinian evolution and points to numerous examples of life structures that seem to require an intelligent cause. In so doing, ID has encouraged advocates of natural theology to reengage the design arguments.

The second scientific development that has encouraged the revival of natural theology has been the accumulation and analysis of fine-tuning data found in countless examples from physics. Interestingly, while this data often sounds very similar to the kind of data offered by the ID movement, proponents of

32. Neal Gillespie, *Charles Darwin and the Problem of Creation* (Chicago: University of Chicago Press, 1979), 83.

33. Gillespie, *Charles Darwin and the Problem of Creation*, 83–84.

34. Jay Wesley Richards, "Proud Obstacles and a Reasonable Hope: The Apologetic Value of Intelligent Design," in *Signs of Intelligence*, ed. William A. Dembski and James M. Kushner (Grand Rapids: Brazos, 2001), 59.

natural theology who use fine-tuning data often take a very different approach than ID advocates. While the ID movement directly attacks the explanatory adequacy of evolution, fine-tuning advocates tend to embrace evolutionary accounts of the physical world and work within that account to show how God must exist as the explanation of the various laws and constants that govern the universe. McGrath is a good example of this. After cataloging a wide variety of fine-tuning examples, he says, "Many would argue that the finely tuned fruitfulness of the world and the intelligibility of the world . . . call for some explanation and understanding which, by its very nature, is likely to go beyond what science itself can provide."[35] McGrath is not alone in this opinion. Fred Hoyle writes, "A common sense interpretation of the facts suggests that a superintellect has monkeyed with physics, as well as with chemistry and biology, and that there are no blind forces worth speaking about in nature."[36]

## Conclusion

As this chapter has shown, natural theology has a long history with various advocates and critics, and its place within Christian theology will continue to be debated. We find traces of divine revelation in the physical world and within the human heart. The more we discover about the world we inhabit, the more inclined we are to consider theological answers to the questions about the universe. As such, natural theology continues to be of great importance in the area of religious epistemology.

35. Alister E. McGrath, *The Open Secret: A New Vision for Natural Theology* (Oxford: Blackwell, 2008), 244.

36. Fred Hoyle, "The Universe: Past and Present Reflections," *Annual Review of Astronomy and Astrophysics* 20, no. 16 (1982): 16.

PART 2

# METAPHYSICS

The world of our everyday experience is awe-inspiring in its complexity, beauty, diversity, order, and abundance. The universe consists of billions and billions of galaxies, each of which has billions and billions of stars. The distance from one end of the universe to the other can be measured only in terms of light years, and the distance is staggering. Focusing in on our solar system, there too we find a fascinating place consisting of ringed planets, asteroid belts, moons, a medium-sized star (the sun), and on earth, life. The diversity of life on earth is truly amazing: plants, such as Kentucky bluegrass, a rose bush, an oak tree; and animals, such as single-celled amoebas, worms, squirrels, horses, giraffes, humans. Yet even here we find unity too; the flora and fauna of this world can be classified into natural classes of things. All of it—the earth and its inhabitants, the solar system, the galaxies—form an integrated whole, or so it seems.

The world is perplexing too. What *kinds* of things are these objects of our everyday experience? Moreover, how do they fit together? How is it that we find unity amid such diversity? **Metaphysics** is the branch of philosophy that asks and tries to answer such questions. The subject matter of metaphysics is "being" itself. In other words, metaphysics is the philosophical study of the nature and structure of reality. In this section, we will explore some of the big questions that surface when we begin to seek to understand the world of everyday experience.

We begin our exploration of metaphysics in chapter 7 with the question of ultimate reality. Is reality, at rock bottom, something physical, nonphysical, or both? A common story today, given the hegemony of science, is that the only kinds of things that exist are material things. On this story, the universe—meaning the concrete material reality—is all there is. Others have argued for a richer view of reality. On these dualistic accounts, there is more to reality than the concrete material reality. In addition to physical things, there exist abstract things or mental things or immaterial things. Others—the idealists—say (along with the materialists) that there is only one kind of thing, but that one kind of thing is not material: instead, everything is mental.

Moving on, a key observation is that there are charactered objects in the world. Consider a dog, Fido. Fido is a thing, a particular, that has characteristics. One important question metaphysics asks and seeks to answer is this: In addition to charactered objects, are there characteristics? Chapter 8 explores the question of characteristics—properties—and what reasons there are to think they exist. Chapter 9 picks up the character-objects thread, exploring different ways philosophers have understood the notion of being a composite object.

We humans, of course, are part of reality. We exist, and it is natural to ask, What kind of thing are we? What does it mean to be a human, a person, and a human person? Moreover, are we significantly free such that, in some sense, we are self-determiners of our character and actions? Or are we in some way determined by the laws of nature or even God to act as we do? Do we have, in addition to our bodies, a soul—an immaterial part—that can survive the death of our bodies? In other words, is it reasonable to think that the afterlife is possible? These questions will be explored in chapters 10 and 11.

These aren't the only questions metaphysics deals with, but they are a good start. Other distinctly metaphysical topics not directly addressed here include the nature of space and time, the question of persistence and change over time, causation, modality, and more.

# 7

# The Nature of Reality

Metaphysics is the branch of philosophy that studies the nature and structure of reality. Questions metaphysicians ask and try to answer include the following: What exists? How do the different kinds of things that exist relate to one another? What aspects of reality are fundamental and derivative? These questions, and many more like them, have been asked as long as human beings have sought to provide a rational account of the world.

These questions are not trivial. Metaphysics matters. The beliefs we hold about the world shape our *experience* of the world and our *behavior* in the world. Even our eternal destinies are at stake, as C. S. Lewis (1898–1963) powerfully illustrates through a series of fictitious letters between a senior devil and a junior/apprentice devil named Wormwood. In the first of these imaginary letters, the senior devil instructs Wormwood as follows:

> Jargon, not argument, is your best ally in keeping him [that is, the patient whom they are trying to keep from becoming a Christian] from the Church. Don't waste time trying to make him think that materialism is true! Make him think it is strong, or stark or courageous—that it is the philosophy of the future. . . . The trouble about argument is that it moves the whole struggle onto the Enemy's [God's] own ground. He can argue too; whereas in really practical propaganda of the kind I am suggesting He has been shown for centuries to be greatly the inferior of Our Father Below. By the very act of arguing, you awake the patient's reason; and once it is awake, who can foresee the result? Even if a particular train of thought can be twisted so as to end

> in our favour, you will find that you have been strengthening in your patient the fatal habit of attending to universal issues and withdrawing his attention from the stream of immediate sense experiences. Your business is to fix his attention on the stream. Teach him to call it "real life" and don't let him ask what he means by "real."[1]

The book, of course, was Lewis's classic *The Screwtape Letters*. He painted for us, in a wonderfully delightful way, a picture of the battle taking place between the forces of good and the forces of evil over humans' beliefs regarding the nature of reality.

This battle over the nature of reality has been going on for some time.[2] In the *Sophist*, Plato describes "something like a battle of gods and giants," an interminable "dispute" over the nature of reality. In one camp, the giants "drag everything down to earth from the heavenly region of the invisible," arguing that true reality is found only in the world of our sensible experience. In the other camp, the gods maintain that "true being is certain nonbodily [i.e., immaterial] forms."[3] In our own day, the battle over the nature of reality continues to rage. For example, in a well-known series of lectures delivered in 1960 at the University of Pittsburgh, the philosopher Wilfrid Sellars distinguishes between the "manifest image" of the world—our ordinary perception of the world as rational, beautiful, and mysterious—and the "scientific image" of the world, a disenchanted world of mathematical formulas, particles in motion, and blind forces.[4] Sellars argues that the two perspectives of the world are incommensurate and that our manifest image—the world of "appearance"—is not the world in reality; in reality, the world is the complex physical system of the "scientific image."

In this chapter we shall consider, in broad outline, three prominent views about ultimate reality, highlighting their merits and drawbacks, as we seek to answer our fundamental questions about the nature and structure of reality.[5] We begin with perhaps *the* dominant views of our day, the view of Plato's giants and Sellars's "scientific image."

1. C. S. Lewis, *The Screwtape Letters* (Westwood, NJ: Barbour Books, 1990), 11–12.

2. Given Christian theism, it could be argued that this battle over reality has been going on since at least the fall of Adam and Eve.

3. Plato, *Sophist* 246a–c, in *Plato: Complete Works*, ed. John M. Cooper (Indianapolis: Hackett, 1997), 267–68.

4. These lectures were later published in Wilfrid Sellars, *Science, Perception, and Reality* (London: Routledge & Kegan Paul, 1963), 1–40.

5. While discussing materialism, dualism, and idealism, in rough outline we follow Steven B. Cowan and James S. Spiegel's discussion of ultimate reality in *The Love of Wisdom* (Nashville: B&H, 2009), 152–72.

## Materialism

According to **materialism**, everything that exists is material. The material cosmos is "one gigantic spatio-temporal whole," composed of (in ascending order) particles, molecules, medium-sized objects, planets, stars, and galaxies.[6] Materialism is a kind of **monism**. There is just one kind of thing that exists: the material thing.

Closely associated with this theory of reality is a theory of knowledge called empiricism. Roughly, empiricism is the idea that all knowledge is of the sense-perceptible kind. It is currently more fashionable to speak of "the scientific" instead of "the sense perceptible," and thus many in our culture who adopt a materialistic metaphysics also adopt a theory of knowledge called scientism.[7] According to a particularly strong version of scientism, all knowledge comes from the deliverances of science. If you want knowledge, you must turn to the scientist.

For the materialist, notice the tight connection between epistemology and metaphysics, as articulated by the philosopher Alex Rosenberg: "If we're going to be scientistic, then we have to attain our view of reality from what physics tells us about it. Actually, we'll have to do more than that: we'll have to embrace physics as *the whole truth about reality*."[8] Science today, as Rosenberg's comment shows, is exalted as the paradigm of rationality. If you want to be reasonable (and who doesn't?), then you must be scientistic, and if you are going to be scientistic, then you must embrace that all of reality is captured by physics. Rosenberg continues: "Why buy the reality that physics paints? Well, it's simple, really. We trust science as the only way to acquire knowledge."[9] This is a bold statement, especially since it is self-defeating![10] But let that pass. We want to notice one implication of scientism as a theory of knowledge and materialism as a theory of reality: **naturalism**, the view that there is no *super*natural aspect to reality.

6. Reinhardt Grossmann, *The Existence of the World: An Introduction to Ontology* (New York: Routledge, 1992), 8.

7. Dallas Willard, "Knowledge and Naturalism," *Naturalism: A Critical Analysis*, ed. William Lane Craig and J. P. Moreland (New York: Routledge, 2000), 25.

8. Alex Rosenberg, *The Atheist's Guide to Reality: Enjoying Life without Illusions* (New York: Norton, 2011), 20 (emphasis in original).

9. Rosenberg, *Atheist's Guide to Reality*, 20.

10. Notice that the claim "Science is the only way to acquire knowledge" is itself a piece of knowledge. But importantly, this piece of knowledge is not a deliverance from science. Rather, it is a philosophical statement about the nature of knowledge. But then, if scientism is true, it is false. It is self-defeating. So there is, contrary to Rosenberg's claim, at least one piece of knowledge that does not come from science. If there is one piece of knowledge, it is reasonable to think there may be other pieces of knowledge from nonscientistic sources.

As Rosenberg concludes, since physics tells us everything about reality, "that is why we are so confident about atheism."[11] Thus if materialism is true, then so is naturalism: there is no God, no immaterial soul, and no abstract reality (more on this below).

The materialistic view of reality has a lot going for it. As already noted, it is widely thought to be the view of reality backed by the scientific enterprise. Given the fact that science is often equated with reason, there are strong sociological factors for thinking materialism to be true. No one, after all, wants to be labeled as antiscience. Moreover, philosophically, materialism is a simple theory, positing one kind of thing only, the material; since simplicity is a theoretical virtue (and hence truth indicative), we have a reason to think that materialism is rationally preferable to its competitors.

Materialism is not without problems, however. One theoretical virtue, such as ontological simplicity, must be weighed against other theoretical virtues, including explanatory power and scope. Many argue that materialism fails miserably in its ability to adequately explain many of the phenomena of the "manifest image"—in particular, facts about human persons and their mental lives.[12]

Two features of our mental lives that seem to be at odds with a materialist metaphysics are the **first-person perspective** and intentionality. When I (Paul) say I am hungry, I am in pain, I am here, and the like, I am reporting something about which I cannot be mistaken. I have privileged access to these mental states. They are mine. I am a self-conscious agent who can refer to myself using **indexicals** such as "I" and "here" and "now." However, as Thomas Nagel has pointed out, there is no place for indexicals in science: a complete scientific description of the world, identifying all particles and forces and their locations in space and time (from a third-person perspective) would leave something out: me.[13] As Roger Scruton states, "Science cannot tell me who I am, let alone where, when or how."[14]

**Intentionality** is the "aboutness" or "ofness" of my mental life. I have a thought of my wife, a belief about London, a hope for the afterlife. This aboutness that characterizes our mental life is, again, very difficult to account for on a purely materialistic metaphysics. Materialists typically try to

11. Rosenberg, *Atheist's Guide to Reality*, 20.

12. Other phenomena that are difficult to explain in a materialistic metaphysic include free will (see chap. 10); morality (see chap. 16); knowledge (see chaps. 2 and 3); meaning (see chap. 17); the unity amid the diversity in the world (see chaps. 8 and 9); and the origin of the universe itself (see chap. 12).

13. Thomas Nagel, *The View from Nowhere* (New York: Oxford University Press, 1986). Cited in Roger Scruton, *The Soul of the World* (Princeton: Princeton University Press, 2014), 31.

14. Scruton, *Soul of the World*, 31.

reduce intentionality to physical causal relations of input and output.[15] My thought of London is reduced to certain inputs (I see a picture of Big Ben), which in turn produce an output, a certain behavior, such as my claiming that London is a grand city. John Searle, however, has advanced the famous Chinese Room Argument, showing how attempts to explain intentionality in terms of physical causal inputs and outputs fails.[16] What is left out, according to Searle, is genuine understanding: physical inputs and outputs can *mimic* understanding, but they do not *possess* it, and thus they do not adequately account for the phenomenon of intentionality. Moreover, intentionality possesses qualities that physical states do not (e.g., intentionality can be about nonexistent entities; physical causal relations hold only between existent entities), and this provides reason to think that intentionality cannot be reduced to the purely material.[17]

A deeper problem for materialism concerns its intelligibility. As Lewis puts it, "Thus a strict materialism refutes itself for the reason given long ago by Professor Haldane: 'If my mental processes are determined wholly by the motions of atoms in my brain, I have no reason to suppose that my beliefs are true, . . . and hence I have no reason for supposing my brain to be composed of atoms.'"[18]

Lewis is noticing a deep conflict between materialism and the reliability of our cognitive faculties. More recently, Alvin Plantinga has advanced a more rigorous argument highlighting the self-defeating nature of materialism.[19] The basic idea is this: The conjunction of materialism and evolution means that our cognitive faculties select beliefs for their survival value rather than truth. But then, if my beliefs are selected for their survival value and not truth, I

15. For more, see J. P. Moreland, *The Recalcitrant* Imago Dei*: Human Persons and the Failure of Naturalism* (Norwich, UK: SCM, 2009), 92–95.

16. John Searle, "Minds, Brains, and Programs," *Behavioral and Brain Sciences* 3 (1980): 417–57.

17. For a discussion of six differences between intentionality and physical states, see Moreland, *The Recalcitrant* Imago Dei, 91–92. For another argument from the reality of conscious intentional states to the falsity of materialism, see Laurence BonJour, "Against Materialism," in *The Waning of Materialism*, ed. Robert C. Koons and George Bealer (Oxford: Oxford University Press, 2010), 15–21. For a sustained argument that the reality of consciousness cannot be accounted for by a materialist metaphysic of human persons, see the collection of essays included in *Waning of Materialism*. As the editors state in the introduction, "It is . . . surprising [given the supposed dominance of a materialist metaphysics regarding human persons] that an examination of the major philosophers active in [philosophy of mind over the last sixty years] reveals that a majority, or something approaching a majority, either reject materialism or had serious and specific doubts about its ultimate viability." *Waning of Materialism*, ix.

18. C. S. Lewis, *Miracles* (New York: Touchstone, 1975), 24.

19. See, e.g., Alvin Plantinga, *Where the Conflict Really Lies* (Oxford: Oxford University Press, 2011), chap. 10.

have no good reason to think my beliefs are true. But then, if I have no good reason to think my beliefs are true, I have no good reason to think materialism is true. Therefore if materialism is true, I have no good reason to believe materialism is true. Materialism is self-defeating.

While much more could be said, we offer one final thought. If Christian theism is true, then materialism is a nonstarter. If God, an immaterial self-conscious substance, exists, then materialism is false. Moreover, if theism is true, advances in science are just discoveries of the world that God has created, not evidence for materialism.

### Dualism

**Metaphysical dualism** is the view that two kinds of things exist in the world. One prominent form of metaphysical dualism is called **Platonism**, roughly the view that in addition to the material cosmos, there exists an abstract realm of nonmaterial objects. Platonism, as the name implies, has its roots in the thought of Plato (427–347 BC), who argued that reality is constituted by a visible world, which is temporal, changing, and contingent, and by an invisible world of the Intelligible Forms, which is eternal, unchanging, and the source of all in the visible realm.

Another prominent form of metaphysical dualism, advocated in the seventeenth century by René Descartes (1596–1650), is called substance dualism. According to substance dualism, each human is composed of two basic kinds of substances, an immaterial soul and a material body. Descartes argued that the body operates according to mechanical laws of nature and is extended through and located in space. The soul, however, has no spatial location or extension; is that which thinks, feels, and wills; can survive the death of the body; and causally interacts with the body through the pineal gland (located in the brain).

Finally, Christian theism is another important kind of metaphysical dualism. As noted above, according to Christian theism there exists, in addition to the material cosmos, an immaterial divine substance. Since the viability of substance dualism and God's existence are discussed in detail in chapters 11, 12, and 15, in the remainder of this section we shall focus on Platonism and the claim that, in addition to the spatiotemporal universe, there exists an abstract realm of reality populated by entities such as properties, relations, propositions, sets, numbers, states of affairs, possible worlds, and the like.

It will be helpful to first understand just what an abstract object is and how it differs from a concrete object. While the issue is debated, there is somewhat of a consensus among philosophers as to the following: An abstract object is a nonspatial, nontemporal, necessarily existing,[20] causally impotent entity. A concrete object—a table, chair, rock, electron, or star—is defined, in contrast, as that which is not abstract.[21]

Why think that abstract objects exist? Two important arguments for Platonism are the One over Many Argument, to be discussed in chapter 8, and the Indispensability Argument, which we shall explore here. The Indispensability Argument can be formulated as follows:

1. If a simple sentence is literally true, then the objects its singular terms denote exist.
2. There are literally true simple sentences containing singular terms that refer to things that could be only abstract objects.
3. Therefore, abstract objects exist.[22]

Consider familiar sentences of the form "*a* is F" such as "The apple is red" or "Socrates is wise." In these sentences, the subject terms—the apple and Socrates—are the singular terms, and if these singular terms are part of a true sentence, then it is reasonable to think that the objects referred to by way of these singular terms really exist. If it is true that "the apple is red," then the object denoted by the singular term—the apple—really exists and is red. (In chap. 8 we'll discuss the question of what to do ontologically with the predicate "is red.") If it is true that Socrates is wise, then the object denoted by the singular term—Socrates—really exists and is wise. Premise 1 rests on a criterion of ontological commitment, in a tradition that broadly follows the work of Willard V. O. Quine, such that we are ontologically committed to singular terms and existential expressions (we focus here only on singular terms) of literally true simple sentences.[23]

20. This sets aside sets with contingent members, which are traditionally considered abstract but nonnecessary.

21. See, e.g., J. P. Moreland, *Universals* (Montreal: McGill-Queen's University Press, 2001), 17–18; Grossmann, *Existence of the World*, 7; and E. J. Lowe, *The Possibility of Metaphysics: Substance, Identity, and Time* (Oxford: Clarendon, 1998), 212–13.

22. This formulation of the Indispensability Argument is from Mark Balaguer, who calls this "The Singular Term Argument" in "Platonism in Metaphysics," in *The Stanford Encyclopedia of Philosophy*, ed. Edward N. Zalta, last modified March 9, 2016, §4, http://plato.stanford.edu/entries/platonism. The Indispensability Argument is historically associated with Willard V. O. Quine and Hilary Putnam and was originally formulated as an argument for the reality of abstract objects within mathematics. For other formulations of the Indispensability Argument, see Mark Colyvan, *The Indispensability of Mathematics* (New York: Oxford University Press, 2001).

23. See Willard V. O. Quine, "On What There Is?," in *From a Logical Point of View* (Cambridge: Harvard University Press, 1953), 1–19. Quine thought we are committed ontologically

Regarding premise 2, consider the sentences "Two is prime" and "Courage is a virtue." Assuming both are true, the singular terms refer, according to the criterion of ontological commitment, to the objects denoted by the singular terms. But in this case, the objects denoted by the singular terms are not concrete objects: they are abstract objects—the number two and the property *courage*, or *being courageous*. Thus if the criterion of ontological commitment is true and there are true atomic sentences in which the singular term can be understood only as an abstract object, it follows that abstract objects exist (and Platonism is true).

Since the Indispensability Argument is valid, the nominalist, who denies the existence of abstract objects, must deny either premise 1 or premise 2. William Lane Craig, for example, rejects premise 1 and the criterion of ontological commitment that undergirds it. Craig finds it astonishing that so many philosophers take existential expressions ("There is/are") and singular terms to be ontologically committing. When considering singular terms, Craig argues, "Far too many philosophers, I think, are still in the thrall of a sort of picture theory of language according to which successfully referring terms have corresponding objects in the world."[24] To support this claim, Craig lists example sentences, such as "Wednesday falls between Tuesday and Thursday" or "He did it for my sake and the children's," arguing that it would be absurd to think that there really are *Wednesdays* or *sakes* in the real world. Craig thinks singular terms that refer to real-world objects are probably the exception rather than the norm.[25]

We are in deep waters here. Questions about how to establish whether something exists, what "ontological commitment" means, and the relationship between language and the world are perennial topics of philosophical dispute. By way of reply to Craig, it won't do simply to assert the unbelievability of a thesis. The fact that Craig finds such recondite objects as *Wednesdays* or *sakes* as absurd is beside the point. What is needed are philosophical reasons for thinking that the criterion of ontological commitment is defective. One advantage of the Quinean approach to ontological commitment is that it offers a clean and straightforward way to determine

---

only by existential expressions and not singular terms, but as Balaguer notes, most philosophers today consider both singular terms and existential quantifiers to be ontologically committing when considering a broadly Quinean criterion of ontological commitment. See Balaguer, "Platonism in Metaphysics," §4. In fact, simple sentences with singular terms seem to entail true existential expressions; for example, "The apple is red" logically entails "There is something that is red."

24. William Lane Craig, "Anti-Platonism," in *Beyond the Control of God? Six Views on the Problem of God and Abstract Objects*, ed. Paul M. Gould (New York: Bloomsbury, 2014), 121.

25. Craig, "Anti-Platonism," 121.

what exists: "to be is to be the value of a bound variable" (for existential claims), or "the function of a singular term is to refer to existent objects."[26] For certain kinds of Meinongians, who think existential expressions and singular terms are not ontologically committing in any sense, the question becomes, How, given your view, do we establish that something exists?[27] Whatever answer is given to this question may prove more troubling than the Quinean approach.[28]

Two prominent attempts to reject premise 2 are (a) the paraphrase strategy, which accepts the truth of the sentences in question yet finds a nominalist-friendly paraphrase that gets rid of the purported abstract object; and (b) the fictionalist strategy, which holds that the sentences in question are literally false and thus do not denote abstract objects.[29] According to paraphrase nominalism, sentences such as "Two is prime" and "Courage is a virtue" can be paraphrased without loss of meaning as, for example, "If there were numbers, two would be prime" and "Courageous persons are virtuous persons."[30] As long as the paraphrase removes the troubling entity (the number two, the property *being courageous*) without a corresponding loss of meaning, we have found a nominalistically acceptable sentence. The problem, however, is that the proposed paraphrases, and many others, seem to fail. As Balaguer observes, the proposed paraphrases do not seem to capture the ordinary meaning of such simple sentences. "Two is prime" is about the number two, whereas the proposed paraphrase is about what would be the case if there were numbers.[31] With respect to the sentence "Courage is a virtue," the proposed paraphrase doesn't even share the same truth value (and thus, again, does not share the same meaning). While "Courage is a virtue" is a necessary truth, the truth value for the sentence "Courageous persons are virtuous persons" is

26. For a defense of the Quinean criterion of ontological commitment, see Peter van Inwagen, "Being, Existence, and Ontological Commitment," in *Metametaphysics: New Essays on the Foundation of Ontology*, ed. David J. Chalmers, David Manley, and Ryan Wasserman (Oxford: Oxford University Press, 2009), 472–506.

27. For more on Meinongians (named after Alexius Meinong, 1853–1920) and linguistic approaches to ontology, see Matti Eklund, "Metaontology," *Philosophy Compass* 1, no. 3 (2006): 317–34.

28. With respect to existential expressions, Craig favors a theory defended by Jody Azzouni called neutralism, where the quantifier of first-order logic does not imply any ontological commitments, and a deflationary theory of reference (defended by Arvid Bave) with respect to singular terms, where a person can use singular terms without thereby committing to the existence of the objects to which one is referring. See Craig, "Anti-Platonism," 119–23.

29. Balaguer, "Platonism in Metaphysics," §4.1.

30. The first, according to Balaguer, is an example of what is known as if-thenism ("Platonism in Metaphysics," §4.1). The second is discussed by Michael J. Loux, *Metaphysics: A Contemporary Introduction*, 3rd ed. (New York: Routledge, 2006), 57–58.

31. Balaguer, "Platonism in Metaphysics," §4.1.

contingent: it could turn out that a courageous person is in fact not virtuous, given moral or intellectual vices in other areas.[32]

The fictionalist isn't worried about translating sentences into proper nominalistic form. Rather, all sentences that appear to commit us to the existence of abstract objects are false. The sentences "Two is prime" and "Courage is a virtue" should be treated the same way as the sentence "Oliver Twist is an orphan." Oliver Twist doesn't exist, yet we can still coherently make reference to him as long as we understand that we are talking about a fictional character in a story written by Charles Dickens. In the same way, argues the fictionalist, we are to construe talk about numbers, properties, and the like as make-believe. The fictionalist proposal strikes many as implausible. It seems too easy: if you don't like the ontological implications of certain sentences, then just deny that the sentence is true. However, it seems obvious that "Two is prime" or "Courage is a virtue" are true, and necessarily so. For these reasons, while there are sophisticated proposals on offer, many are unwilling to follow the fictionalist down the antirealist path.[33]

## Idealism

The final view of ultimate reality we shall consider is **idealism**. While there are many versions of idealism, we shall focus on a particularly influential one developed by the British empiricist George Berkeley (1685–1753). The only kind of things that exist, according to Berkeleyan idealism, are mental things: minds and ideas. To be is to be perceived or to be a perceiver.[34] While the denial of material objects seems to go against common sense, idealism is important to consider for at least two reasons. First, the arguments in favor of idealism are a good bit stronger than one might initially suppose and thus warrant further investigation. Second, there is renewed interest in Berkeleyan idealism today, particularly among Christian theologians and philosophers, and thus it is important to understand why

32. Loux, *Metaphysics*, 57–58.

33. For a sophisticated defense of fictionalism that tries to dispense with numbers in science, see Hartry Field, *Science without Numbers* (Princeton: Princeton University Press, 1980). For a robust defense of nominalism with respect to the Indispensability Argument, see Craig, "Anti-Platonism," in *Beyond the Control of God?*, chap. 4, including the response to Craig by Keith Yandell, Paul M. Gould, Richard Brian Davis, Greg Welty, Scott A. Shalkowski, and Graham Oppy.

34. The classic articulation and defense of Berkeleyan idealism can be found in George Berkeley, Principles of Human Knowledge *and* Three Dialogues, ed. Howard Robinson (New York: Oxford University Press, 1999).

Christians in particular find this theory of reality attractive and superior to its competitors.[35]

The starting point on the path toward idealism is the modern era's debate over the nature of perception. A commonsensical theory of perception, called **direct realism**, holds that what one is directly aware of in perceptual experience is a mind-independent reality. For example, in perceiving the table, I am directly aware of the table itself. The problem with direct realism is that it does not seem to adequately account for special cases, such as illusion. Consider a straight stick that appears bent when placed in water. If the object of perceptual experience is the stick itself, then according to direct realism there should be no difference between appearance and reality.

In order to handle the problem of illusion, early modern philosophers such as Descartes and John Locke (1632–1704) advocated a theory of perception called **representative realism**. According to representative realism, in perception we are directly aware of a mental item—our sensory ideas—and indirectly aware of a mind-independent reality. We perceive physical objects—tables, rocks, trees—by way of our sensory ideas. By making a distinction between direct and indirect awareness, the representative realist can account for why, in the case of illusions, reality and appearance are distinct. For example, in the case of the straight stick, in normal circumstances the only medium between the stick and our sensory idea of the stick is the air. In the illusory case, however, the additional medium of water causes the light from the bottom part of the stick to refract, generating a difference between our sensory idea of the stick and the stick as it is in reality.

Berkeley agreed with the representative realist that the objects of our direct awareness are sensory ideas. He disagreed, however, that the objects of our sensory experience point beyond themselves to some mind-independent reality. This is because in the end, argued Berkeley, representative realism leads to skepticism. How, he asked, could we ever know that our sensory idea of a table is caused by a mind-independent table instead of a mad scientist or an evil demon? By arguing that there is only the mind-dependent reality of sensory ideas, the threat of skepticism is removed once and for all. It is important to emphasize: Berkeley is not denying that tables, rocks, and trees exist. He is simply denying their mind-independence. Physical objects are collections of ideas. Whose ideas? For Berkeley there could be only one answer: God's

35. For recent works by Christian theologians and philosophers defending Berkeleyan idealism, see the two-volume series Idealism and Christianity, with James S. Spiegel as general editor, published in New York by Bloomsbury in 2016: vol. 1, *Idealism and Christian Theology*, ed. Joshua R. Farris and S. Mark Hamilton; vol. 2, *Idealism and Christian Philosophy*, ed. Steven B. Cowan and James S. Spiegel.

ideas. Thus there are, according to Berkeleyan idealism, two kinds of minds, divine and nondivine, and two kinds of ideas, sensory and imaginary (sensory ideas are "given"; we are passive recipients of them, whereas imaginary ideas are ideas that we "dream up" or produce through the activity of thinking).

Berkeleyan idealism, with its focus on the primacy of the mental, has a lot working in its favor, particularly for the Christian theist. For example, as a version of substance monism (only immaterial substances exist), it is simpler than pluralistic ontologies, such as metaphysical dualism; all things being equal (i.e., assuming the two types of ontologies are explanatorily on par), simplicity counts in its favor. Moreover, the idealist theory of perception is argued to be more consistent with the findings of quantum mechanics and is immune to skepticism since what we are directly aware of in perception is the mind-dependent physical reality.[36] Finally, if, as its adherents claim, it is consistent with Christian orthodoxy, then, contrary to initial reactions, idealism is a viable option for many theists.

However, Berkeleyan idealism is not without problems. On reflection, it is not obviously simpler than its dualist competitors. For example, idealists argue that the problem of causal interaction between immaterial and material substances dissolves under idealism, since all causal interactions are between mental objects only.[37] Unfortunately, the causal interaction problem is not solved: it is relocated.[38] Consider the age-old mind-body problem. The question becomes, How does my mind enjoy two-way causal interaction with the collection of divine ideas that is my body? If, as those following Berkeley think, occasionalism is true, then the interaction problem dissolves again (since God is the only causal agent in the universe), but the explanatory benefits accrued to the idealist are negated (for many philosophers) by an unattractive theory of causation. Moreover, in the end it is not clear that Berkeleyan idealism is consistent with Christian orthodoxy. Consider this: if divine ideas are part of God (and how could they not be?) and physical objects are collections of

36. For a discussion of quantum mechanics and idealism, see especially Howard Robinson, "Idealism and Perception: Why Berkeleyan Idealism Is Not as Counterintuitive as It Seems," in Cowan and Spiegel, *Idealism and Christian Philosophy*, 84–87.

37. James Spiegel argues this way in "Idealism and the Reasonableness of Theistic Belief," in Cowan and Spiegel, *Idealism and Christian Philosophy*, 16–17.

38. It could be argued that the interaction problem is about how two radically different kinds of substances, material and immaterial, interact and thus, by removing material objects from the furniture of the world, idealism does dissolve the interaction problem. If this is correct, the general point still stands; however, another kind of problem surfaces, a near cousin of the original, now over how an immaterial substance relates to the collections of divine ideas that constitute its material body. The latter problem is not the same as the former, but it is within the vicinity of it, and the question of how two radically different kinds of things interact still stands.

divine ideas, then physical objects are part of God. But then creation is part of God, panentheism is true, and Christian orthodoxy is called into question.[39] Finally, it could be argued that there are more sophisticated versions of direct realism that handle the problem of illusion (and other related issues) adequately. If so, then a chief motivation for idealism is significantly undercut.[40]

## Conclusion

In this chapter we've explored three prominent views of reality: materialism, dualism, and idealism. Each view has something going for it as well as certain costs or problems that need to be overcome. Given Christian theism, we think that materialism is a nonstarter. We're not particularly attracted to idealism either but think it should be given its due. For our part, we can learn from the materialist to value the physical world—in its beauty, diversity, and abundance—as part of the giftedness of creation. We can also learn from the idealist to remember the primacy of the spiritual or immaterial. Mind is before matter in a very important sense because God—an immaterial Mind—is the source of all concrete finite reality. Moreover, there is more to life than the constant stream of sensual and physical experience. There are immaterial and spiritual goods too, including, most importantly, communion with God through the union of our finite spirit with the infinite Spirit. Much more, of course, can be said about each of these views and more besides. What should be clear is that the interminable battle over the nature of reality shows no signs of waning anytime soon.[41]

39. For a defense of the orthodoxy of Christian idealism with respect to panentheism, see Adam Groza, "Idealism and the Nature of God," in Cowan and Spiegel, *Idealism and Christian Philosophy*, chap. 6.

40. For more sophisticated contemporary defenses of direct realism, see J. P. Moreland and Garrett DeWeese, "The Premature Report of Foundationalism's Demise," in *Reclaiming the Center*, ed. Millard J. Erickson, Paul Kjoss Helseth, and Justin Taylor (Wheaton: Crossway, 2004), chap. 4; and Dallas Willard, "How Concepts Relate the Mind to Its Objects: The 'God's Eye View' Vindicated," *Philosophia Christi* 1, no. 2 (1999): 5–20.

41. Thanks to Ross Inman for comments on an early draft of this chapter.

# 8

# Properties and Universals

There is unity and distinctiveness in the world. Regarding distinctiveness, notice that things—**particulars**—have characters. Things in the world are charactered objects. Socrates is wise, snub-nosed, and the teacher of Plato, for example. Regarding unity, consider that there are natural classes of things: red things, human things, sweet things, round things, and the like. Two key questions are these: First, do we need to postulate characters in addition to charactered objects, properties in addition to particulars? Second, how do we explain the similarities among charactered objects? Do we need to postulate shareable properties—**universals**—or just particular properties that exactly resemble? Questions about the existence and nature of properties are traditionally associated with the age-old debate over the problem of universals.

Willard V. O. Quine put the problem of universals as follows: "Now let us turn to the ontological problem of universals. . . . Speaking of attributes, he [McX] says: 'There are red houses, red roses, red sunsets; this much is prephilosophical common sense in which we must all agree. These houses, roses, and sunsets, then, have something in common; and this which they have in common is all I mean by the attribute of redness.'"[1] Quine's imaginary interlocutor McX thinks there are two facts about the world that are just obvious: (1) there are attributes and (2) similar things share one and the same attribute. McX here is representing the position of the metaphysical

1. Willard V. O. Quine, "On What There Is," in *From a Logical Point of View* (Cambridge, MA: Harvard University Press, 1953), 9–10.

realist, the believer in universals, where a universal is understood as a shareable property that can be possessed by distinct particulars, individual things, at once. Those who deny the existence of universals are called nominalists. Some nominalists—trope theorists—think there are properties but deny they are shareable: all properties are particularized properties. Other nominalists go further, denying the existence of properties themselves, believing in charactered objects but not in characteristics. In this chapter we shall explore the debate over the existence and nature of properties. We begin with the question of whether properties exist at all.

## Do Properties Exist?

Those who think properties exist are called property realists. Those who deny that properties exist are called extreme nominalists. There are two kinds of extreme **nominalism**: **ostrich nominalism**, characterized by denial that resemblance facts need to be explained or grounded in any way, and **reductive nominalism**, which purports there is a general explanation for resemblance.[2]

The ostrich nominalist thinks that only charactered objects exist. The ostrich nominalists don't deny that charactered objects are similar in various ways; rather, they deny that this poses any real problem. This is why the realist David Armstrong dubbed them "ostrich nominalists."[3] They stick their heads in the sand when it comes to the problem of explaining resemblance. True sentences of the form "*a* and *b* are both *F*" are analyzed as "*a* is *F* and *b* is *F*." As long as these qualitative facts can be accounted for in nominalistically friendly ways, so too can the conjunction of these qualitative facts and the various similarities among charactered objects. So, for example, the fact that grass and gummy bears are green is explained in terms of the fact that there is green grass and there are green gummy bears. No ontological commitment to properties, let alone *shareable* properties, is needed. There are only charactered objects: green things, sweet things, round things, human things, tree things, dog things, and so on. Period. As Michael Devitt puts it, "We have nothing to say about what makes *a* [to be] *F*, it just *is F*; that is a basic and inexplicable fact about the universe."[4] Or as Quine responds to McX,

2. Robert C. Koons and Timothy H. Pickavance, *Metaphysics: The Fundamentals* (Malden, MA: Wiley Blackwell, 2015), 85–86.

3. David Armstrong, *Universals and Scientific Realism*, vol. 1, *Nominalism and Realism* (Cambridge: Cambridge University Press, 1978), 16; and Armstrong, "Against 'Ostrich' Nominalism: A Reply to Michael Devitt," *Pacific Philosophical Quarterly* 61 (1980): 440–49.

4. Michael Devitt, "'Ostrich Nominalism' or 'Mirage Realism'?," *Pacific Philosophical Quarterly* 61 (1980): 436.

"That the houses and roses and sunsets are all of them red may be taken as ultimate and irreducible."[5]

In reply to the ostrich nominalist, some have argued that resemblance facts cannot be magically waved away by a mere sleight of hand.[6] The idea is that "*a* and *b* are both *F*" is not explanatorily equivalent with "*a* is *F* and *b* is *F*" but rather with "*a* is *F* and *b* is *F* and the *F*'s of *a* and *b* resemble each other." If so, then resemblance facts remain among the inventory of the world in need of an explanation or ontological ground. It is open to the ostrich to reply, as Quine does above, that resemblance facts, if they are genuine facts at all, are brute too. This is a fair move, but it comes with a cost. Typically it is thought that the more economical a theory, either in terms of its number of undefined predicates (ideological economy) or in terms of the number of entities the theory postulates (ontological economy), the better. For the ostrich, however, the amount of primitive or unexplained facts is quite high, and thus ostrich nominalism will be less ideologically parsimonious, and hence worse off, than other theories in terms of ideological economy (such as property realism) that don't require as many primitive facts.

Suppose that it could be established that ostrich nominalism is explanatorily on par with its property realist competitors. Would this establish the rational preferability of ostrich nominalism, since it postulates fewer entities than theories that rely on properties? Perhaps, surprisingly, it could be argued that ostrich nominalism is ontologically less parsimonious than realism, and this too provides reason to think the view false.[7] Philosophers distinguish between qualitative and quantitative economy. A theory's qualitative economy is measured in terms of the number of *kinds* of fundamental things the theory posits, whereas a theory's quantitative economy is measured in terms of the *number* of fundamental things posited. For the property realist, depending on the specifics, there are a handful of fundamental kinds of things. For example, according to the metaphysical realist (to be discussed below), the sentence "Socrates is wise" ontologically commits the speaker to the particular (Socrates), to the universal (wisdom), and to the exemplification relation (tying Socrates and wisdom together): three *kinds* of fundamental things (particulars, universals, and the exemplification relation). However, the ostrich nominalist is committed to as many fundamental kinds of things as there are charactered objects that are similar along various

5. Quine, "On What There Is," 10.

6. See, e.g., Paul M. Gould, "The Problem of Universals, Realism, and God," *Metaphysica* 13, no. 2 (2012): 183–94.

7. The argument summarized in this paragraph is from Bryan Pickel and Nicholas Mantegani, "A Quinean Critique of Ostrich Nominalism," *Philosophers' Imprint* 12, no. 6 (2012): 1–21.

dimensions. Assuming there are more similarities in the world than three, it follows that ostrich nominalism is costlier in terms of qualitative economy than realism. Since, as it is argued, qualitative economy is more important than quantitative economy, ostrich nominalism is costlier ontologically than realist theories.

Reductive nominalists deny the existence of properties by offering a reductive analysis of sentences that seem to be about properties, identifying predicates (e.g., "is red") with nominalistically friendly objects such as words, concepts, classes, or particulars. The main versions of reductive nominalism include predicate nominalism, concept nominalism, mereological nominalism, class nominalism, and resemblance nominalism.

**Predicate nominalism** and **concept nominalism** are similar enough to be considered together. According to predicate nominalism, "*a* is *F*" is further analyzed as "*a* falls under the predicate *F*"; for concept nominalism, "*a* is *F*" is further analyzed as "*a* falls under the concept *F*." A notoriously difficult problem for the predicate and concept nominalist is that if there were no speakers or thinkers, there would be no charactered objects in the world. But a sunset, for example, undoubtedly would still be red even if there were no human speakers or thinkers to enjoy it. Even if there are human speakers and thinkers, however, it seems possible that there are charactered objects such as undiscovered scientific properties for which no predicates or concepts exist now (and perhaps never will exist).[8] A further problem is that predicates and concepts seem to be *types* and not merely *tokens*. The predicate "is red" applies to both the ball and the fire truck. But then predicate (and concept) nominalism substitutes one kind of universal (a property) for another kind of universal (semantic or conceptual).[9] If it is argued that there are only *token* predicates or concepts, then it must be held, implausibly, that if our language/thoughts were just a bit different, a red truck would not have been red or an electron would not have been negatively charged.[10]

8. If God exists, this objection can be averted because there is always a *divine* mind that thinks and speaks. While this is an option for theists, many extreme nominalists are motivated by a commitment to naturalism and would not be able to avail themselves of this move. For a nice defense of theistic conceptualism, see Greg Welty, "Theistic Conceptual Realism," in *Beyond the Control of God? Six Views on the Problem of God and Abstract Objects*, ed. Paul M. Gould (New York: Bloomsbury, 2014), chap. 3. For more on extreme nominalism and naturalism, see J. P. Moreland, "Naturalism and the Ontological Status of Properties," in *Naturalism: A Critical Analysis*, ed. William Lane Craig and J. P. Moreland (New York: Routledge, 2000), chap. 4.

9. D. M. Armstrong, *Universals: An Opinionated Introduction* (Boulder, CO: Westview, 1989), 10–11.

10. Robert K. Garcia, "Platonism and the Haunted Universe," in *Loving God with Your Mind: Essays in Honor of J. P. Moreland*, ed. Paul M. Gould and Richard Brian Davis (Chicago: Moody, 2014), 39.

Another extreme nominalism is **mereological nominalism**, according to which "*a* is *F*" is further analyzed as "*a* is a part of the aggregate *F* thing." Something is red by virtue of being a part of the aggregate of red things. This aggregate of red things is a particular thing, but it is a rather odd particular thing: a scattered object located everywhere and only where there is something red. A problem with mereological nominalism is that it seems to get the explanatory relationship backward.[11] It is natural to think that something is a part of an aggregate of red things because it is red, not that something is red by virtue of being a part of an aggregate of red things. Moreover, mereological nominalism requires the acceptance of a counterintuitive view called mereological universalism, the idea that any mereological aggregate of parts is an object, no matter how scattered and disparate the parts.[12]

Two related but better views are **class nominalism**, according to which "*a* is *F*" is analyzed as "*a* is a member of the class of *F* things," and resemblance nominalism, according to which "*a* is *F*" is analyzed as "*a* is a member of a class of resembling *F* things." For class nominalism, properties are classes of things. So, for example, the property of *being red* is just the class of red things, the property of *being round* is just the class of round things, and the property of *being sweet* is just the class of sweet things. For an apple to exemplify redness is just for the apple to be a member of the class of red things. Regarding resemblance facts, two red things resemble just in case they are both members of the same class, the class of red things (which is the property of *being red*).

Two serious problems for class nominalism are the Companionship Problem and the Naturalness Problem.[13] The Companionship Problem is this: some pairs of properties are coextensive such that every time one property is possessed by a charactered object, so too is the other. For example, the class of things with a heart is coextensive with the class of things with a kidney, the class of featherless bipeds is coextensive with the class of things having a sense of humor, and the class of triangular things is coextensive with the class of trilateral things. What this means, according to class nominalism, is that the property of *being a heart* is identical with the property of *being a kidney*, and so on for each coextensive property. This is because properties are identified with classes, and classes are identical if they have the same members.

11. Francesco Berto and Mateo Plebani, *Ontology and Metaontology: A Contemporary Guide* (New York: Bloomsbury, 2015), 224.

12. Berto and Plebani, *Ontology and Metaontology*, 224.

13. The Companionship Problem was coined by Nelson Goodman: see *The Structure of Appearance* (Cambridge, MA: Harvard University Press, 1951), 160–61. The Naturalness Problem is developed in David Manley, "Properties and Resemblance Classes," *Nous* 36, no. 1 (2002): 75–96.

But then class nominalism postulates an identity where there isn't one: the property of *being a heart* is not the same as the property of *being a kidney*.

The class nominalist can respond to the Companionship Problem by construing properties as classes of actual and *possible* objects.[14] It certainly seems possible that there are creatures with hearts but not kidneys. If so, then the property *being a heart* is not coextensive with the property *being a kidney* since there are possible worlds, and thus possible creatures, and classes of actual and possible objects, with hearts but not kidneys. This response is problematic, however, even if we set aside that contentious issue of taking possible worlds and possible creatures as equally real with each other and with the actual world, for there are coextensive properties that are *necessarily* coextensive and thus range over all possible worlds (including the actual world) such as the properties *being triangular* and *being trilateral*.

The Naturalness Problem gains traction by noting that class nominalism is an abundant theory of properties. Since properties are just classes of objects, then for any unique class there is a unique property. So consider the class of objects constituted by my left eye, the White House, Alpha Centauri, and my copy of Plato's *Republic*. Call this class Jumble and the corresponding property *jumble*. Next, consider the class of humans and the corresponding property *being human*. Since according to class nominalism no class is metaphysically more fundamental than any other class, it follows that there is no explanation for why the class of humans is pretheoretically natural whereas the class Jumble is nonnatural. The problem of explaining why reality seems to be easily categorized in terms of natural classes of charactered objects is called the Naturalness Problem.

**Resemblance nominalism** presents a solution to the Naturalness Problem by offering a way to distinguish between natural and nonnatural classes. Resemblance nominalism privileges natural classes (such as the class of humans) in terms of the notion of resemblance. Resemblance is metaphysically fundamental: it does not need to be explained; it does the explaining. The character of objects is grounded in the metaphysically fundamental resemblance relation between objects in the resemblance class. The similarity between objects is grounded in the fact that they are members of the same resemblance class. As Gonzalo Rodriguez-Pereyra explains it, red things do not resemble one another because they are red; rather, red things are red because they resemble one another; something is red because it resembles other red things.[15]

14. This is what David Lewis does in *On the Plurality of Worlds* (Oxford: Blackwell, 1986), 50–69.

15. Gonzalo Rodriguez-Pereyra, "Nominalism in Metaphysics," in *The Stanford Encyclopedia of Philosophy*, ed. Edward N. Zalta, last modified April 1, 2015, §4.1, http://plato.stanford.edu/entries/nominalism-metaphysics.

Object classes that resemble one another in certain respects form resemblance classes, and resemblance classes are the only classes that can serve as natural properties. Thus resemblance nominalism offers a way to explain why reality is easily categorized into natural classes of things: there are privileged resemblance classes that explain why certain classes—such as the classes of human things, red things, and sweet things—exhibit a natural unity whereas other classes such as Jumble do not.

Resemblance nominalism is not without problems, however. Some problems that plague class nominalism, such as the Companionship Problem, plague resemblance nominalism too. The same proffered solution of appealing to both actual and possible object classes helps only with properties that are contingently coextensive and requires a commitment to a highly controversial theory of possible worlds. Yet there are other problems unique to resemblance nominalism that appear devastating. One such problem is called the Imperfect Community Problem.[16] Consider a class of three objects, called Mishmash, of the following kinds: a blue round thing, a metal round thing, and a blue metal thing. Since each of these objects resembles every other to a certain degree (all sharing either color or shape or material), Mishmash is a resemblance class. Yet Mishmash does not have any significant degree of naturalness since the only candidate property that all and only the members of Mishmash share is a "cooked" property, the property *mishmash* (or alternatively, the nonnatural disjunctive property *being the same color or shape or material*). So, there are resemblance classes that can't serve as natural properties, and the Naturalness Problem surfaces again. The most plausible solution to this problem is to abandon resemblance nominalism in favor of trope nominalism and to admit that there are, after all, properties (even if they are not shareable).

## Are Properties Shareable?

According to **trope nominalism**, properties are unshareable tropes. A red ball, for example, is red by virtue of a red trope and round by virtue of a round trope. Thickly charactered objects have multiple tropes, then; each individual trope grounds one dimension of character within a fully characterized object. Similarity among red things or sweet things or round things is grounded in the various degrees of resemblance relations that obtain between the classes of red tropes, sweet tropes, and round tropes, respectively. Since

16. Raised and developed by Goodman, *Structure of Appearance*, 162–64.

resemblance classes are constituted by tropes—particularized properties—instead of thickly charactered objects, trope nominalism avoids the worries raised by the Companionship and Naturalness Problems. Coextensive tropes belong to different resemblance classes, unproblematically referring to different properties, and the color, shape, and material tropes from Jumble form resemblance classes that do pick out natural properties.

Additionally, trope nominalism is thought to be superior to metaphysical realism because tropes are thought to be perfectly respectable objects, whereas universals are not. Tropes, for example, are wholly located where and only where the objects that have them are, can stand in causal relations, and are the objects of perception. Universals, however, misbehave—either being multiply located at nonoverlapping places at once (according to **immanent realism**) or being multiply instantiated without being located at all (according to **Platonic realism**). What is hopefully obvious by now is that the fundamental divide between trope theories and realist theories of properties has to do with the issue of shareability. According to the trope theorist, properties are not shareable, whereas according to the metaphysical realist, some properties are shareable.[17] A shareable property is a universal: a multiply instantiable property that can be had by distinct particulars at once.

Unfortunately for trope nominalism, there is an ambiguity in how tropes are understood that undermines its viability.[18] The issue has to do with how tropes ground the character of the thickly charactered objects that have them. Tropes, according to the philosopher Robert Garcia, come in two varieties. Modular tropes are self-exemplifying tropes; modifier tropes are non-self-exemplifying tropes.[19] Thus, according to modular trope theory, a red ball is red by virtue of its red trope and round by virtue of its round trope, and the tropes are themselves red and round, respectively. According to modifier trope theory, a red ball is red by virtue of its red trope and round by virtue of its round trope, and the tropes themselves are neither red nor round, respectively. Modifier tropes, like realist universals, confer character on objects without themselves being the character they confer.

While each version of trope theory has advantages over the other, Garcia importantly points out that they are both unstable. Modular trope theory threatens to collapse into ostrich nominalism, and modifier trope theory

17. The metaphysical realist need not think that all properties are shareable, however. Some properties, such as the property *being identical with Socrates*, are only instantiated by one substance if at all.

18. See Robert K. Garcia, "Two Ways to Particularize a Property," *Journal of the American Philosophical Association* 1, no. 4 (2015): 635–52.

19. Garcia, "Two Ways to Particularize a Property," 637.

threatens to collapse into metaphysical realism.[20] Either way, the viability of trope theory is called into question, or so the argument goes.

Modular tropes are singly charactered properties. Thus, according to modular trope theory, a red trope is red and only red. However, some thin particulars plausibly just don't stay thin. Red things, it seems, must also be shaped things, and shaped things must be extended things.[21] Thus it seems that our red modular trope is not singly charactered after all. It is multiply charactered. It is red, shaped, and extended. The modular theorist must either deny very plausible "Thickening Principles"[22] or allow for multiply charactered tropes that ground the character of fully characterized objects. If the modular theorist goes for the second option (allowing for multiply charactered tropes), then the view threatens to collapse into ostrich nominalism. The reason why, as Garcia notes, is that both the modular theorist and the ostrich nominalist now agree that no analysis of multiply charactered objects is necessary.[23] The character of multiply charactered objects is a primitive fact. It is in this sense that modular trope theory is said to be unstable.

Regarding modifier trope theory, we may ask, What guarantees the unshareability of modifier tropes? Recall that modifier tropes are non-self-exemplifying; they have no intrinsic character of their own beyond purely formal characteristics such as *being self-identical*, *being a particular*, *being a trope*, and the like. A typical answer offered by trope theorists is that the distinctness of a trope is grounded by its location.[24] In other words, tropes are individuated by their location, being wholly located wherever the object that has them is located. A trope is a respectable, perfectly behaving particular had by only one thickly charactered object and individuated by being wholly located at the same place as the thickly charactered object of which it is a part. The problem is that being located is incompatible with a plausible Thickening Principle such that "spatially located objects have a definite size and shape."[25] Again, the trope theorist, on modifier trope theory, is faced with a dilemma, needing either to give up an extremely plausible thickening principle or to admit that location does not individuate tropes (and thus does not guarantee unshareability).

Going for the second option has its own costs. If it is maintained that *being unshareable* is part of the formal character of modifier tropes, modifier trope

20. Garcia, "Two Ways to Particularize a Property," 645–49.
21. See Koons and Pickavance, *Metaphysics*, 99.
22. Koons and Pickavance, *Metaphysics*, 99. They borrow the term from Robert Garcia.
23. Garcia, "Two Ways to Particularize a Property," 649.
24. Koons and Pickavance, *Metaphysics*, 107.
25. Koons and Pickavance, *Metaphysics*, 108.

theory threatens to collapse into realism for at least two reasons. First, tropes are no longer respectable. Since modifier tropes lack an intrinsic nature—round tropes are not themselves round, for example—it seems that they lack shape, size, mass, and so on. But then modifier tropes are not, after all, the immediate objects of sense perception or the sorts of entities that play a direct causal role. Worse, as Garcia argues, it is difficult to see how modifier tropes can be located in space and time.[26] After all, they lack a definite size and shape. Thus it seems that modifier tropes are nonspatiotemporal, and for this reason they are no longer respectable. Second, modifier tropes ground the character of a located object without being wholly located where that object is located.[27] Modifier tropes seem to behave more and more like universals (at least according to Platonic realism), and in this sense modifier trope theory threatens to collapse into realism.

In the end, however, even if these worries about misbehaving can be set aside, in stipulating primitively distinct modifier tropes, modifier trope theory is quantitatively less parsimonious than metaphysical realism.[28] Where realism postulates a distinct universal, *redness*, had by the class of red things, modifier trope nominalism postulates a distinct property $redness_1$–$redness_n$ for each red thing, and so on for every distinct characteristic had by thickly charactered objects. Moreover, with respect to resemblance facts, trope nominalism (of either variety) is explanatorily inferior to realism. Realism explains why the *F*'s of *a* and *b* resemble (a shared universal), whereas nominalism must settle for primitive resemblances among classes of tropes. For at least these reasons, many philosophers are attracted to realism, the view that there are universals.

## Are Universals Transcendent?

The main divide among versions of **metaphysical realism** is over the nature of universals: Are universals spatiotemporal? As already noted, the immanent realist thinks universals are wholly located at distinct places at once.[29] Universals are concrete shareable properties located in space and time. The Platonic realist, however, thinks universals are multiply instantiated without being located at a place.[30] According to the Platonic realist, universals are

26. Garcia, "Two Ways to Particularize a Property," 646.
27. Garcia, "Two Ways to Particularize a Property," 646.
28. Koons and Pickavance, *Metaphysics*, 108.
29. A prominent defender of immanent realism is David Armstrong; see, e.g., Armstrong, *Universals*.
30. A prominent defender of Platonic realism is J. P. Moreland; see, e.g., Moreland, *Universals* (Montreal: McGill-Queen's University Press, 2001).

abstract objects that either (1) are nonspatially "in" concrete particulars as metaphysical parts (according to the constituent ontologist) or (2) are possessed by concrete particulars via a sui generis exemplification relation without being metaphysical parts of the objects that have them (according to the relational ontologist).[31]

The debate over immanent and Platonic versions of realism depends on what one thinks regarding what Reinhardt Grossmann calls the "axiom of localization." The axiom of localization is the principle such that "no entity whatsoever can exist at different places at once or at interrupted time intervals."[32] The immanent realist rejects the axiom of localization whereas the Platonic realist accepts it. The Platonic realist argues that if the axiom of localization is rejected, then absurdities follow. The immanent realist, in response, argues that the conjunction of the axiom of localization with realism leads to the abandonment of naturalism, and it is better to reject the axiom of localization than to abandon naturalism. In other words, immanent realism is consistent with naturalism, and Platonic realism is not; if one wants to be a naturalist and a realist, then the only viable option is to endorse immanent realism.

Consider two yellow balls, $b_1$ held in my right hand and $b_2$ held in my left.[33] According to realism, each individual ball exemplifies the shared universal *yellowness* or *being yellow*. On immanent realism, *yellowness* is wholly located where $b_1$ is located (in my right hand) and where $b_2$ is located (in my left hand). But it is absurd for one and the same thing to be located at two distinct places at once, or so it seems. It gets worse, however. As I move my hands toward each other and then away, *yellowness* moves both toward itself and then away from itself. This picture, argues the Platonic realist, is absurd and implausible and provides reasons in favor of Platonic realism.

On the Platonic realist picture, the yellowness exemplified by each ball is not spatially located where the ball is: it is either nonspatially "in" the ball as a metaphysical part or nonspatially tied to the ball relationally via exemplification. Either way, the absurdities of rejecting the axiom of localization are avoided. In reply, the immanent realist retorts that ordinary objects, in the hands of Platonic realists, become queer or spooky.[34] How is it, they won-

31. For a nice canvassing of the issues and options for realist versions of constituent and relational ontologies, see Koons and Pickavance, *Metaphysics*, 104–25, as well as the discussion in chap. 9 below.

32. Reinhardt Grossmann, *The Existence of the World: An Introduction to Ontology* (New York: Routledge, 1992), 13.

33. This example is from Garcia, "Platonism and the Haunted Universe," 46.

34. For more on the queerness worry, see Paul M. Gould and Stan Wallace, "On What There Is: Theism, Platonism, and Explanation," in Gould and Davis, *Loving God with Your Mind*, 26–27.

der, that the ordinary objects of everyday experience, firmly located in space and time, have properties that are nonspatial? Either way, something must be given up, says the immanent realist: either the axiom of localization or commonsense notions about how ordinary concrete objects have properties.

By maintaining a commitment to naturalism, the immanent realist thinks the gains outweigh any cost associated with rejecting the axiom of localization. The Platonic realist thinks, alternatively, that the costs in rejecting the axiom of localization are too high and the charge of queerness is not particularly troublesome. This is especially so if one is not wed to naturalism in general, or physicalism in particular, since it seems that mental properties (thoughts, beliefs, desires) can be nonspatially in the minds that have them, and thus the concept of being nonspatially "in" something is not entirely implausible.

## Conclusion

In this chapter we've considered three questions that provided structure to our philosophical investigation of the characteristics of charactered objects: Do properties exist? Are properties shareable? Are universals transcendent? It is easy to wonder after reading a chapter like this why it all matters. What is the "real world" pay-off? We sympathize. We also think the debate over the existence and nature of universals is of utmost importance, as are many debates in philosophy, even if not initially obvious. To tip our hands a bit, we think universals do important work and that some version of realism is not only rationally preferable in its own right but usefully employed in other areas of philosophy (e.g., appeal to universals in the philosophy of language can help secure objective meaning) and theology (e.g., in helping us understand how the incarnate Christ can share a nature with humans). Undoubtedly the debate over the existence and nature of universals will continue.[35] It is, in many ways, the central issue in the age-old quarrel between the gods and giants over the nature of reality.

35. The debate over the problem of universals becomes even more complicated when God is added to the picture. For an introduction to the issue of God and the problem of universals, see Paul M. Gould, ed., *Beyond the Control of God? Six Views on the Problem of God and Abstract Objects* (New York: Bloomsbury, 2014); Gould, "The Problem of Universals, Realism, and God"; and Brian Leftow, "God and the Problem of Universals," *Oxford Studies in Metaphysics*, ed. Dean Zimmerman (Oxford: Clarendon, 2006), 2:325–56.

# 9

# Particulars

In the last chapter we noted that there are charactered objects and characteristics. We learned that the character of charactered objects is best explained by postulating properties. Rosie the chicken has the properties (or better, the universals) *being red* and *being a chicken*. Properties are predicables, things that we predicate or assert of other things. But what about Rosie? What kind of thing, ontologically speaking, is she? The first thing to note about Rosie is that she is not a property. She is not "had" or "possessed" by something else in the same way the property *being red* is had by chickens and balls. Rosie is not a predicate: she is a subject. Rosie does the "having" and not the other way around. Rosie, this chicken in my backyard, is a concrete particular. Notice too that Rosie is a composite: she is a whole that has parts (her left foot, red feathers, carbon atoms, etc.) and properties (*being red*, *being a chicken*) that stand in various relations to one another. Rosie is not the only concrete particular in my backyard. This pile of trash next to Rosie, according to some philosophers, is also a concrete particular.[1] Like Rosie it has parts (that piece of paper, those dust molecules, that aluminum can, and so forth) and properties (*being a pile of trash*, *being*

1. A so-called universalist about mereology (from *meros* = parts, thus *mereology* = the study of parts and wholes) thinks any combination of concrete objects fuses or forms another concrete object, no matter how disparate. So my left toe, the moon, and that nail holding a board together at the White House form an object on this view. We ultimately side with common sense here and deny that such a nonnatural fusion forms a concrete whole. Still, for completeness we include things like piles or perhaps better, heaps of sand, which are at least somewhat naturally understood to be concrete objects even if the border between object and nonobject in those cases is somewhat fuzzy.

*shaped*, etc.) that stand in various relations to one another. This car is also a concrete particular. It too has parts and properties that stand in various relations to one another.

A key question to be explored in this chapter is how to make sense of familiar concrete objects such as chickens, cars, and piles of trash. It is currently fashionable to think that the familiar concrete objects of everyday experience are "built up" out of more fundamental parts and properties. If so, then the composite whole (Rosie, the trash pile, the car) is metaphysically posterior to its parts and properties. This reductionist picture makes the most sense, we believe, for things like cars (ordered aggregates) and things like piles of trash (heaps). But for things like Rosie (living organisms), this picture is counterintuitive. Rosie, the composite whole, is fundamental, or so it seems.

There is, however, another historically prominent way to think of concrete particulars that does treat some wholes as fundamental sorts of thing. On this view, found notably in Aristotle, Rosie is a substance, a concrete particular in which the whole is metaphysically more fundamental than its parts and properties. In this chapter we shall argue for an Aristotelian view of concrete particulars, which distinguishes between ordered aggregates and heaps, on the one hand, and substances, on the other hand. With the former, the parts and properties of the thing are metaphysically prior to the whole. With the latter, the whole is metaphysically prior to its parts and properties. The main area of debate to be settled is whether the idea of whole-priority for composite objects is plausible. In other words, are there good reasons to think that Aristotelian substances exist? To enter into the debate, we begin by canvassing the two most prominent bottom-up approaches for understanding concrete particulars such as humans and chickens.

## Bottom-Up Accounts of Concrete Particulars

It is natural to think that Rosie, the composite whole, "has" or possesses her properties. The properties are in some sense "in" Rosie. Yet two questions arise: What, exactly, does the "having"? And how is this "having" relation to be understood? On one prominent story—call it the **substratum theory**—if Rosie were placed under a metaphysical microscope, we would find three constituent entities: her properties, a bare substratum, and the exemplification relation joining the two together. The bare substratum is a featureless particular (a pincushion) that exemplifies the properties (the pins) had, loosely speaking, by Rosie. The sentence

1. Rosie is a chicken

is understood strictly and philosophically as

2. Rosie's bare substratum ($BS_R$) exemplifies the property *being a chicken.*

The literal bearer of a thing's properties is not the composite whole but a constituent part of the whole, the bare substratum.

Why think that Rosie's bare substratum, instead of Rosie herself, is the literal bearer of properties? The idea is that the bearer of a thing's properties must be apprehended or conceived of independently of its properties, but Rosie, the complex whole, is not a thing that is apprehended or conceived of independently of her properties and therefore cannot be the literal bearer of her properties.[2] The literal bearer of Rosie's properties, $BS_R$, is "bare" because it stands under or supports Rosie's properties, like the pincushion to its pins, without itself having properties. It is a propertyless bearer of properties.

In order to highlight a key motivation of substratum theory, we must first set out another prominent bottom-up approach to complex objects: **bundle theory**. According to bundle theory, Rosie is a complex object constituted by her properties. Rosie is a *bundle* of properties, whether properties are understood as tropes or universals.[3] Sentence 1—"Rosie is a chicken"—is understood by the bundle theorist as

3. Rosie is a bundle of compresent properties (either universals or tropes), including the property *being a chicken.*

The compresence relation is a kind of building relation that joins together a plurality of properties into a composite whole.

Now that we've set out the two most prominent bottom-up theories of concrete particulars, we are able to see a key motivation for substratum theories by raising a problem for bundle theory. Imagine two qualitatively indistinguishable objects: red sphere *a* and red sphere *b*. This scenario seems possible.[4] Each object has qualitative properties such as *being red*

2. Michael J. Loux and Thomas M. Crisp, *Metaphysics: A Contemporary Introduction*, 4th ed. (New York: Routledge, 2017), 85.

3. Recall from chap. 8 that a trope is a nonshareable property, but a universal is a shareable property.

4. The classic statement of this kind of scenario is found in Max Black, "The Identity of Indiscernibles," *Mind* 61 (1952): 153–64.

and *being a sphere*. Assuming metaphysical realism, the properties had by objects *a* and *b* are universals—shareable properties. Assuming bundle theory, then objects *a* and *b* are bundles of universals.[5] However, given a plausible principle for identifying complex wholes in virtue of their constituents (i.e., same constituents, same whole), a problem arises. More formally, a **principle of constituent identity** (PCI) can be formulated as follows:

> PCI: If object *a* and object *b* have all the same constituents standing in all the same relations, then *a* is numerically identical to *b*.[6]

The problem, given metaphysical realism, bundle theory, and PCI, is that our imagined scenario is *not* possible. It is not possible for two qualitatively indistinguishable objects to exist. But the scenario *seems* possible, and if it is, then either metaphysical realism, bundle theory, or PCI must be rejected. The principle of constituent identity, PCI, is as good a principle as any, "a regulative principle that does nothing more than state a condition on the use of the terms 'constituent' and 'whole'";[7] thus there is no good reason to reject it. If one is a metaphysical realist, bundle theory must be rejected.

The bundle theorist might not need to concede defeat, however, if it could be maintained, contrary to appearances, that objects *a* and *b* are not qualitatively indistinguishable. Perhaps, it could be argued, object *a* has a relational property not had by object *b*, and vice versa. Object *a* has the property (let's say) *being to the left of b*, and object *b* has the property *being to the right of a*. If so, objects *a* and *b* are individuated by their relational properties; they are not numerically identical objects by virtue of each exemplifying a unique relational property. In this way, bundle theory can be salvaged, or so it seems, for the metaphysical realist.

Unfortunately, the appeal to relational properties won't work. Recall that for the bundle theorist, the only constituents of composite objects are properties. For the metaphysical realist, properties are universals, and so universals are the basic building blocks of composite objects. As basic or fundamental objects, properties are metaphysically prior to their wholes. But the relational property *being to the left of b* (had by object *a*)

5. For more on metaphysical realism—the view that properties exist, many of which are universals—see chap. 8.

6. For an explication of PCI, see Loux and Crisp, *Metaphysics*, 95–96; and Robert C. Koons and Timothy H. Pickavance, *Metaphysics: The Fundamentals* (Malden, MA: Wiley Blackwell, 2015), 110.

7. Loux and Crisp, *Metaphysics*, 96.

presupposes the existence of object *a*, object *b*, and a spatial relation between them. In the same way, the relational property *being to the right of a* (had by object *b*) presupposes the existence of object *a*, object *b*, and the spatial relationship between them. The problem is that objects *a* and *b* must already exist as individuals in order to stand in spatial relationships to each other.[8] But if they already exist, then relational properties cannot individuate the one from the other. Relational properties, if they exist at all, are not *fundamental* properties. They are not basic building blocks for composite wholes. Each object already exists as an individual metaphysically prior to standing in the spatial relationships that generate these relational properties. If so, then relational properties cannot individuate qualitatively indistinguishable objects. It seems that bundle theory (for the metaphysical realist) must go.

We are now able to see a key motivation for substratum theory, for according to the substratum theorists, there is, in addition to a thing's properties, a bare substratum "in" each composite whole. Thus object *a* has a constituent ($BS_a$) that object *b* doesn't have, and vice versa (object *b* has a bare substratum $BS_b$). Different constituents form different objects, according to PCI. Thus if one is a metaphysical realist there are good reasons to endorse substratum theory. We also learn that, in addition to being the literal bearer of a thing's properties, a bare substratum can be employed to play the individuator role, grounding the numeric diversity of distinct particulars (even if they are qualitatively indistinguishable).

Unfortunately for the substratum theorist, however, there is a potentially devastating problem. Many philosophers think the idea of a bare substratum, a propertyless simple that has properties, is incoherent. It is not hard to see why. We are told that a bare substratum is *bare*. It has no properties. But we are also told that a bare substratum is literally the bearer of a thing's properties. If so, then it has properties. So a bare substratum is a thing that both has and doesn't have properties. This is as clear a case of a contradictory notion as there can be, or so it seems.

There are, however, defenders of bare substrata who think the apparent incoherence is easily sidestepped. For example, J. P. Moreland distinguishes two

8. This example assumes the relationalist view of space (roughly, the idea that space is constituted by the relations that obtain between objects). If the substantival view of space is assumed (roughly, the idea that space is a substance in its own right, existing independently from the objects "in" it), the show is up for the bundle theorist, unfortunately. On the substantival view of space, an object is individuated by something like a bare substratum, a point in space-time that is a particular. Thus since the only constituents of objects according to bundle theory are properties, substantival conceptions of space entail the falsity of bundle theory (assuming metaphysical realism and PCI).

different senses for how particulars can have properties.[9] A composite whole (called a substance by Moreland) has properties "rooted within" it, whereas a bare substratum (called a bare particular by Moreland) has properties "tied to" it. There is a sense, then, in which bare substrata do have properties: properties are tied to an ontologically simple particular. Bare substrata are "bare" because they have no properties as constituents; they are ontologically structureless blobs. Still, since properties are tied to them, it is true that they are the literal bearers of properties. While the rooted-in or tied-to distinction does seem to remove the incoherence worry for the metaphysical realist, there are additional problems in the neighborhood.

Defenders of bare substrata usually claim that bare substrata have no essential properties themselves. All the properties tied to bare substrata are contingently tied to them. But it seems that bare substrata do have natures, or essential properties: the property of *being bare*, the property of *being a particular*, the property of *being simple*, and so on. If so, then it seems that bare substrata are not ontologically simple: they have properties, and those properties need a literal bearer too. It is natural to think, since the bearer of a thing's properties must be apprehended independently of its properties (as we noted above), that if a bare substratum has essential properties, those properties will be tied to its own lower-level bare substratum, a further constituent of our original substratum. Not only are bare substrata not simple on this picture: worse, it seems we are on the verge of generating an infinite regress of bare substrata with essential properties at descending levels "all the way down."[10]

Moreland's reply to this worry is to adopt a sparse theory of properties: some predicates—"is bare," "is particular," "is simple," and so on—do not refer to properties.[11] In this way it can be maintained that bare substrata have no essential properties or nature. While avoiding the threat of an infinite regress of metaphysical parts with properties for each bare substratum, this move comes at a cost: the denial of an abundant theory of properties. Some predicates, given the suggested adjustment, do not refer to properties. This concession might, it could be argued, undercut some of the original motivation in favor of metaphysical realism. We do not think this cost must be paid, nor do we think the threat of infinite regress is real, however. Let us explain.

9. J. P. Moreland, *Universals* (Montreal: McGill-Queen's University Press, 2001), 140–57; Moreland, "Exemplification and Constituent Realism: A Clarification and Modest Defense," *Axiomathes* 23, no. 2 (2013): 247–59.

10. For more on this worry, see Loux and Crisp, *Metaphysics*, 103–4.

11. J. P. Moreland and Timothy Pickavance, "Bare Particulars and Individuation: Reply to Mertz," *Australasian Journal of Philosophy* 81, no. 1 (2003): 1–13.

In the discussion thus far, we have been adopting a constituent framework for understanding concrete particulars. Constituent ontologies account for the character of ordinary concrete objects, such as Rosie the chicken, in terms of physical and metaphysical parts had by the whole. On a different approach, the relational approach, ordinary concrete objects such as Rosie do not literally have metaphysical parts, even if they do have physical parts (carbon atoms, feathers, beaks, etc.). On the relational approach, the concrete particular, Rosie, stands in some external relation to its properties; for example, the properties are "tied to" Rosie via exemplification.[12] In terms of metaphysical structure, constituent ontologies are "layer cake" ontologies and relational ontologies are "blob" ontologies.[13] In other words, if you were to look at Rosie under your metaphysical microscope, if in fact the relational approach truly describes the metaphysical structure of things, you would see a structureless blob (an internally simple thing) with properties tied to it (somewhat like a flower connected to its petals). If, however, the constituent way of looking at things were in fact true, you would see various metaphysical parts standing in various relationships and forming a complex whole, like a cake if *it* were placed under a metaphysical microscope.

With this distinction in hand, it seems that the defender of bare substrata can adopt a hybrid approach such that complex wholes (substances) have properties as constituents whereas simple wholes (bare substrata) have properties in the relational way, and that the bare substrata, along with the properties they exemplified, are nonseparable parts of the whole (the substance) that has them. It could then be maintained that while a bare substratum has no constituents, it does (on an abundant theory of properties) have properties, and some essentially (i.e., the properties that pick out *its* nature). We think this scenario is possible. The notion of bare substrata is coherent and doesn't require the rejection of an abundant theory of properties.

Even if bare substrata are perfectly respectable entities in their own right, there is a further question, however, regarding bare substratum *theory*. There are two reasons to think, as a stand-alone theory, that bare substratum views won't work. First, even if the bare substratum has a nature, and thus some essential properties that ground *its* nature, bare substratum theory does not allow for structured wholes—everyday particulars—to have essential properties. All the complex/structured wholes' properties are exemplified contingently by the bare substratum, even if (as we allow) the bare substratum

12. For a nice overview of the issues and options with respect to relational and constituent ontologies, see Koons and Pickavance, *Metaphysics*, 104–25.

13. Moreland, "Exemplification and Constituent Realism," 248.

has some essential properties that ground *its* nature. None of the complex whole's attributes are intrinsic to the bare substratum; they are, as Michael Loux states, "always accidental to its bearer."[14] For those who think, as we do, that Rosie the chicken, for example, has some essential properties (*being a chicken, being a particular*) in addition to her accidental properties (*being red, being five pounds*, etc.), bare substratum theories in the end fall short. Second, the rooted-in or tied-to distinction employed to render the concept of bare substrata coherent pushes in the direction of a different theory of ordinary objects, a theory that allows for fundamental wholes that are in some sense metaphysically prior to their constituent parts (otherwise it is hard to make sense of the rooted-in locution). We shall explore this top-down approach to concrete objects below. Before we do so, it will be helpful to see if bundle theory, in which properties are construed as tropes, might be able to unproblematically accommodate the distinction between essential and accidental properties for ordinary objects. If so, then one of the central motivations in favor of Aristotelian substances (to be discussed shortly) would be undercut.

Consider again our loveable pet chicken, Rosie. According to trope bundle theory, Rosie, the composite object, is a bundle of compresent tropes. The "is" in this last sentence is the "is" of identity: Rosie, the composite whole, is identical to her bundle of compresent tropes. But then, contrary to appearance, all of Rosie's tropes belong to her essentially. If Rosie were to grow an inch in height, she would lose a trope (*being ten inches tall*) and gain a new trope (*being eleven inches tall*). The problem is that the new emerging bundle of compresent tropes is a numerically distinct bundle. Rosie no longer exists. In her place is a new composite object, Rosie*. Thus bundle theory cannot accommodate (accidental—i.e., nonessential) change.

In reply, defenders of bundle theory have developed accounts that allow the possibility of change. The so-called nuclear bundle theory distinguishes two kinds of bundling relations: nuclear and peripheral compresence.[15] On this view, since we are exploring trope theoretic versions of bundle theory, Rosie is identical with the set of nuclear tropes—tropes that pick out her essence. In addition to her nuclear tropes, she has peripheral tropes standing in the peripheral compresence relation. These peripheral tropes can come and go, but Rosie, along with her nucleus, will survive the gaining and losing of peripheral tropes. Nuclear bundle theory is an improvement on so-called classical bundle theory since it allows the commonsense distinction between

14. Loux and Crisp, *Metaphysics*, 108.

15. Peter Simons, "Particulars in Particular Clothing: Three Trope Theories of Substance," *Philosophy and Phenomenological Research* 54, no. 3 (1994): 553–75.

essential and accidental properties, as well as the possibility of survival through change. The cost, however, is in terms of an additional primitive; there are now two primitive building relations for the bundle theorist: nuclear compresence and peripheral compresence.[16] While the benefit—compatibility with a robust theory of change—seems worth the cost, it does bring focus to one final problem for the bundle theorist, a problem that affects all versions (i.e., realist and trope nominalist). The problem has to do with the nature of the building relation itself.

According to Robert Garcia, a bundle theorist takes compresence to be an object-making relation.[17] In the context of bundle theory, compresence is supposed to take something from one category—property—and make or generate (out of a plurality or bundle of properties) something in another category—object. But what is the resultant entity that compresence makes? The resultant entity, according to Garcia, is most plausibly understood to be a state of affairs: the compresence of *being a chicken* and *being red* results in the state of affairs *chickenhood being compresent with redhood*. The problem with this story is that it leaves a critical explanatory gap at the heart of bundle theory. The explanatory gap has to do with how a plurality of properties yields a distinct entity that is characterized by those properties. As Garcia puts it, states of affairs are entities "*involving* those properties," but they are not entities "*charactered* by those properties."[18] In other words, consider the state of affairs *chickenhood being compresent with redhood*. The latter involves the properties *being a chicken* and *being red*, but the state of affairs *itself* is neither red nor a chicken. Since according to Garcia explanatory gap problems affect any version of the object-making relation, then on bundle theory "it is simply *axiomatic* . . . that properties go together to generate non-properties which are charactered in the ways specified by those properties; . . . object-making is an explanatory black box. . . . [It is] relatively weak with respect to its explanatory power."[19] The bundle theorist must take it

16. Koons and Pickavance, *Metaphysics*, 114.

17. In addition to compresence (also called collocation), Garcia explores other proposals concerning the nature of this relationship including fusion and interdependence. See Robert K. Garcia, "Bundle Theory's Black Box: Gap Challenges for the Bundle Theory of Substance," *Philosophia* 42, no. 1 (2014): 115–26.

18. Garcia, "Bundle Theory's Black Box," 123. This problem also infects substratum theories: the product of properties tied to bare substrata, according to Michael Loux, are states of affairs. If so, the explanatory gap problem infects substratum theories too: the resultant entity that is the complex whole (the state of affairs) *involves* properties but is not *charactered* by those properties. See Michael Loux, "Aristotle's Constituent Ontology," in *Oxford Studies in Metaphysics*, ed. Dean Zimmerman (Oxford: Clarendon, 2006), 2:216.

19. Garcia, "Bundle Theory's Black Box," 125 (emphasis in original).

as a given that properties go together to form objects. The inability to explain *how* this takes place is an ideological cost for the theory. Given bundle theory's lack of explanatory power, as well as the problems associated with substratum theories, it would be wise to consider top-down approaches to concrete objects like Rosie.

We now turn to consider Aristotelian substances, a top-down approach to some concrete objects that views the whole as a fundamental unity of parts, properties, and powers.

## Top-Down Accounts of Some Concrete Particulars

We are considering ordinary concrete objects like Rosie the chicken. One observation about Rosie and other living organisms is that she exhibits a kind of natural unity and fundamentality. Rosie, according to the Aristotelian tradition, is a **substance**: a fundamental unity of parts, properties, and powers. As a fundamental unity, a substance "enjoys a certain naturalness or completeness or rounded-offness"[20] not enjoyed by cars or piles of trash. We shall follow Aristotle in distinguishing between fundamental (natural) unities (substances) and nonfundamental (lesser or artificial) unities such as ordered aggregates or heaps.

In what sense are substances such as Rosie fundamental unities? One way to understand this is in terms of how Rosie, the composite whole, has her physical and metaphysical parts. As a substance, Rosie's parts are *nonseparable* parts of Rosie. To say of some part that it is a nonseparable part of some whole is not to be understood as the claim that the part is essential to the whole; rather, it's the claim that being a part of the whole is essential *to the part*.[21] Consider this car's spark plugs. These spark plugs are separable parts of the car. They are metaphysically prior to the whole they find themselves in. If the spark plugs were removed from the car, they would still be the same spark plugs; their nature and existence is indifferent to the whole of which they are a part. On the contrary, Rosie's heart, as a part of a fundamental whole, is an inseparable part of Rosie. Rosie's heart is defined in terms of the functional role it plays as part of the composite whole; take Rosie's heart out of Rosie, and it is no longer a heart (or so we claim, following Aristotle). The heart, in some sense, survives its removal from Rosie. The thing that formerly

20. Barry Smith, "On Substance, Accidents and Universals: In Defense of Constituent Ontology," *Philosophical Papers* 26, no. 1 (1997): 108.

21. Patrick Toner, "On Substance," *American Catholic Philosophical Quarterly* 84, no. 1 (2010): 27.

was Rosie's heart, when removed from Rosie, becomes a clump of matter. Yet that clump of matter is no longer Rosie's heart, strictly speaking.

As fundamental unities of parts, properties, and powers, Aristotelian substances exhibit top-down, whole-to-part priority. Philosophers who endorse this picture reject the bottom-up approach to concrete particulars (of a certain kind) where wholes are built up out of more basic constituents. Rather, the substance, on this account, is a "particularized-nature"[22] that has (nonseparable) parts, properties, and powers. The claim is not that substances *have* natures but rather that substances *are* natures.[23] The essential properties of a substance flow out of or are determined by the kind of thing the substance is. The kinds of accidental properties a substance can have are also determined by its nature (e.g., a chicken can't have the property *being wise* or *being an English speaker*, but it can have the property *being red* or *being five pounds*; the latter are accidental properties that come and go in chickens, guided by the stable patterns grounded in the thing's nature). In this way, the unity of a substance can be explained in terms of final causation: the particularized nature is the final cause of its parts, properties (essential and accidental), and powers. Thus the natures function teleologically. As Loux explains, on Aristotle's account of living organisms (i.e., substances), "Natures impose a top-down organization on the members of the relevant kind in the sense that the nature dictates a specific pattern of functional organization in which the various organic parts of a living being get their identity from the role they play in the overall functional economy imposed by the nature. What we have, then, is a single, unified form of being or life that spreads itself over the parts and subordinates them to the whole."[24]

Thus it is possible, and we think plausible, to distinguish between a thing's nature and its (essential and accidental) properties: a substance just is a particularized nature—a dog, a chicken, a geranium—that has properties, parts, and powers.[25]

22. Ross D. Inman, *Substance and the Fundamentality of the Familiar: A Neo-Aristotelian Mereology* (New York: Routledge, 2018), 20.

23. In the Aristotelian tradition, this nature is sometimes called the thing's form, and the material parts of the whole are called its matter. On this reading, Aristotelian substances are fundamental unities of form and matter. This view is also called *hylomorphism*, a term spliced together from two Greek roots: *hylē* (matter) and *morphē* (form). For contemporary articulations and defenses of hylomorphism, see Michael C. Rea, "Hylomorphism Reconditioned," *Philosophical Perspectives* 25 (2011): 341–58; and Robert Koons, "Staunch vs. Faint-Hearted Hylomorphism: Toward an Aristotelian Account of Composition," *Res Philosophica* 91, no. 2 (2014): 151–77.

24. Loux, "Aristotle's Constituent Ontology," 246.

25. For a defense of the distinction between natures and essential (and accidental) properties, see Paul M. Gould and Richard Brian Davis, "Where the Bootstrapping Really Lies: A Neo-Aristotelian Reply to Panchuk," *International Philosophical Quarterly* 57, no. 4 (2017): 415–28.

As noted above, Moreland is a contemporary defender of Aristotelian substances. How does Moreland explicate our now-familiar sentence about Rosie? According to Moreland,

1. Rosie is a chicken

can be analyzed as

4. The property *being a chicken* inheres in Rosie as a constituent

and

2. Rosie's bare substratum ($BS_R$) exemplifies the property *being a chicken.*

Following Aristotle, Moreland employs a constituent framework for understanding ordinary concrete objects.[26] Statements 4 and 2 are understood as follows: The concrete material substance, the particularized nature, Rosie, has as a constituent property (Moreland is a Platonist regarding properties: properties are universals) *being a chicken.*[27] Hence the property inheres in or is rooted in Rosie. Moreover, the property *being a chicken* is tied to or exemplified by a further constituent of Rosie, Rosie's individuator $BS_R$.[28] Thus Moreland employs at least two "building relations" to join together a plurality of properties into a composite whole: the exemplification relation (or tie) and the inherence relation.[29]

26. See Moreland, *Universals*; Moreland, "Exemplification and Constituent Realism."

27. Here is a possible objection: You say substances have nonseparable parts, but if Platonism is true, then properties are separable parts, necessarily existing abstract objects that can (and do) exist apart from the substances that have them. Solution: Strictly speaking, the nonseparable part of the substance is the property-instance, a complex entity with three constituents: the property, the exemplification relation, and the bare substratum. The property-instance is the nonseparable part of Rosie, even if the property/universal can and does exist independently (and is thus metaphysically prior to Rosie). Thus this fix, if one follows Moreland, is to say that substances have no *integral* separable parts (even if they have separable metaphysical parts) where an integral part is a spatial part of a substance (e.g., atoms, molecules, cells, my left arm, my head, the whiteness of my toe, etc.). For more on the possibility of blending Platonism about properties with Aristotelian substances, see Paul Gould, "How Does an Aristotelian Substance Have Its Platonic Properties? Issues and Options," *Axiomathes* 23, no. 2 (2013): 343–64.

28. Not all defenders of Aristotelian substances appeal to bare substrata. Some, such as Loux, argue that substances just come individuated by virtue of being a member of a substantial kind. Others posit different individuators such as thin particulars, matter, regions of space-time, individual essences, or complexes of parts. For more on the problem of individuation for Aristotelian substances, see Loux and Crisp, *Metaphysics*, 108–14.

29. For more on the idea of "building relations" that join pluralities of things into unities, see Karen Bennett, "Construction Area (No Hard Hat Required)," *Philosophical Studies* 154 (2011): 79–104.

Endorsing this nonreductive picture, at least for living organisms and perhaps for other concrete (material or immaterial) objects, has certain benefits. For starters, belief in Aristotelian substances accommodates many of our prephilosophical intuitions such as belief that Rosie, for example, is a fundamental thing, a deep unity, and capable of surviving accidental change.

The view is not without worries, however. Two prominent worries are worth noting. First, it is not obvious that living organisms have only nonseparable parts. The trouble for the Aristotelian view begins with things like atoms.[30] It certainly seems that atoms are separable parts of living organisms. Take one of Rosie's carbon atoms. It is now a part of her. Next week, after she scratches it off her face (she likes to rub her face on the side of the pen), the carbon atom will no longer be a part of her. Then it will be a part of the ground and will soon be absorbed into that weed. It seems that the carbon atom, contrary to the claim made by the Aristotelian, is a separable part of Rosie. The reply to this worry is simplicity itself. When carbon atoms exist independently of some whole, they are genuine Aristotelian substances. When they are incorporated into some other substance as a part, they cease being a substance in their own right and become virtual or pseudosubstances.[31]

If accepted, this reply surfaces the second prominent worry. It seems that the resultant account of living organisms doesn't cohere with things we know from science. Science tells us that carbon atoms (among other atoms, molecules, and cells) do work in the organism. But if there are only "carbon-atomish parts,"[32] how can they do the work science says they do? Patrick Toner offers the following reply: "Everything we want to say about the work that gets done in organisms because of carbon atoms can all still be said. We just can't endow such claims with too much metaphysical baggage."[33] In other words, the scientist can truly and coherently talk about carbon atoms (and other atoms, molecules, and cells) within living organisms. What the scientist can't say, at least as a scientist, is that those carbon atoms are substances when existing apart from things and are nonsubstances or pseudosubstances when existing as nonseparable parts of things. Those claims are philosophical claims. The upshot is that there is no obvious conflict between the things

30. Both worries discussed here are from Toner, "On Substance," 42–46.

31. Toner, "On Substance," 44. See also James D. Madden, *Mind, Matter, and Nature* (Washington, DC: Catholic University of America Press, 2013), 240–42.

32. Toner, "On Substance," 44.

33. Toner, "On Substance," 44. As Madden writes, "The elements [i.e., atoms, molecules, cells] are present in the sense that their essential capacities [i.e., their active and passive powers] have been adopted by the substance, what we call *virtual presence* as distinguished from *substantial presence*, but they strictly speaking do not exist as discrete parts of the substance." *Mind, Matter, and Nature*, 241 (emphasis in original).

scientists want to say about living organisms and the kinds of things (Aristotelian) philosophers want to say about living organisms.[34]

Since there are benefits to believing in substances and nothing important needs to be given up along the way, we think it best to admit them into our ontology.[35] Summarizing then, some particulars (living organisms, atoms, maybe more) exist as fundamental unities, whereas others (ordered aggregates and piles) are constructions out of more basic parts.

## The Divine Substance

Finally, we think the foregoing discussion helps us to better understand the divine substance. God is an immaterial concrete particular. A natural reading of Scripture suggests that God too has properties (e.g., being omnipotent, being omniscient, and being omnibenevolent) and other constituent parts (e.g., ideas, thoughts, volitions, a will, an intellect). One traditionally held view argues that this natural understanding of the divine is problematic. The idea is that if God has parts and properties, then in some sense God depends on those parts and properties for his existence and nature. If so, then God is not ultimate. Thus it is argued that God is *simple*, completely devoid of any metaphysical parts. This doctrine of **divine simplicity** was held by thinkers such as Augustine, Anselm, and Aquinas in order to secure God's supremacy.[36] Many today, however, think the doctrine of divine simplicity is itself implausible.[37] Whether or not the doctrine of divine simplicity can be salvaged, we want to highlight a further benefit to the Aristotelian view. The defender of Aristotelian substance can secure God's supremacy even if there is complexity within the divine being. If God, as we maintain, is an Aristotelian substance, then he is a fundamental unity, a particularized nature, and thus

34. For a book-length defense of this claim, see William M. R. Simpson, Robert C. Koons, and Nicholas J. Teh, *Neo-Aristotelian Perspectives on Contemporary Science* (New York: Routledge, 2017). But see also Howard Robinson, "Modern Hylomorphism and the Reality and Causal Power of Structure: A Skeptical Investigation," *Res Philosophica* 91, no. 2 (2014): 203–14.

35. In addition to the benefits cited in this section, Toner argues that the Aristotelian view of substance can solve philosophical problems such as the Problem of Material Constitution, the Problem of the Many, the Problem of Overdetermination, and the Problem of Vagueness. See Patrick Toner, "Emergent Substance," *Philosophical Studies* 141 (2008): 281–97. To see how Aristotelian substances have been employed to solve problems regarding God's relationship to abstract objects, see Gould and Davis, "Where the Bootstrapping Really Lies."

36. See Augustine, *Confessions* 7.1.1; Augustine, *City of God* 11.10; Anselm, *Proslogion* 18; Aquinas, *Summa Theologiae* 1.3.

37. For a clear and powerful statement of the contemporary challenge to the doctrine of divine simplicity, see Alvin Plantinga, *Does God Have a Nature?* (Milwaukee: Marquette University Press, 2007).

metaphysically prior to his parts. As creator of all distinct reality, God depends on nothing outside his borders for his existence and nature, and as an Aristotelian substance, everything within God's borders ultimately depends on God, the composite whole who is the final cause of his constituent parts and properties. In this way, we submit, Aristotelian substances can do important work not only in philosophy and science but in theology too.

## Conclusion

In this chapter we've considered how to make sense of the concrete objects, or particulars, of our everyday experience. Some particulars are best thought of from the "bottom-up": piles of trash and ordered aggregates like cars and computers are best thought of in this way, or so we've argued. Other particulars—atoms, organisms, God—are best thought of from the "top-down," as substances or fundamental unities. In arguing for top-down dependency relations and whole-priority for some particulars, we are pushing back on the now dominant neo-Humean and reductionistic trend that prioritizes the microphysical over the macrophysical and the "scientistic" over the "manifest" image of reality.

# 10

# Freedom and Determinism

It is a datum of human experience that our actions *seem* to be free. For most, this is good reason to think that we are in *fact* free. Moreover, we tend to think this to be a good thing. We think it a good thing to be self-determiners of our actions, our character, and the story of our lives. This freedom grounds our moral ascriptions of praise and blame with respect to the actions, character, and life story of others and ourselves. "Free will" is what we call this *ability* or *power to choose* our actions, character, and life story.[1] But there is a problem lurking below the surface with respect to free will. Consider the following dilemma:

1. If determinism is true, free will is an illusion.
2. If determinism is not true, free will is arbitrary.

Determinism—roughly, the idea that the future is fixed—is either true or not. Either way, free will seems to be impossible. The tension between claims 1 and 2 highlights what is often called the problem of free will. In this chapter we shall explore the problem of free will. We will be particularly interested in whether there are strategies that can be plausibly employed in order to avoid one or both horns of the dilemma highlighted by claims 1 and 2. We begin by considering determinism.

1. Meghan Griffith, *Free Will: The Basics* (New York: Routledge, 2013), 3.

### Determinism

There are basically three versions of determinism: logical, theological, and physical (see fig. 10.1). In all versions of **determinism**, the future is fixed by some determining factor. With logical determinism, the determining factor is the fact that propositions about the future are already true or false. Consider the act of reading *Harry Potter and the Sorcerer's Stone* on your twelfth birthday. One hundred years prior to your twelfth birthday, the proposition P, "You will read *Harry Potter and the Sorcerer's Stone* on your twelfth birthday," was either true or false. Assume that the proposition P was true. If P was true, then necessarily, on your twelfth birthday, you would read *Harry Potter and the Sorcerer's Stone*. But if you had no choice regarding the truth of P one hundred years ago (and how could you?), then you have no choice about reading Harry Potter on your birthday either. By the time of your twelfth birthday, it was too late: you couldn't prevent P from being true a hundred years earlier, and it is also too late to prevent what necessarily follows from the truth of P (namely, your reading the book on your twelfth birthday). While many remain unmoved by the threat of logical determinism, the task of deciding what exactly is wrong with the above line of reasoning has proved difficult, quickly moving into areas of fundamental metaphysics regarding the nature of truth, time, dependence, and explanation.[2]

Theological determinism moves not from prior *truths* about what you do but from either prior *divine decrees* or *divine beliefs* about what you do.[3] An example of theological determinism grounded in the decrees of God is Calvinism, which endorses the claim that God is the sufficient cause of everything that happens in the world, including the good and evil actions of humans.[4] In a later section we will consider an example of theological determinism grounded in divine beliefs about future contingent acts of humans. For the remainder of this section, we'll consider physical determinism.

Consider the event of my hand raising at time $t_1$. According to physical determinism, the event of my hand raising at $t_1$ is a consequence of the past history of the universe (prior to time $t_1$) and the laws of nature. The past history of the universe and the laws of nature are the determining factors of the event of my hand raising. In other words, given the past and the laws

2. For an excellent overview of the current debate over logical determinism (often called logical fatalism), see the introduction by John Martin Fischer and Patrick Todd to *Freedom, Fatalism, and Foreknowledge*, ed. Fischer and Todd (Oxford: Oxford University Press, 2015), 1–38.

3. Fischer and Todd, *Freedom, Fatalism, and Foreknowledge*, 22.

4. Robert Kane, *A Contemporary Introduction to Free Will* (Oxford: Oxford University Press, 2005), 148.

Figure 10.1
**Kinds of Determinism**

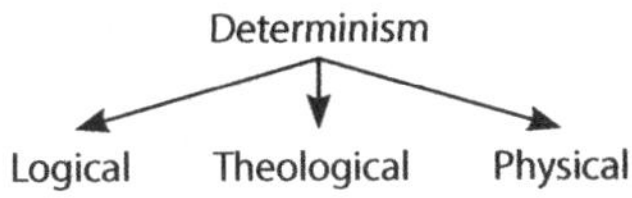


of nature, I could not have done otherwise than raise my hand at time $t_1$. At any time before $t_1$, the future was fixed for me: it was determined that I would raise my hand at time $t_1$. If my choices and actions are inevitable, given the past and the laws of nature, then I am not free. Thus the argument goes: if determinism is true, free will is an illusion (i.e., claim 1 of our dilemma is true).

At this point the defender of free will has two options. Such a person can deny the first part of claim 1 and argue that determinism is false or deny the second part of claim 1 and argue that freedom is *compatible* with determinism. Let's consider the first part of claim 1. Is physical determinism true? Most philosophers think the answer to this question is an empirical matter, investigated by discovering the nature of the world.[5] It certainly seems as if the world operates according to fixed laws of nature. Each day is followed by night, each spring is followed by summer, acorns fall to the ground when released by oak trees, and so on. The world seems to be a grand machine operating according to the exceptionless laws of classical (Newtonian) physics. Indeed, many philosophers in the eighteenth and nineteenth centuries thought classical science entailed physical determinism.[6] However, this picture of the world is no longer taken for granted due to the advent of contemporary quantum mechanics and the possibility of probabilistic laws of nature.

If the world of elementary particles (the microworld governed by quantum mechanics) is in fact indeterministic, then physical determinism is false. While the issue is by no means settled, there seems to be somewhat of a consensus that the quantum world is indeterministic.[7] Let us, for the sake of argument, assume that the quantum world is indeterministic. Does the indeterminancy of the quantum world ground the possibility of genuine freedom? It is not clear that it does. While quantum indeterminancy is relevant to elementary

5. Kevin Timpe, *Free Will in Philosophical Theology* (New York: Bloomsbury, 2014), 8.

6. But for an argument that classical science does not entail physical determinism, see Alvin Plantinga, *Where the Conflict Really Lies* (Oxford: Oxford University Press, 2011), chap. 3.

7. For a helpful discussion of the relevant issues in interpreting quantum mechanics, see Tim Maudlin, "Distilling Metaphysics from Quantum Physics," in *The Oxford Handbook of Metaphysics*, ed. Michael J. Loux and Dean W. Zimmerman (Oxford: Oxford University Press, 2003), 461–87.

particles and their behavior, it is not obviously relevant to larger-scale physical objects such as the human brain and body (presumably the seat of our deliberations and actions). If somehow indeterministic microevents were "amplified" so that they could produce large-scale effects within the human brain and body, such effects, like their microbase, would also happen by chance.[8] These large-scale effects, which result from indeterministic "quantum jumps," are unpredictable and uncontrollable—more like a sudden twitch of the face or a random thought traversing through the mind than a responsible and hence free action.[9] But then we've avoided, in this first attempt, the rocky heights of claim 1, only to be shattered on the crags of claim 2. It is time to consider the second option for the defender of free will with respect to claim 1: the idea that freedom is compatible with determinism and therefore not an illusion. We begin by considering the nature of freedom.

## Freedom

What are the necessary conditions for genuine freedom? Intuitively, an action or choice is free if it is one of a number of alternative possibilities. So on this way of thinking, for example, I am free with regard to my choice to wear the blue shirt if it is the case that I could also choose the red, black, or green shirt instead. This intuition undergirds claim 1 of our dilemma. If the future is not "open" in any genuine sense, if there is no power to do otherwise, then there is no freedom. Many philosophers think this is the sine qua non—the essential condition—of freedom; without it, an action or choice is simply not free. In addition, many think freedom requires that each agent is ultimately responsible for their own actions and choices. The agent must be the ultimate source or origin of the action or choice and not merely a passive conduit of external causes that are outside the agent's control (such as the past, the laws of nature, or the decree of God). If alternative possibilities (AP) and ultimate responsibility (UR) are necessary conditions for freedom, it is not difficult to see how determinism poses a threat to the possibility of freedom.

Not all, however, think freedom is incompatible with determinism. Some philosophers argue that there is no conflict between freedom and determinism. This view, known as **compatibilism**, argues that claim 1 of our dilemma

8. Robert C. Bishop considers various routes for amplification such as Chaos Theory and Nonequilibrium Statistical Mechanics, in "Chaos, Indeterminism, and Free Will," in *The Oxford Handbook of Free Will*, ed. Robert Kane (Oxford: Oxford University Press, 2002), 119–21.

9. Kane, *Introduction to Free Will*, 9.

is false. A compatibilist who also thinks that we do have free will is called a soft determinist. In fact, the soft determinist often thinks freedom *requires* determinism. This is because, as claim 2 states, if determinism is false our actions and choices seem arbitrary, either uncaused, in which case the agent is not ultimately responsible, or caused (by reasons or desires) but not necessitated, in which case the agent acts or chooses irrationally or randomly. All that is required for freedom, says the compatibilist, is the "agent's unhindered ability to do [or choose] what he wants."[10] As long as the agent does or chooses what this agent wants to do or choose, and does so without coercion, the act or choice is free even if determined.

But what about AP and UR? Does the compatibilist reject our intuitively plausible conditions for genuine freedom? With respect to AP, the compatibilist (ironically!) has options. One can either provide a Conditional Analysis of AP or deny that AP is a necessary condition for freedom. The compatibilist who thinks AP is true can offer a Conditional Analysis of "what I could have done otherwise" that is consistent with being determined. To say "I could have become an accountant instead of a philosopher" is analyzed by the compatibilist as "I would have become an accountant instead of a philosopher, if I had wanted to." There is a sense, then, says the compatibilist, in which I could have done otherwise, even though my actions and choices are determined. And if the conditional analysis of "could have done otherwise" is acceptable, then it seems the compatibilist can also affirm an important condition of what it means to be free.

Unfortunately, many philosophers think the Conditional Analysis fails. If what I want is determined, then it doesn't seem, after all, that I really have any alternative possibilities. Recall my act of hand raising at time $t_1$. If at $t_1$ I want to raise my hand and nothing prevents me from doing what I want with respect to my hand raising at $t_1$, then my act is done freely, according to the compatibilist. But at $t_1$ there are no genuine alternative possibilities before me. Given my want, a want over which I have no control, I could act in only one way. What are needed, argues the incompatibilist, are genuine alternative possibilities *at the time of* the action or choice. But given determinism, there is only one alternative at the time of the action or choice, so the conditional analysis gives the wrong results.[11]

The second option, to deny that AP is a necessary condition for freedom, seems more promising for the compatibilist. As it turns out, there are powerful

10. Griffith, *Free Will*, 41. This is the view of the "classic compatibilist" of the seventeenth and eighteenth centuries, such as Hobbes and Hume.

11. Griffith, *Free Will*, 42.

reasons provided by compatibilists for thinking the principle of alternative possibilities is false. In 1969, the philosopher Harry Frankfurt published an influential paper that ignited the debate over the truth of AP.[12] Frankfurt gives various examples designed to show that someone could be responsible, and hence free, even if there was no ability to do otherwise. If these "Frankfurt-style counterexamples," as they have come to be called, are successful, then AP is false; alternative possibilities are not required for moral responsibility or freedom. A typical Frankfurt-style counterexample is this: Suppose that Black wants Jones to kill Smith. If Jones kills Smith on his own, then Black will not intervene. If when the moment comes, however, it appears that Jones will not kill Smith (Black is an expert at reading people), then Black, who has secretly planted a chip in Jones's brain, will press a button, manipulating Jones's brain so that he will kill Smith. Suppose Jones wants to kill Smith and does so. Black remains in the background, and the chip in Jones's brain is dormant. Did Jones act responsibly, and hence freely, in killing Smith? It seems that he did. We blame Jones because he killed Smith on his own and wanted to. But he could not have done otherwise. Black was ready to intervene if needed. Therefore, we have a counterexample to the claim that freedom requires AP.

There is considerable debate over whether Frankfurt-style counterexamples are successful. The defender of AP might argue that there are in fact genuine alternative possibilities in these cases. For example, while Jones does not have the alternatives of "kill Smith" or "not kill Smith," he does have the alternative of "kill Smith on my own" or "kill Smith as a result of Black's manipulation."[13] The defender of Frankfurt-style counterexamples in turn retorts that this "flicker of freedom . . . is too thin a reed on which to rest moral responsibility."[14] Alternatively, the defender of AP might argue that Frankfurt-style counterexamples presuppose the truth of determinism and thus beg the

12. Harry Frankfurt, "Alternative Possibilities and Moral Responsibility," *Journal of Philosophy* 66 (1969): 829–39. Frankfurt's principle of alternative possibilities (PAP) focuses on moral responsibility, whereas AP above focuses on freedom. We are treating Frankfurt's PAP as roughly synonymous with AP, since it is widely held that agents are morally responsible for their own actions or choices only if free.

13. Griffith, *Free Will*, 45.

14. John Martin Fischer, "Frankfurt-type Examples and Semi-Compatibilism," in Kane, *Oxford Handbook of Free Will*, 289. This essay is an excellent overview of the debate about Frankfurt-style counterexamples. Fischer's own view is that determinism probably does rule out alternative possibilities, but moral responsibility and freedom do not require alternative possibilities. This view is called semicompatibilism. Alternatively, some argue that even if AP (alternative possibilities) is false, determinism does rule out responsibility and freedom since freedom and responsibility require only UR (ultimate responsibility). This incompatibilist view is called source incompatibilism.

question against **indeterminism.**[15] If freedom requires indeterminism, then the only way Black can ensure that Jones will kill Smith is to act in advance to bring it about that Jones kills Smith (after all, Black cannot ensure that he *reliably* predicts Jones's actions given indeterminism). But if it is necessary that Black *actually* needs to intervene to ensure that Jones kills Smith, then while it is true that Jones could not have done otherwise, it is also the case that Jones is not responsible. Thus moral responsibility (and freedom) does require AP if indeterminism is true. At this point, there seems to be somewhat of a stalemate between the compatibilist and the incompatibilist. It is not clear whether AP is required for freedom.

What is clear is that if compatibilism is true, we must give up UR as a necessary condition for freedom.[16] Given compatibilism, an agent *contributes* to action—for example, I contribute to the action of raising my hand at time $t_1$ by choosing to do so and moving my body in order to bring about the event of my hand raising—but the agent still is not the *ultimate* source of action. To be the ultimate source of action, nothing outside the agent guarantees the action. But, given physical determinism, the past and the laws of nature do guarantee the action. Thus the compatibilist requires that we give up on at least one, and maybe both, of the parts of our prephilosophical intuition regarding freedom.[17]

## Incompatibilism

The incompatibilist argues that determinism is incompatible with freedom. That is, claim 1 of our dilemma is true. A powerful argument called the Consequence Argument has been advanced to show the incompatibility of determinism and freedom.[18] Informally stated, the argument is as follows: Assume determinism is true. If determinism is true, my act of hand raising at time $t_1$ is the necessary consequence of the past and the laws of nature. There is nothing I can do to change the past and the laws of nature; they are beyond my control. But if my hand raising at $t_1$ is a necessary consequence

15. This objection is called "The Indeterminist World Objection" by Kane. See Kane, *Introduction to Free Will*, 87–88.

16. For what follows in this paragraph, see Griffith, *Free Will*, 47.

17. For an overview of more sophisticated new compatibilist theories, see Kane, *Introduction to Free Will*, chaps. 9 and 10; and Griffith, *Free Will*, chap. 4.

18. The Consequence Argument has been ably defended by, among others, Peter van Inwagen, *An Essay on Free Will* (Oxford: Clarendon, 1983); Carl Ginet, *On Action* (Cambridge: Cambridge University Press, 1990); and Timothy O'Connor, "Indeterminism and Free Agency: Three Recent Views," *Philosophy and Phenomenological Research* 53 (1993): 499–526.

of the past and the laws of nature, and the past and the laws of nature are beyond my control, then my hand raising at $t_1$ is also beyond my control. Generalized, since all my actions are determined, it follows that all my actions are beyond my control. That is, if determinism is true, there is no freedom.

The key inference of the Consequence Argument is the Principle Beta: "If there is nothing agent S can do about X, and Y is a necessary consequence of X, then there is nothing agent S can do about Y either." Principle Beta seems intuitively true. The compatibilist, of course, rejects the Consequence Argument and focuses attention on the viability of Principle Beta. One strategy, as we have already seen, is to offer a Conditional Analysis of the word "can" found within Principle Beta and the premises of the Consequence Argument: "You can do action A" means "You would do action A if you wanted to." But as we have seen, many think the Conditional Analysis fails. This does not mean incompatibilism wins; there are other compatibilist counterexamples to Principle Beta on offer. Still, it is safe to say that the burden of proof is on the compatibilist to provide a viable account of "can" and "could have done otherwise" that either undercuts Principle Beta or refutes other premises of the Consequence Argument.[19]

Assume the Consequence Argument is sound, and thus determinism is incompatible with freedom. It does not follow that there *is* freedom in the world. There are three kinds of **incompatibilism**: **hard determinism, hard incompatibilism**, and **libertarianism** (see fig. 10.2). The hard determinist thinks incompatibilism and determinism are true and denies the reality of genuine freedom. The hard incompatibilist thinks incompatibilism is true and is unsure whether determinism is true or false, but either way denies the reality of genuine freedom. The libertarian (about free will, not politics) thinks incompatibilism is true and affirms genuine freedom. All accept claim 1 of our dilemma. The defender of libertarian freedom rejects claim 2. It is time to consider whether indeterminism is compatible with freedom.

The problem is that the denial of determinism isn't enough to secure the reality of genuine freedom. J. J. C. Smart succinctly captures the worry. He argues that all events are the result of either deterministic forces (what he calls "unbroken causal continuity") or chance. But if our actions result from

19. For a nice overview of contemporary compatibilist responses to the Consequence Argument, see Tomis Kapitan, "A Master Argument for Incompatibilism?," in Kane, *The Oxford Handbook of Free Will*, chap. 6. See also Peter van Inwagen, "Free Will Remains a Mystery," in Kane, *The Oxford Handbook of Free Will*, chap. 7, for van Inwagen's discussion of a successful counterexample to one understanding of Principle Beta and his fix. Van Inwagen remains convinced that Principle Beta is valid and the Consequence Argument sound.

Figure 10.2

**The Free Will Landscape**

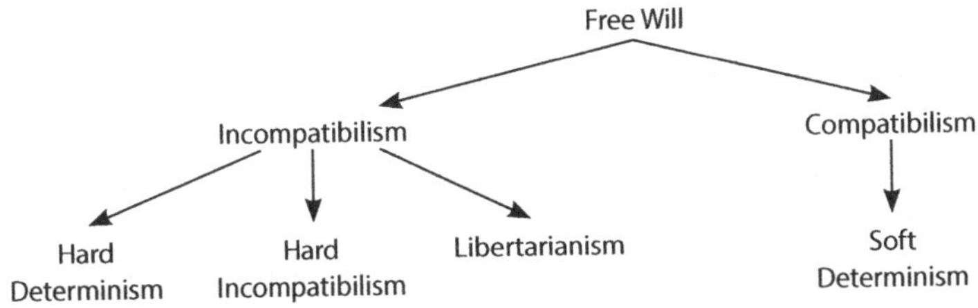


chance, they are not under our control; hence, they are not *free* actions.[20] The idea is that there is no "space" for genuine (libertarian) freedom between something being undetermined and its happening as a matter of chance or luck. What is needed is some "extra factor" to ground libertarian freedom.[21] Many defenders of libertarian freedom have responded to this challenge by postulating **agents** as the needed "extra factor": agents are the cause of undetermined yet free actions.

## Agent Causation

Consider again the act of my hand raising at time $t_1$. Suppose the children next door are playing backyard football, and a wayward pass results in the football hitting my raised hand at time $t_2$. The event of the football hitting my hand at $t_2$ brings about the event of the football coming to rest on the ground at $t_3$. This is an example of **event causation**. But what about the act of my hand raising at $t_1$? Is this also an example of event causation? Some think another kind of causation is at work in this act of mine, called **agent causation**. On this view, I am a substance, a continuant that is the "first cause" of my action. As an agent cause, I am a self-determiner of my actions, character, and life story. Thus I am ultimately responsible (UR) and in many cases (if not all cases, depending on the role of character in influencing choices and actions) able to do otherwise (AP). As Roderick Chisholm puts it, "Each of us, when we act, is a prime mover unmoved. In doing what we do, we cause certain events to happen, and nothing—or no one—causes us to cause those events to happen."[22]

While agency theory is an attractive "extra factor," a factor that seems to capture the way we experience our own choices and activity, many find

20. J. J. C. Smart, "Free Will, Praise and Blame," in *Free Will*, ed. Gary Watson, 2nd ed. (Oxford: Oxford University Press, 2003), 63.

21. Kane, *Introduction to Free Will*, 39.

22. Roderick M. Chisholm, "Human Freedom and the Self," in Watson, *Free Will*, 34.

the idea at worst incoherent or at best deeply mysterious. A prominent objection to agent causation is that it does not eliminate randomness: if the free actions of agents are undetermined, then given the *exact* prior circumstances, an agent could have chosen (say) A or B. But then it seems that the actual choice made by the agent is entirely random and arbitrary. Hence, it is argued, agent causation is incoherent. In response, the agent theorist points out that the reasons and purposes of an agent can play a role, as motivating factors, in the agent's self-determining choices. Reasons and purposes influence the agent's choices without causing them. I raised my hand at $t_1$ because I wanted to; I was exercising (let's say) in order to remain healthy. This reason ("I wanted to") and purpose ("in order to remain healthy") influenced my decision to raise my hand at $t_1$. If so, then the choices and actions of agents are not random: they are done for reasons.[23] Regarding the charge of mystery, while it can be granted that agent causation is to some extent mysterious, it is no more mysterious than the concept of causation itself (which, as Hume and others have taught us, is notoriously difficult to analyze). Moreover, the worry of mystery is mitigated by the fact that we are more familiar with agent causation, via introspection into our own experience, than we are with event causation. It is more basic; our concept of event causation is arguably parasitic on our experience as causal agents. Finally, while agent causation might be difficult to reconcile with naturalism and its preference for event causation, it fits nicely within a broadly theistic view of the world. If God exists and is the first cause of the physical universe, agent causation is one of the most basic facts of reality.[24] We conclude: there are good reasons to think that agent causation is the necessary "extra factor" for libertarian freedom.[25]

In summary, if there is to be genuine (libertarian) freedom, the following four conditions must be met: (1) incompatibilism is true, (2) the agent is ultimately responsible for his or her choices and actions (UR), (3) agent

23. For a robust defense of agent causation, including reasons and explanations for actions, see Timothy O'Connor, "Agent Causation," in *Agents, Causes, and Events: Essays on Indeterminism and Free Will*, ed. Timothy O'Connor (Oxford: Oxford University Press, 1995), chap. 10.

24. For more on the difficulty of squaring agent causation with materialism, see J. A. Cover and John O'Leary-Hawthorne, "Free Agency and Materialism," in *Faith, Freedom, and Rationality*, ed. Daniel Howard-Snyder and Jeff Jordan (Lanham, MD: Rowman & Littlefield, 1996), 47–72. For an argument that libertarian free will is incompatible with naturalism, see Jason Turner, "The Incompatibility of Free Will and Naturalism," *Australasian Journal of Philosophy* 87, no. 4 (2009): 565–87.

25. For a survey of alternative "extra factor" strategies for the defender of libertarian freedom, see Kane, *Introduction to Free Will*, chap. 5; and Griffith, *Free Will*, chap. 5.

causation is true, and (4) at least sometimes there are alternative possibilities (AP) (see table 10.1).[26]

**Table 10.1. Necessary Conditions for Libertarian Freedom**

| | |
|---|---|
| Incompatibilism | Freedom is not compatible with being determined. |
| Ultimate Responsibility (UR) | The agent is the ultimate source of the self's choices and actions. |
| Agent Causation | The agent is the "first cause" of one's own choices and actions. |
| Alternative Possibilities (AP) | The agent "could have done otherwise" with respect to choices or actions (either at the time of the choice or action or at earlier "will-setting moments"). |

## God and Freedom

The debate over the problem of free will intensifies when the existence and nature of God are factored in. Consider the question of whether human freedom is compatible with divine foreknowledge. The problem is this: God, as traditionally conceived, is omniscient. From eternity past, God knows that I will raise my hand at time $t_1$ (i.e., God foreknows the future). God's past belief about what I will do at $t_1$ is something over which I have no control. Moreover, since God cannot be mistaken in his beliefs, I will necessarily raise my hand at $t_1$. But if I will necessarily raise my hand at $t_1$, then I am not free.

In order to understand prominent responses to the problem of divine foreknowledge and human freedom, consider the following set of jointly inconsistent claims:

3. God has exhaustive foreknowledge of the future.
4. I have no control over God's past beliefs about the future.
5. Determinism is true.
6. There is libertarian freedom.

26. Virtue Libertarianism, a view consistent with the above conditions for freedom, allows that an agent might not have genuine alternative possibilities at the time of an action. Still, the agent did, at some point in the near or distant past, have alternative possibilities and thus is responsible for the self's character. Thus if we understand AP broadly as alternative possibilities at the time of a decision or action or some time in the causal past (at key "will-setting moments"), we can preserve the connection between alternative possibilities and responsibility and allow a role for character in our account of libertarian freedom. Virtue Libertarianism is a version of Soft Libertarianism, which is the view that alternative possibilities are not always required for genuine freedom (or not always required at the time of the action or choice). For more on Virtue Libertarianism, see Timpe, *Free Will in Philosophical Theology*.

In order to render this set consistent, one or more of these claims must be rejected. The compatibilist accepts claims 3–5 and rejects claim 6. Human freedom is compatible with being determined. However, many think theistic compatibilism is unacceptable.[27] While it is difficult with all versions of compatibilism to account for human moral responsibility, theistic compatibilism seems to render God as the ultimate cause of all human actions and thereby the author of sin and evil. Moreover, it is not clear, on theistic compatibilism, that God desires all to be saved (contrary to 1 Tim. 2:4). The damned are consigned to hell by virtue of God's sovereign decree, a decree issued long before they were born. As a result, it is hard to make sense of the claim that God is wholly good. Given the apparent insuperability of these worries, many theists will be attracted to libertarian accounts of freedom.[28]

The defender of libertarian freedom will, of course, reject claim 5, but in order to do so will also need to reject either claim 3 or claim 4 since, as we have seen, 5 is entailed by 3 and 4. The open theist rejects claim 3: God does not have exhaustive foreknowledge of the future. The future is "open"; God is a "risk taker" who in love willingly exposes himself to the real possibility of failure and disappointment.[29] While there are important defenders of open theism, it has not garnered wide acceptance among traditional theists.[30] This is partly because open theism seems to undermine the phenomenon of biblical prophecy and calls into question God's ability to bring his plan for the world to fulfillment.

Others reject claim 4. The Molinist, for example, argues that in addition to foreknowledge, God possesses "middle knowledge": knowledge of what

27. See, e.g., Jerry L. Walls, "Why No Classical Theist, Let Alone Orthodox Christian, Should Ever Be a Compatibilist," *Philosophia Christi* 13, no. 1 (2011): 75–104. In reply, see Steven B. Cowan and Greg A. Welty, "*Pharaoh's Magicians Redivivus*: A Response to Jerry Walls on Christian Compatibilism," *Philosophia Christi* 17, no. 1 (2015): 151–73. But see Jerry Walls, "Pharaoh's Magicians Foiled Again: Reply to Cowan and Welty," *Philosophia Christi* 17, no. 2 (2015): 411–26, and in response Steven B. Cowan and Greg A. Welty, "Won't Get Foiled Again: A Rejoinder to Jerry Walls," *Philosophia Christi* 17, no. 2 (2015): 427–42.

28. Arguably, the biblical position on human freedom is underdetermined. It may be that Scripture is *consistent* with both compatibilism and libertarianism (yet see the preceding footnote for Walls's arguments that Scripture *demands* libertarianism). For an excellent discussion of how to understand the biblical teaching on the nature of human freedom, see Thomas H. McCall, *An Invitation to Analytic Christian Theology* (Downers Grove, IL: IVP Academic, 2015), chap. 2.

29. William Hasker, "A Philosophical Perspective," in *The Openness of God: A Biblical Challenge to the Traditional Understanding of God*, by Clark Pinnock et al. (Downers Grove, IL: InterVarsity, 1994), 151.

30. In addition to Hasker and other contributors to *The Openness of God*, important defenders of Open Theism include Richard Swinburne and Peter van Inwagen. For bibliographical information on key philosophical defenders of Open Theism, see the introduction to Fischer and Todd, *Freedom, Fatalism, and Foreknowledge*, 26–27.

libertarianly free creatures *would* do in any particular situation.[31] Thus, given **Molinism** (named after Luis de Molina [1535–1600]), we do have a kind of power over the past; we have *counterfactual power* over God's past beliefs. If I were to act differently at time $t_1$ (e.g., and not raise my hand), God's middle knowledge would have been different, and he would have foreknown that I will not raise my hand at $t_1$. God's past beliefs *track* our future choices, but (given Molinism) they do not determine (or cause) our future choices.[32] **Ockhamism** is another view that rejects claim 4. The Ockhamist solution, first put forth by William of Ockham (1285–1347), makes a distinction between hard facts (facts simply about the past) and soft facts (facts not simply about the past since they depend on something that happens in the future). With this distinction in place, the Ockhamist claims that while it is not in our power to affect hard facts about the past, it is in our power to affect soft facts about the past, and God's past beliefs about what I will do are all soft facts.[33] While Molinism or Ockhamism are not without problems, they represent attractive solutions to the problem of divine foreknowledge and human freedom that account for our prephilosophical intuitions about the nature of freedom and moral responsibility, all the while preserving a high view of divine sovereignty, a robust doctrine of divine omniscience, and belief in the goodness of God.

## Conclusion

In this chapter we've explored "the problem of free will." The problem is multifaceted, requiring attention to the question of determinism, the nature of moral responsibility, the possibility of agent causation, and the role of character in choice and action. Adding God into the mix further complicates things. While we side with the incompatibilist (and the virtue libertarian), we think there is freedom here to maneuver as a Christian and, as with many areas of philosophical and theological investigation, would encourage you to hold your position as thoughtfully as you can with intellectual humility and theological modesty.

31. For more on Molinism, see the discussion in chapter 14.

32. For more, see William Lane Craig, "Middle Knowledge: A Calvinist-Arminian Rapprochement?," in *The Grace of God and the Will of Man*, ed. Clark H. Pinnock (Grand Rapids: Zondervan, 1989), 141–64.

33. For more, see Alvin Plantinga, "On Ockham's Way Out," *Faith and Philosophy* 3, no. 3 (1986): 235–69.

# 11

# Minds, Bodies, and Human Persons

Philosophers ask questions about all sorts of things. We wonder about the nature of reality, the existence of God, the possibility of gaining knowledge of the world, and the basis of our moral inclinations. But philosophers also ask questions about persons in general and what it means to be a *human* person in particular. What exactly is a human being? What makes us unique? And how is it that we manage to continue existing across time? These might sound like bizarre or even unnecessary questions, but a casual reflection on our lives in the world suggests that these questions are highly important. What are we exactly? How are we put together? What is my relationship to my body? And is there more to me than just my body?

Questions like these have been a central topic of debate throughout the history of philosophy, but especially in contemporary philosophy. Generally speaking, substance dualist philosophers—such as Plato in the ancient world and the seventeenth-century philosopher René Descartes—made a sharp distinction between bodies and souls (or minds), suggesting that they were two distinct kinds of things. In addition to this, Plato and Descartes argued that persons were to be identified with the soul (or mind) and not the body. This view has been widely held throughout most of philosophical history and continues to have able defenders to this day.[1] Nevertheless, Plato and Des-

1. See, e.g., J. P. Moreland and Scott B. Rae, *Body and Soul: Human Nature and the Crisis in Ethics* (Downers Grove, IL: InterVarsity, 2000); and Richard Swinburne, *Mind, Brain, and Free Will* (Oxford: Oxford University Press, 2013).

cartes's view has not been the only one. In the modern period, for example, philosophers like Locke and Hume rejected such substantival views, arguing instead that persons are nothing more than a cluster of psychological dispositions, beliefs, and memories. Still later, a long list of other philosophers from modernity to the present have argued that human persons are material beings through and through.

The purpose of this chapter is not so much to trace the history of these debates, as important as they may be. Rather, the purpose is to sift through the various topics, concepts, and questions that guide philosophers in the current discussion and to help students find their footing in such discussions. To do this, we will first lay out some basic terms and concepts at play in the conversation, highlighting some of the most important questions on the subject along the way. After that, we will offer a quick survey of the most common positions on the questions of human nature and constitution.

## Basic Terms and Concepts

In one sense, terms like "mind," "soul," "body," "person," and "human person" seem to be rather straightforward and understandable. We use them every day with ease, and we know what they mean when people use them in general conversation. But other terms, like "substances," are less familiar and can cause confusion. Furthermore, even with the more familiar terms like "minds," "souls," and "persons," philosophers tend to use them in unique ways and with layers of nuance and technicality. Hence, given the nuance and technical nature of the philosophical debate around these issues, it is important to begin the discussion with a quick survey of how they are used in philosophical discourse.

### *Substances*

The notion of "substance" is as old as philosophy itself and comes into play within the broader field of metaphysics. It was first introduced by Aristotle, but similar notions can be found with thinkers before him. According to Aristotle, a substance is something that is composed of both matter and form. Consider a cup that you drink from. What is it that makes it a cup? Aristotle would describe the cup as composed of the material stuff of wood or heat-cured clay as well as the form that is imposed on the material to give it the structure of a cup. Only when the two come together do we have the substance of a cup.

As we saw in chapter 9, discussions about substances have evolved over time. Contemporary philosophers, for example, tend to think about substances differently than Aristotle conceived of them. In these discussions, philosophers typically focus their attention on the kinds of criteria that must be met in order to identify a thing as a substance. According to Peter Simons, various factors have been suggested in recent history. Summarizing the discussion of Aristotelian substance from chapter 9, four distinct criteria seem to be most common. First, substances are often thought of as the bearers of properties. Consider, once again, Rosie the chicken. Notice how I mentioned that she is a chicken. That is to say, Rosie has the property of being a chicken. As such, she is the bearer of a property. Metaphysicians regularly note that this is a major feature of substances. They bear properties or qualities but are not themselves a property or quality of some other thing.

Second, substances can be conceived as allowing for individuation. In other words, substances allow for things to be individuated and distinct from other things. Consider the two chickens Rosie and Ronnie. They are two distinct chickens, not one. Each individual chicken is a substance that is distinct from the other, no matter how similar they appear to be physically. As substances they are individuated from each other.

Third, substances are the kinds of things that can exist on their own. This is not to say that they don't have to have a cause for their existence. Rather, it is to say that their existence does not ride on some other thing such that if that other thing ceased to exist, then the substance would too. Consider the shadow of a tree. If the tree were not there to block the rays of the sun, then surely the shadow would not be there. In this case, the shadow cannot exist on its own. Substances are different since they are the kinds of things that don't need some other thing to exist. Rosie sits by herself and does not depend on anything else around or beside her.

Finally, substances can be thought of as things that are capable of surviving changes. That is, a substance can sustain a change of some kind and continue to be what it is and continue to be the one that it was.[2] Again, Rosie is helpful. When Rosie first hatched from her eggshell, she had yellow feathers. But as she grew and developed, she lost her yellow feathers and replaced them with reddish brown feathers. Did Rosie change in some way? Yes, of course. Yet is she still a chicken? Yes, of course. Is she the same chicken she once was? Again, yes, of course! These four criteria are helpful for our purposes in this

2. See David Robb, "Substances," in *The Routledge Companion to Metaphysics*, ed. Robin Le Poidevin et al. (New York: Routledge, 2012), 256–64.

chapter since much of the debate on the topic of human persons revolves around the validity of substance dualism.

### *Minds and Souls*

Setting forth the meaning of words like "minds" and "souls" in the current debates is a little more difficult. For starters, these terms can be used interchangeably by theologians and philosophers. This interchange is somewhat understandable since there is indeed much overlap in what is meant by each term. But they do not always mean exactly the same thing. Another difficulty comes from the fact that each term seems to carry a different level of meaning depending on the particular view held by the person treating the question. In other words, different theories of mind define minds differently; so also different views of the soul define souls differently. What philosophers and theologians mean by these terms depends at least in part on who is speaking and the view they espouse. Despite these tendencies, however, we shall offer a quick survey of the ways these terms are used.

So what are minds? At minimum, minds are entities that facilitate rational processes and process intelligent functions. But if this is all they are, then there is no reason to say that humans, animals, angels, or divine persons are all that could qualify as having minds. On this view, we could also include computers as minds. For most philosophers, however, this definition is not enough. Most go beyond this to include other important features in their conception of minds. Most views of the mind suggest that minds are thinking things, thus capable of reflection and metacognition. Regardless of what kinds of stuff minds are composed of—physical brains or spiritual substances—most philosophers throughout history have generally agreed that minds are the kinds of things that think, reason, and reflect. But this raises the question of what exactly it is that composes minds, and this takes us into another view of minds. As suggested above, while some believe that physical brains are capable by themselves of facilitating such metacognitive thought, philosophers like Plato, Descartes, and many more have argued that only immaterial substances could ever think. And so, for Plato and Descartes, minds are distinct from physical brains and physical bodies and are instead composed of something nonphysical.[3] On this view, minds have a spiritual element over and above the brain, even if minds are intimately connected with brains.

With this in view, it is easy to see why terms like "mind" and "soul" are used interchangeably. Those employing the term "soul" typically use that term to

3. See René Descartes, *Meditations on First Philosophy*, trans. Donald A. Cress, 4th ed. (Indianapolis: Hackett, 1993). See especially meditation 2.

refer to immaterial substances that are capable of thought, reflection, desire, intention, direction, and conscious experiences. As we shall see below, this is the view espoused by substance dualists. But once again, this is not the only way the word "soul" is used. For hylomorphists (Greek: *hylē* = matter; *morphē* = form), a soul is not actually a spiritual immaterial substance. Rather, it is the substantial form—the organizing principle that gives life and structure to the physical body—of the body that it gives life to.[4]

### *Persons and Human Persons*

Most of us never wonder what it means to be a person. We don't struggle to recognize and categorize the various beings we encounter into the proper categories in which they belong. When we meet a new dog, for example, we don't wonder if it is a person. We recognize it as a dog and would likely dispute any suggestion by others that the dog is a person. But if we had to dispute the claim that dogs are persons, how would we do it? What does the dog lack that we possess? This question forces us to ask a broader question: What exactly is a person?

Some initial answers might go as follows. Perhaps persons are beings or entities with minds and therefore capable of thought and reflection as described above. While most philosophers would agree that having a mind is a necessary condition for persons, they would also tend to agree that it is not a sufficient condition for personhood. That is, having a mind may be a minimal criterion but would not by itself make something a person. In short, while animals like dogs clearly and significantly differ from human beings in their mental life, it is also the case that animals think. Perhaps, then, one might say that persons have conscious experiences like tasting sugar or hearing wind blow and that this is what makes us persons. But again, it surely seems as though dogs do the same thing. They clearly like certain kinds of foods and respond to the sound of our voices. It certainly looks as though they have some kind of conscious experience. Or perhaps one may say that the difference between us and dogs that makes it possible to say that humans are persons and dogs are not is that humans are just more intelligent. While this is certainly true, it again doesn't seem to convey the distinction between animals and persons. It seems like there is something more.

Lynne Rudder Baker's work is helpful on this point. She argues that persons have two distinct qualities that other nonperson animals don't: intentional states and first-person perspective. The intentional-states criterion requires

4. See Aristotle, *De Anima* 11.1, trans. Hugh Lawson-Tancred (New York: Penguin, 1986), 157.

that, at minimum, a person has mental states like desiring, intending, and planning. So, for example, persons are the kinds of things that desire to get married, intend to do so, and then develop a plan to go about accomplishing this. But here again, this criterion is clearly not a sufficient condition for personhood since many animals demonstrate these capacities on a regular basis. Baker adds an additional condition that is the most important one for us to consider. According to Baker, a person is some kind of being that has first-person perspective. She says, "To be a person—whether God, an angel, a human person, or a Martian person—one must have the capacity for a first-person perspective."[5] She explains this further, saying, "The defining characteristic of person is a first-person perspective."[6] But what does this mean? In other words, first-person perspective requires more than me being able to have desires, intentions, and plans: it is a metacognition about myself that requires me to realize that *it is I who has such desires, intentions, and plans*. It is this first-person awareness of my mental states that seems to be the key for Baker's account. Baker's criteria seem to get at something that truly differentiates persons from nonpersons. Even still, we might add at least one additional component to our understanding of persons: moral inclinations. Persons are the kinds of beings that operate and act in moral categories. We have a sense of oughtness and responsibility that drives and shapes us. This is a major difference from animals and nonpersons. Thus we suggest that persons are beings with intentional states, first-person perspective, and moral inclinations.

Notice that the above discussion is about persons in general. It does not distinguish specific kinds of persons. Because of this, we need to say something more with regard to what it means to be a *human* person. Nevertheless, what we have said thus far about persons in general will apply to the question of human persons, even if there is more to say about this specific case. In addition to being entities with intentional states, first-person perspective, and moral inclinations, human persons are persons who are related in some way to human bodies. The relationship of person to the human body is a matter of debate between the various positions. For materialist views, that relationship is very strong. On these views, the human person either is identical to the living human body or is at least constituted by the living human body. According to substance dualist views, however, the relationship to the human body is not as strong. On this view, the human person is just the soul/mind, and its

5. Lynne Rudder Baker, *Persons and Bodies: A Constitution View* (Cambridge: Cambridge University Press, 2000), 92.

6. Lynne Rudder Baker, "When Does a Person Begin?," in *Social Philosophy and Policy* 22 (2005): 28.

relationship to the body is one of possession. In other words, the person is the soul and has a body.

Scores of views might be enumerated here, but three major views have tended to dominate the debates of the past and the present: (1) substance dualism, (2) materialism and physicalism, and (3) some middle position between the first two that we might call hylomorphism. We shall see the differences of these views as we go forward.

### Substance Dualism

The most widely held view throughout philosophical history is called **substance dualism**. This was the view of Plato and, later, Descartes. Plato, Descartes, and others who hold this view typically make two distinct ontological claims regarding human constitution. First, substance dualists make what we might call a stuff distinction claim. On this view, there are two distinct kinds of stuff with regard to human persons: physical bodies and nonphysical souls or minds. Bodies and souls are radically different from each other and must be thought of as fundamentally different substances. Being different substances, the body and the soul have different identities, bear different properties, survive different kinds of events, and can exist apart from each other.

Substance dualists, however, make an additional claim, and this is the one that is most essential to understand. The second claim is the person/soul identity claim: while there may be two distinct kinds of stuff, persons are distinct from their bodies and identical to their souls. In this claim, in other words, substance dualists contend that human persons are not their physical bodies. Human persons may have physical bodies, but they are not their bodies. Instead, substance dualists argue that human persons are souls that inhabit or possess their bodies. As J. P. Moreland and Scott Rae suggest in their account, "Human persons are identical to immaterial substances, namely, to souls."[7] Or as Stewart Goetz puts it, "One of the things that I, as an ordinary person, believe about myself is that I am a soul that is distinct from my physical (material) body."[8]

Like other views, substance dualism has its strengths and weaknesses. This view, for example, seems to have a rather easy time accounting for things like conscious experience and personal persistence across time. Consider

7. Moreland and Rae, *Body and Soul*, 121.

8. Stewart Goetz, "Substance Dualism," in *In Search of the Soul: Four Views of the Mind-Body Problem*, ed. Joel B. Green and Stuart L. Palmer (Downers Grove, IL: InterVarsity, 2005), 33.

the experience we have when we taste a soda. In this case there clearly are particular kinds of physical events that take place on a chemical level on the tongue and in the mouth. With these, there are also corresponding brain events in the neural firings of the brain. Interestingly, however, the actual experience of *tasting* the soda doesn't appear to be reducible to the physical events of the mouth or the brain event in the neurons. To account for the actual experience of tasting, it looks as though something beyond the physical body and brain is required. John Searle puts it this way: "Materialists have a problem: once you have described the material facts in the world, you still seem to have a lot of mental phenomena left over. Once you have described the facts about my body and my brain, for example, you still seem to have a lot of facts left over about my beliefs, desires, pains, etc."[9] Searle goes on to state that this problem has often led materialists to try to simply explain consciousness away or eliminate consciousness. But this is rather problematic since consciousness is so obviously real. Searle observes that getting rid of consciousness "is not an easy thing to do. It sounds too implausible to say right out that pains and beliefs and desires don't exist, though some philosophers have said that."[10] Substance dualists have no such problem. In their ontology, there is plenty of space for the mental life and conscious experience, and it seems far easier to account for such things with the existence of the soul.

Substance dualists also appear to have an easier time accounting for the persistence of the person across time. Consider what happens in our experience. Take, for example, Bernie's development and change throughout his life. Bernie was born in 1976, his body was twenty-one inches long, he weighed six pounds and thirteen ounces, and he had no hair. Of course, his body didn't stay that way. It grew and changed over time as he ate food and his body metabolized it. By the time he was three years old, he was forty inches tall, weighed thirty-eight pounds, and had curly blond hair. The process of growth and development continued over time until he reached his full growth potential of five feet, eleven inches in height, weighed two hundred pounds, and had thick brown hair that was still a little curly.

Two things are interesting about this growth process. First, to put it roughly, his body experienced significant changes over time and was even composed of different parts along the way as his body metabolized food and discarded old parts that wore out. Second, despite these changes Bernie continued to

9. John Searle, *The Mystery of Consciousness* (New York: New York Review of Books, 1997), 136.

10. Searle, *Mystery of Consciousness*, 136.

be exactly the same person he was at the earlier moments of life, when his body was very different. That is, Bernie of 1976 and Bernie of today are exactly the same person. What allowed for Bernie to continue being Bernie even though his body was constantly changing? Substance dualists have a rather straightforward and easy answer to this question: his soul. No matter what one thinks about substance dualism in general, and despite what other materialistic answers might be given to the question of personal persistence across time, one has to respect the simplicity and elegance of the substance dualist's answer to this question.

But, as is well noted throughout history, substance dualism seems to face a rather perplexing issue known as the mind-body interaction problem. This problem involves a seeming impossibility of immaterial minds interacting with the material body. If, as substance dualists say, bodies and souls are radically different substances, one being material and the other being immaterial, how is it that the two interact with each other? As we consider the nature of bodies and souls as described by substance dualists, our normal understanding of causation seems to go out the window.

Consider the case of two dominoes that fall in a causal sequence. Why is it that domino B fell? It fell because domino A caused it to fall when it fell and hit domino B. And how exactly did A's hitting B cause B to fall? It caused it to fall by (1) coming into contact with B and (2) transferring energy from itself into B. Can this understanding of causation work for bodies and souls? It doesn't seem so, since immaterial souls have no mass and do not take up space. Therefore the body and the soul (1) cannot come into contact with each other and (2) cannot transfer energy to each other. Or at least so it seems. Perplexing questions like these have caused philosophers over the centuries to reject substance dualism. In Descartes's own time, Princess Elisabeth of Bohemia raised this very concern: "I admit that it would be easier for me to concede matter and extension to the soul than to concede the capacity to move a body and to be moved by it to an immaterial thing."[11] In other words, for Princess Elisabeth, the interaction problem was so significant that she found it easier just to believe that minds/souls were material things than it was to believe that an immaterial thing could interact with material objects. To this day, many philosophers continue to think that this concern is a defeater for substance dualism. But, of course, defenders of the position disagree. The debate rages on!

11. Princess Elisabeth of Bohemia, "Elisabeth to Descartes—10 June 1643," in *The Correspondence between Princess Elisabeth of Bohemia and René Descartes*, ed. and trans. Lisa Shapiro (Chicago: University of Chicago Press, 2007), 68.

## Materialism and Physicalism

Generally speaking, in philosophical discussions of human persons the terms "materialism" and "physicalism" are synonymous and interchangeable. Some may make certain subtle distinctions between the two, but we shall use them interchangeably in what follows. Materialists take a much different approach to the question of human persons than substance dualists. Specifically, they reject the existence of immaterial substances like souls or minds. While distinct materialistic views share this belief in "material monism," the actual details of distinct views can vary considerably. We won't have the space to address all of them, but a sampling of some of the most common views can be offered.

### *Psychological Continuity Model*

One notable view, adopted by Descartes's contemporary John Locke (1632–1704), is called the psychological continuity model of persons. This view rejects the notion of immaterial souls/minds and affirms the idea that the "self" is a bundle or cluster of psychological properties composed of memories, beliefs, and psychological dispositions. Moreover, some particular "self," or we could say more generally "person," persists across time as long as there is psychological continuity across time. Locke famously says:

> For as far as any intelligent being can repeat the *idea* of any past action with the same consciousness it had of it at first, and with the same consciousness it has of any present action; so far it is the same *personal self*. For it is by the consciousness it has its present thoughts and actions, that it is *self* to *itself* now, and so will be the same *self*, as far as the same consciousness can extend to actions past or to come, . . . with . . . the same consciousness uniting those distant actions into the same *person*, whatever substances contributed to their production.[12]

That is, as long as the psychological bundle of properties—beliefs, desires, dispositions, and so forth—continue to exist, the person continues to exist.

### *Eliminativism*

In recent philosophical history, a more radical materialist ontology known as **eliminativism** has been adopted by some philosophers. This is a radical

12. John Locke, *An Essay Concerning Human Understanding* (Oxford: Clarendon, 1975), 2.27.10 (emphasis added).

view because it suggests that the best way to handle mental properties and states is simply to deny them altogether, or at least to deny the vast majority of them. In this model, there are no such things as "beliefs," "pains," "desires," or "feels." Some advocates of this view would even say that there is no such thing as free will or the self. On this account of minds, there are only brains and brain events. This view is called eliminativism because it eliminates minds and mental properties entirely.

Technically speaking, by eliminating the mental, this view says that no one ever feels pain or tastes anything. As one might imagine, this is not a very popular view among materialists, simply because it seems so counterintuitive. Even though they universally reject immaterial substances, materialists generally recognize the reality of our experiences of pain, tastes, hopes, and joys. The eliminativist's attempt to get rid of such things just doesn't seem to work.

### *Reductionism and Identity Theory*

Other materialists offer a slightly less radical account of the mental. Reductionists, for example, do not deny that we feel pain, taste sugar, or have hope. Rather, they simply reduce those things, which are typically thought of as mental events or properties, to brain events or physical properties. That is, those phenomena are just, or are nothing but, physical properties or events in the brain. One very common expression of this is called **identity theory**, which claims that minds and brains are identical to each other. To describe a mind is just to describe a brain. Hence our understanding of the mind is nothing more than our understanding of the brain. On the surface, it may seem as though the reductionists and identity theorists are saying exactly the same thing as the eliminativist, but they actually aren't. Pete Mandik offers a helpful comparison:

> The simple form of mind-brain identity theory says that pains are nothing but a certain kind of brain state—c-fibers firing. The simple form of eliminative materialism says that there are no pains—there are only c-fibers firing. Both theories agree that c-fibers firing exist. But do both agree that there are no pains, that pains do not exist? No, they do not, and this is the key difference between them. The mind-brain identity theorist's statement in terms of "nothing but" may make it seem like the existence of pains is being denied, but this is not so. The "nothing but" claim—the claim that pains are nothing but c-fibers firing—is not telling us that pains are nothing at all. Instead, it is simply saying that pains are nothing additional, they are nothing beyond c-fibers. . . . In contrast, the eliminative materialist is outright denying that pains are identical to c-fibers

firing. Pains aren't identical to anything at all—they don't even exist according to the eliminative materialist.[13]

As Mandik makes clear, reductionist views like identity theory have some similarities to eliminativist accounts of the mind, but identity theory is a less radical view that doesn't reject the commonsense notion that pain and other such experiences are real. It does, however, reduce mental aspects of our lives to the physical events and components of our brains. In the end, it maintains that everything is reducible to, and thus explainable by, the physical.

### *Nonreductive Physicalism*

A much more common materialist view, at least among Christian materialists, contends that the reductive account also goes too far. They may agree with their fellow materialist that immaterial souls do not exist and that only material substances do, but they reject the idea that everything—namely, the mental—is reducible to the physical. That is to say, on their view there may be only one kind of stuff that accounts for human beings on a basic ontological level, but that doesn't mean that mental stuff is reducible to brain stuff. This **nonreductive physicalism** is a form of physicalism, since it holds that, ontologically, human persons are nothing more than living physical organisms. At the same time, however, it does not reduce the mental to physical objects, events, or states. On this view, the mental is something distinct from the physical. Nancey Murphy, one of nonreductive physicalism's most able defenders, says that when applied "to the specific area of studies of consciousness, it denies the existence of a nonmaterial entity, the mind (or soul) but does not deny the existence of consciousness (a position in philosophy of mind called eliminative materialism) or the significance of conscious states or other mental (note the adjectival form) phenomena."[14] She then adds, "In brief, this is the view that the human nervous system, operating in concert with the rest of the body in its environment, is the seat of consciousness (and also of human spiritual or religious capacities). Consciousness and religious awareness are emergent properties and they have a top-down causal influence on the body."[15]

Several features of Murphy's description are worthy of comment. First, notice that this view affirms conscious experiences. It does so without reducing

13. Pete Mandik, *This Is Philosophy of Mind: An Introduction* (Malden, MA: Wiley-Blackwell, 2014), 140.

14. Nancey Murphy, "Nonreductive Physicalism: Philosophical Issues," in *Whatever Happened to the Soul?*, ed. Warren S. Brown, Nancey Murphy, and H. Newton Malony (Minneapolis: Fortress, 1998), 130–31.

15. Murphy, "Nonreductive Physicalism," 131.

the content of conscious experiences, mental content, or mental properties to physical brain states. As often pointed out, this view holds that while there may not be a dualism of substances, there is a dualism of properties. In other words, this view rejects substance dualism but embraces property dualism. Property dualism claims that mental properties are distinct from physical properties and that mental events are distinct from brain events, even if they occur in conjunction with each other. In the philosophical literature, the kind of mental properties we have in view here are often referred to as *qualia*, which is the Latin for "qualities." In our conscious experiences of things, we experience qualities like sweetness, redness, bitterness, or coldness. Thus there is something that it is like, a mental experience, that we possess in these moments. Property dualism affirms that mental properties and *qualia* are not reducible to physical brain events, but it does so while also maintaining physicalism.

Second, these properties are emergent in that they arise out of the complex neurological system within the brain. Third, once such properties have emerged, they exercise a downward causation on the lower systems of the brain and the rest of the body. This understanding of downward causation, sometimes called top-down causation, is best understood by setting it in contrast to bottom-up causation. As Murphy and Brown explain, bottom-up refers to "the assumption that behavior of an entity is determined by the behavior (or laws governing the behavior) of its parts."[16] By contrast, a downward-causation model suggests that "phenomena at some higher level or organization of a complex system had a downward causal influence on the events that were being studied at a lower level."[17]

### *Functionalism*

Another very popular view among materialist philosophers is known as **functionalism**. Though functionalism is technically noncommittal about the number of substances involved in a human person, the overwhelming majority of those who hold this view come from the materialist camp. Generally speaking, functionalists think the "number of substances" question is the wrong question. In their view, the better and more important question is, What is a mind? And as their name implies, functionalists define minds as those entities capable of intelligent function, contending that there are any number of entities—humans, computers, machines, and so forth—that might qualify

16. Nancey Murphy and Warren S. Brown, *Did My Neurons Make Me Do It?* (New York: Oxford University Press, 2007), 62.

17. Murphy and Brown, *Did My Neurons Make Me Do It?*, 63.

as minds. A helpful illustration of the functionalist conception of minds is the illustration of a hand and a fist. What exactly is a fist? It is a hand that punches. When the hand is balled up into a fist, no new thing comes into existence. Rather, all that happens is that the hand now takes on the function of punching. The same is the case with a brain. When it thinks, no new thing comes into existence. Rather, the brain simply takes on the function of thinking. As already implied, this view of minds raises questions about machines, robots, computers, and much more. Do computers have minds? Are they able to think? While some philosophers believe this is possible, others continue to resist the notion: it is not at all clear that computer processing comes anywhere close to achieving the same kind of thing humans do when we think, reflect, desire, and deliberate.

### *Constitutionalism*

One final materialist view is worth considering. **Constitutionalism** is the view that human persons are constituted by their physical bodies even if they are not identical to them. Kevin Corcoran offers an illustration to help clarify the point: "For example, statues are often constituted by a piece of marble, copper, or bronze, but statues are not identical with pieces of marble, copper, or bronze that constitute them. Likewise, dollar bills, diplomas, and dust jackets are often constituted by pieces of paper, but none of those things is identical with the piece of paper that constitutes it."[18]

Like other materialists, constitutionalists reject the idea of there being immaterial substances like souls. On a brute ontological level, there is nothing beyond the physical body that constitutes—or makes up—the person. Yet, interestingly, constitutionalists insist that persons are not the same thing as their bodies. To see this, consider the different ways that a single dollar coin can be instantiated and the kinds of events it can survive. If the coin were thrown into a hot fire and left for a sufficient amount of time, it would eventually melt, and the dollar would be ruined. And as constitutionalists would point out, the metal of the coin would survive in a different form, but the dollar would be lost. The metal that constitutes the dollar is such that it is able to survive the fire, but the dollar constituted by the metal is such that it cannot survive the fire. If the metal and the dollar have different properties—one has the property of being able to survive a fire and the other has the property of not being able to survive the fire—then the metal and the dollar are not the same thing. Similarly, constitutionalists argue against immaterial souls and

18. Kevin Corcoran, *Rethinking Human Nature* (Grand Rapids: Baker Academic, 2006), 65–66.

claim that human persons are constituted by their physical bodies even if they are not the same thing as their bodies.

One additional observation is worth making about constitutionalism: there are two types of constitutionalism, type I and type II. Type-I constitutionalism, maintained by Corcoran, affirms that human persons have to be *constituted by the specific bodies* that they have. In other words, Dew has a particular body, and he must have the body that he has. Likewise, Gould has a particular body, and he must have the body that he has. On type-I constitutionalism, it would not be possible for Dew and Gould to switch bodies. But on type-II materialism, maintained by Lynne Rudder Baker, it is not necessary that we each have the specific bodies that we have. All that is required is that we each *have some body or another*. She says, "I find the traditional thought experiments about bodily transfer—for example the Prince and the Cobbler—utterly convincing when considered from a first-person point of view."[19] So then, while constitutionalists agree that human persons are constituted by their bodies, even if they are not identical to them, they differ over which body is necessary for a person to be thereby constituted.

---

So what shall we make of materialism in general? On the positive side, materialists have been helpful in forcing us to see the significance of the body as it relates to human persons. Our brains and bodies have much to do with who we are, what we are like, and what we do. Moreover, philosophers over the past several centuries have generally felt that materialism has a significant advantage over dualism in accounting for mind-body interaction. While dualism struggles to explain how it is that an immaterial mind interacts with material bodies, since they never touch and therefore cannot transfer energy one to another, materialism seems to have no such difficulty. Material seems to enjoy a parsimony and elegance of explanation that gives it a significant advantage over dualism. Yet philosophers have also noticed that materialism is not without problems of its own. In particular, while it might have a better explanation of mind-body interaction than does dualism, it seems to have great difficulty accounting for consciousness in general and *qualia* in particular. Thomas Nagel puts the problem rather bluntly: "Consciousness is the most conspicuous obstacle to a comprehensive naturalism that relies only on the resources of physical science. The existence of consciousness seems to imply that the physical description of the universe, in spite of its richness

19. Baker, *Persons and Bodies*, 141. Given that Baker identifies the human person and the being with a first-person perspective, it is not surprising that she finds the Prince and Cobbler thought experiment convincing. Such is certainly consistent with her view.

and explanatory power, is only part of the truth, and that the natural order is far less austere than it would be if physics and chemistry accounted for everything."[20] Dualists are well aware of this difficulty and often make use of consciousness to critique materialism and to make arguments in favor of substance dualism.

## Hylomorphism

In earlier sections of this chapter we discussed the various categories of views that philosophers put forward regarding human persons. Substance dualists tend to make two distinct claims: (1) for "stuff distinction," the view that there are two radically distinct kinds of things, or two distinct substances, and (2) for "person-soul identity," the view that the person is a soul who has a body. By contrast, materialists and physicalists reject the immaterial soul and argue that (1) there is only one substance, which is physical, and that (2) human persons are identical to or are at least constituted by their human body. In this last section, we shall briefly describe one final category put forward by Aristotle and Thomas Aquinas, a theory known as **hylomorphism**.

Hylomorphism is sometimes regarded as a version of dualism and sometimes as a version of materialism. In contrast to the substance dualists who argue for two distinct substances, hylomorphists argue that there is but one substance: a human person. In contrast to materialists, however, hylomorphists argue that the one substance (human person) has two distinct causes: material and formal. The word "hylomorphism" comes from two Greek words: *hylē* (matter or, more literally, wood) and *morphē* (form). In the case of the human person, which is a substance, the person is constituted by the material body and the soul, which is the form (life principle or organizing and structuring agent) of the body.

There are at least two important things to notice about this account. First, it understands the concept of substances as it relates to human persons

20. Thomas Nagel, *Mind and Cosmos: Why the Materialist Neo-Darwinian Conception of Nature Is Almost Certainly False* (New York: Oxford University Press, 2012), 35. Notice here that Nagel mentions this problem with specific application toward naturalism. To be clear, naturalism is not exactly the same thing as materialism or physicalism. Materialism and physicalism are generally used synonymously and interchangeably to refer to views suggesting that *only* material or physical objects are included in our ontological discussion. Neither materialism nor physicalism, however, assume a particular view of God. Nevertheless naturalism assumes materialism and physicalism and goes a step farther by rejecting theism and embracing atheism. Yet if consciousness is a problem for naturalism, it is also a problem for materialism and physicalism.

differently than both substance dualists and materialists. For substance dualists, a human body and a human soul are two distinct substances. Hylomorphists reject that notion and instead argue that there is only one substance: just the human person. For materialists there may be only one substance (the human body), and souls do not exist. Hylomorphists agree that there is only one substance but reject the idea that the substance is just the physical body. On this view, the substance of a human person is composed of both body and soul. Second, and flowing out of the first observation, hylomorphists contend for an ontological unity within the person. In other words, hylomorphists reject the substance dualist's idea of "person-soul identity" described above, which says that persons *are* their souls and that they *have* bodies. In his discussion regarding human sensation, for example, Aquinas says, "Since, then, sensation is an operation of man, but not proper to him, it is clear that man is not a soul only, but something composed of soul and body."[21] According to hylomorphism, human persons *are both* body and soul essentially.

Philosophers and theologians vary on their opinions of hylomorphism. Those who embrace it think that it allows for a unified understanding of human nature while also affirming the biblical categories of body and soul. Critics, however, are more skeptical about the view being helpful, contending that it collapses back down into either materialism or substance dualism. As with dualism and materialism, the debates continue.[22]

## Conclusion

In this chapter we have offered a survey of various discussions surrounding the philosophical debates about human nature. It began with an overview of the basic terms and concepts involved in the discussion and then summarized a variety of positions. It has been our aim to offer a survey only, leaving our readers to decide for themselves. We shall see some of these issues again in other chapters, and especially in chapter 15 as we take a look at the possibility

21. Thomas Aquinas, *Summa Theologica*, trans. Fathers of the English Dominican Province (Notre Dame, IN: Christian Classics, 1947), 1.75.4.

22. For those who defend a substance dualist view of human persons, see examples such as John Cooper, *Body, Soul and Life Everlasting* (Grand Rapids: Eerdmans, 1989); and Moreland and Rae, *Body and Soul*. For examples of those who defend materialism's compatibility with Christianity, see Trenton Merricks, "How to Live Forever without Saving Your Soul: Physicalism and Immortality," in *Soul, Body, and Survival: Essays on the Metaphysics of Human Persons*, ed. Kevin Corcoran (Ithaca, NY: Cornell University Press, 2001), 183–200; Peter van Inwagen, "A Materialist Ontology of the Human Person," in *Persons: Human and Divine*, ed. Peter van Inwagen and Dean Zimmerman (Oxford: Oxford University Press, 2007), 199–215; and Nancey Murphy, *Bodies and Souls, or Spirited Bodies?* (New York: Cambridge University Press, 2006).

of life after death. For now, let us simply note that various Christian thinkers have defended materialism, substance dualism, and hylomorphism. For our part, we are inclined to think that minds and bodies are distinct kinds of things and that human beings are composed of both. As such, we are inclined to hold some form of either substance dualism or hylomorphism.

PART 3

# PHILOSOPHY OF RELIGION

In the human quest to understand the world and our place in it, the religious impulse is on full display. We instinctively postulate a sacred order to the world in order to find meaning, purpose, and value. We seek a divine source of solace from the ravages of this world. We find hope too, by believing in an afterlife: eternal life in the presence of God and loved ones. Given the prevalence of religion within all cultures throughout human history, it is not unreasonable to think that humans are inherently religious. Christianity, of course, confirms this religious impulse. The most fundamental fact about reality is spiritual. God, a spiritual being, is the causal source of all distinct reality. This means humans can understand themselves, as John Calvin famously put it, only in first understanding God. Philosophy of religion is the area of philosophy where ultimate questions of a religious nature are explored.

Chief among these questions is the question of God's existence and nature. Does God exist? If so, what is God like? Can we know God? Does God want us to know him? Can we show others that God exists? Can we know God apart from arguments? Has God revealed himself to his creation? In chapter 12 we explore the question of God's existence by examining three of the four classic arguments for God: the ontological, cosmological, and teleological arguments (the moral argument will be examined in chap. 16).

While we think that the arguments for God are sound, it is also important to consider the most powerful objections to the rationality of belief in God. If

God exists and is all-good, all-powerful, and all-knowing, then how is it that there is evil? Moreover, much of the pain and suffering we find in the world seems utterly pointless. Does the horrific nature and amount of apparently pointless evil give us reason to doubt God's existence? If God is perfectly loving, wouldn't he make himself more obvious? How is it that, as far as we can tell, there are instances of reasonable nonbelief? These questions and others like them surface what are known as the problems of evil and of divine hiddenness. In establishing the case for the truth, goodness, and beauty of the Christian God, it is important to address the questions raised from the realities of evil and of divine silence. These topics will be explored in chapter 13.

Once God's existence and nature are established, there are issues regarding how God interacts with the world. This family of questions, to be explored in chapter 14, centers on the question of divine intervention in the world. How is divine creation and sustenance to be understood? Does God interact in any meaningful way with the world? Does he respond to our prayers? Does God heal us? Are such miracles possible? Does God's providential care for the world extend to every detail? If so, does a high view of divine control rule out significant human freedom? Relatedly, does God's foreknowledge rule out significant human freedom? How is it even possible to know future contingent acts, even for God?

Most religious stories carry a belief in some kind of afterlife, whether it is a heaven or hell, a state of nonbeing, a state of bliss or nirvana, or some combination of these views. Questions about the possibility of an afterlife hinge on whether human beings can survive the death of the body. Are there good reasons to believe in a soul? How, going by the Christian story, do we make sense of the claim that our souls are reunited with our bodies at the resurrection? These questions are explored in chapter 15.

The philosophy of religion is a rich and fertile field of study, integrating insights from metaphysics, ethics, logic, and epistemology, as well as from science and theology. Additional areas of exploration in the philosophy of religion not directly addressed in this section include the question of religious experience, religious disagreement and diversity, the topic of nontheistic religions, and more fine-grained discussions regarding the divine attributes and other key Christian doctrines, such as the incarnation and the Trinity.

# 12

# The Existence of God

Humans seem to be fundamentally religious. Belief in God or gods plays a significant role in every culture throughout history. Even so-called secular societies define themselves (often quite intentionally) by what they are against: no supernatural causes, no nonphysical reality, nothing sacred or divine. Today in the West, the bastion of secularism, religions flourish. In fact, sociologists tell us we now live in a postsecular age. Religion and belief in God are not waning. Rather, religion will likely play a significant role in the twenty-first century.[1]

Atheists have noticed this unwelcome state of affairs and have responded with vigor: "Belief in God is delusional." "Religion poisons everything." "We must break the spell of the religious."[2] With planes flying into buildings in the name of Allah and many other horrors perpetrated in the name of God, it is not hard to see their point. However, these so-called New Atheists do not offer much in terms of new *reasons* to doubt God's existence. Rather, the *rhetoric* is novel. It is angry, loud, accusative, and impatient: for them, belief in God is dangerous, delusional, and destructive.[3] The debate over

1. Douglas Jacobsen and Rhonda Hustedt Jacobsen, "Postsecular American: A New Context for Higher Education," in *The American University in a Postsecular Age*, ed. Douglas Jacobsen and Rhonda Hustedt Jacobsen (Oxford: Oxford University Press, 2008), 10.

2. See Richard Dawkins, *The God Delusion* (Boston: Houghton Mifflin, 2006); Christopher Hitchens, *God Is Not Great: How Religion Poisons Everything* (New York: Hachette, 2007); and Daniel C. Dennett, *Breaking the Spell: Religion as a Natural Phenomenon* (New York: Viking, 2006).

3. Thanks to Greg Koukl for this description of New Atheism's rhetoric. For a good overview of New Atheism, see his talk "The New Atheists: Old Arguments, New Attitudes," Apologetics Canada, Aug. 28, 2012, https://www.youtube.com/watch?v=DWBPTuZq2xU.

God's existence and nature shows no signs of abating anytime soon. Given its fundamental importance to all of life, it is doubtful this controversy will ever cease this side of eternity (or, for those thus inclined, until humanity passes into oblivion).

The fact remains: the human is a worshiping animal. There is a universal longing to render praise to that which absorbs our hearts and captures our imagination. Two questions press for explanation. First, in this world of objects, what are we? Each day the sun rises and sets. The earth turns on its axis. The universe continues its expansion. People are born. People die. Lives change. Lives continue as before. The story of the world goes on, and it does so without our permission. We are not the author of the story of the world, let alone of every aspect of our lives. But neither are we merely a member of the audience. We are participants. We've got skin in the game. We, one and all, look for a story to enter into and to help us find meaning, value, and purpose. This leads to a second pressing question: In this world of objects, is that which we worship as ultimate *worthy* of our devotion? In short, is the object of our worship, well, God? These two questions, as John Calvin pointed out many years ago, are related: in understanding the truth about God's existence and nature, we come to understand ourselves too.[4] In this chapter we shall explore the question of God's existence.

## Does God Exist?

The question of God's existence is a big deal. On the one hand, if God exists then our search for happiness, love, beauty, goodness, truth, justice, and significance leads us, if we allow it, to a fitting object of our longings.[5] If, on the other hand, God does not exist, then we must seek for each of these things within a godless universe. We must scratch our itch in another way.

4. John Calvin, *Institutes of the Christian Religion*, ed. John T. McNeill, trans. Ford Lewis Battles (Philadelphia: Westminster, 1960), 1.1.1.

5. Compare C. S. Lewis's discussion of his childhood experience of a kind of intense longing, a longing aroused when he came into contact with inanimate nature and marvelous literature, which ultimately led him to God:

> It appeared to me therefore that if a man diligently followed this desire, pursuing the false objects until their falsity appeared and then resolutely abandoning them, he must come out at last into the clear knowledge that the human soul was made to enjoy some object that is never fully given—nay cannot even be imagined as given—in our present mode of subjective and spatio-temporal experience. . . . The dialectic of Desire, faithfully followed, would retrieve all mistakes, head you off from all false paths, and force you not to propound, but to live through, a sort of ontological proof. (*The Pilgrim's Regress* [Grand Rapids: Eerdmans, 2002], 204–5)

Some try to re-create the beauty and splendor of the God-bathed picture of reality within a godless world. Others shrug their shoulders and grab a beer. Many take Prozac.[6] This issue, the question of God's existence, is as basic as questions get. And the trajectory of our lives is set by the answer we give.

We think that there are good reasons for believing in God and that it is rational to believe God exists. Moreover, there are signs or clues of his existence everywhere. As the psalmist proclaims, "The heavens declare the glory of God; the skies proclaim the work of his hands" (Ps. 19:1 NIV). In the New Testament, the apostle Paul affirms that the knowledge of God is available to all: "For since the creation of the world God's invisible qualities—his eternal power and divine nature—have been clearly seen, being understood from what has been made, so that people are without excuse" (Rom. 1:20 NIV).

These signs are, as the philosopher Stephen Evans notes, *widely available* yet *easily resistible*.[7] They are widely available because God desires humans to love and serve him, and thus he has provided evidence of his existence for all. They are easily resistible because God desires our love and service to be freely given. As the great philosopher and mathematician Blaise Pascal (1623–62) summarizes: "Thus wishing to appear openly to those who seek him with all their heart and hidden from those who shun him with all their heart, he has qualified our knowledge of him by giving signs which can be seen by those who seek him and not by those who do not."[8]

The evidence for God is available, especially for those who have eyes to see and ears to hear (cf. Matt. 13:16). When Christians develop arguments for God's existence, the goal is partly to help others *see* how the evidence functions to point to God. The arguments also help us to think about what God is like. Given that, as the Christian claims, the evidence for God is ubiquitous, we might expect a wide variety of arguments for God's existence. In fact, this is the case. Christian philosophers have developed arguments for God from the existence of the universe itself, from the fine-tuning of the universe for life, and from freedom, consciousness, knowledge, numbers, logic, morality, and more.[9] We shall briefly consider four of the traditional arguments for God,

6. In *The Atheist's Guide to Reality: Enjoying Life without Illusion* (New York: Norton, 2011), chap. 12, the atheist philosopher Alex Rosenberg suggests that we should take antidepressants if we are struggling with the truth of atheism.

7. C. Stephen Evans, *Natural Signs and the Knowledge of God* (Oxford: Oxford University Press, 2010), 12–17.

8. Blaise Pascal, *Pensées* (New York: E. P. Dutton, 1958), 118, quoted in Evans, *Natural Signs*, 16.

9. For a nice survey of many of these phenomena and how they figure into arguments for God, see Alvin Plantinga, "Two Dozen (or so) Theistic Arguments," in *Alvin Plantinga*, ed. Deane-Peter Baker (Cambridge: Cambridge University Press, 2007), 203–27.

three in this chapter and one, the moral argument, in chapter 16. In the next chapter we shall consider arguments against God's existence that begin with the realities of pain, suffering, and the hiddenness of God.

### *The Ontological Argument*

One famous line of thinking on the topic of God's existence begins with our idea of God. According to Anselm of Canterbury (1033–1109), God is "something than which nothing greater can be thought."[10] To get at what Anselm means, consider a slightly exaggerated and canned example of the kind of discussion in which I found myself as a teenager:

> ME: Michael Jordan is a basketball player than which nothing greater can be thought.
>
> FRIEND: Oh, you mean Michael Jordan is the greatest basketball player ever to play the game—better than Wilt Chamberlain or Magic Johnson or Bill Russell?
>
> ME (with *slight* exaggeration): No, I'm not saying just that Jordan is the best player alive or the best player who ever has or ever will play basketball. I'm saying that Michael Jordan is the greatest imaginable basketball player. You can't even conceive of one who is better!

Now, if I really were claiming that Michael Jordan is a basketball player than which nothing greater can be thought, the claim would clearly be false. We can quite easily imagine a better basketball player: a player who never misses; a player who wins seven instead of six NBA championships; a player who blocks his opponent every time. But when it comes to God, Anselm claims, it is impossible to think of a being that is greater. Beginning with this exalted conception of God, Anselm quickly proceeds to the conclusion that God must actually exist, for, he reasons, it is greater to exist in reality than in the understanding alone. Thus God, the greatest conceivable being, must exist in reality and not just in our minds. Therefore, God exists.

It is easy to feel as if one has been tricked even if it is not easy to point out how. Gaunilo (an eleventh-century Benedictine monk) thought Anselm's reasoning could be used to argue for a most perfect island that does not actually exist. Just because we can conceive of such an island, Gaunilo argued, it does not follow that the island actually exists.[11] But Gaunilo's response misses its mark. Anselm's point is that we can reason from an idea to reality only when

10. Anselm, *Proslogion*, in *Basic Writings*, ed. Thomas Williams (Indianapolis: Hackett, 2007), 81.

11. Gaunilo, "In Behalf of the Fool," in Anselm, *Basic Writings*, 99–103.

considering the greatest conceivable being whatsoever, not the greatest conceivable being of one kind (such as an island). Immanuel Kant's (1724–1804) objection that existence is not a predicate does, however, provide a serious problem for the ontological argument.[12] Kant's point is that asserting the existence of a thing does not add new content to the concept of a thing and thus is not a real predicate. Existence is not some property a thing possesses or fails to possess. Rather, to exist is to possess the properties predicated of a thing. A lion, for example, if it exists, possesses the property *being a lion* (among other properties). God, if he exists, possesses the property *being divine* (among other properties) but does not, according to Kant, possess the property of existence. Thus it is false to claim that existence in reality is greater than existence in the mind alone; existence adds nothing to the concept of a thing.

Still, the ontological argument continues to fascinate philosophers. More recently the ontological argument has been given a tune-up in the hands of the Christian philosopher Alvin Plantinga.[13] Using the tools of contemporary modal logic, Plantinga hopes to avoid Kant's charge that existence isn't a real property. The central premise of the more sophisticated argument hinges on the possibility of a being that has "maximal greatness"—a being that is omniscient, omnipotent, and morally perfect in every possible world. If one thinks such a being possible, then we have found a good argument for God's existence.

But how so? How is it that modal logic helps us make ontological arguments stronger? And what do we mean by modal ontological arguments? The term "modal" refers to a particular way of reasoning that hinges on different kinds (or modes) of existence. For example, some things have "necessary" existence. Things with necessary existence must exist: they cannot not exist. One way philosophers like to talk about necessary existence is in terms of possible worlds: maximal ways or stories about how things could go. On this way of speaking, a necessarily existing being is a being that exists in every possible world. Other things have mere possible existence. The term "possible" in this case refers to a thing that exists but does not have to exist. Or put another way, it exists in some worlds but not in every possible world. Finally, some "things" have impossible existence. We can articulate them with our language, but on reflection we find such things could never exist in this world or in any possible world. For example, it is impossible for "a stick with one end" to exist. So what do these modal terms do for our considerations about

12. See Immanuel Kant, *Critique of Pure Reason*, trans. Werner S. Pluhar (Indianapolis: Hackett, 1996), 578–86.

13. Alvin Plantinga, *The Nature of Necessity* (Oxford: Clarendon, 1974), chap. 10.

God's existence? In short, some philosophers believe it is possible to employ these terms to reframe the ontological argument. Such arguments might go something like this:

1. If God exists, he is a necessary being.
2. It is possible that God exists.
3. Therefore, God exists necessarily.

How does this argument work? Premise 1 is rather straightforward and has been affirmed by both theists and atheists: many think necessary existence is just part of what it means to be God. Premise 2 is key. If it is possible that God exists, given the meaning of the modal term "possible," then that means there is a possible world where God exists. But if God exists in some possible world, then God exists there as a necessary being. And as we saw above, a necessary being is one that exists in every possible world. Therefore, premise 3: God exists necessarily.

Yet intuitions about ontological arguments waiver. It is not clear to all that such a being is possible.[14] We think such a being is possible, and so we think the argument is sound. But, it is reasonable to ask, are there any good reasons to think God exists that proceed from empirical premises and not just from our idea of God? To explore that question, we now turn to the cosmological argument.

### *The Cosmological Argument*

The great medieval theologian Thomas Aquinas (1224–75) thought God's existence "must be demonstrated through what is more evident to us, . . . through God's effects."[15] Thus his arguments begin not from our conception of God but from some empirical premise. The idea is rather simple. Look around. Pick some phenomenon of the world. Any will do since, as Gerard

14. Plantinga's own conclusion is as follows: "The only question of interest, it seems to me, is whether its main premiss—that indeed unsurpassable greatness is possibly exemplified, that there is an essence entailing unsurpassable greatness—is *true* [in our simplified version, this idea is captured in premise 2]. I think this premiss is indeed true. Accordingly, I think this version of the Ontological Argument is sound." *Nature of Necessity*, 216–17. More recently, on further reflection, Plantinga has stated that the ontological argument is "just as satisfactory as most serious arguments philosophers give for important conclusions." "Self-Profile," in *Alvin Plantinga*, ed. James E. Tomberlin and Peter van Inwagen (Dordrecht: D. Reidel, 1985), 71.

15. Thomas Aquinas, *Summa Theologiae* 1.2.1, in *The Treatise on the Divine Nature*, trans. Brian J. Shanley, OP (Indianapolis: Hackett, 2006), 19.

Manley Hopkins writes, "the world is charged with the grandeur of God."[16] Take that phenomenon and plug it into a premise of a philosophical argument. Search for the best explanation of the phenomenon in question. The result? A theological conclusion. This is a rough but accurate characterization of Aquinas's approach. He picked five aspects of our world—the reality of motion, efficient causes, contingent beings, morality, and design—plugged each into a philosophical argument as evidence, and generated a theological conclusion; each of his "Five Ways" ends with the phrase "and this all understand to be God."[17]

Cosmological arguments seek to demonstrate that there is a First Cause (i.e., the Kalam cosmological argument), or Sufficient Reason (i.e., the Leibnizian cosmological argument), or Ground of Being of the universe (i.e., the Thomist cosmological argument).[18] Each of these basic types of arguments has been advanced in our own day with increasing rigor and strength. As we learn more about our world, the evidence for God mounts. For example, in Aquinas's day it was an open question whether the universe was eternal. Today the scientific evidence suggests that the universe began to exist a finite time ago. At the moment of the Big Bang, all matter, energy, time, and space came into being out of nothing. The obvious question is, How? What best explains the origin of the universe? If there is no God, then the beginning of the universe is utterly inexplicable. But if God exists, we have a ready explanation for the beginning of the universe: a personal agent of immense power and intellect brought the universe into being in virtue of his willing it so.

The above reasoning can be formalized as follows:

1. Whatever begins to exist has a cause.
2. The universe began to exist.
3. Therefore, the universe has a cause.

This argument, called the Kalam cosmological argument—originally articulated and defended by early Christian theologians and subsequently by medieval Jewish, Muslim, and Christian theologians—has been given new life in the hands of the contemporary Christian philosopher William Lane

16. "God's Grandeur," in *The Poems of Gerard Manley Hopkins*, ed. W. H. Gardner and N. H. MacKenzie, 4th ed. (New York: Oxford University Press, 1967), 66.

17. Thomas Aquinas, *Summa Theologiae* 1.21.

18. William Lane Craig and James D. Sinclair, "The Kalam Cosmological Argument," in *The Blackwell Companion to Natural Theology*, ed. William Lane Craig and J. P. Moreland (Malden, MA: Blackwell, 2012), 101.

Craig.[19] The argument is deductively valid: if the premises are true, the conclusion inescapably follows. Moreover, there are good reasons to think that the premises are true (or minimally, more plausible than their denials).

Consider premise 1. This premise, as Craig notes, is "rooted in the metaphysical intuition that something cannot come into being from nothing."[20] To argue that anything—Twinkies or computers or universes—can pop into existence out of nothing is absurd. The claim made by some, such as the scientist Lawrence Krauss, that quantum physics provides a counterexample to premise 1 is false.[21] So-called virtual particles do not, as Krauss claims, come into being out of literally nothing. Rather, the "nothing" of which virtual particles come from is the quantum vacuum, a "something" characterized as a "sea of fluctuating energy endowed with a rich structure and subject to physical laws."[22] Additionally, the truth of premise 1 is supported by everyday experience, an experience that undergirds the foundation of science itself: our confidence that every effect has a cause sustains scientific investigation.

Premise 2 is supported by philosophical argument and scientific evidence. First, Craig argues that an actual infinite, as opposed to a potentially infinite, series of temporal events is impossible, and an eternal universe would constitute an actually infinite series of temporal events. Second, Craig points to (a) the expansion of the universe (noted above) and (b) the Second Law of Thermodynamics as evidence that the universe began a finite time ago. According to the Second Law of Thermodynamics, the amount of usable energy decreases over time in a closed system. The universe, understood as the totality of all physical reality, is a closed system. Given that there is still usable energy in the universe, it follows that the universe cannot be eternal, for if it were eternal, the universe would have reached "heat death" an infinite time ago. While debate over the truth of premise 2 will undoubtedly continue, it is reasonable to conclude that the universe began to exist. If so, the conclusion necessarily follows: there is a cause to the universe.

Given the nature of the case, what can we learn about this cause of the universe? For starters, the cause of the universe must be transcendent to the

19. William Lane Craig's first major work on an updated Kalam cosmological argument is found in *The Kalam Cosmological Argument* (London: Macmillan, 1979). More accessible discussions of the argument are found in Craig, *Reasonable Faith*, 3rd ed. (Wheaton: Crossway, 2008), chap. 3; and Craig, *On Guard* (Colorado Springs: David C. Cook, 2010), chap. 4. For a recent defense of the Kalam argument that addresses the latest science, see Craig and Sinclair, "The Kalam Cosmological Argument."

20. Craig and Sinclair, "The Kalam Cosmological Argument," 182.

21. Lawrence M. Krauss, *A Universe from Nothing: Why There Is Something Rather than Nothing* (New York: Atria, 2012).

22. Craig and Sinclair, "The Kalam Cosmological Argument," 183.

universe. As Dallas Willard puts it, the universe is "ontologically haunted."[23] There is something beyond the universe that is responsible for the universe. Moreover, this cause must be immaterial (since prior to the Big Bang there was no matter, energy, time, or space). Importantly, this cause must be personal. This is because there are only two kinds of causes: event causation and agent causation.[24] Event causation relates a prior event to a subsequent event as an effect (e.g., the event of my hitting the white ball with a pool cue causes the event of the black ball going into the corner pocket). However, at the moment of the Big Bang—the creation event—there is no prior physical state. The universe comes into being out of nothing. The only kind of cause that can bring about the initial state of the universe is an agent cause. This cause is also, arguably, one (since causes should not be multiplied beyond what is necessary), necessary, eternal (since, otherwise, the cause of the universe would itself need a cause), immensely powerful (if not omnipotent), and incredibly knowledgeable (if not omniscient). In sum, this deceptively simple argument rules out naturalism and nontheistic religions by establishing a transcendent, personal, immaterial, necessary, and eternal singular cause of the universe. While this conception of God is admittedly not as full and rich as the biblical conception of God, importantly, it is consistent with the God of the Bible and thus plays a key role in a cumulative case argument for the God of Christianity.

### *The Teleological Argument*

In Aquinas's Fifth Way we find a classic statement of the teleological argument. Aquinas observes that some things within nature are ordered toward a valuable end—acorns become oaks, human fetuses become adults, and so on. This "beneficial order" cries out for explanation.[25] "But," Aquinas continues, "those things that lack knowledge do not tend toward an end except under the direction of something with knowledge and intelligence, as is the case of an arrow from an archer."[26] Therefore, there is an intelligence that is responsible for the beneficial order found in nature, and, argues Aquinas, this intelligence is God.

As the scientific revolution progressed through the Enlightenment era, the evidence of apparent design continued to mount. William Paley (1743–1805)

23. Dallas Willard, "The Three-Stage Argument for the Existence of God," in *Contemporary Perspectives on Religious Epistemology*, ed. R. Douglas Geivett and Brendan Sweetman (Oxford: Oxford University Press, 1992), 216.

24. Or so we say. For a discussion of agent causation, see chap. 10 above.

25. Evans, *Natural Signs and the Knowledge of God*, chap. 3.

26. Thomas Aquinas, *Summa Theologiae* 1.2.1, in *Treatise on the Divine Nature*, 24.

famously argued that if someone were hiking through a forest and stumbled on a watch, it would be absurd to suggest that there was no explanation for the watch's existence. The complexity, order, and purpose found in watches are marks of intelligence, suggestive of design. Similarly, when considering the universe, it too shares marks of intelligence—complexity, order, and purpose—and it is reasonable to think that the universe (and things within the universe, such as organisms and eyes) also is the product of an intelligent designer.[27]

Paley's design argument is widely thought to have been refuted first by David Hume (1711–76) and finally by Charles Darwin (1809–82).[28] According to Hume (who actually wrote before Paley), the concept of deity entailed by the design argument is *religiously* inadequate.[29] Since the effects in nature are finite and imperfect, all that can be inferred about the cause is that it too is finite and imperfect. Moreover, we cannot infer there was a *single* designer (for all we know there was a committee of designers), nor does the argument require that the designer be the first cause of all reality (like the watchmaker, the designer[s] of the universe could be working with preexisting material). In reply, defenders of the design argument could concede Hume's objection, arguing that the design argument on its own, at least in its analogical form, does not entail a religiously adequate conception of deity. However, as part of a cumulative case argument, the design argument does provide key insight regarding the existence and nature of God. Cosmological arguments show that there is a transcendent personal cause to the universe, and teleological arguments build on this foundation by showing that the personal cause of the universe is also intelligent.

With the publication of Darwin's *Origin of Species* in 1859, design arguments quickly fell out of vogue. Darwin's theory of evolution provided a naturalistic mechanism (natural selection) sufficient to explain apparent design found in nature. It was no longer necessary to postulate an intelligent cause. As Richard Dawkins puts it, "Darwin made it possible to be an intellectually fulfilled atheist."[30] The defenders of the design argument are not without reply, however. Some have argued that the theory of evolution is replete with scientific and

27. William Paley, *Natural Theology: Or Evidence of the Existence and Attributes of the Deity, Collected from the Appearances of Nature* (London: C. Knight, 1845), especially chaps. 1–3.

28. David Hume, *Dialogues Concerning Natural Religion* (1779; repr., London: Penguin, 1990); and Charles Darwin, *On the Origin of Species* (1859; repr., Cambridge, MA: Harvard University Press, 1964).

29. Evans, *Natural Signs and the Knowledge of God*, 79.

30. Richard Dawkins, *The Blind Watchmaker: Why the Evidence of Evolution Reveals a Universe without Design* (New York: Norton, 1996), 6, quoted in Evans, *Natural Signs and the Knowledge of God*, 84.

philosophical problems and thus is not capable of providing a complete explanation of all biological life and complexity.[31] Others have argued that even if the evolutionary story is substantially correct, the theory, shorn of its naturalistic baggage, is compatible with theism and even requires theism.[32] Nevertheless, the design argument suffered a serious setback due to the attacks of Hume and Darwin in the eighteenth and nineteenth centuries. However, teleological arguments have been given new life in our own day, owing to new scientific discoveries regarding the fine-tuning of the universe and empirical markers of intelligent design. While space prohibits a detailed look at contemporary intelligent-design arguments, we shall look briefly at the fine-tuning argument.[33]

New scientific discoveries over the past century have revealed that the universe is fine-tuned for the existence of conscious embodied agents. The evidence for the fine-tuning of the laws of nature, the constants of nature, and the initial conditions of the universe are overwhelming, pointing to a divine creation. Robin Collins, a leading defender of the fine-tuning argument, provides the following examples of fine-tuning: (1) "If the strength of gravity were smaller or larger by an estimated one part in $10^{60}$ of its current value, the universe would have either exploded too quickly for galaxies and stars to form, or collapsed back on itself too quickly for life to evolve";[34] (2) the cosmological constant, which governs the expansion of the universe, is fine-tuned for life to around one part in $10^{120}$;[35] and (3) the low entropy state of the initial universe falls into an exceedingly narrow range for complex life to evolve, and the odds of such conditions arising by chance are about one part in $10^{10^{\wedge}123}$.[36] We could add to this list the spiral shape of the Milky Way galaxy, the position of the earth from the sun, the tilt of the earth, the speed of the earth's spin, the moon's effect on the oceans of the earth, the relative size of the neutron and proton, and more.

31. See, e.g., Michael Denton, *Evolution: A Theory in Crisis* (Bethesda, MA: Adler & Adler, 1985); Michael J. Behe, *Darwin's Black Box* (New York: Free Press, 1996); and Behe, *The Edge of Evolution: The Search for the Limits of Darwinism* (New York: Free Press, 2007).

32. See, e.g., Francis S. Collins, *The Language of God* (New York: Free Press, 2006); Karl W. Giberson, *Saving Darwin* (New York: HarperOne, 2008); and Kenneth R. Miller, *Finding Darwin's God* (New York: Harper Perennial, 1999).

33. For an important recent version of intelligent-design arguments, see William Dembski, *Intelligent Design* (Downers Grove, IL: InterVarsity, 1999); Stephen C. Meyer, *Signature in the Cell* (New York: HarperOne, 2009); and the two books by Behe listed in footnote 30 above.

34. Robin Collins, "The Teleological Argument," in Craig and Moreland, *The Blackwell Companion to Natural Theology*, 215.

35. Robin Collins, "The Anthropic Teleological Argument," in *Philosophy of Religion: Selected Readings*, ed. Michael Peterson et al., 5th ed. (New York: Oxford University Press, 2014), 189.

36. Collins, "Teleological Argument," 220.

That the universe is fine-tuned for life is well established. The question is, What best explains fine-tuning? Many see fine-tuning as powerful evidence for an intelligent creator. For example, one of the leading atheist philosophers of the twentieth century, Antony Flew, converted to theism because of the evidence of fine-tuning.[37] The argument from fine-tuning to God can be formalized as follows:

1. The existence of a fine-tuned universe is not surprising under theism.
2. The existence of a fine-tuned universe is enormously surprising under naturalism.
3. Therefore, by the likelihood principle, the existence of a fine-tuned universe strongly supports theism over naturalism.[38]

In support of premise 1, consider the following. As a being worthy of worship, God in the thought of theists is perfectly rational, free, and good. If a perfectly rational, free, and good God creates at all, we would expect him to bring into being a reality that positively manifests both moral and aesthetic values.[39] The creation of a world suitable for embodied conscious (moral) agents is such a world. Thus, on theism's view, the existence of a fine-tuned universe is not surprising. Regarding premise 2, given the extremely small quantifiable range of possibilities in order for the universe to be able to support life, it is reasonable to think that a fine-tuned universe would be enormously surprising on naturalism's view. Thus, given the likelihood principle—a kind of epistemic probability that "can be thought of as a measure of rational degrees of expectation"[40]—the existence of a fine-tuned universe offers support for theism over naturalism.

One prominent objection to the fine-tuning argument is the "multiverse hypothesis." The idea is that there are either infinite universes (unrestricted version) or an extremely large number of universes (restricted version) that exist parallel to our own with different laws, constants, and initial conditions.[41]

37. Antony Flew and Roy Abraham Varghese, *There Is a God: How the World's Most Notorious Atheist Changed His Mind* (New York: HarperOne, 2007). Flew converted to a kind of Aristotelian theism, not Christian theism, largely because he thinks miracles are impossible. For more, see also Antony Flew and Gary R. Habermas, "My Pilgrimage from Atheism to Theism: A Discussion between Antony Flew and Gary R. Habermas," *Philosophia Christi* 6, no. 2 (2004): 197–211.

38. The argument presented here is a slight modification of a version of the fine-tuning argument advanced by Robin Collins. See Collins, "Teleological Argument," 191.

39. Collins, "Teleological Argument," 254.

40. Collins, "Teleological Argument," 191.

41. For an excellent overview of the various multiverse hypotheses, including critiques of the unrestricted and restricted versions, see Collins, "Teleological Argument," 256–72.

If there were multiple universes, it would not be surprising for one of them to be conducive to life. Thus the atheist could argue that premise 2, supplemented by the multiverse hypothesis, is false. In reply, theists have argued that in its unrestricted version (i.e., all possible worlds exist in reality causally inaccessible to one another), there is no empirical evidence for its truth, and in its restricted version (there are many but not infinite universes), the physical process needed to generate the universes must itself be designed. Either way, the multiverse hypothesis does not help the atheist. If so, the fine-tuning argument should be considered a powerful argument for God's existence.

### *The Moral Argument*

A final traditional argument for God's existence begins with the reality of moral obligations. A detailed analysis of the moral argument for God is explored in chapter 16. Here in this chapter it is sufficient to observe that if we live in a moral universe and there is something beyond the universe that is the source of morality, then we have reason to be uneasy. There is a moral law, and none of us live up to it. This moment of self-realization points us beyond mere theism. It prompts us to hope for further divine disclosure and action on our behalf. In short, it points us to the Triune God of Christianity, who has revealed himself not only through that which he has made but also in Scripture and in the person of Jesus Christ.

## Conclusion

We have considered four traditional arguments for God's existence. The ontological argument begins with our intuition that any being deserving the title "God" must be worthy of worship, a greatest conceivable being. The cosmological argument teaches us that there is a personal transcendent cause of the universe. The teleological argument tells us there is a cosmic intelligence. The moral argument points us toward a cosmic morality. Considered together, the traditional arguments for God suggest that God is personal, good (if not all-good), immensely knowledgeable (if not all-knowing), immensely powerful (if not all-powerful), necessary, eternal, and the creator and sustainer of all distinct reality. In the chapters that follow, we shall test this exalted conception of God as we explore the problems of evil, hiddenness, and hell and as we wrestle with the question of divine providence.

# 13

# Evil and the Hiddenness of God

The problem of evil and the closely related problem of divine hiding provide reasons for the unbeliever to deny God's existence. They also raise important questions for the believer in God and can be a chief source of doubt regarding the goodness of God. In this chapter we shall explore these problems as well as the resources theists can employ in responding to the problems in all of their forms. Two prominent versions of the problem of evil are the logical and the evidential problem of evil. We begin with an exploration of the logical problem of evil.

## The Logical Problem of Evil

In his *Dialogues Concerning Natural Religion*, David Hume nicely summarizes the logical problem regarding God and evil: "Epicurus' old questions are yet unanswered. Is he willing to prevent evil, but not able? then is he impotent. Is he able, but not willing? then is he malevolent. Is he both able and willing? whence then is evil?"[1] A rough sketch of the challenge can be formalized as follows:[2]

1. The character that expresses these questions in the dialogue is Philo, widely assumed to represent the voice of Hume. See David Hume, *Dialogues Concerning Natural Religion* (London: Penguin, 1990), 63.

2. I (Paul) first came across this way of formalizing the logical problem of evil as a graduate assistant for Michael Bergmann's undergraduate philosophy of religion class at Purdue University. This is not the only way to formalize the logical problem of evil, but I have found it to be an accessible way to introduce the topic to those unfamiliar with it. For other formulations

1. If God is not able to prevent evil, then God is not all-powerful.
2. If God is not willing to prevent evil, then God is not perfectly good.
3. If God were willing and able to prevent evil, then there would be no evil.

But,

4. There is evil.
5. Therefore, God (an all-powerful and perfectly good being) does not exist.

What the argument, if sound, shows is that God's existence is incompatible with the reality of evil. In the same way that it is impossible for there to be married bachelors or round squares, it is *impossible* that God and evil coexist. The argument, as stated, is formally valid. If the premises are true, the conclusion inescapably follows. What can then be said for each premise of the argument?

Premise 4 is obviously true. Pain and suffering is in itself a bad thing, an evil. It is, as the philosopher Richard Gale puts it, "an ought-not-to-be, an 'Oh no!'"[3] The Christian tradition as well as human experience affirms the truth of premise 4. If there is a way out of the challenge posed by the logical problem of evil, it will have to be found elsewhere.

Alvin Plantinga famously argues that premise 1 is not necessarily true by offering what is called the Free Will Defense: if premise 1 is not necessarily true, then it is logically possible that God and evil coexist. The Free Will Defense doesn't need to show that premise 1 is false, just that it is not necessarily true in order to solve the logical problem of evil. The basic idea of the Free Will Defense is this:

> God cannot do the logically impossible (and this fact does not count against God's omnipotence). No being (God or otherwise) can actualize logically impossible states of affairs such as *being a married bachelor* or *being a square circle*; no being (God or otherwise) can make it true that 2 + 2 = 5 or that *God exists and simultaneously God doesn't exist*. In fact, if God could do such things, he would not be perfectly rational and hence not worthy of worship. God *wants* (at least some of) his creatures to be self-determiners of their actions

of the logical problem of evil, see J. L. Mackie, "Evil and Omnipotence," *Mind* 64, no. 254 (1955): 200–212; and Alvin Plantinga, *God, Freedom, and Evil* (Grand Rapids: Eerdmans, 1977).

3. Richard Gale, "Evil as Evidence against God," in *Debating Christian Theism*, ed. J. P. Moreland, Chad V. Meister, and Khaldoun A. Sweis (Oxford: Oxford University Press, 2013), 197.

> and character. In other words, God has created (libertarianly) free creatures, creatures that, for at least some actions, are free to perform the action or refrain from the action. Given the fact that God has created free creatures, he cannot guarantee that in every instance they will always perform morally right actions. God could remove their freedom, thereby guaranteeing that creatures never do wrong, but what God cannot do is *cause* free creatures to never do wrong. *Causing free creatures to act in a particular way* is a logically impossible state of affairs. Hence, when free creatures misuse their creaturely freedom and do wrong, evil results. God permits the possibility of evil, but free creatures actualize evil by doing wrong.

If the above scenario is possible, then premise 1 is not necessarily true and Plantinga has successfully shown that there is no logical incompatibility between God and evil. As Plantinga summarizes, "The heart of the Free Will Defense is the claim that it is *possible* that God could not have created a universe containing moral good (or as much moral good as this world contains) without creating one that also contained moral evil. And if so, then it is possible that God has a good reason for creating a world containing evil."[4]

A prominent reply to the Free Will Defense is called the Free but Perfect objection. Isn't it possible, it is suggested, for God to create (libertarianly) free creatures who never do wrong?[5] Perhaps whenever a free creature intends wrong, God intervenes to stop the action or the intended effect. In reply, Plantinga provocatively argues that, for all we know, there are no "free but perfect" creatures; every free creature suffers from what Plantinga calls "transworld depravity": in every possible world, free creatures do at least one wrong action, an action that is morally evil.[6] If so, then God, though omnipotent, could not have created a world containing just "free but perfect" creatures. If Plantinga is correct, then there is reason to think the Free Will Defense successful.

Suppose, however, the Free Will Defense fails and premise 1 is a necessary truth. What about premise 2? Again, it seems that premise 2 is not necessarily true. In everyday life there are many instances where, for example, a parent allows a child to undergo pain and suffering because of some morally sufficient reason. So too, it is possible that God has a morally sufficient reason for

4. Plantinga, *God, Freedom, and Evil*, 31 (emphasis in original).

5. This objection was raised forcefully by Mackie in his 1955 article "Evil and Omnipotence."

6. Plantinga calls the idea that God can create any world he wants "Leibniz's Lapse." While there are many worlds that God could create that contain moral good but no moral evil, there are, for all we know, no possible worlds that contain free creatures and no moral evil. This was, according to Plantinga, the mistake Leibniz made. For more on transworld depravity, see Plantinga, *God, Freedom, and Evil*, 34–55.

allowing pain and suffering. We shall explore some of those possible reasons in the next section, when considering the evidential argument from evil. The point here is that premise 2 is not necessarily true, and thus we find another reason to think the logical problem of evil fails. Yet premise 3, it could be argued, is clearly false. Just because I am able to buy a new computer (I have the money) and I want to buy a new computer (my current one is annoyingly slow), it does not follow that I will purchase a new computer. I am willing and able to purchase the new computer, but I do not because I also want to pay my mortgage. The paying of my mortgage (and my desire to stay in my home) is an overriding value for me. I want to stay in my home more than I want a new computer. In the same way, God could have an overriding reason—for example, the high value of (libertarianly) free moral creatures—that justifies his allowing evil.

The result is that the hope of finding some kind of logical incompatibility between God and evil is significantly diminished. Many theist and atheist philosophers agree that there is no actual logical problem of evil. Many philosophers think that Plantinga's Free Will Defense solved the logical problem of evil. As we have seen, even if that is not the case, there are other reasons to think that the logical problem of evil fails. As a result, the discussion regarding the problem of evil has shifted to the evidential problem of evil. It is that formulation of the problem to which we shall now turn.

## The Evidential Problem of Evil

Struck by lightning, a baby deer suffers in agony for a week before finding death. On New Year's Eve, as the family celebrates in another room, a child is kidnapped, tortured, raped, and murdered.[7] An earthquake devastates a nation, killing many and leaving the rest destitute. Daily we are confronted with evil both in the world and within the human heart. If God exists, he must have a good reason for permitting evil. But much evil appears pointless. Why did the deer have to suffer in agony for a week before death instead of instantaneously dying or (better) not being struck by lightning at all? What possible reason is there for allowing a child to be kidnapped, tortured, raped, and then murdered? How could God be morally justified in allowing an earthquake that brings pain and suffering to the righteous and the unrighteous without distinction? Given the intensity, distribution, and amount of pain

7. Both of these examples of horrendous evils are prominent in the literature. See, e.g., Daniel Howard-Snyder, Michael Bergmann, and William L. Rowe, "An Exchange on the Problem of Evil," in *God and the Problem of Evil*, ed. William L. Rowe (Malden, MA: Blackwell, 2001), 126.

and suffering in the world, much of which appears pointless, it is likely, the argument goes, that God does not exist. This is the evidential problem of evil.

The evidential problem of evil can be formulated as follows:

1. If God exists, pointless evil does not exist.
2. Probably, pointless evil exists.
3. Therefore, probably God does not exist.

The evidential problem of evil concedes that God and evil are logically compatible. Still, given the intensity, distribution, and amount of evil in the world, it is argued that God *probably* doesn't exist. While some theists deny premise 1, most accept it as true and therefore focus their attention on premise 2, arguing that there is (contrary to appearances) no pointless evil.[8] God has a morally justified reason for allowing evil in all cases. There are two main strategies employed by theists in arguing against the truth of premise 2.

The first strategy is to give a theodicy. A "theodicy" is a God-justifying reason for evil. When providing a theodicy, a theist is saying, "Here is the reason why God allows evil. This is it." While there are many theodicies on offer, two historically prominent theodicies are the Free Will Theodicy, argued notably by Augustine of Hippo (354–430), and the Soul-Making Theodicy, suggested in the writings of the early church father Irenaeus (130–202) and rigorously formulated more recently by John Hick (1922–2012).[9]

The basic outline of the Free Will Theodicy has already been provided (above) with Plantinga's Free Will Defense. To better understand how theodicies work, it is important to understand the difference between a theodicy and a defense. A **theodicy** is different from a defense in that the former provides God's *actual* justification for evil, whereas a **defense** provides a *possible* justification for evil. In offering a Free Will Defense, Plantinga gives a *possible* justification for evil; in offering a Free Will Theodicy, Augustine (and those who follow him) is saying, in effect, that such *possible* justification for evil is God's *actual* justification for evil. God really did create free creatures. Free

8. For an example of a Christian who thinks there is pointless evil, see Kirk R. MacGregor, "The Existence and Irrelevance of Gratuitous Evil," *Philosophia Christi* 14 (2012): 165–82. In reply, see Ross Inman, "Gratuitous Evil Unmotivated: A Reply to Kirk R. MacGregor," *Philosophia Christi* 15 (2013): 435–45.

9. See Augustine, *On Free Choice of the Will*, trans. Thomas Williams (Indianapolis: Hackett, 1993); Irenaeus, "Against Heresies," in *Ante-Nicene Fathers*, vol. 1, ed. Alexander Roberts and James Donaldson (Peabody, MA: Hendrickson, 1994); and John Hick, "Soul-Making Theodicy," in Rowe, *God and the Problem of Evil*, 265–81.

creatures really did, through the misuse of their creaturely freedom, bring about evil.[10]

Although the Free Will Theodicy is an effective response to the problem of evil, it obviously is not a complete response; thus, on its own, it is not clear that the Free Will Theodicy provides the resources to deny premise 2 of the evidential problem. The Free Will Theodicy does a nice job of explaining much (perhaps all) of the moral evil of this world, but what about natural evil: earthquakes, tornadoes, tsunamis, disease, and the like? One reply, suggested by Plantinga and defended by many early Christian apologists, is to argue that natural evil, like moral evil, is also the result of a misuse of creaturely freedom. The creatures in view with respect to natural evil, however, are not human creatures, but angelic creatures: Satan and his cohorts are responsible for the deep-seated disorder found in nature and the resultant natural evil.[11] If this suggestion is correct—and it is a genuine possibility given a theistic worldview—then perhaps the Free Will Theodicy on its own is enough to show the falsity of premise 2. Suppose, however, that it is not correct. In other words, suppose there are instances of evil left unexplained and therefore unjustified, given the Free Will Theodicy. Does this mean that premise 2 is true and the evidential problem of evil cogent? Not at all. The theodicist at this point may simply offer up additional theodicies in order to provide the actual God-justifying reason for the remaining evils in question.

Historically, while the **Soul-Making Theodicy** has been seen as the chief alternative to the Free Will Theodicy, it can also be thought of as playing a complementary role to the Free Will Theodicy.[12] The intuition behind the Soul-Making Theodicy is that pain and suffering produce character. As John Hick puts it, God did not initially create humans as wholly good free beings because "virtues which have been formed within the agent as a hard-won deposit of his own right decisions in situations of challenge and temptation are intrinsically more valuable than virtues created within him ready made and without any effort on his own part."[13] The moral, intellectual, and spiritual development of humans requires a challenging environment and a dangerous

10. For an excellent discussion of Augustine's Free Will Theodicy, see R. Douglas Geivett, "Augustine and the Problem of Evil," in *God and Evil: The Case for God in a World Filled with Pain*, ed. Chad Meister and James K. Dew Jr. (Downers Grove, IL: IVP Books, 2013), chap. 5.

11. See, e.g., Plantinga, *God, Freedom, and Evil*, 58; and Plantinga, "Supralapsarianism, or 'O Felix Culpa,'" in *Christian Faith and the Problem of Evil*, ed. Peter van Inwagen (Grand Rapids: Eerdmans, 2004), 16–17.

12. James Spiegel, "The Irenaean Soul-Making Theodicy," in Meister and Dew, *God and Evil*, 81. Spiegel argues that the Free Will Theodicy addresses the question of the *origin* of evil; the Soul-Making Theodicy addresses the question of God's *purpose* for evil.

13. John Hick, "Soul-Making Theodicy," in Rowe, *God and the Problem of Evil*, 271.

world. Thus natural evil is explained as part of the required environment for character development. It is a necessary aspect "of the present stage of the process through which God is gradually creating perfected finite persons."[14]

While this theodicy seems to explain much of the natural evil in the world, it is not obvious that it explains all instances of natural evil. What about those whose life is cut short by a natural disaster or disease and so don't have any real chance of growth from the experience? How is the Soul-Making Theodicy supposed to help them? There are a number of plausible replies available. First, it could be argued that, for all we know, these natural evils might bring about character growth in those associated with the person suffering. Second, perhaps the apparent pointlessness of natural evil is a necessary feature of a soul-making world. As Hick observes, "The very fact that disasters afflict human beings in contingent, undirected and haphazard ways is itself a necessary feature of a world that calls forth mutual aid and builds up mutual caring and love."[15] If so, then the fact that much of the natural evil appears pointless does not count in favor of its actually being pointless. Third, for those who suffer and die without an opportunity for growth in this life, the possibility remains that such growth will continue in the afterlife. While this eschatological dimension of the Soul-Making Theodicy is helpful, it also reveals a weakness of the theodicy. As James Spiegel notes, there are two categories of sufferers for whom moral growth in the afterlife is not an option: *animals*, such as the fawn discussed earlier, and *humans who go to hell*.[16] Perhaps it could be argued that animal suffering is for human benefit, a means to building our moral character as we respond with compassion and kindness to animal suffering. This reply, while initially plausible, seems weak given the amount of animal suffering in this world brought about by humans (consider, e.g., intensive animal farming and the deplorable conditions of animal lives as they are prepared for slaughter). Regarding humans in hell, in the traditional account hell is a place of eternal conscious torment. Since the damned are beyond redemption, it is not clear that their suffering serves the higher good of character formation. This has led some philosophers, such as Hick and Marilyn Adams, to endorse universalism and the idea that all will eventually be united with God.[17] For those not willing to embrace

14. Hick, "Soul-Making Theodicy," 276.

15. Hick, "Soul-Making Theodicy," 278–79.

16. Spiegel, "The Irenaean Soul-Making Theodicy," 92.

17. In addition to the Hick article already cited, see Marilyn McCord Adams, "The Problem of Hell: A Problem of Evil for Christians," in *Reasoned Faith: Essays in Philosophical Theology in Honor of Norman Kretzmann*, ed. Eleonore Stump (Ithaca, NY: Cornell University Press, 1993), 301–27; included in Rowe, *God and the Problem of Evil*, 282–309.

universalism, it seems that the Soul-Making Theodicy, while helpful, cannot (obviously) account for all instances of evil.

At this point the defender of theodicies can continue to offer additional theodicies, attempting to explain the remaining apparently pointless evils. Many theodicies have been and continue to be offered by philosophers and theologians.[18] Many people find various theodicies helpful, even comforting, when experiencing pain and suffering. Still, as a response to the evidential problem of evil, it is not obvious that a theodicy strategy is ultimately successful. Even if the full panoply of theodicies has been employed in order to defeat premise 2, doubts remain. Why the tremendous *amount* of evil instead of a lot less? Why six million Jews killed in the Holocaust instead of five million? Why these *types*—rape, genocide, cancer—of evil? Why does God allow those? Couldn't humans be genuinely free, for example, without the ability to commit rape? Why this *instance* of evil?[19] Is it really necessary to maintain human freedom or moral growth or whatever by allowing this murder or this rape? Moreover, Christian Scripture provides reason to think we will not be able to understand God's justifying reason for evil in all cases. As the apostle Paul proclaims of God, "How unsearchable his judgments, and his paths beyond tracing out!" (Rom. 11:33 NIV). Considerations like these suggest that perhaps, as a response to the evidential problem of evil, another strategy might be more promising.

The second prominent strategy employed by the theist to refute premise 2 is to argue that while God has a morally justified reason for allowing evil, we humans are just not in a position to know what that reason is. This response to the evidential problem of evil is called **skeptical theism**. The theist is not skeptical that God exists. Rather, the theist is skeptical that we are in a position to *know* God's reasons for evil. While this strategy might appear at first to be a cop-out, an illicit punt to mystery, on further reflection it can be shown that the theist is rational in endorsing a skeptical stance with respect to God's reasons for evil.

18. For a nice book-length introduction to seven historically prominent theodicies, see Richard Rice, *Suffering and the Search for Meaning: Contemporary Responses to the Problem of Pain* (Downers Grove, IL: InterVarsity, 2014). For an excellent discussion of theodicies, including their shortcomings, see Daniel Howard-Snyder's essay "God, Evil, and Suffering," in *Reason for the Hope Within*, ed. Michael Murray (Grand Rapids: Eerdmans, 1999), 86–101.

19. Some theists argue that while there are God-justifying reasons for *types* of evils, there are not, in many cases, God-justifying reasons for *tokens* of evils. See, e.g., Peter van Inwagen, "The Place of Chance in a World Sustained by God," in *Divine and Human Action*, ed. Thomas V. Morris (Ithaca, NY: Cornell University Press, 1988), 211–35. However, even if there is no reason for a particular token of evil, it does not follow that it is all-things-considered pointless. That is, it does not follow that, just because an evil is token-gratuitous, it is all-things-considered gratuitous. See Inman, "Gratuitous Evil Unmotivated," 436–38.

Consider how the atheist presses the evidential problem. Particular instances of evil—the baby deer suffering and dying; the torture, rape, and murder of a young child—are pointed out, and it is argued that for all the goods that we know, there is no good that would justify God's permitting the evil. The atheist offers a "No-see-um Argument": "As far as we can tell, there is no reason that justifies God in allowing so much or any particular instance of evil. Therefore, it is very likely that there is no such reason."[20] The inference at the heart of the No-see-um Argument is: "So far as we can tell, there is no *x*; so, probably there is no *x*."[21] Is the no-see-um inference a good inference, capable of providing a reason to think premise 2 is true? Sometimes the no-see-um inference is a good inference. If I open up my fridge and exclaim, "As far as I can tell, there is no milk in the fridge. So probably there is no milk in the fridge," I properly infer the absence of milk. However, if when sitting on my back porch I proclaim, "As far as I can tell, there are no fire ants on the hill over there [over a thousand yards away]; so probably there are no fire ants on the hill over there," I have made a bad no-see-um inference. The salient difference is that, in the case of the milk, I was in a position to see the milk if it was in the fridge, whereas in the case of the fire ants on the far-off hill, I was not in a position to likely see them if they were there. My perceptual abilities are such that I can perceive medium-sized objects a couple yards away but not very small objects (like fire ants) over a thousand yards away.

Applied to the problem of evil, the question becomes: Are we humans in a position to see, or apprehend, God's morally justified reason for every instance of evil if there is one? As we have seen, we are able to discern some of God's reasons for evil. But there are reasons to think that we are not in a position to understand all of God's reasons for evil. Humans are finite, limited in time, space, and knowledge in a way that God is not. God knows the beginning from the end and has providentially ordered human history, taking into account the free actions of humans (and angelic beings) in order to accomplish his purpose. It seems unreasonable to think that we should be able to discern God's reasons for evil in every case. Our perceptual and intellectual capacities are just not powerful enough to discern the overall story that God is weaving throughout human history. Thus, in the case of evil, the no-see-um inference is a bad inference. Therefore premise 2 of the evidential argument is false, and there is no reason to think, given the reality of apparently pointless evil, that there is pointless evil.

20. Howard-Snyder, "God, Evil, and Suffering," 105.
21. Howard-Snyder, "God, Evil, and Suffering," 103.

What this brief survey has shown is that the problem of evil does not render belief in God irrational. There is no logical inconsistency involved in postulating the existence of God and evil. Moreover, the reality of evil does not render God's existence unlikely. When we move from considerations regarding mere theism to considering Christianity in particular, we find, as Peter Kreeft puts it, God's solution to the problem of evil.[22] God's solution is Christ on the cross. On the cross Jesus took all pain and suffering on himself, providing a way for those who believe to find hope instead of despair in the face of evil.

## Divine Hiddenness

The problem of **divine hiddenness** is a source of *unbelief* and, for the believer, a source of *doubt* about the goodness of God. Consider the question of divine hiding from the atheist's point of view. Both theists and atheists agree that God's existence is not obvious to everyone. However, the atheist presses, if as Christians claim (a) God is perfectly loving and (b) humankind's greatest need is to know and love God, it seems that God's existence *ought* to be obvious to everyone. God *should* make himself maximally obvious so that there would be no reasonable unbelief. If God were maximally obvious, all unbelief would be unreasonable and thus all unbelievers would be morally culpable in their unbelief. As it stands, the fact that there is (or seems to be) reasonable unbelief—sincere seekers who don't see plausible evidence for God—provides a reason to doubt that a perfectly loving God exists.

The argument from hiddenness for atheism can be formalized as follows:

1. If God exists, he is perfectly loving.
2. If a perfectly loving God exists, reasonable nonbelief does not occur.
3. Reasonable nonbelief does occur.
4. Therefore (from 2 and 3), no perfectly loving God exists.
5. Therefore (from 1 and 4), God does not exist.[23]

The above argument is formally valid. If the premises are true, the conclusions 4 and 5 logically follow. A central tenet of Christian theism is that God

22. Peter Kreeft, *Making Sense out of Suffering* (Ann Arbor, MI: Servant Books, 1986), chap. 7.

23. This version of the hiddenness argument is from Chad Meister, "Evil and the Hiddenness of God," in Meister and Dew, *God and Evil*, 142. For more fine-grained versions of the argument, see John L. Schellenberg, *Divine Hiddenness and Human Reason* (Ithaca, NY: Cornell University Press, 1993).

is perfectly loving (cf. 1 John 4:8), so premise 1 is secure. If the argument from hiddenness is to be shown as unsound, either premise 2 or premise 3 will need to be rejected. As it turns out, Christian theism offers good reasons for thinking both (2 and 3) are false.

Consider premise 3. Given the doctrine of original sin, it is plausible to think there is no such thing as reasonable nonbelief. As the apostle Paul states in Romans 1:20, God's existence and nature have been revealed to all through that which he has made "so that people are without excuse" (NIV). All unbelief is unreasonable, a case of self-deception: moral rebellion and the desire to reject God prevent an accurate assessment of the evidence. Such widespread self-deception is a genuine possibility. Many people simply do not want there to be a God and are morally culpable in their unbelief and rebellion against God.[24] Still, it could be argued that in Romans 1 Paul is not referring to all humanity. Rather, Paul is referring to the godless and wicked people "who suppress the truth by their wickedness" (Rom. 1:18 NIV).[25] Perhaps there are those (e.g., from a non-Western context) who have never considered whether God exists. Or perhaps, through no fault of their own, some people do not know that God exists because of some deeply rooted emotional, social, or intellectual barrier that prevents them from believing.

Assume that there is reasonable nonbelief (and that, for now, premise 3 is secure). What about premise 2? Are there good reasons to think that a perfectly loving God might allow reasonable nonbelief? Philosophers have offered a number of plausible reasons why God hides.[26] Paul Moser, for example, has argued that for many, if God were too obvious, it would elicit an improper response.[27] If God were to rearrange the stars each night to read "Made by God" or to imprint on each DNA strand "Made lovingly by Yahweh," it is possible that it would produce mere belief *that* God exists without resulting in genuine belief and trust *in* God. Or perhaps, as Michael Rea argues, divine silence is just God's preferred mode of interacting with us humans. Maybe God's silence speaks louder of his love and care for us than verbiage, and, therefore, "we need not experience his silence as *absence*—especially if we see Biblical narratives and liturgies as things that in some sense mediate the

24. Consider the oft-quoted admission of Thomas Nagel: "I don't want there to be a God; I don't want the universe to be like that." *The Last Word* (New York: Oxford University Press, 1997), 130.

25. Meister argues this way in "Evil and the Hiddenness of God," 144.

26. See, e.g., the collection of essays in *Divine Hiddenness: New Essays*, ed. Daniel Howard-Snyder and Paul K. Moser (Cambridge: Cambridge University Press, 2002).

27. Moser calls this the "Divine Purposes Reply" to hiddenness. See his "Cognitive Idolatry and Divine Hiding," in Howard-Snyder and Moser, *Divine Hiddenness*, chap. 6.

presence of God to us."[28] The general point is that a greater good is secured by God in hiding, and therefore God is morally justified even if there is reasonable nonbelief. If these replies or those like it are plausible, then there is no reason to think that premise 2 is true. In conclusion, it is open to the theist to reject either premise 2 or 3 of the argument from hiddenness. The reality of divine hiding does not provide a reason to think that God does not exist.

The problem of divine hiddenness, as we've noted, is also a problem for those who believe in God. Often our prayers seem to go no higher than the ceiling. In times of deep anguish, God remains silent, distant, and uninvolved. This problem is not just for "normal" believers. Exemplars of the faith, such as Mother Teresa, regularly experience divine silence.[29]

In closing, we offer some thoughts from J. P. Moreland for those who struggle with divine hiding as a source of doubt.[30] First, don't be overly anxious in times of divine hiding. A look at the lives of saints both past and present reveals moments of God's manifest presence as well as times of divine absence. This is normal for the Christian life. Second, God uses times of divine hiding to mature and deepen our trust and reliance on him. In these times we learn to trust in God and God alone, not in our experience of God or our expectations for God. Finally, God hides to give us an opportunity to seek him with all of our heart. As God proclaims through the prophet Jeremiah, "You will seek me and find me when you seek me with all your heart" (Jer. 29:13 NIV).

## Conclusion

In this chapter we've considered the problems of evil and divine hiddenness. We've argued that neither provides reason to think that a perfectly loving God doesn't exist. This doesn't mean that the lived experience of suffering, tragedy, divine silence, and loss are easy. Just the opposite is the case. But—and this is good news—it does mean there is *always* hope. In the Christian story, tragedy doesn't get the last word. Death is not the end. One day our pain and grief will be no more. In those moments when it seems like all is lost, there is Jesus. As Christians, we can find comfort in God's pursuing and passionate love. And we look forward to a time when all will be made right again and we will experience the unmediated presence of God forever.

28. Michael Rea, "Divine Hiddenness, Divine Silence," in *Philosophy of Religion: An Anthology*, ed. Louis Pojman and Michael Rea, 6th ed. (Boston: Wadsworth/Cengage, 2012), 273.

29. See Mother Teresa, *Come Be My Light: The Private Writings of the Saint of Calcutta*, ed. Brian Kolodiejchuck (New York: Doubleday, 2007).

30. See J. P. Moreland's sermon on divine hiding at http://www.jpmoreland.com/media/the-god-who-hides/.

# 14

# Divine Interaction

## *Miracles and Prayer*

In the two previous chapters we explored some of the major arguments for and against the existence of God. There we saw that, in favor of God's existence, philosophers have offered ontological, cosmological, teleological, and moral arguments. Against God's existence, atheists have typically argued that the problem of evil either disproves God's existence or at least makes it improbable. Most recently, skeptics have argued that the hiddenness of God is also troubling for theistic belief.

In this chapter we will explore an additional philosophical puzzle related to Christian theism: the question of divine interaction. Generally speaking, theists—at least Christian theists—affirm at least five different ways that God interacts with his world. First, Christian theism maintains that God interacts in a basic ontological way with creation by holding all things together continually. Second, Christian theism claims that God interacts spiritually with his creatures through the ongoing encounter with the Holy Spirit. Third, Christian theism holds that in the incarnation, God has interacted with his world by being bodily present. Fourth, Christian theism holds that at times God performs miracles within the natural order. And finally, Christian theism claims that God works providentially in response to prayer. Such affirmations may raise any number of interesting questions. But three particular questions seem most pressing: (1) What is a miracle? (2) Are miracles really possible? (3) How does God's providence work? We begin with the first question about miracles.

### What Is a Miracle?

Throughout history, reports of **miracles** abound, especially within religious literature and in religious contexts. In the Bible, for example, we are told of bushes that burn but are not consumed, seas that divide, ax heads that float, blind people made to see, lame people healed, and people raised from the dead, just to name a few. In each case, something supernatural and spectacular takes place that defies ordinary explanation. In the section below we will explore the question of whether this really happens.

Before jumping in to answer this question, we must first define miracles. There is actually a significant amount of debate about the definition of miracles, but by most accounts something like the following could serve as a general definition. Perhaps most famously, for example, David Hume suggests that a "miracle is a violation of the laws of nature."[1] But while this rather abrupt statement begins to get at what he understands a miracle to be, it does not reflect the more precise definition that he offers in his footnotes, where he says, "[A] miracle may be accurately defined, a transgression of a law of nature by a particular volition of the Deity, or by the interposition of some invisible agent."[2] Generally speaking, definitions like these have been very popular in discussions on miracles. Most recently, Yujin Nagasawa offers the following definition: "A miracle is a violation of the laws of nature that is caused by an intentional agent; and it has religious significance."[3]

What these popular definitions have in common is that (1) they understand miracles as a violation of the laws of nature, (2) they have an agent behind them, and (3) they relate to God in some way. Despite our agreement with some aspects of these definitions, we suspect that such definitions don't fully, or accurately, reflect the way miracles are understood within the Christian faith. Therefore we offer this definition:

> Miracle = A God-caused event that suspends the regular flow of the natural order to accomplish some divine purpose.

There are several significant features of this definition that call for our attention. First, this definition is clear about the cause of such events. While

1. David Hume, *An Inquiry concerning Human Understanding* (New York: Oxford University Press, 2007), 83; specifically, see his essay "Of Miracles," 79–95, for his detailed treatment of the possibility of miracles.

2. Hume, *Inquiry concerning Human Understanding*, 127; this elaboration on the nature of miracles comes via footnote 11 in part 1, paragraph 12, of the essay "Of Miracles," in *Inquiry concerning Human Understanding*.

3. Yujin Nagasawa, *Miracles: A Very Short Introduction* (New York: Oxford University Press, 2017), 18.

miracles may involve human agents, ultimately God is the one who causes the miracle to take place.

Second, we dispute the language of "violation" and instead contend that miracles should be thought of as a "suspension" of the regular flow of nature. If God's miraculous work is a violation of the laws of nature, then this seems to strip the laws of their inherent integrity. Moreover, since God is the author of the laws of nature, the notion of violation suggests that he is now working against his own original intentions. Likewise, to use the language of "breaking" the laws of nature is problematic. If the laws are broken, does this now suggest that nature is dysfunctional and that God is at fault? Either way, we suggest that the language of "violation" or "breaking" prejudices the case against miracles and thus is unhelpful. A miracle is more rightly thought of as a suspension of the laws of nature. Winfried Corduan offers a helpful analogy to show what this involves. He uses the example of a car coming to a stoplight where the driver would expect to find a traffic light directing traffic. Instead, the driver comes to the light, sees it working, but notices a police officer waving traffic along in a different order than the traffic lights would be doing. In this case, the traffic lights are still in place and unbroken, but they are simply suspended by the police officer in the intersection. While traffic lights are what normally facilitate the flow of traffic in the intersection, there are still times when, due to factors we may not know or understand, law enforcement officers supersede the lights and direct traffic differently. This type of understanding appears to be a better way to think about the laws of nature. The laws of nature do not appear to possess absolute power for how things *must* work. Rather, they appear to serve as guidelines for what *normally* happens.[4]

Third, as this definition makes clear, miracles are productive toward some divine end. When God performs a miracle, he does so for some eschatological reason, where he secures or achieves something that furthers the coming of his kingdom. Take, for example, the exodus encounter with Pharaoh when God uses Moses to part the Red Sea. Why did he do that? On this account we would say that God performed a miracle to save his people, Israel. And why does he care to do that? He cares to do that because he has committed himself to protecting them and because they carry the bloodline of the Messiah. If Israel is snuffed out by the Red Sea, then the bloodline of Christ is cut off, and this would prevent the Messiah from coming, thus thwarting God's divine plan for the world. In cases like these, God performs miracles when he sees the need to protect or advance the outflow of his kingdom. But now comes the bigger question: Are such things really possible?

4. Winfried Corduan, *No Doubt about It* (Nashville: B&H, 1997), 151–52.

## Are Miracles Really Possible?

Debates about the possibility of miracles almost always center on the work of David Hume, who by all accounts offers the most influential and important objections. His argument against miracles is multifaceted and has been represented in a variety of different ways. Perhaps the best way to describe his argument, however, is by understanding it as an inductive argument that contends for the improbability of miracles. He says, for example, that a "wise man, therefore, proportions his belief to the evidence."[5] In other words, when it comes to things like miracles, wise people will always believe what is most probable in light of the evidence. To make his case against miracles, he considers the evidence on both sides.

To support miracles, Hume notes that believers typically rely on the testimony of those who say they have experienced a miracle. So, for example, for the miraculous claim that Jesus was raised from the dead, believers point to the testimony of those who claimed to have seen Christ after the tomb was discovered to be empty. But as you might expect, Hume is unpersuaded by such claims and raises at least four criticisms.

First, he argues that "there is not to be found, in all history, any miracle attested by a sufficient number of men, of such unquestioned good-sense, education, and learning, as to secure us against all delusion in themselves; of such undoubted integrity, as to place them beyond all suspicion of any design to deceive others."[6] In other words, Hume thinks there are an insufficient number of witnesses to establish miracles and that those who claim to have experienced them are of the wrong kind of character. Second, suggests Hume, testimonies that support miracles are given by those who have a bias toward religion. He says, "But if the spirit of religion join itself to the love of wonder, there is an end of common sense; and human testimony, in these circumstances, loses all pretensions to authority. A religionist may be an enthusiast, and imagine he sees what has no reality: he may know his narrative to be false, and yet persevere in it, with the best intentions in the world, for the sake of promoting so holy a cause."[7] Third, Hume argues that miracles are never attested to by intelligent, upstanding, and civilized people, but always by the poor, uneducated, and ignorant. He says, for example, "It forms a strong presumption against all supernatural and miraculous relations, that they are observed chiefly to abound among ignorant and barbarous nations; or if a civilized people has ever given admission to any of them, that people

5. Hume, *Inquiry concerning Human Understanding*, 80.
6. Hume, *Inquiry concerning Human Understanding*, 84.
7. Hume, *Inquiry concerning Human Understanding*, 85.

will be found to have received them from ignorant and barbarous ancestors, who transmitted them with that inviolable sanction and authority, which always attend received opinions."[8]

Fourth and finally, Hume notes that miraculous claims from one religion are often countered by miraculous claims in another religion. He says, "There is no testimony for any, even those which have not been expressly detected, that is not opposed by an infinite number of witnesses."[9]

These are Hume's objections to the testimonial evidence offered in support of miracles. We shall respond to his concerns shortly, but before we do that, we must first hear the rest of his argument. What we just described above is Hume's rebuttal to the evidence put forward in favor of miracles. But what about the evidence against miracles? Against the possibility of miracles, Hume famously says: "A miracle is a violation of the laws of nature; and as a firm and unalterable experience has established these laws, the proof against a miracle, from the very nature of the fact, is as entire as any argument from experience can possibly be imagined."[10] So in other words, Hume is committed to something like the following:

1. Miracles, if they happened, would be a violation of the laws of nature.
2. But uniform experience suggests that the laws of nature cannot be violated in this way.
3. Therefore, given the laws of nature, miracles cannot happen.

Putting it all together, Hume believes that evidential support for miracles is rather weak and that, by contrast, the evidential argument against miracles (per 1–3 above) is strong. So then, the wise person who "proportions . . . belief to the evidence" should not believe in miracles.

But how strong is this argument? Is it sufficiently strong to defeat the possibility of miracles? While some people may find Hume convincing, we suggest that his argument has some problems. Let's begin by responding to his criticisms of the testimonial evidence in favor of miracles. To be fair, Hume raises several interesting and important insights about the nature of these testimonies. And yet there is a very serious and troubling brand of snobbery, overstatement, and bias present within Hume's criticisms. For example, consider his first criticism, that miracles are not sufficiently attested to. The problem here is that Hume never actually tells us how many witnesses would

8. Hume, *Inquiry concerning Human Understanding*, 86.
9. Hume, *Inquiry concerning Human Understanding*, 87.
10. Hume, *Inquiry concerning Human Understanding*, 83.

be needed and what their level of education must be. As Nagasawa notes, "It is not clear, for example, how many witnesses are required or what sort of educational backgrounds they must have. Hume, however, gives the impression that a miracle report cannot be considered authentic without a very large number of witnesses who are perhaps comparable to Hume himself in terms of education, reputation, and social status."[11] But as Nagasawa points out, this "sets the standard too high"[12] and prevents us from affirming a wide variety of things that are reasonable to affirm.

Or consider his second criticism of testimonial evidence, that those who report miracles typically have a desire to believe them for religious reasons. As Nagasawa states, this may be an insightful sociological observation, but it doesn't follow from this that such testimonies are therefore false.[13] Our desire to believe something doesn't indicate anything about the truth of the belief. Furthermore, as in the case of the apostle Paul and James, the half brother of Jesus, some people hold their religious motivations to be a result of the miraculous events they have experienced.

Hume's third criticism—that such reports come from ignorant, uneducated, and poor people and therefore are suspect—is deeply problematic. In short, Hume's criticism here amounts to bias and snobbery, not philosophical reasoning. It is a good example of what philosophers refer to as the genetic fallacy: rejecting an idea or argument because of where or who it comes from. Are we really to believe that only people with a certain level of education are worth listening to? Just because someone doesn't hold an academic degree doesn't mean they are stupid or unreliable.

And finally, Hume's fourth criticism, that competing religions offer competing accounts of miracles, fails to undercut the testimonial value of miracles. It may be true that competing religions affirm different sets of miracles, yet this is completely irrelevant to the possibility of them happening or to the possibility that we can experience them. As Nagasawa reports, "Even though Christian witnesses of miracles and Muslim witnesses of miracles make conflicting claims with respect to which religion is true[,] they are in agreement with respect to the possible occurrence of miracles. [Criticism] 4, therefore, fails to undermine belief in miracles."[14]

Hume's criticisms regarding the testimonial support in favor of miracles raises some interesting points for consideration but ultimately fail to undermine testimony as an evidential basis for belief in miracles. But we still aren't

11. Nagasawa, *Miracles*, 73.
12. Nagasawa, *Miracles*, 74.
13. Nagasawa, *Miracles*, 74.
14. Nagasawa, *Miracles*, 77.

off the hook yet. What about his case against the very possibility of miracles based on the laws of nature? Again, we could summarize his account this way:

1. Miracles, if they happened, would be a violation of the laws of nature.
2. But uniform experience suggests that the laws of nature cannot be violated in this way.
3. Therefore, given the laws of nature, miracles cannot happen.

This is perhaps a more significant objection to miracles. In the above section we have already rejected premise 1 in the way we defined miracles as "a God-caused event that suspends the regular flow of the natural order to accomplish some divine purpose." Nevertheless, we suspect that this will not be enough of a response to the argument, since Hume, or someone like him, could simply reformulate the argument this way:

1′. Miracles, if they happened, would be a suspension of the laws of nature.
2′. But uniform experience suggests that the laws of nature cannot be suspended in this way.
3. Therefore, given the laws of nature, miracles cannot happen.

To respond to this kind of argument, we must address premises 2 and 2′, and the key issue here is the regularity of the laws of nature. What premises 2 and 2′ seem to imply is that the laws of nature are so constant and regular that the universe is guaranteed to obey them and that nothing outside of their purview can interrupt or act in nature contrary to these laws. Put another way, Hume and contemporary naturalists who follow in his footsteps seem to be suggesting that the laws of nature display a regularity that renders the universe to be a closed system. If the universe is a "closed system," nothing outside the universe can step in and act on it. Causes from outside this system of physical laws, like the supernatural being God, are out of bounds, off-limits, or utterly impossible. Therefore, what happens inside the universe is a result of the physical objects, forces, and laws within nature itself. In addition to Hume's emphasis on the regularity of the laws of nature, the idea of a closed system was further strengthened by the mechanistic picture of the universe often associated with Isaac Newton. As Alvin Plantinga explains, the universe on this account is understood as

> a collection including material particles and the things made of them, evolving according to the laws of classical mechanics. Theologically, the idea is that the world is a great divine mechanical artifact that runs according to the fixed laws

> of classical science, the laws prescribed for it by God. The world is mechanical in that the laws of physics are sufficient to describe its behavior; no additional laws—of chemistry or biology, for example—are needed, and if there are such laws, they are reducible . . . to the laws of physics.[15]

From the Humean emphasis on the regularity of the laws of nature and the Newtonian picture of a mechanistic universe, the idea that the universe is a closed system came to be the orthodox opinion of the naturalists. As John Heil suggests, this is precisely what naturalists believe the scientific picture of the universe is committed to. He says, "Modern science is premised on the assumption that the material world is a causally closed system. This means, roughly, that every event in the material world is caused by some other material event (if it is caused by any event) and has as effects only material events."[16] Or as Jaegwon Kim puts it, "One way of stating the principle of physical causal closure is this: If you pick any physical event and trace out its causal ancestry or posterity, that will never take you outside the physical domain. That is, no causal chain will ever cross the boundary between the physical and the nonphysical."[17]

But is this view correct? There can be no doubt that the laws of nature act and operate with an astounding regularity and dependability. To deny this would be incredibly foolish. The real question is whether the regularity of the laws of nature actually establishes the mechanistic view of the universe that eliminates the possibility of activity from outside the system. We contend that such regularity is not enough to demonstrate that the universe is closed. First, as Plantinga notes, while it is true that Newton painted a rather mechanistic picture of the universe, we must remember that Newton himself did not take this to mean that it was a closed system. Plantinga says, "But the Newtonian picture is nowhere nearly sufficient for hands-off theology. First, Newton himself (one hopes) accepted the Newtonian picture, but he didn't accept hands-off theology. He believed that God providentially guides the world. He also believed that God regularly adjusts the orbits of the planets; according to his calculations, their orbits would otherwise spiral off into chaos."[18]

But this is not all. Plantinga continues, "More important, however: according to Newton and classical mechanics, natural laws describe how the world

15. Alvin Plantinga, *Where the Conflict Really Lies* (New York: Oxford University Press, 2011), 77.

16. John Heil, *Philosophy of Mind: A Contemporary Introduction*, 3rd ed. (London: Routledge, 2012), 23.

17. Jaegwon Kim, *Mind in a Physical World: An Essay on the Mind-Body Problem and Mental Causation* (Cambridge, MA: MIT Press, 2001), 40.

18. Plantinga, *Where the Conflict Really Lies*, 77.

works *when, or provided that the world is a closed (isolated) system, subject to no outside causal influence*."[19] So as Plantinga states and as the case of Newton himself seems to indicate, even if the mechanical view of the universe is correct, there is nothing contradictory in holding that mechanical view of the universe and at the same time holding that God is still able to interact with it. But more important for those who understand the regularity of the laws of nature, demonstrating causal closure seems to make a logical leap. What *normally* happens does not indicate what *must* happen, as they seem to think. As Plantinga indicates, the uniformity of the laws of nature shows us what normally happens when the universe is left to run on its own. But the uniformity of the laws of nature "don't purport to tell us how things *always* go; they tell us, instead, how things go when no agency outside the universe acts in it."[20] As such, on the basis of the regularity and uniformity of the laws of nature, we have no reason to argue that the universe is a closed system.

But before we move on from this issue, there is one further reason to challenge the Humean argument against miracles from the uniformity of nature. In short, more recent developments and discoveries in physics suggest that the Newtonian picture of a mechanistic universe might not tell us everything we need to know about the world. While Newton's laws hold true for most objects in the universe (atoms, rocks, planets, stars, solar systems, etc.), his laws don't seem to apply to objects on the quantum level. The discovery of quantum particles has changed our understanding of physics significantly. As best we can tell, particles at this level do not operate in a deterministic fashion. Rather, their movements and operations function only with varying levels of probability. What this means is that we now have even fewer reasons to think that the laws of nature are causally closed to agents from outside the system. As such, the case against miracles from the regularity of the laws of nature, causal closure, and naturalism seems rather weak. We conclude, therefore, that premises 2 and 2′ are both false.

## What Is Providence and How Does It Work?

Another major question we must explore is the issue of **divine providence**: God's governing mode of interaction with the world. Christians believe, for example, that God can interact with the world in miraculous ways, as argued above, but they also believe that God interacts with people in the way he governs the world toward his ends in response to prayer. This way of interacting

19. Plantinga, *Where the Conflict Really Lies*, 78 (emphasis in original).
20. Plantinga, *Where the Conflict Really Lies*, 79.

with the world is often referred to as God's providence. The challenge to understanding how this mode of interaction works lies not in the nature of physical laws, as in the case of miracles. Rather, the key to understanding this mode of divine interaction resides in the kinds of historical, moral, and theological concerns that must be kept in balance. So, for example, in God's providential interaction, factors relating to human freedom and divine purpose must be kept in balance or held in tension. How this is done is understood in different ways by theologians throughout history.

Generally speaking, theologians have offered both theistic (a view that affirms a creator of the world who is personal in nature and remains actively involved in the world) and nontheistic (views that affirm some kind of God or gods that differ in nature from theistic portrayals) accounts of how to think of God's providence. Some examples of nontheistic views include deism or pantheism. According to deism, God created the universe but is impersonal and therefore inactive in the world. According to pantheism, God and the universe are the same thing, and since the universe is ever in the process of evolving and developing, God is constantly becoming something new. These perspectives have had numerous advocates over the centuries and are worthy of serious attention. But given their distinct views about the nature of God, they are not compatible with Christian theism, and we will not elaborate on them here.

By contrast, the God of Christianity is clearly a theistic God. That is, God is a personal being who created the world ex nihilo (out of nothing) and remains actively involved in the world he created. Within that framework some of the most common accounts of divine providence include open theism, Calvinism, and Molinism.[21] We shall explore each of these views very briefly.

### *Open Theism*

**Open theism** is a theistic view: God is thought of as a personal creator and involved in his world. Open theism holds a distinct understanding about the kinds of knowledge God has. Generally speaking, open theists affirm that God is omniscient (knows everything) but suggest that this applies to events, objects, and states of affairs about only the history and present state of the world. God's knowledge does not include knowledge of events, objects, or states of affairs about the future, since the future does not exist to be known, because knowing such future states would eliminate human freedom. God is therefore "open" regarding the future. Terrance Tiessen offers a helpful summary of the view:

21. One might also offer a Thomist account of providence, but space issues forbid such in this chapter.

> The openness model gets its name from the proposition that God is open to his creatures, to whom he has given libertarian freedom, and that the future is open because it will be brought about to a large degree by the decisions those creatures make. God is omnipotent, but he has freely limited his own ability to control every event within creation by giving libertarian freedom to moral creatures, human and spiritual. God is personal in his relationships with these creatures, and so he is affected by them as well as having an effect upon them. There were risks in creating this kind of world, but God decided that it was better to have a world in which free creatures love and obey him than to have one in which he could guarantee that his own will would always be done. God is faithful to himself and unchanging in his moral nature, but he is not absolutely immutable, as though he had formed a comprehensive plan for his creation, in eternity, and was now working out all the details of that plan, in the time and space that he created.[22]

So then, according to open theism, God providentially balances his purposes with human freedom by giving human beings a significant degree of autonomy. But, as critics of this view have noted, this view of God's knowledge seems hard to reconcile with the teachings of Scripture and the teachings of Christianity. Biblically, God is described as a God who knows the past, present, and future of free creatures like us. As a result, many Christians are hesitant to embrace this view.

### *Calvinism*

As we saw, open theism tries to balance the divine purposes that God may have with human freedom by limiting the extent of God's knowledge to include only the past and present. Going in the opposite direction, **Calvinism** embraces God's sovereign right and power to determine what takes place in the universe and limits the scope and nature of human freedom. Tiessen is again helpful: "[The] Calvinist model believes that God's comprehensive determination can only be coordinated with a creaturely freedom that is volitional or voluntary. Creatures do what they want to do but what they do is always within God's overall determination."[23] Thomas Morris describes this approach by showing how some theists "endorse the idea that God has eternally predestined, or predetermined, the course of history in every detail. [For these theists] God is to be thought of as the omnipotent creator of all things. It is typically taken to be a corollary of this that God is sovereign over

22. Terrance Tiessen, *Providence and Prayer: How Does God Work in the World?* (Downers Grove, IL: InterVarsity, 2000), 71.
23. Tiessen, *Providence and Prayer*, 232.

all things."[24] John Feinberg calls this approach hard determinism. He says, "Hard determinism removes the idea of inevitability more than does fatalism. A hard determinist believes that all that happens is causally determined. As a result, there is no human free will of any sort. That is, some hard determinists agree with libertarians that the only notion of genuine freedom is libertarian free will, but they add that since everything is causally determined, no one has such freedom."[25]

Taken to its logical conclusion, God would be understood as the author of sin and evil. While some may not see this as a problem, it is difficult to see how this can be reconciled with the notion of God's goodness. Thus some who recognize the difficulties with hard determinism attempt to soften it with the notion of compatibilistic freedom. The basic idea here, as discussed in chapter 10, is that each person does as each truly desires to do, even if the choice is determined or caused. That the causation or determinism is in keeping with the desires of the agent renders them as compatible with each other, even if the choice is fully caused. Bruce Ware advocates this view when he states that

> our freedom consists in our choosing and doing according to what we are inclined most, or what we desire most, to do. . . . Compatibilist freedom . . . insists that regardless of what struggles we go through in making our choices or deciding what action to perform, in the end, when we choose and act, we do so from prevailing desires which explain exactly why this choice and not another is made. This obviously means, however, that when we choose, all things being just what they are, we must choose as we do![26]

Feinberg takes a similar view but refers to it as **soft determinism**: "Soft determinism says that genuine free human action is compatible with causal conditions that decisively incline the will without constraining it. The causal conditions are sufficient to move the agent to choose one option over another, but the choice and resultant action are free as long as the person acts without constraint. Acting under constraint means that one is forced to act contrary to one's wishes or desires."[27]

What the Calvinist model succeeds in doing is providing an account that retains the classical Christian ideas that God is the sovereign king over all creation. As sovereign, God determines (in either hard or soft versions) the

24. Thomas V. Morris, *Our Idea of God* (Vancouver: Regent College Publishing, 1991), 89.
25. John S. Feinberg, *No One Like Him* (Wheaton: Crossway, 2001), 635.
26. Bruce A. Ware, *God's Greater Glory* (Wheaton: Crossway, 2004), 25–26.
27. Feinberg, *No One Like Him*, 637.

course of nature and the future of the world. Critics, however, have suggested that this view is problematic since it eliminates human freedom and, as a result, suggests a deeply problematic view of God, meaning that God is either the author of evil or at least morally culpable for evil.

### *Molinism*

While open theism accounts for God's providential work by limiting the knowledge that God has and Calvinism accounts for it by limiting (or maybe redefining) human freedom, Molinism takes the unique approach of expanding God's knowledge to include the doctrine of middle knowledge. This doctrine is a bit more complex than the open theist or Calvinist accounts and will require a little more attention. The doctrine of middle knowledge was first developed in the sixteenth century during the Counter-Reformation by a Spanish Jesuit priest named Luis de Molina (1535–1600).[28] This doctrine was largely forgotten until the early 1970s, when Plantinga seems to have rediscovered it and made considerable use of it in his work titled *The Nature of Necessity*.[29] Since then the doctrine has enjoyed the support of such scholars as Thomas Flint[30] and William Lane Craig,[31] to name just two.

As Craig explains, the doctrine of middle knowledge deals with God's knowledge of what are often referred to as counterfactuals of freedom. He says counterfactuals "are conditional statements in the subjunctive mood: for example, 'If I were rich, I would buy a Mercedes'; 'If Barry Goldwater had been elected president, he would have won the Vietnam War'; and 'If you were to ask her, she would say yes.' Counterfactuals are so called because the antecedent or consequent clauses are typically contrary to fact."[32] That is, they are contrary to the actual world that we live in. Up until the time of Friedrich Schleiermacher (1768–1834), theologians commonly affirmed that God had counterfactual knowledge. What they debated was at what point or when God had this knowledge logically.[33]

28. Luis de Molina, *On Divine Foreknowledge: Part IV of the "Concordia,"* trans. Alfred J. Freddoso (Ithaca, NY: Cornell University Press, 1988).

29. Alvin Plantinga, *The Nature of Necessity* (Oxford: Clarendon, 1974).

30. Thomas P. Flint, *Divine Providence: The Molinist Account* (Ithaca, NY: Cornell University Press, 1998).

31. William Lane Craig, "The Middle Knowledge View," in *Divine Foreknowledge: Four Views*, ed. James K. Beilby and Paul R. Eddy (Downers Grove, IL: InterVarsity, 2001), 119–43; and Craig, *The Only Wise God: The Compatibility of Divine Foreknowledge and Human Freedom* (Eugene, OR: Wipf & Stock, 1999).

32. Craig, "Middle Knowledge View," 120.

33. Craig, "Middle Knowledge View," 120.

Before moving forward, it will be helpful to determine what is meant by asking "when" God knows something. The question of "when" God knows something does not refer to a *temporal* moment in time. Rather, it refers to the *logical* moment or point when God has a certain aspect of knowledge. In Craig's view, "To say that something is logically prior to something else is not to say that the one occurs before the other in time. Temporally, they could be simultaneous. Rather, logical priority means that something serves to explain something else. The one provides the grounds or basis for the other."[34] Craig explains that according to the Dominican view, against which Molina is arguing, "God's counterfactual knowledge is logically subsequent to his decree to create a certain world. They maintained that in decreeing that a particular world exist, God also decreed which counterfactual statements are true. Logically prior to the divine decree, there are no counterfactual truths to be known. All God knows at that logical moment are the necessary truths, including all the various possibilities."[35]

In other words, on the Dominican view, God gave the decree for the world and the details therein, and after this possessed counterfactual knowledge. This understanding of counterfactuals leads to determinism and the elimination of human freedom.

In opposition to this, Molina's Jesuit view suggests that God has counterfactual knowledge logically prior to the decree for the world, which locates this knowledge logically between his natural and free knowledge.[36] Craig says, "The Molinists charged that the Dominicans had in effect obliterated human freedom by making counterfactual truths a consequence of God's decree, for on the Dominican account it is God who determines what each person will do in whatever circumstances he finds himself. By contrast, the Molinists, by placing God's counterfactual knowledge prior to the divine decree, made room for creaturely freedom by exempting counterfactual truths from God's decree."[37] Thus, as Morris puts it,

> The Molinist view is based on a distinctive conception of the makeup of God's knowledge. The range of divine knowledge is thought of as divided into three types: natural knowledge—knowledge God has prior to (conceptually prior to) any act of creation, concerning what all the possibilities of creation are; free knowledge—knowledge of everything that will actually happen in the world

34. Craig, *Only Wise God*, 127.
35. Craig, "Middle Knowledge View," 121.
36. God's natural knowledge is typically understood to refer to God's knowledge of all necessary truth. His free knowledge is understood to be the knowledge that God possesses about the actual world after the decree has been given.
37. Craig, "Middle Knowledge View," 122.

given God's free choice of which possibilities of creation to actualize; and middle knowledge—comprehensive knowledge of what contingently, as a matter of fact, would result from any creative decision he might make.[38]

With this, we could sketch the Molinist model this way:

Natural Knowledge = God has knowledge of all necessary truths, including all the possible worlds he might create. This gives him knowledge of what could be. This knowledge serves as the parameters in which any possible world might develop.

Middle Knowledge = God has knowledge of how each contingent being in any possible world would freely react to the given circumstances if those circumstances were actual. That is, God knows all the counterfactuals of each world before he actualizes one world.

---

Divine Decree to Actualize a World

---

Free Knowledge = Logically subsequent to his decree to create a particular world, God knows all the contingent truths about the actual world, including its past, present, and future. This includes all of God's knowledge of what will be in the actual world.

As you will notice, the Divine Decree is placed between God's Middle Knowledge and his Free Knowledge. But why? In short, this is one of the distinct philosophical moves that Molina makes to provide a way of balancing God's foreknowledge of our future choices with our libertarian freedom. If the Divine Decree came prior to God's Middle Knowledge (specifically, his counterfactual knowledge entailed within Middle Knowledge), then this would entail a rather hard version of determinism, as this would require God to determine what will be without our choices having a chance to play out beforehand. By placing the Divine Decree where he does, Molina thinks that God's choice of what will be in the world comes logically after his knowledge of what could be given our free choices.

So what does the Molinist account of providence do for the questions of divine purposes and human freedom? According to many philosophers and theologians, the doctrine of middle knowledge offers an attractive proposal for reconciling the foreknowledge of God with human freedom. In Garrett DeWeese's view, "Molina's theory of Middle Knowledge represents a remarkable

38. Morris, *Our Idea of God*, 95.

advance in the understanding of the problem of God's foreknowledge and human freedom."[39] Craig also sees this as a valuable doctrine and says, "Once one grasps the concept of middle knowledge, one will find it astonishing in its subtlety and power. Indeed, I would venture to say that it is the single most fruitful theological concept I have ever encountered."[40] Critics, however, have suggested that Molinism is implausible, since the future does not yet exist and thus there is no reality to ground God's middle knowledge. Like most philosophical questions, debates about its merit continue.

## Conclusion

As we have seen, questions about the way God interacts with his world are complex and much debated. Some, like Hume and the naturalists who follow him, suggest that the evidential support for miracles is weak and that the regularities of the laws of nature suggest that miracles could never happen. We've explored those claims in this chapter and have found them wanting. We have also explored the question of God's providence. How is it that God balanced the concerns of his own divine purposes in creation with the seeming reality of human freedom? To answer this question, theologians have offered a variety of different accounts, but three of the most popular contemporary accounts are open theism, Calvinism, and Molinism. In the end, Christian philosophy seems to be fully capable of dealing with the complex issues relating to divine interaction.

39. Garrett DeWeese, *God and the Nature of Time* (Burlington, VT: Ashgate, 2004), 204.

40. Craig, "Middle Knowledge View," 125. He adds, "In my own work, I have applied it to the issues of Christian particularism, perseverance of the saints and biblical inspiration." For Craig's treatment of particularism, see William Lane Craig, "'No Other Name': A Middle Knowledge Perspective on the Exclusivity of Salvation through Christ," *Faith and Philosophy* 6 (1989): 172–88; for his treatment of perseverance of the saints, see Craig, "'Lest Anyone Should Fall': A Middle Knowledge Perspective on Perseverance and Apostolic Warnings," *International Journal for Philosophy of Religion* 29 (1991): 65–74; for his work on biblical inspiration, see Craig, "'Men Moved by the Holy Spirit Spoke from God' (2 Peter 1.21): A Middle Knowledge Perspective on Divine Inspiration," *Philosophia Christi* 1 (1999): 45–82.

# 15

# The Possibility of Life after Death

Philosophy of religion deals with all sorts of issues that human beings care about very deeply. It deals with questions about God's existence and nature, his purposes in the world, and why he allows evil and suffering in the world. In addition to this, philosophy of religion deals with questions about miracles, prayer, and the way God interacts with the world. Moreover, as we will see in this chapter, philosophy of religion deals with the possibility of life after death.

Christians all over the world and throughout history have rejected the idea that death is the final and conclusive result of our existence. Christians have instead affirmed the reality of heaven and the idea that believers live forever in God's presence and enjoy eternal bliss. Christians have not been the only ones to affirm ideas like this. Throughout the world and the various religions that people practice, the possibility of an afterlife is a widely held idea. In short, human beings generally believe that life goes on even after we die.

Despite how widespread these ideas are, however, they are not without difficulty and questions. Is it really possible to live after we die? If so, how does that work, and what should we expect it to be like? This chapter explores these kinds of questions, but it does so from within a Christian point of view. We shall first set forth what is entailed within a Christian understanding of life after death and will then explore the kinds of problems that must be addressed. After that, we will explore the rationales we have for belief in the existence of the soul and the possibility of bodily resurrection.

## A Christian View of Life after Death

Throughout history, Christians have typically been the most vocal and insistent that we survive our deaths and continue to experience life. At the same time, Christians, at least in recent history, can also be guilty of offering nothing more than a very general and simplistic account of this life after death. If asked what happens to people when they die, they might simply respond with something like, "They go to heaven." But, of course, Christianity has more to say about this matter, and as we delve into the above questions, it is important to make sure we have a grasp of some of its primary teachings on the subject. Christianity does affirm that there is a heaven and a hell, and that people will go to one or the other. When Christianity speaks about the afterlife, there are two general kinds of ideas that seem to drive much of the discussion.

First, Christianity seems to affirm that human beings have souls that survive the death of the body. At death, the soul departs and goes to a spiritual realm of reward or punishment. The spiritual realm of reward has been referred to as the **intermediate state** in the presence of Christ, where the soul awaits the resurrection of the body. Thomas Aquinas describes this view in rather blunt fashion: "Since a place is assigned to souls in keeping with their reward or punishment, as soon as the soul is set free from the body it is either plunged into hell or soars to heaven."[1] Operating within a different theological tradition, John Calvin offers a similar summary of Christian thought on this point. Noting numerous allusions to it in Scripture, he says,

> The apostle banishes doubt when he teaches that we have been gathered "to the spirits of just men" [Heb. 12:23 NKJV]. By these words he means that we are in fellowship with the holy patriarchs who, although dead, cultivate the same godliness as we, so that we cannot be members of Christ unless we unite ourselves with them. And if souls when divested of their bodies did not still retain their essence, and have capacity of blessed glory, Christ would not have said to the thief: "Today you will be with me in paradise" [Luke 23:43 NKJV]. Relying on such clear testimonies, in dying let us not hesitate, after Christ's example, to entrust our souls to God [Luke 23:46], or, after Stephen's example, to commit them into Christ's keeping [Acts 7:59], who is called with good reason their faithful "Shepherd and Bishop" [1 Pet. 2:25 KJV].[2]

1. Thomas Aquinas, *Summa Theologica*, trans. Fathers of the English Dominican Province (Notre Dame, IN: Christian Classics, 1947), 3.69.2, supp.

2. John Calvin, *Institutes of the Christian Religion*, ed. John T. McNeill, trans. Ford Lewis Battles (Philadelphia: Westminster, 1960), 3.25.6.

What Calvin affirms here is the existence of the intermediate state. He is less willing, however, to say much about the nature of this state. He adds, "Scripture goes no farther than to say that Christ is present with them, and receives them into paradise [cf. John 12:32] that they may obtain consolation, while the souls of the reprobate suffer such torments as they deserve."[3] Passages like these from Aquinas and Calvin suggest a wide-ranging affirmation of the doctrine from within the Catholic and Protestant traditions. Yet this is only one of the major ideas affirmed by these traditions.

Second, in addition to affirming the intermediate state, both the Catholic and Protestant traditions have also affirmed the necessity of bodily resurrection. That is, both traditions hold that, in the eschaton, Christ will return and raise our bodies from the grave. Again, Aquinas and Calvin make this clear. Aquinas, for example, says, "Further, the members should be conformed to the Head. Now our Head lives and will live eternally in body and soul, since *Christ rising again from the dead dieth now no more* (Rom. vi. 8). Therefore men who are His members will love in body and soul; consequently there must needs be a resurrection of the body."[4] Calvin agrees, but goes one step further by adding that the body we shall receive in the resurrection will be the same body that we currently possess. He says that we must believe "that as to substance we shall be raised again in the same flesh we now bear."[5]

Thus, generally speaking, the major traditions of Christianity have affirmed two major ideas regarding life after death for Christians: the soul's presence with Christ in the intermediate state and bodily resurrection in the eschaton. There are, however, concerns with both of these ideas. For the intermediate state, the concern revolves around the existence of the soul. Since the intermediate state suggests a time of disembodied existence in Christ's presence, it requires the existence of something immaterial about human persons to persist. Most commonly, Christians have pointed to the existence of an immaterial soul as what makes such disembodied existence possible. In other words, when Granny dies and we go to the funeral, we might hear the pastor suggest that Granny is not here. He might say, for example, "Her body is here, but her soul is in heaven with Christ." On this account of Granny's person and death, she is composed of body and soul, and at death the two are separated, with one remaining behind and the other moving on to the heavenly realm. Hence this view depends on the existence of an immaterial soul to account for the intermediate state. Yet, as we saw in chapter 11, there are questions

3. Calvin, *Institutes* 3.25.6.
4. Aquinas, *Summa Theologica* 3.75.1 (emphasis in original).
5. Calvin, *Institutes* 3.25.8.

about the existence of the soul. For materialist accounts of human persons, there is not a soul, since persons are composed of nothing beyond their physical bodies. If this account is true, then Granny's soul is not in the presence of Christ, since it does not exist in the first place. To be clear, materialists have their reasons for taking this position. As we saw, the difficulties surrounding mind-body interaction seem to suggest that materialism might be true. So if a Christian account of life after death is correct, it seems as though a defense of the soul is required.

A second problem for the Christian account of life after death concerns the possibility of bodily resurrection. Christians almost universally affirm this possibility. Yet, at the same time, none of us have ever experienced such a strange phenomenon. Moreover, it seems like this could actually be impossible given what we know about the decomposition of human bodies in the grave, in cremation, in cases of cannibalism, or in other cases where a body might be completely obliterated by some natural process. In short, how can the same body come back in the eschaton if it is completely destroyed through one of the processes described above?

These are two of the major problems that must be addressed to support a Christian view of life after death. In what follows we shall offer a brief account of how the Christian view of life after death might be defended.

## Arguments for the Soul

So what about the soul? In chapter 11 we outlined the various views that philosophers and theologians have taken over the years. Some of those views affirm the existence of the soul, and some do not. We are now interested in seeing if there are perhaps good reasons for thinking that such a thing actually exists. Over the centuries dozens, or even hundreds, of different kinds of arguments have been offered for the soul. Obviously, we cannot look at all or even most of those arguments. Instead, we will simply focus on a few arguments that have either been very popular or that we think have considerable merit. Here are a few that could be set forth to contend for an immaterial soul.

### *An Argument from Doubt*

René Descartes (1596–1650) is sometimes referred to as the father of modern philosophy. The reason for this is that his work launched the modern emphasis on epistemology and, as a corollary, a major interest in mind-body relations. Growing ever more suspicious about the possibility of gaining sure and certain knowledge, he set out to find a foundation for knowledge that was completely trustworthy. He recognized that it was at least possible that all his perceptions were illusions. To see if he could overcome this possibility, he chose to doubt everything that was possible to doubt in an attempt to find any particular idea or ideas that were sure and certain. Of particular suspicion was the knowledge we gain of the physical world through our senses. He noticed that our perceptions are sometimes wrong and thought that we should not place much confidence in the information derived from them. Hence he admitted that it was possible that all of his beliefs about the physical world could be wrong. Because of this, all of our beliefs about the physical world should be doubted. He could doubt the tree in front of him, the lake beside him, the person speaking to him, and so on.

With great consistency, Descartes also considered his physical body. As a physical object, it too could be nothing more than an illusion. But here Descartes stumbled on an important idea. While he could doubt that his body existed, he could not doubt that he existed. For to doubt is to think, and to think requires that he must exist to think. With this Descartes gives one of the most well-known statements in the history of philosophy: "*Cogito ergo sum* [I think, therefore I am]." The fundamental idea here is that bodies are of such a nature that they can be doubted, while souls/minds are of such a nature that they cannot be doubted. Therefore, souls/minds are different things. We could state the argument this way:

1. All physical objects are such that they can be doubted.
2. My body is a physical object, and thus I can doubt it.
3. My soul/mind is such that it cannot be doubted.
4. My soul/mind is distinct from my body.
5. Therefore, my soul/mind exists.

Premise 1 seems rather straightforward and intuitive. If premise 1 is true, then premise 2 would also be true. The key premise here is premise 3. As Descartes points out, the very act of doubting requires a being to do the doubting. Thus while it is possible to doubt our physical bodies, it does not seem possible to doubt our souls/minds.

Philosophers are divided on this argument. Advocates believe that the argument has intuitive appeal, while critics suggest that perhaps there is a bit of smoke and mirrors being employed. While they agree that "something" must exist to doubt, they do not believe that Descartes has shown us that it must be an "I" or a soul/mind. We (the authors) remain convinced that this thing that thinks and doubts is in fact the mind or the soul.

### *An Argument from Persistence of Personal Identity*

Another argument for the soul comes from the fact that persons persist across time even as their bodies experience change. Consider, for example, that a person named Bob lives from 1976 to 1988 and perhaps beyond. During his life, his body is constantly changing parts through the regular metabolic process of eating food and discarding waste. Over a sufficient amount of time, his body replaces the parts that compose his body. Yet, through this process of change Bob continues to exist and to be the very same person he was at an earlier time. What is it that allows his identity to continue? Advocates of the soul could argue that it is the soul that allows Bob to continue existing. We could put an argument along these lines of thought this way:

1. Bob exists in 1976 and his body is composed of parts *a*, *b*, *c*.
2. Bob exists in 1980 and his body is composed of parts *b*, *c*, *d*.
3. Bob exists in 1984 and his body is composed of parts *c*, *d*, *e*.
4. Bob exists in 1988 and his body is composed of parts *d*, *e*, *f*.
5. From (1–4), Bob persists across time from 1976 to 1988 and is the same person at both times.
6. From (1) and (4), Bob's body is composed of completely different parts in 1976 and 1988.
7. Bob is, or has, something over and above his physical body.

Premises 1–4 are uncontroversial. They simply state the process of change in Bob's body throughout the years. Likewise, premise 5 affirms that it is Bob himself who experiences these changes in his body. Premise 6 makes it clear that Bob's body in 1988 is composed of completely different parts than it was in 1976. Now if such a process takes place, then the conclusion derived in 7 seems to follow: Bob either is, or at least has, something over and above his physical body.

Here again, philosophers differ on the merits of the argument. There is some question about whether the body completely replaces its parts over time. If it does not, then the argument would seem to have a fatal flaw. If it does, then the argument seems to succeed. Just how many of the parts get replaced is beyond our attention here. For now, we note that the body does replace the vast majority of parts at minimum and possibly all of its parts. At the same time, something remains and is consistent throughout the process. We contend that the soul plays a vital role in making this happen.

*An Argument from Consciousness*

Another argument for the soul comes from the experience of consciousness. Recall that in chapter 11 we introduced the concept of *qualia*, which refers to a specific kind of mental properties—namely, our experiences of what certain things are like. Or, put another way, *qualia* are qualities that are felt directly and immediately. When we eat a jelly donut, for example, there is a particular kind of experience that we have. We do not just have a brain event of electrochemical firings when we ingest sugar. Rather, we actually *taste* the sugar. That is, there is "something that it is like" to taste sugar, and this is very real. Now as we saw in chapter 11, on this basis most philosophers grant a distinction between brain properties and mental properties—what we call property dualism. Yet some philosophers suggest that property dualism does not go far enough.[6] They contend that such mental properties likely require a corresponding kind of entity to bear them. In other words, if property dualism is true, then it is likely that some form of substance dualism is also true. We could put an argument for this as follows:

1. Human persons have both mental properties and brain properties.
2. Mental properties and brain properties are distinct from each other.
3. Distinct kinds of properties require corresponding entities as the basis for each property.
4. Human persons have both bodies and souls.

Again, premise 1 is rather uncontroversial. It would be rejected by eliminativists (discussed in chap. 11) but would be affirmed by most philosophers. Premise 2 is also rather uncontroversial, though identity theorists might push back against it. Nevertheless, again we find that the majority of philosophers would accept it. The important move of the above argument is in premise 3, which suggests that each kind of property must have a corresponding kind of entity to bear them. So, for example, a physical property will be one that belongs to a physical object. In this case, the physical properties and the physical events that take place in eating a jelly donut are had by and take place in the brain. By contrast, nonphysical properties are had by nonphysical things. In this case, mental properties like *qualia* are had by immaterial entities like souls. As Richard Swinburne has put it, "A man's body is that to which his physical properties belong. If a man weighs ten stone then his body weighs

6. See Dean Zimmerman, "From Property Dualism to Substance Dualism," in *Proceedings of the Aristotelian Society*, Supplementary vol. 84 (2010): 119–50.

ten stone. A man's soul is that to which the (pure) mental properties of a man belong. If a man imagines a cat, then, the dualist will say, his soul imagines a cat. . . . On the dualist account the whole man has the properties he does because his constituent parts have the properties they do."[7]

There is good reason to think that Swinburne is right about this. Materialist accounts such as eliminativism and identity theory have been unsuccessful in explaining away mental properties and conscious experiences. The various other versions of materialism that allow for the existence of mental properties like *qualia* have had a difficult time accounting for the way that brains give rise to *qualia* and mental properties. How is it, exactly, that the neural firings in the brain give rise to the taste of the jelly donut and the feel of the wind blowing through your hair? It looks as though all attempts to explain this within a materialist framework are doomed to fail. Perhaps it is just the case, then, that the existence of mental properties requires the existence of mental substances to have them.

## A Case for Bodily Resurrection

If there are good reasons to think that souls exist, then it follows that there are good reasons to think that the intermediate state is also indeed possible. Even if that is so, however, what should we make about the concerns that surround the seeming impossibility of bodily resurrection? Again, as we stated before, the difficulty with this possibility seems to come from what we know about the destruction of our bodies after death from a variety of different causes. If our bodies are completely destroyed, then is it possible for them to be raised from the dead?

To answer this question, we must first get straight on exactly what we mean when we say that the body raised in the eschaton is the "same" as the body that we currently possess. In this case, what does "same" mean? Here an important distinction will help us to navigate the question. Philosophers use the word "same" in at least two different ways. The first is called **numerical sameness**, which refers to the very same object existing at two different times, even if the object has encountered changes of some kind along the way. In this case, some particular object $O_2$ at $t_2$ is the very same object as $O_1$ at $t_1$. That is to say, a single object O has continued to exist through various moments of time. $O_2$ just is $O_1$ from the earlier moment. Whatever changes might occur in O from $t_1$ to $t_2$ are merely changes in the qualities it has at

7. Richard Swinburne, *The Evolution of the Soul* (New York: Oxford University Press, 2007), 145.

different moments. This brings us to the second way that philosophers use the word "same." Philosophers also speak of **qualitative sameness**, which merely refers to the sameness of qualities that two numerically distinct objects might possess. So, for example, consider two numerically distinct objects *A* and *B* that both exist at a given moment $t_1$. Interestingly, *A* possesses properties *x*, *y*, *z*, and *B* also possess qualities *x*, *y*, *z*. Therefore *A* and *B* share qualitative sameness, even though they are in fact different objects.

A good example that illustrates this distinction even further would be the case of two Ford F-150s that just rolled off the assembly line. Let's call them no. 1 and no. 2. Then no. 1 will always be no. 1, no matter what dings, scratches, dents, or changes of paint color it might encounter over the years of its life. Likewise, no. 2 will always be no. 2, no matter what dings, scratches, dents, or changes of paint color it encounters over the years of its life. In this case, no. 1 is numerically identical to itself at all points of its life, and the same is true of no. 2. As such, no. 1 and no. 2 are numerically distinct. But now also imagine that no. 1 and no. 2 are qualitatively identical. That is, both no. 1 and no. 2 have exactly the same qualities. They are both white, have an extended cab, have brown leather seats, and are four-wheel drive. Since they possess all and exactly the same qualities (they are physically indistinguishable), they are qualitatively the same, even though they are numerically distinct.

The distinction of numerical and qualitative sameness is deeply influential on the way we answer the question of bodily resurrection. Christianity promises that God will raise our bodies from the grave in the eschaton. Yet we must ask what exactly it is that God must raise. Must the body that God raises be numerically identical to the body we currently possess (i.e., must he raise these exact bodies), or is it only necessary for him to raise a body that is qualitatively the same as the one we currently have (i.e., a physical duplicate)?

How we answer that question of resurrection depends entirely on what we say human persons are. Recall the different views we surveyed in chapter 11. For the substance dualist who affirms person/soul identity (the idea that human persons are just their souls), apparently all that is necessary in the resurrection is for God to raise a body that is a physical duplicate of our current bodies. This is because, on this view, the person just is one's own soul and is distinct from the body. If so, the current body possessed is not necessary for that person to exist. If this is all that is necessary, then this is very good news, for surely God is able to construct bodies that duplicate the bodies we currently possess. If so, then it really doesn't matter if our current bodies are completely destroyed. Our existence and identity is not tied to them, so there is not a real resurrection problem.

But what if a duplicate body will not do the trick? What if it turns out that we must have the very same (i.e., numerically identical) body in the resurrection? Such would be the case if it turned out that substance dualism's person/soul identity claim is false. For example, what if some version of materialism is true and our current bodies are essential to our existence and identity? If so, it would seem that a duplicate body would not secure life after death since a numerically distinct body would yield a numerically distinct person. In this case, while the eschaton might have some person there who looks and acts just like you (a phenomenological duplicate), it's not you: it's just a good copy of you. This would be (1) of no comfort for us as we face death and (2) thus a deviation from the promises of Christianity.

Likewise, what if we affirmed the substance dualist's first claim of stuff distinction (the idea that persons have both immaterial souls and material bodies) but, like materialists, reject the substance dualist's claim of person/soul identity? In other words, what if a dualist agreed that there is a difference between bodies and souls but said that the human person is a composite of both? In this case, some person named Bruce *is* his body and his soul. He is not just his soul. It seems like this kind of dualist—let's call this "dualistic holism"—has the same problem that the materialists would have. For both the materialist and the dualistic holist's account of resurrection, what is required is a numerically identical body in the resurrection. While substance dualists have a rather easy time answering the question of resurrection, the materialists and dualistic holists seem to have a much more difficult time. This is because (1) our bodies often experience total destruction after death, and (2) these views require us to get those very same—numerically identical—bodies back. The million-dollar question is whether this is really possible.

As Caroline Bynum Walker notes, one of the most common and popular answers to these questions in the early church was the **reassembly model** of resurrection.[8] On this model, God secures numerically identical bodies for us in the resurrection by going out, retrieving all the old parts that used to compose our bodies, and then reassembling them together into the previous order and structure that once composed our current bodies. In short, God just puts us back together and then reunites our souls (which have been in the presence of Christ in the intermediate state) with the reassembled bodies. As a result, the very same person, Bruce, is once again alive and will now live again forever and ever.

8. See Caroline Bynum Walker, *The Resurrection of the Body in Western Christianity, 200–1336* (New York: Columbia University Press, 1995).

As straightforward and simple as this model seems to be, it does have a rather significant problem that is as old as the theory itself. Namely, what would happen if Bruce's old parts came to compose some other person's, Keith's, body? Perhaps after Bruce died, his body decomposed in the ground, its parts were sucked up as nutrients for an apple tree, and Keith ate one of the apples. It looks as though some parts that once composed Bruce's body now compose Keith's body. In the resurrection, it looks as though God cannot give the numerically same parts to both Bruce and Keith. This same objection dates back to the time of Athenagoras (AD 133–190). Stated in provocative (and somewhat creepy) form, Athenagoras's critics put forward what has come to be known as the cannibal objection. Athenagoras says, "Then to this they tragically add the devouring of offspring perpetrated by people in famine madness, and the children eaten by their own parents through the contrivance of enemies, and the celebrated Median feast, and the tragic banquet of Thyestes; and they add, moreover, other such like unheard-of occurrences which have taken place among Greeks and barbarians."[9] He later adds, "From these things they establish, as they suppose, the impossibility of the Resurrection, on the ground that the same parts cannot rise again with one set of bodies, and with another as well; for that either the bodies of the former possessor cannot be reconstituted, the parts which compose them having passed into others, or that, these having been restored to the former, the bodies of the last possessors will come short."[10]

So what about the scenario that Athenagoras describes? The cannibal objection points to a problem whereby two persons both end up being composed of the same set of parts at different times. For example, what if Bruce's body was composed of parts *a*, *b*, and *c* at the last moment of his life, when he was murdered by Keith, and that on murdering Bruce, Keith decided to eat Bruce's body, thereby consuming parts *a*, *b*, and *c*. Now that Keith's body is composed of parts *a*, *b*, and *c*, it looks as though there is a significant problem for the reassembly model of bodily resurrection. In short, now that two persons' bodies are composed of the numerically same set of parts at the last moments of their lives, it seems impossible that God could raise them both via reassembly and give them both the same sets of parts. One set of parts can constitute only one physical body, not two. Several contemporary philosophers consider this objection to be a defeater for the reassembly model of resurrection.[11]

9. Athenagoras, *The Resurrection of the Dead*, in *Ante-Nicene Fathers*, ed. Alexander Roberts and James Donaldson (Peabody, MA: Hendrickson, 2004), 2:151.

10. Athenagoras, *Resurrection of the Dead*, 2:151.

11. Trenton Merricks, "How to Live Forever without Saving Your Soul: Physicalism and Immortality," in *Soul, Body, and Survival: Essays on the Metaphysics of Human Persons*, ed.

Despite the difficulties that the reassembly model faces, Christian philosophers have not rejected the possibility of life after death in a physical body. They simply offer some alternative ways that such a thing could take place. Philosophers like Peter van Inwagen, Dean Zimmerman, and Kevin Corcoran, for example, offer two different possibilities for life after death in our physical bodies. Before describing two popular examples of this, however, two notes of clarification about their suggestions are vital. First, their accounts are not necessarily accounts of "resurrection" per se. Rather, they are accounts that allow for our bodies to survive the death event in such a way that we can resume living in these bodies in the life to come. Second, their suggestions are offered only as *merely logical possibilities*. In neither case do they think that what they describe is what will actually happen.

So why take such an approach? As van Inwagen declares, "What is important is that God can accomplish it this way or some other [way]."[12] Both van Inwagen and Corcoran contend that such responses disprove the naturalist's claim that "it is impossible" for us to survive death if (1) we need our bodies to survive and (2) our bodies get destroyed through some process or another. The "logically possible" response they offer helps us to identify at least a few ways that it is possible. If we can figure a few ways that it is possible, then surely a God who is omniscient, omnipotent, and perfectly wise can figure out a better way to bring this about. As such, one need not necessarily endorse these approaches in order to use them against the naturalist's accusation that embodied survival of death is impossible given what we know about decomposition and destruction of our physical bodies after death. With these clarifications out of the way, we now consider two different examples of logically possible accounts of bodily persistence.

### *Brain-Snatching Model*

Van Inwagen is a Christian materialist about human persons. He rejects the soul and argues that human persons are the life events that are to be identified with their living organisms. Like others, van Inwagen argues that material beings, such as human persons, continue to exist over time via immanent causal connections. On this view, person *P* persists over time via the causal sequences of $P_1$ at $t_1$ causing $P_2$ at $t_2$, $P_2$ at $t_2$ causing $P_3$ at $t_3$, $P_3$ at $t_3$ causing $P_4$

Kevin Corcoran (Ithaca, NY: Cornell University Press, 2001), 186–87; Kevin Corcoran, *Rethinking Human Nature* (Grand Rapids: Baker Academic, 2006), 124–25.

12. Peter van Inwagen, "The Possibility of Resurrection," *International Journal for Philosophy of Religion* 9, no. 2 (1978): 121.

at $t_4$, and $P_4$ at $t_4$ causing $P_5$ at $t_5$ to exist. So, in other words, the persistence of $P$ over a span of time from, say, $t_1$ to $t_5$ would be as follows:

$$\text{Persistence} = P_1 \rightarrow P_2 \rightarrow P_3 \rightarrow P_4 \rightarrow P_5 \ldots$$

On this view, a person *P* persists over time as long as that person's living organism continues in the causal sequence of personal life and is uninterrupted. If, however, that life is disrupted (i.e., ended in such a way that the individual's organism is disassembled), then that person does not continue. On such an account, van Inwagen rejects the reassembly model of bodily resurrection, arguing that the deconstruction of a person *P*'s body brings an end to that life and therefore breaks the possibility of it causing the organism to persist. Once the life of a person *P* has ended, van Inwagen believes that it is impossible for *P* to come back into existence. He says, "If a man should be totally destroyed, then it is very hard to see how any man who comes into existence thereafter could be the *same* man."[13] As he goes on to explain, any reassembled body in the resurrection would be a person, called *Q*, numerically distinct from the current person *P*, even if *Q* looked just like *P* and was assembled out of *P*'s old parts.

Two important points need to be noted about van Inwagen's view. First, he is a materialist about human persons, which means that for *P* to survive her death, *P* must have a numerically identical body to the current body. A duplicate body will not achieve life after death. Second, for *P*'s body at a later moment to be numerically identical to the current body, there cannot be any temporal gaps in *P*'s life. In other words, the person cannot stop existing. For both of these reasons, van Inwagen thinks that reassembly will not do. So to solve the problem, van Inwagen suggests the logical possibility of brain snatching: "Perhaps at the moment of each man's death, God removes his corpse and replaces it with a simulacrum which is what is burned or rots. Or perhaps God is not quite so wholesale as this: perhaps He removes for 'safekeeping' only the 'core person'—the brain and central nervous system—or even some special part of it. These are details."[14] Again, van Inwagen's point is to say that it is logically possible that such a thing as this could happen. And if this **brain-snatching model** could be possible, then surviving death is not impossible. If it is not impossible, then it is something that God can do, and Christians are justified in believing in life after death.

13. Van Inwagen, "Possibility of Resurrection," 118.
14. Van Inwagen, "Possibility of Resurrection," 121.

### *The Body-Fission Model*

Other philosophers like Dean Zimmerman[15] and Kevin Corcoran[16] have suggested an alternative way—the **body-fission model**—to allow for *P* to survive death if numerical identity is required and there cannot be any temporal gaps in *P*'s life. Suppose, they say, *P*'s body exists at some point ($t_1$) prior to a fission event. Then, at $t_2$ just prior to death, *P*'s body experiences a fission event (it splits into two different bodies). That is, at $t_2$, God allows every particle of our bodies to divide into two distinct particles, and this fission event of particles thereby produces two sets of particles so that each set looks the same as *P*'s body prior to the fission event. Let's call these later bodies produced by the fission event at $t_2$ bodies *Q* and *R*. Suppose further, they say, that one of these sets of particles, *Q*, "takes" the life of *P* and the other set, *R*, does not. We could diagram this as shown in figure 15.1.

Figure 15.1

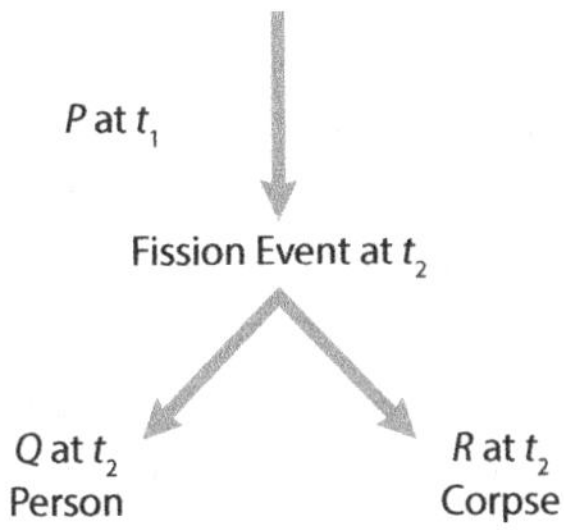


Phenomenologically and Physically, $Q = R$ at $t_2$
Numerically, $Q \neq R$ at $t_2$

If such were the case, then Zimmerman and Corcoran believe that the materialist should have everything needed to account for surviving death and continuing the life of *P*. In this case, they have provided a logically possible way that a body could survive death that is immanently and causally connected to the previous body, making it possible to say that the surviving body *Q* is numerically identical to *P* and that it did not experience a temporal gap.

15. Dean W. Zimmerman, "The Compatibility of Materialism and Survival: The 'Falling Elevator' Model," *Faith and Philosophy* 16, no. 2 (April 1999): 194–213. Unlike van Inwagen and Corcoran, Zimmerman is not himself a materialist about human persons. He simply offers this as a way to achieve bodily survival for our physical bodies.

16. Kevin J. Corcoran, "Persons and Bodies," *Faith and Philosophy* 15, no. 3 (July 1998): 324–40; and Corcoran, "Dualism, Materialism, and the Problem of Postmortem Survival," *Philosophia Christi* 4, no. 2 (2002): 411–25.

Again we should emphasize that such proposals are given only as a way to demonstrate logical possibilities and thus the real possibility of our bodies surviving death. So if we can figure out a way that it could happen, no matter how unlikely our account may be, then surely God can figure out a way to make it happen. As mentioned above, what these accounts give us are not accounts of resurrection per se but rather a demonstration of the logical possibility of our bodies surviving death. As such, if these accounts are successful, materialists might have everything they need to account for life after death.

### *Back to Reassembly*

While the brain-snatching and body-fission models might give us a way for a body to survive death, they do not give us a resurrection. The concept of resurrection entails the idea of a body experiencing death (possibly even being completely destroyed) and then coming back to life at some later time. Therefore, although the brain-snatching and body-fission accounts might argue for some kind of postmortem survival, they do not seem to do justice to the concept of resurrection. Hence, once again, we turn to consider whether the reassembly model should be dismissed so quickly. As we saw, the major problem of this model comes from the possibility that two different physical bodies might be composed of the same set of parts at different times. As the cannibal objection highlights, if the parts that once composed Bruce's body now come to compose Keith's body, then it looks as though God has a problem for resurrecting them both via the reassembly model. After all, God can't give back the same parts to both Bruce and Keith. What should we make of this problem?

Space will allow only a short response to the problem. We admit that the scenario outlined by the cannibal objection is a genuine problem under certain conditions. The question that must be asked is: In order for two bodies separated by time to be numerically identical to each other, must they possess *all and exactly* the same set of parts? Let's call this the "all-and-exactly principle." In other words, suppose that $A$ at $t_1$ is made up of parts $a$, $b$, $c$, and $d$. If $B$ at $t_2$ is to be numerically identical to $A$ at $t_1$, must $B$ at $t_2$ also be made up of parts $a$, $b$, $c$, and $d$? If the answer to that question is yes, then it looks like the cannibal objection defeats the reassembly model. But is the all-and-exactly principle true? Perhaps it is not. What about the changes our bodies experience over time through the normal metabolic process of eating food and eliminating waste? It looks like our bodies are constantly changing parts while also maintaining numerical identity. In other words, our bodies change parts without ceasing to be the very same bodies they were at some earlier time. If so, then our current bodies are not composed of *all and exactly* the same set of parts that once composed them.

So what does this mean for the reassembly model? At minimum, it looks like the cannibal objection is not the defeater for reassembly that some have thought it to be. Perhaps it is not necessary for God to use all and exactly the same set of parts in our reassembled bodies as were once present in our original bodies. Perhaps all that is needed is a sufficient set of the original parts for the eschaton body to be the resurrected body. If those are real possibilities, then it looks like the reassembly model is still in play.

## Conclusion

In this chapter we sought to provide a rationale for a Christian view of life after death. As we saw, such an approach requires us to affirm at least two things. First, it requires us to say something about the possibility of disembodied existence in the intermediate state. Such a possibility requires an immaterial soul, and so we explored various arguments in favor of the soul. Second, a Christian view must also say something about the possibility of bodily resurrection. Here we saw that while the accounts of van Inwagen and Corcoran provide us with a logical possibility of how our bodies might survive death, they are not actually accounts of resurrection. We have also argued that despite the traditional concerns about the reassembly model of resurrection, it is not at all clear that such a model is implausible. It looks as though there is sufficient ground for the possibility of life after death.

# PART 4

# ETHICS

Ethics, the study of morality, is the branch of philosophy that perhaps most people are familiar with. In every age people have wondered about what is right, what is wrong, and how we are supposed to live. Moreover, ethical questions come from all angles and in every aspect of life. Consider a few examples: Politically speaking, we debate the morality of welfare, abortion, public education, taxes, and marital rights. In our personal lives, we take very strong stances on things like marital fidelity, parenting styles, and education choices. Indeed, ethical discussions are an integral aspect of every facet of our lives.

But moral discussions about the above issues represent only one aspect of our ethical considerations. The examples we've just described are good examples of an area within the field of ethics known as **applied ethics**. This field of ethics deals with our ethical decisions about very particular moral questions we face. While this area of ethics is vitally important to us, these are not the kind of questions we will address in the following section. Rather, in this section we hope to survey two other branches of ethics that are a bit more theoretical in nature and therefore serve as the theoretical foundations for applied ethics. In this section we will consider metaethics and normative ethics.

**Metaethics** is a particular branch of philosophy and ethics that is concerned with semantic, metaphysical, and epistemological aspects of morality. For example, regarding semantic questions, metaethics attempts to answer questions about the meaning of moral terms like "goodness," "ought," and "right." Take "goodness" as one instance. If we were to say that little Timmy's actions are "good," what exactly would we mean when we say this? In exactly what way are they "good"? Metaethics also deals with metaphysical questions about the existence of moral values. So, for example, most people tend to think that there are such things as objective moral standards. These would be moral in the sense that they inform our actions and choices. They would be objective in the sense that they don't appear to be based on any cultural or subjective factors that are based on individual people or groups. But if there are such standards, what grounds them? If they don't come from particular peoples or groups, where do they come from? Metaethics attempts to answer these kinds of questions.

In addition to these semantic and metaphysical questions, metaethics also tries to say something about the epistemic conditions of our knowing moral truths. Consider the very commonly held moral belief that it is wrong to murder. Let's assume that this moral claim is true, and let's assume that we know how it is grounded. There is another question that we still need to answer: How do we know that it is wrong to murder? Is this moral truth something we infer from reason, a divine command, a social construction, or something else? Such are the concerns of metaethics. We consider these kinds of questions in chapter 16 and offer a survey of the various ways to explore the issues.

In contrast to metaethics, **normative ethics** is that branch of ethics that deals with the "how" of morality. In other words, normative ethics deals with the various ethical systems that attempt to provide a framework for our moral systems of thought. In chapter 17 we explore three major approaches, with some examples of each along the way. First, we explore the teleological approaches to morality. According to these moral systems, morality is not a matter of rules or rule keeping. Rather, morality is a matter of character or the "end" of our actions. For example, on Aristotle's virtue approach to morality, our primary concern in the moral life is to develop the right character and virtues. By contrast, John Stuart Mill's utilitarianism is focused on the end, outcome, or result of our actions and choices.

Deontological approaches to moral systems take the opposite approach, focusing on the actual rules we follow and actions we take. And once again, there are various schools of thought that fit under this category. According to Immanuel Kant's deontological approach to moral systems, certain rules must be followed and applied to all people. He based this, as we shall see, on something called the categorical imperative. Or, according to divine-command theory, for example, God has commanded particular actions, and the moral life is about following these commands. What is important to note at this point is simply that deontological approaches to morality ground morality in rules to be followed.

One final moral system we consider in our chapter on normative ethics is often referred to as contemporary virtue ethics. As we shall see, thinkers like Alasdair MacIntyre take great exception to the idea that we have been working with the same general notions of morality throughout the course of Western history. In his mind, the trajectory of Western thought has so fragmented our moral categories that it is no longer possible to work within the traditional concepts given to us by the great thinkers within the traditions. MacIntyre, and the contemporary virtue ethicists that follow him, suggest that we should embrace the sociotemporal realities we find ourselves in and work to dialogue with other moral traditions in hope of building a moral system of our own. In his mind, this allows our moral declarations to evolve and expand with the increase of knowledge over time.

These are the kinds of philosophical issues that metaethics and normative ethics deal with. In this section we explore some of these issues in depth by considering the major ideas that have shaped our contemporary discussions and views. Once again, we trust that these chapters will be profitable for you.

# 16

# Metaethics

In the *Republic*, the question arises, Why be moral? What if, Plato asks, you had a magic ring that made you invisible?[1] Would you still be moral if you could do whatever you wanted without being found out or penalized? Plato's own conclusion, after a good deal of dialogue, is that the moral life is inherently valuable. We ought to be moral, according to Plato, because being moral is a great good: the moral life is intrinsically worthwhile.

How you answer this question depends a great deal on your view regarding the nature of reality. For Plato, there is a moral dimension to reality; moral properties are part of the furniture of the world. To put this another way, if you, like Plato, think that, in addition to physical facts, there are mind-independent moral facts, then you will likely think the answer to our question is something to be discovered. The answer depends on the way the world is. If, however, you think that either there are no moral facts or that all moral facts are mind-dependent in some way (indexed to what an individual or group of individuals believe), then you will be tempted to think morality is, in an important sense, an invention.

Ethics is the branch of philosophy that explores morality. The field of ethics can be subdivided into two main areas: normative ethics and metaethics (see fig. 16.1). Normative ethics attempts to answer moral questions and settle issues of *what to do* or *how to be*. Examples of moral questions that normative

1. Glaucon, Plato's brother, raises this question in book 2 of the *Republic* and illustrates the contention that no one is willingly moral with the story about Gyges and the magic ring in 359d–360e. Fans of Middle Earth may be surprised that the idea of an invisibility ring does not originate with J. R. R. Tolkien.

Figure 16.1
**The Field of Ethics**

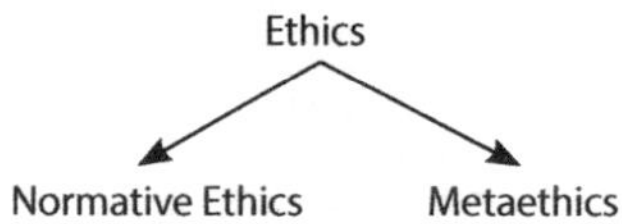


ethics tries to answer include: What makes an action morally right or wrong? What kind of person ought I to be? Is abortion wrong? Is homosexuality permissible? Is courage a virtue? Metaethics, however, attempts to answer *nonmoral* questions about morality. The question of why to be moral is a metaethical question: in asking the question, we are seeking reasons why one ought to adopt the moral point of view.[2] This chapter will focus on metaethics.

In this chapter we survey prominent metaethical theories, noting each theory's account of the nature and existence of moral facts (moral metaphysics), the meaning of moral statements (moral semantics), and the justification for and knowledge of moral statements (moral epistemology).[3] A helpful way to think about subdividing metaethical theories is in terms of the theory's fundamental view of morality as either invented or discovered.[4] **Subjectivist metaethical theories** are antirealist and regard morality as invented. **Objectivist metaethical theories**, alternatively, are realist and regard morality as discovered. Subjectivist metaethical theories can be further subdivided into noncognitive and cognitive, and objectivist metaethical theories can be further subdivided into naturalist and nonnaturalistic (see fig. 16.2).

As we consider each theory, noticing costs and benefits along the way, it will be argued that theistic nonnaturalism is the rationally preferred theory, best accommodating the curious facts, as C. S. Lewis maintains, that "human beings . . . ought to behave in a certain way, . . . [and] they do not in fact behave in that way."[5] We depart from our usual approach of offering an opinionated introduction to the philosophic topic under discussion since in this chapter we are building toward the moral argument for God and will make the case for its soundness.

2. The "ought" here is best understood as a *rational ought*. We are seeking reasons for why someone would be rationally justified in adopting the moral point of view. For more on the distinction between the moral ought and the rational ought, see J. P. Moreland and William Lane Craig, *Philosophical Foundations for a Christian Worldview* (Downers Grove, IL: InterVarsity, 2003), 403–4.

3. For a nice explanation of moral semantics, moral metaphysics, and moral epistemology, see Mark Timmons, *Moral Theory*, 2nd ed. (Lanham, MD: Rowman & Littlefield, 2013), 19.

4. David McNaughton, *Moral Vision* (Cambridge, MA: Blackwell, 1988), 3–16.

5. C. S. Lewis, *Mere Christianity* (San Francisco: HarperOne, 2001), 8.

Figure 16.2

**Metaethical Theories**

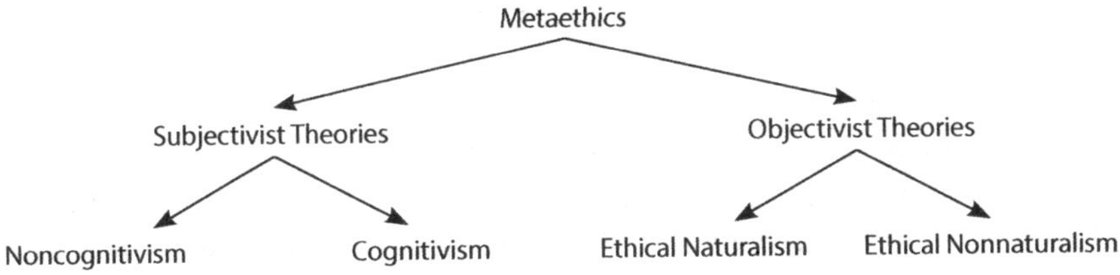


## Subjectivist Theories

Subjectivist metaethical theories all agree that moral properties are not part of the mind-independent world. Rather, morality is grounded in the beliefs (cognitive states) or attitudes (noncognitive states) of individuals or groups of individuals. When it comes to the nature and meaning of moral statements, noncognitivist and cognitivist theories significantly differ. The noncognitivist denies, whereas the cognitivist affirms, that moral statements are indicative statements and thus can be either true or false. Consider the sentence "The dog is brown." This sentence is in the indicative mood: it purports to be about reality. It asserts the existence of a particular substance—a dog—that has a property, *being brown*. The sentence has, as philosophers like to put it, ontological import. Additionally, as an indicative sentence, it can be either true or false.

In the same way, it is natural to think that moral statements, such as the sentence "Murder is wrong," also have ontological implications and can be either true or false. The noncognitivist denies all of this. Moral statements are not indicative: they do not represent reality. Since moral statements do not express genuine facts, they cannot be either true or false.

### *Noncognitivism*

Two prominent versions of **noncognitivism** are emotivism and prescriptivism. According to **emotivism**, moral statements are expressions of emotion. To say "Murder is wrong" expresses a feeling of disapproval toward murder. Alternatively, to say "Truth-telling is right" expresses a feeling of approval toward truth-telling. As the prominent twentieth-century emotivist A. J. Ayer puts it, "The function of the relevant ethical word is purely 'emotive.' It is used to express feeling about certain objects, but not to make any assertion about them."[6]

6. A. J. Ayer, *Language, Truth, and Logic* (New York: Dover, 1952), 108. There is a prescriptive element in Ayer's emotivism: moral statements are also used to stimulate similar feelings in others

According to **prescriptivism**, moral statements function as commands: "Murder is wrong" means "Do not murder"; "Truth-telling is right" means "Tell the truth." Moral statements, for the prescriptivist, are imperatives that prescribe actions.

Noncognitivism fails to adequately account for the nature of morality for at least three reasons. First, the denial that moral statements can be true or false is problematic. The claim that "It is wrong to kill babies for fun" is plausibly true. The claim that "It is right to dedicate one's life to the counting of peas in a pan" (as the asthmatic Spaniard did in Camus's *The Plague*) is plausibly false. That we are sometimes correct and incorrect in our moral judgments attests to the reality of genuine moral facts.[7] But if noncognitivism is correct that there are no moral facts, then our moral judgments regarding such things as the torture of babies and a life devoted to counting peas are beyond reproach, mere expressions of attitudes, which cannot be true or false. This result, to say the least, is counterintuitive.

Second, noncognitivism fails to adequately capture the nature of moral disagreement. Since moral judgments lack cognitive content, moral disagreements are recast as being about what to do instead of about what to believe. But notice that the noncognitivist cannot offer reasons for one course of action over another. Moral disagreements become, as Alasdair MacIntyre explains, "a clash of antagonistic wills, each determined by some set of arbitrary choices of its own."[8] But our actual moral discourse suggests otherwise. There is a "nearly universal appearance" in moral disagreement of "an exercise of our rational powers."[9] In other words, the fact that we argue for the truth of our moral statements is hard to square with the claim, made by the noncognitivist, that moral disagreement is merely a clash of wills, devoid of rational content. Any metaethical theory that removes even the possibility of rational engagement from our moral discourse is implausible, oversimplifying the nature of moral arguments and reducing attempts to influence behavior to a form of manipulation.

Finally, there is the "embedding problem," the problem of figuring out the meaning of complex sentences that embed simpler moral sentences and moral terms.[10] Consider conditional sentences, such as "If Brett Favre throws

---

and encourage them to act accordingly. For another prominent twentieth-century defense of emotivism, see C. L. Stevenson, *Ethics and Language* (New Haven: Yale University Press, 1944).

7. James Rachels, *The Elements of Moral Philosophy*, 6th ed., with Stuart Rachels (New York: McGraw-Hill, 2010), 38–39.

8. Alasdair MacIntyre, *After Virtue*, 3rd ed. (Notre Dame, IN: University of Notre Dame Press, 2007), 9.

9. MacIntyre, *After Virtue*, 9, 11.

10. Also sometimes called the Frege-Geach problem. For a helpful discussion of the problem, see Mark van Roojen, *Metaethics* (New York: Routledge, 2015), 149–50.

the ball, then the Green Bay Packers will win." Conditional sentences are complex, composed of two simpler sentences and a connective. In our sample sentence, "Brett Favre throws the ball" and "the Green Bay Packers will win" are the simple sentences, and "if . . . then" is the connective; it connects the two simple sentences into a complex sentence that is a conditional.

The problem for the noncognitivist is that moral terms can appear in conditional sentences without expressing any emotion of the speaker (or prescribing any action). Consider the following argument (inspired by the television show *Gotham*):

1. If murder is wrong, then getting Jim Gordon to murder is wrong.
2. Murder is wrong.
3. Therefore, getting Jim Gordon to murder is wrong.

The argument appears valid. For the argument to avoid committing the fallacy of equivocation, the moral terms (in this case "is wrong") must have the same meaning in each of the statements 1–3. However, the moral term "is wrong" expresses disapproval (on emotivism) only in statement 2. The problem is that moral terms don't function to express disapproval when embedded in complex sentences (such as conditionals). To see this more clearly, if "Murder is wrong" means "Boo! Murder" as the emotivist claims, then the above argument becomes incoherent:

1′ If "Boo! Murder," then getting Jim Gordon to "Boo! Murder."
2′ "Boo! Murder."
3′ Therefore, getting Jim Gordon to "Boo! Murder."

The challenge for the noncognitivist is to provide an account of moral semantics that enables the meaning of moral sentences to remain the same whether freestanding or embedded. While there are attempts by noncognitivists to meet this challenge, many think this problem, along with the others, renders the theory implausible.[11]

### *Cognitivism*

Cognitivist views of subjectivist theories hold moral statements to be either true or false. According to **simple subjectivism**, the truth value of a moral

11. For a nice discussion of noncognitivist responses to the embedding problem, see van Roojen, *Metaethics*, 150–56.

statement depends on the belief of the individual, and the belief of the individual is based on the individual's psychological state. Thus the truths of morality turn out to be truths of psychology. If Jones believes that the claim "Abortion is wrong" is true, then Jones disapproves of abortion, and "abortion is wrong" for Jones. If Smith believes the claim "Abortion is wrong" is false, then Smith approves of abortion, and abortion is right for Smith. Notice that, according to simple subjectivism, whatever an individual believes to be true is true (for that person).

This feature of simple subjectivism leads to bizarre consequences. First, if mere belief, albeit grounded in a psychological state, is sufficient to make something true, then the individual believer is infallible, not able to go wrong; to believe *X* (because *X* is approved) is to make *X* true. This is why subjectivism is also antirealist: moral truths depend on the subjective states (attitudes and beliefs) of the individual, not mind-independent facts in the world. The problem, however, is that individuals are not infallible. Their fallibility is shown by everyday experience: we can be and often are wrong about many things. Second, simple subjectivism entails relativism, rendering moral disagreement pointless since everyone is right and all beliefs are true by virtue of a person holding them.

**Cultural relativism** trades individual infallibility for group infallibility. According to cultural relativism, whatever a group of individuals (or usually, the majority of a group of individuals) believe to be true is true for them. Like simple subjectivism, what a group of individuals believes to be true is based on the psychological state of the individuals within the group. For example, the moral judgment that an action is wrong would be true if most members of the relevant group disapproved of the action.

We might ask, however: Is it wise to trade individual infallibility for group infallibility? It seems not. History attests to the fact that groups of individuals have been wrong about many things, including the morality of slavery, the moral status of women or Jews, and the so-called divine right of kings. Moreover, the question of which group of individuals constitute the relevant group for rendering moral judgments is notoriously difficult to specify. Neither simple subjectivism nor cultural relativism offers an adequate treatment of the nature of morality.[12] The main difficulty—for all versions of subjectivism—is that the beliefs and various psychological states of individuals or groups of individuals do not provide a firm enough foundation to ground our moral intuitions and experience. For this reason, many are attracted to objectivist

12. For a more fine-grained discussion of versions of subjectivism that have evolved in response to objections like those noted above, see van Roojen, *Metaethics*, 99–140.

metaethical theories that hold morality to be a discoverable feature of the world: morality is objective, something completely independent of anyone's attitudes or beliefs. It is to objectivist metaethical theories that we now turn.

## Objectivist Theories

Objectivist theories are cognitivist and realist metaethical theories: moral judgments express beliefs that can be true or false, and these beliefs are about discoverable features of the world. For example, according to objectivist theories, the claim "Murder is wrong" picks out a genuine moral property, the property of *being wrong*, that attaches to the act of murder, and the moral judgment is true if in fact murder is wrong. Likewise, the claim "Truth-telling is right" picks out a genuine moral property, the property of *being right*, that attaches to the act of truth-telling, and the moral judgment is true if in fact truth-telling is right.

Granted, this moral reality is a bit mysterious: moral facts seem to be different from everyday physical facts. Still, the objectivist argues, belief in the reality of a distinct moral realm is justified in order to make sense of our common beliefs regarding morality.[13] The two major versions of objectivist theories differ on the nature of moral properties. The ethical naturalist says the moral properties we ascribe to persons or acts are not as mysterious as they initially appear: rather, they are reducible to natural (meaning nonmoral) properties. The ethical nonnaturalist, however, says moral properties are irreducible.

### *Ethical Naturalism*

Attempts to reduce or define one thing in terms of something else are common in philosophy. In the debate over properties, for example, the nominalist attempts to reduce properties to classes of charactered objects (class nominalism) or classes of objects that resemble charactered objects (resemblance class nominalism). In philosophy of mind, some materialists offer a reductive analysis of mental properties in terms of physical properties; mental properties are just C-fiber firings in the brain. In the debate over causation, the Humean offers a reductive analysis of causation in terms of one type of event regularly following another type of event; causation is just the regular succession of types of events. In these examples, and many others, *X* is reducible to *Y* if and only if *X* can be defined by or identified with *Y*.

13. For a nice discussion of the phenomena of morality that lead to a presumption of moral realism—e.g., moral agreement and disagreement, moral mistakes, and moral progress—see Andrew Fisher, *Metaethics: An Introduction* (New York: Routledge, 2014), 56–60.

For the ethical naturalist, moral properties are identified with natural properties, properties that are the subject matter of the natural sciences such as biology, psychology, or sociology. For example, the term "right" in the moral judgment "X is right" could mean one of the following, according to the ethical naturalist: "conducive for survival" or "pleasurable" or "what is approved by most people."[14] A virtue of **ethical naturalism** then is that moral properties are not so mysterious after all. They are safely located within the bounds of the naturalistic universe, empirically measurable in the same way that other natural properties, such as mass and velocity, are measurable.

The main problem with ethical naturalism is that it doesn't adequately account for the normative nature of morality. Given the fact that cheating is wrong, it follows that you ought not to cheat. Given the fact that it is right to keep promises, it follows that you should keep your promises. In other words, when we make moral judgments, there is an inherent oughtness to the judgment, and it is for this reason that we rightly ascribe blame or praise to our actions. The problem for the ethical naturalist is that natural properties are not normative: they don't motivate us in the right way. They don't tell us what we ought to do or what is worth pursuing or what reasons we have for doing anything. Normativity is the ethical naturalist's Achilles' heel, according to the philosopher Alvin Plantinga: "There is no room, within naturalism, for right and wrong, or good or bad."[15] Given the action-guiding nature of moral properties, there are good reasons to think they are not natural properties. In other words, if moral properties exist, as the moral realist insists, then there are good reasons to think they are nonnatural.

### *Ethical Nonnaturalism*

Throughout the mid-twentieth century, **ethical nonnaturalism** was not viewed as a viable option. Of late, however, due to the work of Russ Shafer-Landau and Terence Cuneo, ethical nonnaturalism is making a comeback.[16] It is now considered a metaethical view worthy of serious consideration.

14. Moreland and Craig, *Philosophical Foundations*, 401. For a more detailed discussion of how ethical naturalists go about reducing moral properties to natural properties, including the a priori methods of Frank Jackson's "Canberra Plan" and the a posteriori methods of the so-called Cornell realists, see Fisher, *Metaethics*, 60–70; and van Roojen, *Metaethics*, 210–52.

15. Alvin Plantinga, "Afterword," in *The Analytic Theist: An Alvin Plantinga Reader*, ed. James Sennett (Grand Rapids: Eerdmans, 1998), 356, quoted in Fisher, *Metaethics*, 75.

16. See especially Russ Shafer-Landau, *Moral Realism: A Defense* (Oxford: Clarendon, 2003); and Terence Cuneo and Russ Shafer-Landau, "The Moral Fixed Points: New Directions for Moral Nonnaturalism," *Philosophical Studies* 17, no. 1 (2014): 399–443.

Shafer-Landau's central claim is that there are moral truths and moral properties that exist as fundamental aspects of reality and are discoverable a priori. We don't discover the morality of genocide or rape, for example, by empirical methods. Thus moral judgments and moral properties are not reducible to the deliverances of the natural sciences. There are sui generis nonnatural moral properties that are intrinsically action-guiding.

Versions of ethical nonnaturalism divide, however, on the question of how to best account for moral properties. The **theistic ethical nonnaturalist** claims that God's existence is the best explanation for moral properties. The **atheistic ethical nonnaturalist**, alternatively, argues that moral properties are brute realities; there is no need to postulate a divine being in order to account for objective morality. In the remainder of this chapter, we shall consider the relationship between God and morality. In doing so, we also fulfill a promissory note issued in chapter 12 to further explore the moral argument for God's existence.

The moral argument for God can be formulated as follows:

1. If God does not exist, there are no objective moral properties.
2. Objective moral properties exist.
3. Therefore, God exists.

Moral arguments for God have a rich history, defended by thinkers as diverse as Plato, Aquinas, and Kant, and more recently by C. S. Lewis, Richard Swinburne, William Lane Craig, and Mark Linville.[17]

The moral argument begins by highlighting the inadequacy of atheism to ground objective morality: if God doesn't exist, then there are no objective moral properties. Atheists who think objective morality stands or falls with the question of God are not hard to find. The atheist Bertrand Russell (1872–1970), for example, argues that if God does not exist and humans are just the "outcome of accidental collocations of atoms," then there is no objective morality.[18] All we can do, according to Russell, is build our lives on "the firm foundation of unyielding despair."[19] Russell's way out of the moral

17. Lewis's classic defense of the moral argument is given in *Mere Christianity*, chaps. 1–5. See also Richard Swinburne, *The Existence of God* (Oxford: Oxford University Press, 2004), chap. 9; William Lane Craig, *Reasonable Faith*, 3rd ed. (Wheaton: Crossway, 2008), 172–83; and Mark D. Linville, "The Moral Argument," in *The Blackwell Companion to Natural Theology*, ed. William Lane Craig and J. P. Moreland (West Sussex: Wiley-Blackwell, 2009), 392–448.

18. Bertrand Russell, "A Free Man's Worship," in *Why I Am Not a Christian* (New York: Touchstone, 1957), 107.

19. Russell, "Free Man's Worship," 107.

argument, then, is to reject premise 2 and the claim that there are objective moral properties. Russell argues that moral properties are subjective; morality is a matter of personal taste. But what if the atheist is convinced of **moral realism** and thus accepts premise 2? Are there plausible atheistic accounts of morality that do not require the existence of God as the ontological ground of objective morality? In other words, what resources are available to the atheist to plausibly deny premise 1?

As might be expected, there are naturalistic and nonnaturalistic attempts to ground objective morality apart from God. The most plausible naturalistic attempt to ground objective morality appeals to human flourishing. On this view, the "good" is whatever contributes to human flourishing, and the "bad" is whatever doesn't. The problem with this view is that it is arbitrary and implausible.[20] It is arbitrary because, given atheism, it is hard to justify giving priority to humans instead of aardvarks or ants. Given the conjunction of naturalism and atheism, there is no difference in intrinsic value between any species. Thus there is no good reason to think human flourishing, as opposed to aardvark or ant flourishing, is the relevant domain for morality.

The attempt to ground morality in human flourishing is implausible because it is not always the case that what contributes to human flourishing is good and what doesn't is bad. Consider the police officer who, in order to quell a citywide riot, has to kill one vigilante.[21] Surely quelling a citywide rebellion is conducive to human flourishing if anything is, yet it would be wrong for the police officer to kill one vigilante to satisfy the mob's lust for blood. Alternatively, consider the firefighter who rushes into a burning building to save a child. The child's life is spared, but both the child and the firefighter are badly burned and will suffer a great deal for the rest of their lives. It would seem that the act of rushing into the fire, while conducive to human survival, was not conducive, in this case, to human flourishing, yet no one would argue that what the firefighter did was bad. Thus the atheist's attempt to ground morality in human flourishing gives us the wrong result.

The most plausible atheistic attempt to ground objective morality is, in our view, Platonic Atheism. Erick Wielenberg argues for a metaethical view amenable to Platonic Atheism called "*non-natural non-theistic moral realism*."[22]

20. William Lane Craig, *On Guard* (Colorado Springs: David C. Cook, 2010), 138.

21. The example is from C. Stephen Evans, *Natural Signs and the Knowledge of God* (Oxford: Oxford University Press, 2010), 119.

22. See Erick J. Wielenberg, "In Defense of Non-natural Non-theistic Moral Realism," *Faith and Philosophy* 26, no. 1 (2009): 23–41 (emphasis in original). More recently, Wielenberg has dubbed his view "non-theistic robust normative realism." See Wielenberg, *Robust Ethics: The Metaphysics and Epistemology of Godless Normative Realism* (New York: Oxford University Press, 2014).

It is a version of moral realism because it endorses objective moral properties. It is nonnatural in that it endorses the view that brute ethical facts and properties are sui generis, not reducible to purely natural facts and properties. It is nontheistic because objective moral properties do not require a theistic foundation. While Wielenberg's nonnatural nontheistic moral realism doesn't entail atheism (a theist could endorse such a view),[23] it does provide another option for the atheist to respond to premise 1 of the moral argument. Add to Wielenberg's nonnatural nontheistic moral realism the claim that God does not exist, and the result is Platonic Atheism.

If Platonic Atheism is true, then premise 1 in the moral argument is false. Objective morality is a brute fact. As Wielenberg puts it: "[Basic ethical facts] are the foundation of (the rest of) objective morality and rest on no foundation themselves. To ask of such facts, 'where do they come from?' or 'on what foundation do they rest?' is misguided in much the way that, according to many theists, it is misguided to ask of God, 'where does He come from?' or 'on what foundation does He rest?' The answer is the same in both cases: They come from nowhere, and nothing external to themselves grounds their existence."[24] Since both theists and atheists posit a "bottom floor of objective morality" that "ultimately rests on nothing,"[25] there is no reason to prefer the theistic foundation to the atheistic foundation.

In reply, theists such as J. P. Moreland and William Lane Craig criticize Platonic Atheism as unintelligible:

> It is difficult, however, even to comprehend this view. What does it mean to say, for example, that the moral value *justice* just exists? It is hard to know what to make of this. . . . Moral values seem to exist as properties of persons, not as mere abstractions—or at any rate, it is hard to know what it is for a moral value to exist as a mere abstraction. [Platonic Atheists] seem to lack any adequate foundation in reality for moral values but just leave them floating in an unintelligible way.[26]

Wielenberg notes that Moreland and Craig's objection boils down to two claims: (1) all values are properties of persons, and (2) all values have external foundations. Wielenberg simply rejects both claims: "[Moreland and Craig]

23. See, e.g., Keith Yandell, "Moral Essentialism," in *God and Morality: Four Views*, ed. R. Keith Loftin (Downers Grove, IL: IVP Academic, 2012), chap. 3; and Yandell, "God and Propositions," in *Beyond the Control of God? Six Views on the Problem of God and Abstract Objects*, ed. Paul M. Gould (New York: Bloomsbury, 2014), chap. 1.

24. Wielenberg, "Non-natural Non-theistic Moral Realism," 26.

25. Wielenberg, "Non-natural Non-theistic Moral Realism," 40.

26. Moreland and Craig, *Philosophical Foundations*, 492.

provide no arguments for such principles."[27] Moreover, argues Wielenberg, in adopting a version of the divine-command theory, Moreland and Craig violate claim 2, since God is the ultimate brute fact; as a being *worthy* of worship, the ethical fact of *being worthy* is also a brute fact. Given nonnatural nontheistic moral realism, according to Wielenberg, "from valuelessness, value sometimes comes."[28]

In reply, it should be noted that Wielenberg is partially correct: even in theism there are brute ethical facts. This worry is a bit of a red herring, however. The issue isn't whether there are ethical brute facts. Explanation must stop somewhere. The salient issue concerns the appropriateness of the stopping point for explanation. The theist argues that God, as a personal being worthy of worship, is the appropriate stopping point for explanation. God exists *a se* (from himself) as the omniscient, omnipotent, wholly good creator and sustainer of all distinct reality. Therefore moral properties and obligations that attach to finite agents and acts are ultimately grounded in God himself, a morally perfect personal being who is the source of all distinct moral reality.

The issue between the theist and the Platonic Atheist boils down to the question of stopping points. Which is a better stopping point to ground moral facts: God or Platonic moral properties? We find the following consideration persuasive on behalf of theism. Consider that I (Paul) am under no obligation to my chair to weigh less than five hundred pounds. If I did weigh five hundred pounds and sat on my chair and it broke, I would not have wronged the chair. Granted, it would be unfortunate that the chair broke, but I am not obligated to the chair to not sit in it if I were to weigh five hundred pounds. (I might have obligations to myself and others not to weigh five hundred pounds, but not to things such as chairs.) I do, however, have obligations to my students: to tell the truth, to treat them fairly, to not steal their money, and so on. We may ask, Why am I obligated to my students but not to my chair? A plausible answer is that we are obligated to persons, not to things. But according to Platonic Atheism, at rock bottom, my obligations are to things: Platonic moral properties such as the property *being just* or *being honest* or *being fair* and the like. This story strikes many as implausible. We are obligated to people partly because value ultimately resides in persons. Theism accounts for this common moral intuition. Moral properties are ultimately grounded in the supreme person, God himself. The only brute fact is that God exists and has the moral character he has. This, we submit, is the proper stopping place for explanation. Thus theism, and not Platonic Atheism, best explains the fact of objective morality.

27. Wielenberg, "Non-natural Non-theistic Moral Realism," 34.
28. Wielenberg, "Non-natural Non-theistic Moral Realism," 40n68.

It is false that "from valuelessness, value sometimes comes," as Wielenberg suggests. Rather, reality is fundamentally valuable because God exists and is morally perfect. Moreover, the fact that there is a moral law that we constantly fail to live up to provides further reason for thinking *Christian* theism to be true, for only in Christianity does God provide the remedy for humanity's moral failure. Through Christ, a payment has been made for our wrongdoing, and thus the possibility for forgiveness of sins and moral wholeness is offered to all who would believe.

The upshot is this: There is a sound argument from the existence of nonnatural moral properties to the existence of God. Thus, of all the metaethical theories canvassed in this chapter, some version of theistic ethical nonnaturalism is the rationally preferred theory.

## Conclusion

In this chapter we have explored the nature of morality and moral statements. The realist thinks that morality is part of the furniture of the world and that moral facts are discoverable. The anti-realist thinks that morality is not part of mind-independent reality; moral facts are invented. We have argued that there are good reasons to think morality is an objective and discoverable feature of the world. We also think, as we have briefly canvassed, there is a good (and sound) argument from the reality of objective moral properties to God. In the end, it is a good thing that God is the source of the moral law even as humans fail to uphold it. Tragedy and failure don't get the last word. God, in his goodness and mercy, has provided a remedy for our failures through Jesus Christ.

# 17

# Normative Ethics

Roughly speaking, morality is about good and bad action, or, to state it another way, it is about right and wrong. But as we jump into these discussions, we quickly find that things are a bit more complex, since there are unique categories of moral questions and various theories that seek to provide the answers to such questions. For example, in the last chapter we introduced the distinction between two branches of ethical inquiry: metaethics and normative ethics. As we suggested there, metaethics is the branch of ethics that deals with the nonmoral (or perhaps largely philosophical) questions concerning morality. So, for example, metaethics deals with semantic questions about goodness: What does it mean to be good? Metaethics also deals with epistemological questions: How do we know what is good? And finally, metaethics deals with metaphysical moral questions: What is the basis of morality? Why should we be good?

By contrast, normative ethics, the focus of this chapter, deals with questions regarding the "how" of morality. In other words, in normative ethics we concern ourselves most centrally with questions about the way of doing morality. Within this inquiry, normative ethics divides into two further general categories: moral theory and applied ethics. Applied ethics is that branch of normative ethics that tries to answer very specific moral questions like these: Is abortion morally acceptable? How should we treat animals? Is sex before marriage permissible? Should we use the death penalty in the case of murder? Moral theory, the second branch of normative ethics, deals with systems of thought that try to provide a pathway for doing morality itself. Or, as Mark

Timmons has put it, moral theory "attempts to answer very general moral questions about what to do and how to be."[1]

In this chapter we will explore the branch of normative ethics known as moral theory. We will explore three broad approaches to moral theory, including teleological, deontological, and contemporary virtue ethics. In each case we will outline distinct versions of each approach. We will begin with the teleological accounts of moral theory.

## Teleological Theories

When people think about morality, they typically think in terms of right actions, commands, or mandates of some kind. For example, to be moral, one might think, is to avoid doing bad things and instead to do good things. But this is not the way teleological models of moral theory conceive of morality. Indeed, **teleological accounts of morality** build on the notion of *telos* (Greek for "purpose" or "goal"), and suggest that morality be thought of in terms of certain kinds of goals or outcomes, not in terms of actions per se. As John Frame explains, "This tradition understands ethics as a selection of goals and of means to reach those goals."[2] But aside from this general point of agreement, as we will see, the selected teleological moral theories seek to achieve this in different ways. Below we outline Aristotle's virtue account, egoism, and utilitarianism.

### *Aristotle's Virtue Ethics*

Aristotle was a pupil of Plato and one of the greatest philosophers of all time. He wrote on virtually every discipline possible, including physics, metaphysics, the soul, poetics, rhetoric, politics, economics, and ethics.[3] In his *Nicomachean Ethics*, Aristotle offers his teleological account that builds on the concept of virtue. Like other teleological accounts, **Aristotelian virtue ethics** begins with a particular kind of outcome or end that we are to seek. In his case, it the notion of *eudaimonia*, a Greek term often rendered in English as "happiness." But by "happiness," Aristotle does not mean pleasure. Rather, eudaemonia (English spelling) suggests something deeper and more meaningful: it means something more along the lines of well-being or excellence of the soul. What Aristotle suggests is that life in general, and morality

1. Mark Timmons, *Moral Theory*, 2nd ed. (Lanham, MD: Rowman & Littlefield, 2013), 17.
2. John M. Frame, *The Doctrine of the Christian Life* (Phillipsburg, NJ: P&R, 2008), 91.
3. Aristotle, *The Complete Works of Aristotle*, ed. Jonathan Barnes, 2 vols. (Princeton: Princeton University Press, 1984).

in particular, is about achieving the goal of eudaemonia. But how is this done? For Aristotle, the answer lies within virtue and virtuous living. But what are virtues, and how do they help us to achieve eudaemonia?

To understand what a virtue is, we must also say something about its opposite, vice. Both virtues and vices are characteristics or qualities of some kind. In other words, virtues and vices are characteristics that are true of us, or qualities that we possess. Even though virtues and vices are characteristics true of a person, there are very different kinds of characteristics that can be true of a person. Simply put, a vice is some negative characteristic of a person that is debilitating, destructive, or problem-producing in nature. If a person has a vice, possessing some negative characteristic, then that person and all the closely connected people will suffer from the difficulties that come in the wake of that vice. So, for example, we might say that a person has a vice of "being quick tempered." Because of this vice, the person may be prone to lose jobs, destroy relationships, hurt people, or even commit a crime in a rage of anger. The result of the vice is that it hurts or hinders in some way. By contrast, a virtue is some positive characteristic of a person that is life-producing, beneficial, or helpful in nature. If a person has a virtue, some positive characteristic, then that person and all the closely connected people will benefit from that displayed virtue. One other important note should be made about the concepts of virtue and vice. While they are in some sense opposites, they are not necessarily *polar* opposites, with virtue on one side and vice on the other. Rather, it is better to think of virtue as being situated in the middle, and vice being expressed in two polar opposite directions from it. We could diagram this as shown in figure 17.1.

As the diagram visually lays out, Aristotle recognizes that for each virtue there were two opposing vices that move away from each other. He says that virtue is the "mean between two vices, one of excess and one of deficiency."[4] That is, for each virtue, there are vices of excess and vices of deficiency. Consider, for example, the virtue of courage. There are at least two ways that character can be corrupted in opposition to the virtue of courage. On the one hand, there is the utter lack of courage. Cowardice, for instance, is a vice that opposes the virtue of courage. We call it a vice of deficiency because it lacks what courage provides. On the other hand, the vice of rashness is also an opposing vice to courage. In this case, however, it overshoots the concept of courage by being too eager to fight. Courage then is that middle characteristic between the vices of excess and deficiency. Thus Aristotle refers to virtue as

4. Aristotle, *Nicomachean Ethics*, trans. Terrence Irwin, 2nd ed. (Indianapolis: Hackett, 1999), 1107a.

Figure 17.1
**Aristotle on Virtue**

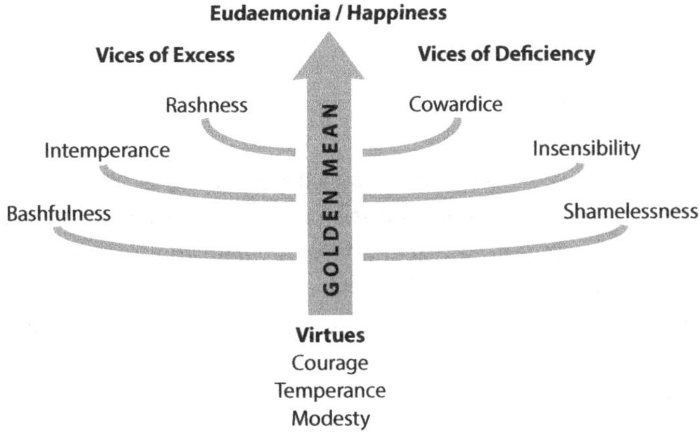


"the **golden mean**," since it produces the right qualities of a person set between the vices of excess and deficiency. By virtue—a positive characteristic that is in contrast to a respective vice—one is able to achieve eudaemonia.

One of the benefits of Aristotle's approach is that it recognizes the need for internal goodness within a person. It is entirely possible for a person to perform good actions and still be rotten on the inside. While such a person may satisfy the expectations and needs of others, surely this is not enough to instantiate true goodness. Aristotle's contention that the character of a person is vital to goodness is helpful and instructive. Critics, however, have suggested that his system inevitably falls back into some kind of rule-based ethic.

Consider how this might be the case. Suppose I am to develop the virtue of courage. How might this virtue develop in me? It seems that I can't develop this virtue by simple reflection or will. I can develop this virtue only in situations that call for me to be courageous. So, for example, imagine that I see a bully roughing up a smaller kid on the playground. To be courageous means that I must go and do something about it. I must stand up to the bully and protect the smaller kid. But if this is true, isn't there some rule that I am obeying after all? Isn't it the case that I am only courageous inasmuch as I follow the rule of "protecting the weak" and that developing the virtue of courage needs rules for such development? As it turns out, Aristotle was well aware of this issue, and his response demonstrates that his view is actually rather balanced. He recognizes that there are certain kinds of actions that need to be performed and certain kinds of actions that need to be avoided. He says, "That is why we need to have had the appropriate upbringing—right from early youth, as Plato says—to make us find enjoyment or pain in the right things."[5]

### *Egoism*

Another variation of teleological moral theory is **egoism**. This is the view that understands morality in terms of the well-being of oneself. Like other teleological views, it rejects the idea that there is some objective moral standard or set of commands that must be obeyed at all costs; instead, it argues that an outcome of some particular kind is what is important to moral thinking. Unique to this teleological view, however, is the idea that what a person should do is consider one's own personal interests in the decision-making. While Aristotle's virtue account was concerned with the well-being of a person, it was not essentially egocentric in the way that egoism turns out. As the twentieth-century naturalist Ayn Rand (1905–82) put it, man "must live for his own sake, neither sacrificing himself to others nor sacrificing others to himself. To live for his own sake means that the achievement of his own happiness is man's highest moral purpose."[6] If such a position sounds radical, it is because it is radical. James Rachels describes it this way: "Ethical egoism does not say that one should promote one's own interest as well as the interests of others. . . . Ethical egoism is the radical view that one's only duty is to promote one's own interests."[7] For many individuals, this radical ethical notion seems hard to accept. But Scott Rae describes the rationale behind it.[8] As Rae notes, egoists have typically argued that (1) looking out for others is generally "a self-defeating pursuit," (2) egoism is "the only moral system that respects the integrity" of individuals, and (3) egoism is the "hidden unity underlying our widely accepted moral duties."[9]

Before moving on from egoism, there are two points of clarification about what such a radical view doesn't entail. First, as Rachels notes, while egoism understands one's own personal interests as the sole moral principle of concern, this does not mean that egoism is necessarily against helping other people and at times looking out for their concerns. After all, there are certainly times in our lives when helping someone else is actually beneficial to us. For example, I might choose to help the man on the side of the road who has a

5. Aristotle, *Nicomachean Ethics* 1105b.
6. Ayn Rand, *The Virtue of Selfishness*, 50th anniv. ed. (New York: Signet, 2014), 30.
7. James Rachels, *The Elements of Moral Philosophy* (New York: McGraw-Hill, 1999), 84.
8. See Scott B. Rae, *Moral Choices: An Introduction to Ethics* (Grand Rapids: Zondervan, 2009). Just to clarify, in providing the rationale behind it, Rae is in no way endorsing this view.
9. Rae, *Moral Choices*, 70.

flat tire because I know that he is president of my company and this would make a good impression on him. Or I might give a sandwich to the homeless person on the street because I know that my companion is watching and will think highly of me for doing such things. So then, as long as helping others helps me in some way, egoism is not against helping others. In this sense, egoism is deeply consequentialist.

Second, egoism also doesn't entail the idea that we should always do what we want to do, since it is often the case that doing what we want to do can lead to harm for us and go against our best interest as a result. For example, if I always did what I want, I'd have ice cream seven times a day and would be incredibly unhealthy. Or if I always did what I most want, I might sleep until noon every day. But if I did this, I wouldn't have a job. So then, while egoism makes moral thinking a matter of personal, and only personal, concern, it doesn't entail that we should never help others or that we should always do what we most want.[10]

The radical theory of egoism is rather difficult to embrace. Nevertheless, egoism's contention—that when all is said and done, self-interest is what actually motivates all of our ethical theories—is insightful. Whatever other moral obligations we may affirm, it is true that we are often concerned with ourselves. But this insight is only partial. Sure, we may be motivated by self-interest, but we are also motivated by plenty more beyond that. When a soldier throws himself on a grenade to save the life of his friend, it seems we can safely say two things: (1) such action is morally praiseworthy, and (2) whatever it is that makes it praiseworthy, it is not merely self-interest. Furthermore, as critics have been right to point out, if egoism were universally accepted, it would lead to absolute anarchy and chaos.[11] When all we have is concern for ourselves, society is destroyed.

### *Utilitarianism*

**Utilitarianism**, initiated by Jeremy Bentham (1748–1832) and popularized by John Stuart Mill (1806–73), is another version of teleological moral theory in that its focus is on the effect of our actions and choices. It contends that morality is judged by the results that follow from our actions, not the nature of the action itself. As such, it rejects the idea of an objective moral standard for our action and locates morality in outcomes. Unlike egoism, however, utilitarianism is concerned with what is good for other people as well as for

10. Rae, *Moral Choices*, 70.

11. Arthur F. Holmes, *Ethics: Approaching Moral Decisions* (Downers Grove, IL: IVP Academic, 2007), 39–42.

the self. While egoism is based solely on personal interests, utilitarianism seeks what is in the best interest of the whole (such as a whole group of people). As Bentham puts it, "It is the greatest happiness of the greatest number that is the measure of right and wrong."[12] Central to this account is the notion of the "utility" of an action. He writes, "By utility is meant that property of something whereby it tends to produce benefit, advantage, pleasure, good, or happiness (all this in the present case comes to the same thing) or (what comes again to the same thing) to prevent the happening of mischief, pain, evil, or unhappiness to the party whose interest is considered."[13]

For Mill, utilitarianism provides a way to think about ethics that doesn't require metaphysical foundations. As he considered the history of philosophy, Mill was convinced that philosophers before him had failed to provide an adequate moral foundation for objective morality. Because of this, he rejects approaches to morality that search for the ontological basis of right and wrong. And while he admitted that utilitarianism could not be proved or demonstrated, he did believe that this account of morality is justified on the basis of the results it produces. He says:

> Whatever can be proved to be good, must be so by being shown to be a means to something admitted to be good without proof. The medical art is proved to be good by its conducing to health; but how is it possible to prove that health is good? The art of music is good, for the reason, among others, that it produces pleasure; but what proof is it possible to give that pleasure is good? If, then, it is asserted that there is a comprehensive formula, including all things which are in themselves good, and that whatever else is good, is not so as an end, but as a mean, the formula may be accepted or rejected, but is not a subject of what is commonly understood by proof.[14]

Utilitarianism is commendable in that it concerns itself with the happiness and well-being of as many people as possible. With its concern for "many people," utilitarianism is an improvement on egoism. Nevertheless, it too has its problems. First, this moral theory is unable to ground moral ideals in anything substantial. As the happiness of the greatest number may change, so too will the laws, rules, and actions of society. Can morality really be summed up in a list of rules that (generally) bring felicity to many people?

12. Jeremy Bentham, A Comment on the Commentaries *and* A Fragment on Government, ed. J. H. Burns and H. L. A. Hart, The Collected Works of Jeremy Bentham (London: Continuum, 1977), 393.

13. Jeremy Bentham, *The Principles of Morals and Legislation* (Buffalo: Prometheus Books, 1988), 2.

14. John Stuart Mill, *Utilitarianism*, 2nd ed. (Malden, MA: Wiley-Blackwell, 2003), 184.

Surely there is something deeper at the heart of morality. Second, utilitarianism never actually says anything about goodness. Third, and building on the first two concerns, without a true account of goodness and a pathway toward it, utilitarianism will be inevitably oppressive to some.

Imagine this example. According to utilitarianism, the "good" and the "right" are determined by whatever brings the greatest amount of happiness to the greatest number of people. Now imagine a society like America in the eighteenth and nineteenth centuries, when slavery was the law of the land. The greatest number of people (the white people) were made happy by the forced labor of the minority (the black people). Sure, this approach brings the greatest amount of happiness to the greatest number of people, but is this really what is good and what is right? Surely not!

As we have seen, moral theories that are teleological in nature ultimately judge morality in terms of the results of actions and rules. On this account, it is the outcomes of our actions that we are after, and ethical systems must be built to bring about these outcomes. Aristotle's virtue ethic seeks eudaemonia and sees virtue—the golden mean—as the only way to achieve this. Egoism, by contrast, maintains that our only duty is to look out for our own best interest, but it doesn't entail that we never help others or that we always do what we most want. The utilitarian ethics of Bentham and Mill seek the greatest amount of happiness for the greatest number of people. Each of these systems has its critics, but each of them has merit as well. We now turn to a different way of doing moral theory: deontology.

## Deontological Theories

In contrast to teleological moral theories, which reject the idea of rules, laws, and mandates and develop their approaches to morality in terms of certain kinds of goals or outcomes, **deontological moral theories** do the opposite. For deontology (from *deō*, Greek for "ought" or "duty"), ethics is typically thought of in terms of obligation. In these systems, morality is grounded in a set of objective standards that prescribe certain kinds of moral actions. As Rae puts it, deontological "systems of ethics are principle-based systems, in which actions are intrinsically right or wrong, dependent on adherence to the relevant moral principles or values."[15] Noting a key difference between the deontologist and the teleologist, Frame

15. Rae, *Moral Choices*, 77.

says, "In the deontological view, seeking happiness is never morally virtuous; indeed, it detracts from the moral quality of any action. So when a writer despises pleasure and exalts principle or self-sacrifice, he is probably a deontologist."[16]

But as we shall see, not all deontological moral theories are the same. "What distinguishes various types of deontological systems," Rae states, "is the sources of the principles that determine morality."[17] Rae's observation is both accurate and helpful. Below we will illustrate this point by exploring deontology and divine-command theory. These two moral theories, while both are deontological, have very different sources for their moral principles. While one looks to the categorical imperative, the other looks to God and the commands that he gives.

### *Kant's Deontology*

The great Enlightenment philosopher Immanuel Kant was one of the leading voices for deontological moral theories. Like other deontologists, Kant sought to ground morality in a fixed set of moral standards and the moral duty that comes from them. But as an Enlightenment philosopher who rejected the possibility of doing ethics on metaphysical or theological foundations, Kant needed to find a way to objectively ground morality without God or the traditional metaphysics of the classical, patristic, and medieval thinkers. Moreover, Kant was equally convinced that such foundations could not be discovered through the empirical observation of the sciences.[18] But how could something like this be done? How can we have objective moral standards that are not grounded in theological or philosophical convictions and are also not discovered by empirical science? Kant's solution was found in a distinction between two kinds of imperatives (commands or moral rules) that we can identify.

On the one hand, Kant considers what he calls the hypothetical imperatives, which have a conditional goodness and operate on an *if/then* logic. Hypothetical imperatives refer to a set of commands or rules that one must follow *if* wanting a particular outcome. So, for example, *if* I want a pay increase for my work, *then* I should work really hard and go over and above what is expected of me. Notice that the imperative in this example—I should work really hard and go over and above what is expected of me—is not universally applicable. This is an imperative that should be obeyed only in some

16. Frame, *Doctrine of the Christian Life*, 101.
17. Rae, *Moral Choices*, 77.
18. Frame, *Doctrine of the Christian Life*, 102.

circumstances—namely, if I want a pay increase. If I do not want an increase in pay, then the imperative is not obligatory. The conditional nature of hypothetical imperatives is too weak to ground morality objectively and as a result cannot be the basis of deontology.

In contrast to hypothetical imperatives, Kant also observed what he called the **categorical imperatives**, which are unconditional in nature. That is, a categorical (applying to all people everywhere) imperative is a rule or command that is universally and objectively applicable. To identify specific cases of the categorical imperative, Kant suggested the following way of thinking: "Act only according to the maxim whereby you can at the same time will that it should become a universal law."[19] What Kant suggests here is that the test for determining whether an imperative is hypothetical or categorical is to ask whether we would want that imperative applied to all people in all circumstances. If we would see it necessary to be applied only in some circumstances, then the imperative is merely hypothetical. But if we find that we would want that imperative applied everywhere to all people, then it is a categorical imperative. Given the universal applicability of these imperatives, Kant believes this is the basis of deontology. In this approach, Kant thought that he had provided a nontheological or empirical basis for moral duty that was, nevertheless, universally applicable to all people.

One of the major assumptions in **Kantian deontological moral theory** is that there is in fact a "universal rationality" shared by all people everywhere. Indeed, this was one of his major assumptions in his entire philosophical system and a central idea within the Enlightenment itself. If it is true that all people everywhere share the same rational patterns of thought and that there really is a universal rationality, then systems like Kant's may indeed be successful. But, as it turns out, increased globalization, discoveries about the way people in different cultures actually think, and the advent of new intellectual disciplines like psychology, sociology, and anthropology have seriously challenged this assumption. As Alister McGrath puts it, "[The] empirical study of cultural rationalities disclosed a very different pattern—namely, that people possessed and possess contested and at times incommensurable notions both of what is 'rational,' 'true and right,' and how those qualities might be justified."[20] As the assumption regarding the "universal rationality" began to erode, so too did the confidence that we could develop a deontological moral theory along the lines that Kant suggested.

19. Immanuel Kant, *Grounding for the Metaphysics of Morals*, trans. James W. Ellington (Indianapolis: Hackett, 1993), 30.

20. Alister E. McGrath, *A Scientific Theology* (Grand Rapids: Eerdmans, 2002), 2:57.

*Divine-Command Theory*

Another example of a deontological moral theory is what philosophers have called **divine-command theory**. Roughly, this theory says that morality is grounded in a fundamental way in whatever it is that God commands. Or as Robert Adams suggests, "This is the theory that ethical wrongness *consists in* being contrary to God's commands, or that the word 'wrong' in ethical contexts *means* 'contrary to God's commands.'"[21] Found in versions of several of the major world religions like Judaism, Islam, and Christianity, this view is commonly associated with religious perspectives on morality. But what exactly is it about morality that is supposed to be grounded in the commands of God? Morality is not a one-dimensional issue. Numerous moral dimensions need to be addressed. For example, questions about goodness and obligation are different philosophical questions. What is ultimately good and what we are obligated to do are different aspects of moral theory, and a failure to recognize this will only muddy the water. When we say that God's commands are what ground morality, are we talking about goodness or obligation?

As Timmons points out, because of questions like these there are actually two different versions of divine-command theory: unrestricted and restricted.[22] As he notes, unrestricted divine-command theory seeks to account for both goodness and obligation via God's commands. On the unrestricted version, (1) we are obligated to do some action *A* (and avoid others) because God says so, *and* (2) *A* is good because God says so. God's commands are what make *A* good or bad, and God's commands are what render us obligated to do *A*. Critics of divine-command theory typically attack this unrestricted version. One major concern with it is that it seems to make goodness an arbitrary matter. If unrestricted divine-command theory is right, then it is possible for God to flip morality on its head and say the very opposite of what he earlier said. If in this world God said love is good and hate is evil, it would be possible for him to say the opposite, that hate is good and love is evil. This seems hard to square with what we know about God and leaves morality as nothing more than a divine whim or coin flip. Surely a God who is all-knowing, all-wise, and all-good has better reasons for doing what he does than that.

Other advocates of divine-command theory have opted for a restricted version, which says that God's commands ground some but not all aspects of morality. On this view, what God's command does ground is our obligation. In other words, God says that we are not to steal or commit adultery. God's commands are what render us obligated. But this view restricts the

21. Robert M. Adams, *The Virtue of Faith* (New York: Oxford, 1987), 97 (emphasis in original).
22. Timmons, *Moral Theory*, 23–33.

grounding of morality to obligation and does not suggest that goodness is grounded in divine commands. Goodness, on this view, is not something that God simply commanded. Rather, it is something that God is. As such, goodness is grounded in God's nature, not in his commands. And what is more, God's commands flow out of his nature. So then, when God says you shall not commit adultery, this is not just an arbitrary coin flip on his part. Rather, the command, which does ground our obligation, flows from his own divine nature, which is good and perfect. God commands us not to commit adultery because he wants us to be faithful. And why does God want that? He wants it because he himself is faithful, and we bear his image. This restricted approach, according to its advocates, seems to bypass the concerns raised above with the unrestricted account.

### Contemporary Virtue Ethics

So far we have considered teleological and deontological accounts of moral theory. We now turn to **contemporary virtue ethics**, which, as we will see, is a bit less precise and thus more difficult to fully grasp. By most accounts, this movement in ethics stems largely from the work of Alasdair MacIntyre in *After Virtue* and *Whose Justice? Which Rationality?*[23] MacIntyre begins with a simple thought experiment. He asks us to imagine that, due to a series of catastrophes that society blames on scientists, riots erupt and the masses seek to destroy the natural sciences from the face of the earth. Laboratories, books, and equipment are burned and destroyed. Scientists are killed, and teaching science in schools is forbidden. For the most part, the masses succeed in destroying modern science. But the masses have not been completely successful, since still remaining are fragments of scientific material and some equipment that survived the destruction. In later generations, some students desire to revive the sciences, and they collect all the remaining artifacts that can be found and begin to attempt reconstruction. The remaining artifacts are enough for them to learn some of the language of science but not sufficient to actually do science or to be successful in their reconstruction. They use the language of "mass," "relativity," and "gravity," but they use that language in a way that differs sharply from the way it was used by scientists prior to the riots and that fails to enable them to actually do science. What is MacIntyre's point with this thought experiment? He suggests that what is imagined in

23. Alasdair MacIntyre, *After Virtue* (Notre Dame, IN: University of Notre Dame Press, 2007); MacIntyre, *Whose Justice? Which Rationality?* (Notre Dame, IN: University of Notre Dame Press, 1988).

the thought experiment about science is precisely what has happened with morality in modern times. He says:

> The hypothesis which I wish to advance is that in the actual world which we inhabit the language of morality is in the same state of grave disorder as the language of natural science in the imaginary world which I described. What we possess, if this view is true, are the fragments of a conceptual scheme, parts which now lack those contexts from which their significance derived. We possess indeed simulacra of morality, we continue to use many of the key expressions. But we have—very largely, if not entirely—lost our comprehension, both theoretical and practical, of morality.[24]

MacIntyre believes the current state of morality is in shambles because of the widespread disagreement about what virtue is in the history of Western thought. Whatever else one might think about MacIntyre's actual virtue ethic, his historical survey of the great thinkers is spectacular. Indeed, he spends much of his time in both *After Virtue* and *Whose Justice? Which Rationality?* summarizing and analyzing the ethical thought of ancient, patristic, medieval, and even modern giants. What he demonstrates in the process is that there has been no agreement on what a virtue is, which characteristics are virtues, which virtues are most important, and what virtue's place in society should be. He asks, "If different writers in different times and places, but all within the history of Western culture, include such different sets and types of items in their lists, what grounds have we for supposing that they do indeed aspire to list items of one and the same kind, that there is any shared concept at all?"[25]

In his view, what the history of ideas shows us we cannot do is construct a unified approach to morality that applies to all people everywhere. He concludes this from his survey of Western thought alone. Matters only worsen when we bring in Native American, Eastern, and African accounts of morality. The sharp and widespread disagreement over what virtue is makes it impossible to ground morality in any universal or objective way. Or as he puts it, "There is no set of independent standards of rational justification by appeal to which the issues between contending traditions can be decided."[26]

But if that is the case, what does MacIntyre suggest we should do? Despite what one might think from the description above, MacIntyre does not (1) disparage the sociotemporal nature of traditions and their respective understandings of virtue or (2) embrace a relativistic notion suggesting that all

24. MacIntyre, *After Virtue*, 2.
25. MacIntyre, *After Virtue*, 183.
26. MacIntyre, *After Virtue*, 49.

traditions are intellectually or morally equal. To be clear, he suggests that virtue requires a tradition as a starting point for moral principles.[27] We start within a particular tradition and its understanding of virtue and then let our understanding of virtue evolve, change, or even expand as we encounter new data about the world we live in or dialogue with people from different traditions. As such, virtue is not conceived of as a fixed set of moral characteristics. Rather, it is thought of as "an acquired human quality the possession and exercise of which tends to enable us to achieve those goods which are internal to practices and the lack of which effectively prevents us from achieving any such goods."[28]

On this view, objective moral principles derived from natural law are not our starting point. Instead, we start with the traditions we inherit and work to improve our understandings of both reality and morality. The intellectual viability of different traditions is judged not by an objective set of intellectual or moral truth, as the Enlightenment suggested, but rather by the ability of a tradition to respond to the problems and inadequacies of its view. MacIntyre describes the process in three stages: "a first [stage] in which the relevant beliefs, texts, and authorities have not been put in question; a second [stage] in which inadequacies of various types have been identified, but not yet remedied; and a third [stage] in which response to those inadequacies has resulted in a set of reformulations, reevaluations, and new formulations and evaluations, designed to remedy inadequacies and overcome limitations."[29]

But what does this mean? What MacIntyre suggests here is that some traditions are superior to others given their ability to continue adapting and reformulating in response to new questions, concerns, and objections that are discovered. As new facts about the world are discovered or objections are raised for a tradition from a rival tradition, the superior tradition will be the one that is able to adapt in such a way that it can address those concerns. What this means for our moral theory is that, while we start from within our own unique tradition, we do not leave our understanding of truth and morality as a set of static beliefs that we came to adopt. Rather, we work from within that set of beliefs, learning new facts about the world while in dialogue with rival traditions to sharpen our beliefs through expansion and adaptation.

As mentioned above, MacIntyre is a master of historical intellectual analysis on the question of virtue. As he's shown us, the history of ideas is indeed filled with various understandings of virtue. His critical work is worthy of

27. MacIntyre, *After Virtue*, 186.
28. MacIntyre, *After Virtue*, 191.
29. MacIntyre, *Whose Justice? Which Rationality?*, 355.

serious attention as a result. But some critics have suggested that his own account of virtue collapses into the same kind of problem that he seeks to avoid. The key to his contemporary virtue account is his rejection of the Enlightenment's notion of a shared universal rationality. But some have suggested that MacIntyre embraces something similar to this regarding his three-stage account for adjudicating between differing traditions. The idea that some traditions are better than others, due to their ability to respond and adapt to new insights and objections, is not an idea that is specific to any particular tradition and thus seems to be an objective criterion. Others have suggested that his approach forces us to reject the idea of absolute truth and, despite his best efforts, results in relativism.

## Conclusion

As we have seen in this chapter, normative ethics is the branch of moral inquiry that tries to provide a way of doing ethics or a pathway for being moral. Of normative ethics' two divisions, this chapter has focused on moral theory. We have sought not to endorse one particular approach over another but rather to survey and describe the various accounts that have been most popular. These debates will no doubt continue for decades and centuries to come, and the moral questions we've considered will continue to be central to our philosophical concerns.

For the Christian, there is actually much to be gleaned from each approach. Like the teleological accounts of moral theory, the Christian Scriptures are very concerned with the character and qualities of human beings. Jesus's "Blessed are those" statements found in the Sermon on the Mount (Matt. 5:3–12) are a good example of this. At the same time, however, the Bible offers a clear set of commands and guidelines to life in both the Old and New Testaments, marking a clear correlation to deontological accounts of moral theory. And while Christians like Augustine insisted that goodness itself is grounded in God's own nature, what we are obligated to do in certain circumstances may very well be a matter of divine volition. As such, philosophical discussions about moral theory have a clear connection to many of the same concerns addressed by the Christian faith.

# Glossary of Terms

**agent**—a subject, person, or mind that is capable of and the ultimate source of enacting change in the world

**agent causation**—the view that agents are a first cause of actions and are not determined by any prior or external event or phenomena

**applied ethics**—the branch of normative ethics that tries to answer very specific moral questions confronting practical, everyday life

**a priori knowledge**—knowledge possessed *prior to* empirical evidence/sense data

**argument**—a set of statements consisting of one or more premises that support, through one or more rules of inference, a conclusion

**Aristotelian virtue ethics**—a teleological normative ethical theory that understands the outcome to which moral actions should be pointed is eudaemonia, well-being, or the excellence of the soul, focusing on character building through enacting and embodying virtues

**atheistic ethical nonnaturalism**—an objectivist metaethical theory claiming that moral properties are brute metaphysical realities and are, therefore, not naturally or divinely derived

**body-fission model**—the account of bodily resurrection suggesting that the body experiences a fission event (split into two, or duplicated) just before death and that one of these two survives death and remains continuous and numerically identical to the person

**brain-snatching model**—an account of a possible method of bodily resurrection wherein God "snatches" the body's brain/nervous system at the point of death, replacing it with a duplicate that decomposes in its place, thus preserving it and the person's immanent causal connections

**bundle theory**—the view that a concrete particular is a bundle of its properties

**Calvinism**—a theological version of determinism such that God's decree determines the course of history and the actions of human beings even as humans are still responsible and free

**categorical imperative**—an ethical rule or command that would be universally and objectively applicable (do not lie, etc.)

**causal theory of knowledge**—the theory claiming justification for a belief as grounded in the causal connection between objects or events outside a person's mind and the corresponding ideas that form as a result

**classical foundationalism**—the view in epistemology claiming that beliefs are either basic or nonbasic and that nonbasic beliefs are *founded* on basic, unmediated beliefs

**class nominalism**—a version of reductive nominalism regarding properties that analyzes the sentence "*a* is *F*" as "*a* is a member of the class of *F* things"

**coherence theory of truth**—the view declaring that truth obtains when a statement or belief coheres within a worldview or set of beliefs

**compatibilism**—the claim that freedom and determinism are compatible

**concept nominalism**—a version of reductive nominalism regarding properties that analyzes the sentence "*a* is *F*" as "*a* falls under the concept *F*"

**constitutionalism**—the view in philosophy of mind holding that human persons are *constituted* by their bodies, even if they are not identical/reducible to them

**contemporary virtue ethics**—the movement, stemming largely from the work of Alasdair MacIntyre, maintaining that we cannot construct a unified approach to morality that applies to all people everywhere, since morality is something inherently tied to cultural systems, contexts, and languages

**correspondence theory of truth**—the view holding that truth obtains when a statement or belief corresponds to reality

**cultural relativism**—a subjectivist metaethical theory maintaining that moral statements are true or false relative to the specific groups making them

**deductive argument**—an argument form where true premises entail the conclusion

**defense**—an explanation (more modest than a full-blown theodicy) of God's *possible* reasons(s) for allowing evil

**deontological moral theories**—normative ethical theories that understand morality in terms of obligations, laws, duties, or commands

**determinism**—the claim that the future is fixed, or determined, either logically, theologically, or physically

**direct realism**—a commonsensical theory of perception holding that what one is directly aware of in perceptual experience is a mind-independent reality

**divine-command theory**—a deontological ethical theory declaring that morality is grounded in a fundamental way in whatever it is that God commands

**divine hiddenness**—the notion that humankind lacks universal or obvious evidence of God, or that God has hidden himself from humanity

**divine providence**—God's governing mode of interaction with the world

**divine simplicity**—the doctrine that God is metaphysically simple, having no temporal or spatial parts or properties

**egoism**—a teleological normative ethical theory that understands morality in terms of the well-being of the self

**eliminativism**—a view that "eliminates" the mind by holding that there are no *actual* things such as "beliefs," "pains," "desires," or "feels"

**emotivism**—a metaethical theory maintaining that moral statements are expressions of emotion

**epistemology**—the branch of philosophy that deals with philosophical notions about knowledge, perception, justification, and truth

**ethical naturalism**—an objectivist metaethical theory attempting to reduce moral properties to or define them as natural properties that are the subject matter of biology, psychology, or sociology

**ethical nonnaturalism**—an objectivist metaethical theory claiming the existence of fundamental moral truths that are not features of the natural world

**event causation**—the view that causation is a relation between events; a prior event (e.g., the event of Smith pulling the trigger) causes, or brings about, a subsequent event (e.g., the event of Smith killing Jones)

**evidentialism**—the view that knowledge should be based on evidence and that claims lacking evidence are not knowledge

**externalism**—the view that what justifies a belief for a person is something external to his or her own perspective

**fideism**—the view of faith and reason that esteems faith and knowledge gained via personal, emotional, and/or spiritual means over and above rational/empirical ones

**first-order discipline**—the primary subject matter of an academic discipline; what the academic discipline is about

**first-person perspective**—the self-awareness of mental life indicating that *it is I who is experiencing* desires, feelings, and so forth; a classic criterion of personhood

**functionalism**—a view in philosophy of mind that seeks to understand the mind only by virtue of what it does, by its function

**global/Pyrrhonian skepticism**—the most radical form of skepticism, claiming that there can be no knowledge

**golden mean**—an Aristotelian ethical notion describing the virtuous place that stands directly between the polar vices of excess and deficiency

**hard determinism**—the view that the future is determined and, therefore, freedom does not exist

**hard incompatibilism**—the view that incompatibilism is true, determinism is either true or false (unsure which), but either way, there is no genuine freedom

**hylomorphism**—the view that the soul is the substantial form of the body and that human persons are composites of bodies and souls

**idealism**—the metaphysical position that the only things existing are mental things: minds and ideas

**identity theory**—the theory (or group of theories) in the philosophy of mind that reduces the mind to the brain

**immanent realism**—the brand of metaphysical realism holding that universals are wholly located at distinct places at any one time

**incompatibilism**—the claim that freedom and determinism are not compatible; also called libertarian freedom

**indeterminism**—the view that freedom is incompatible with being determined

**indexicals**—perspectival words like "I," "here," and "now," used to capture the first-person perspective

**inductive argument**—an argument form where true premises render the conclusion probable

**intentionality**—the "aboutness" or "ofness" of one's mental life or mental states

**intermediate state**—in Christian theism, the time between the physical death of the body on earth and bodily resurrection in the eschaton

**internalism**—the view that what justifies a person in holding a particular belief depends on what is "internal" to his or her own mind, or that the person has first-person awareness of the reasons for the belief

**justification**—in epistemology, what differentiates knowledge from mere true belief or opinion, and is typically understood as either internalistic or externalistic

**Kantian deontological moral theory**—Immanuel Kant's ethical theory, which seeks to ground morality, understood as duty, in objective reality by positing the categorical imperative, which is objectively and universally known and applicable

**libertarianism**—the view that incompatibilism is true and there is genuine freedom

**local/metaphysical skepticism**—a form of skepticism regarding claims to knowledge of metaphysical or supernatural things

**materialism**—the metaphysical position that everything is material

**mereological nominalism**—a version of reductive nominalism regarding properties that analyzes the sentence "*a* is *F*" as "*a* is a part of the aggregate *F* thing"

**metaethics**—the subdiscipline of ethics concerned with answering nonmoral questions about morality

**metaphysical dualism**—the view that there are two kinds of things, as opposed to monism

**metaphysical realism**—the view that universals (shareable properties) exist

**metaphysics**—the branch of philosophy that studies the nature and structure of reality

**methodological skepticism**—a method for gaining knowledge that begins in doubt, famously employed by René Descartes

**miracles**—God-caused events that suspend the regular flow of the natural order to accomplish some divine purpose

**Molinism**—the theological perspective (named after Luis de Molina) claiming that God has "middle knowledge" of what you *would* do in any circumstance, such that God's beliefs *track* our future choices but do not determine them

**monism**—the metaphysical position that just one kind of thing exists (examples of monism include materialism or idealism), as opposed to dualism

**moral realism**—the ethical theory or group of ethical theories claiming that there are objective moral properties or truth

**naturalism**—the view that there is no supernatural aspect to reality

**natural revelation**—the self-disclosure of God through what can be understood in creation, both physical and existential

**natural theology**—a branch of philosophy and theology that tries to draw theological conclusions from nature, often taking the form of arguments or providing warrant for God's existence

**nominalism**—the view that abstract objects do not exist and that universals (shareable properties) do not exist

**noncognitivism**—a subjective metaethical category of theories, including emotivism and prescriptivism, that do not appeal to rational factors to explain moral statements

**nonreductive physicalism**—the view in philosophy of mind claiming that while there are no immaterial souls, there are at least some mental properties that are not reducible to physical ones

**normative ethics**—the subdiscipline of ethics concerned with answering moral questions, such as about *what to do* or *how to be*

**numerical sameness**—a philosophical term that refers to the same object or person over time

**objectivist metaethical theories**—realist metaethical theories holding that morality is discovered

**Ockhamism**—the view, first put forth by William of Ockham, that distinguishes between hard and soft facts about the past in order to understand how the future might not be determined

**open theism**—the theological perspective maintaining that God does not know the future

**ostrich nominalism**—a brand of extreme nominalism holding that all resemblance facts can be explained in terms of the qualitative facts of concrete objects that exactly resemble one another

**particular**—a concrete entity such as a molecule, table, dog, or car occupying a single spatial location at any moment of its existence

**phenomenal conservatism**—holds that undefeated appearances are a source of justification (perhaps the *only* source of justification) for belief

**Platonic realism**—the brand of metaphysical realism claiming that universals are multiply instantiated without being located at a place

**Platonism**—the metaphysical view of Plato, understanding reality in two worlds: the visible, sensational world, which changes, and the invisible world of the forms, which are eternal, unchanging, and the source of all in the visible realm; in contemporary debates, the view that, in addition to the concrete world, abstract objects exist

**pragmatic theory of truth**—the view holding that truth obtains when a statement or belief works or has practical/pragmatic value

**predicate nominalism**—a version of reductive nominalism regarding properties that analyzes the sentence "*a* is *F*" as "*a* falls under the predicate *F*"

**prescriptivism**—a metaethical theory maintaining that moral statements function as commands

**principle of constituent identity**—an intuitive principle for identifying complex wholes in virtue of their constituent parts, properties, and relations, stated as follows: If object *a* and object *b* have all the same constituents standing in all the same relations, then *a* is numerically identical to *b*

**proposition**—a statement about things, states of affairs, places, or people that has a truth value

**qualitative sameness**—a philosophical term that refers to identical properties or qualities in two numerically distinct objects, or in the same object separated by time

**reassembly model**—the most traditional account of bodily resurrection, claiming that God takes the physical cells/atoms that make up a person's (dead) body and reassembles them in the eschaton

**reductive nominalism**—any version of nominalism denying the existence of properties by offering a reductive analysis of sentences that seem to be about properties (e.g., concept nominalism, predicate nominalism, mereological nominalism, class nominalism, resemblance nominalism)

**Reformed epistemology**—an epistemic movement maintaining that religious belief can be rational without argument

**reliabilism**—an externalist theory holding that a belief is justified if it was formed in the appropriate environment and the cognitive faculties of the mind were functioning in a reliable fashion

**representative realism**—the view of perception claiming that we are directly aware of a mental item—our sensory ideas—and indirectly aware of a mind-independent reality

**resemblance nominalism**—a version of reductive nominalism regarding properties that analyzes the sentence "*a* is *F*" as "*a* is a member of a class of resembling *F* things"

**second-order discipline**—a discipline that studies another discipline (e.g., as a second-order discipline, philosophy studies the first-order discipline of physics)

**simple subjectivism**—a subjectivist meta-ethical theory that understands moral statements to be either true or false depending on the belief of the individual

**skeptical theism**—the approach to the problem of evil denying that we are in a position to know God's reasons for evil in the world

**skepticism**—the view that rejects all or some kinds of knowledge claims, divided into three different brands: global, local, and methodological

**soft determinism**—the view, synonymous with compatibilism, that the future is determined yet one can still have freedom

**Soul-Making Theodicy**—the explanation for evil in the world that understands pain and suffering as productive, or even necessary, for building character

**subjectivist metaethical theories**—antirealist metaethical theories, holding that morality is invented

**substance**—a concrete object as a fundamental unity of parts, properties, and powers

**substance dualism**—a view advocated by René Descartes positing two kinds of basic substances: mind and body

**substratum theory**—the view that concrete particulars have a metaphysical substrate that bears properties

**teleological accounts of morality**—theories in normative ethics built on the purpose, end, or telos of a moral action and suggesting that morality be thought of in terms of certain kinds of goals or outcomes, not in terms of actions per se

**theistic ethical nonnaturalism**—an objectivist metaethical theory holding that God is the best explanation for moral values and duties

**theodicy**—an explanation of God's *actual* (as opposed to *possible*) reason(s) for allowing evil

**trope nominalism**—the brand of nominalism that endorses the existence of unshareable properties (e.g., the redness of the truck, ball, and shirt are numerically distinct but exactly resembling properties)

**universals**—shareable properties such as *being red*, *being bald*, or *being wise* that can be possessed by distinct particulars at the same time

**utilitarianism**—a teleological normative ethical view contending that morality is judged, not by the nature of the action itself, but by the results following from our actions and that the goodness of an action is understood as the degree to which it benefits or is good for a community or society

**virtue epistemology**—an approach to knowledge that builds on the notion of intellectual virtues, cognitive characteristics, or qualities that allow a person to think well, acquire knowledge, and avoid epistemological error

# Bibliography


Adams, Marilyn McCord. "The Problem of Hell: A Problem of Evil for Christians." In *Reasoned Faith: Essays in Philosophical Theology in Honor of Norman Kretzmann*, edited by Eleonore Stump, 301–27. Ithaca, NY: Cornell University Press, 1993. Reprinted in *God and the Problem of Evil*, edited by William Rowe, 282–309. Malden, MA: Blackwell, 2001.

Adams, Robert M. *The Virtue of Faith*. New York: Oxford, 1987.

Anselm. *Proslogion*. In *Anselm of Canterbury: The Major Works*, 82–104. New York: Oxford University Press, 2008.

———. *Proslogion*. In *Basic Writings*, edited by Thomas Williams, 75–98. Indianapolis: Hackett, 2007.

Aristotle. *De Anima*. Translated by Hugh Lawson-Tancred. New York: Penguin, 1986.

———. *Metaphysics*. In *The Complete Works of Aristotle*, vol. 2, edited by Jonathan Barnes, 1552–1728. Princeton: Princeton University Press, 1984.

———. *Nicomachean Ethics*. Translated by Terrence Irwin. 2nd ed. Indianapolis: Hackett, 1999.

———. *Physics*. In *The Complete Works of Aristotle*, vol. 1, edited by Jonathan Barnes, 315–446. Princeton: Princeton University Press, 1984.

Armstrong, David. "Against 'Ostrich' Nominalism: A Reply to Michael Devitt." *Pacific Philosophical Quarterly* 61 (1980): 440–49.

———. *Universals and Scientific Realism*. Vol. 1, *Nominalism and Realism*. Cambridge: Cambridge University Press, 1978.

———. *Universals: An Opinionated Introduction*. Boulder, CO: Westview, 1989.

Athenagoras. *The Resurrection of the Dead*. In *Anti-Nicene Fathers*, edited by Alexander Roberts and James Donaldson, 2:149–62. Peabody, MA: Hendrickson, 2004.

Augustine of Hippo. *Concerning the City of God against the Pagans*. Translated by Henry Bettenson. London: Penguin, 1984.

———. *Confessions*. Translated by Henry Chadwick. New York: Oxford University Press, 1998.

———. *On Free Choice of the Will*. Translated by Thomas Williams. Indianapolis: Hackett, 1993.

———. *On the Gospel of St. John*. In *Nicene and Post-Nicene Fathers*, edited by Philip Schaff. First Series, vol. 7. Peabody, MA: Hendrickson, 2004.

Ayer, A. J. *Language, Truth, and Logic*. New York: Dover, 1952.

Baker, Lynne Rudder. *Persons and Bodies: A Constitution View*. Cambridge: Cambridge University Press, 2000.

———. "When Does a Person Begin?" *Social Philosophy and Policy* 22 (2005): 25–48.

Balaguer, Mark. "Platonism in Metaphysics." In *The Stanford Encyclopedia of Philosophy*, edited by Edward N. Zalta. Last modified March 9, 2016. http://plato.stanford.edu/entries/platonism.

Behe, Michael J. *Darwin's Black Box*. New York: Free Press, 1996.

———. *The Edge of Evolution: The Search for the Limits of Darwinism*. New York: Free Press, 2007.

Beilby, James. "Plantinga's Model of Warranted Christian Belief." In *Alvin Plantinga*, edited by Deane-Peter Baker, 125–65. New York: Cambridge University Press, 2007.

Bennett, Karen. "Construction Area (No Hard Hat Required)." *Philosophical Studies* 154 (2011): 79–104.

Bentham, Jeremy. A Comment on the Commentaries *and* A Fragment on Government. Edited by J. H. Burns and H. L. A. Hart. The Collected Works of Jeremy Bentham. London: Continuum, 1977.

———. *The Principles of Morals and Legislation*. Buffalo: Prometheus Books, 1988.

Berkeley, George. Principles of Human Knowledge *and* Three Dialogues. Edited by Howard Robinson. New York: Oxford University Press, 1999.

Berto, Francesco, and Mateo Plebani. *Ontology and Metaontology: A Contemporary Guide*. New York: Bloomsbury, 2015.

Bishop, Robert C. "Chaos, Indeterminism, and Free Will." In *The Oxford Handbook of Free Will*, edited by Robert Kane, 111–26. Oxford: Oxford University Press, 2002.

Black, Max. "The Identity of Indiscernibles." *Mind* 61 (1952): 153–64.

Boa, Kenneth, and Robert Bowman. *Faith Has Its Reasons: An Integrative Approach to Defending Christianity*. Milton Keynes, UK: Paternoster, 2005.

Boethius. *The Consolation of Philosophy*. New York: Oxford University Press, 2000.

Bolos, Anthony. "Is Knowledge of God a Cognitive Achievement?" *Ratio* 59, no. 2 (2016): 186–201.

BonJour, Laurence. "Against Materialism." In *The Waning of Materialism*, edited by Robert C. Koons and George Bealer, 3–24. Oxford: Oxford University Press, 2010.

Byerly, Ryan T. *Introducing Logic and Critical Thinking*. Grand Rapids: Baker Academic, 2017.

Bynum, Caroline Walker. *The Resurrection of the Body in Western Christianity, 200–1336*. New York: Columbia University Press, 1995.

Calvin, John. *Institutes of the Christian Religion*. Edited by John T. McNeill. Translated by Ford Lewis Battles. Philadelphia: Westminster, 1960.

Carroll, Vincent, and David Shiflett. *Christianity on Trial*. San Francisco: Encounter Books, 2002.

Chisholm, Roderick M. *The Foundations of Knowing*. Minneapolis: University of Minnesota Press, 1982.

———. "Human Freedom and the Self." In *Free Will*, edited by Gary Watson, 26–37. 2nd ed. Oxford: Oxford University Press, 2003.

Clark, David K. *To Know and Love God*. Wheaton: Crossway, 2003.

Clifford, W. K. "The Ethics of Belief." Reprinted in *Gateway to the Great Books*, vol. 10, edited by Robert M. Hutchins and Mortimer Adler, 14–36. Chicago: Encyclopedia Britannica, 1963.

Collins, Francis S. *The Language of God*. New York: Free Press, 2006.

Collins, Robin. "The Anthropic Teleological Argument." In *Philosophy of Religion: Selected Readings*, edited by Michael Peterson, William Hasker, Bruce Reichenbach, and David Basinger, 187–96. 5th ed. New York: Oxford University Press, 2014.

———. "The Teleological Argument." In *The Blackwell Companion to Natural Theology*, edited by William Lane Craig and J. P. Moreland, 202–81. Malden, MA: Wiley-Blackwell, 2012.

Colyvan, Mark. *The Indispensability of Mathematics*. New York: Oxford University Press, 2001.

Cooper, John. *Body, Soul and Life Everlasting*. Grand Rapids: Eerdmans, 1989.

Corcoran, Kevin. "Dualism, Materialism, and the Problem of Postmortem Survival." *Philosophia Christi* 4, no. 2 (2002): 411–25.

———. "Persons and Bodies." *Faith and Philosophy* 15, no. 3 (July 1998): 324–40.

———. *Rethinking Human Nature*. Grand Rapids: Baker Academic, 2006.

Corduan, Winfried. *No Doubt about It*. Nashville: B&H, 1997.

Cover, J. A., and John O'Leary-Hawthorne. "Free Agency and Materialism." In *Faith, Freedom, and Rationality*, edited by Daniel Howard-Snyder and Jeff Jordan, 47–72. Lanham, MD: Rowman & Littlefield, 1996.

Cowan, Steven B., and James S. Spiegel, eds. *Idealism and Christian Philosophy*. Idealism and Christianity. New York: Bloomsbury, 2016.

———. *The Love of Wisdom*. Nashville: B&H, 2009.

Cowan, Steven B., and Greg A. Welty. "*Pharaoh's Magicians Redivivus*: A Response to Jerry Walls on Christian Compatibilism." *Philosophia Christi* 17, no. 1 (2015): 151–73.

———. "Won't Get Foiled Again: A Rejoinder to Jerry Walls." *Philosophia Christi* 17, no. 2 (2015): 427–42.

Craig, William Lane. "Anti-Platonism." In *Beyond the Control of God? Six Views on the Problem of God and Abstract Objects*, edited by Paul M. Gould, 113–31. New York: Bloomsbury, 2014.

———. *The Kalam Cosmological Argument*. London: Macmillan, 1979.

———. "Lest Anyone Should Fall: A Middle Knowledge Perspective on Perseverance and Apostolic Warnings." *International Journal for Philosophy* 29 (1991): 65–74.

———. "'Men Moved by the Holy Spirit Spoke from God' (2 Peter 1.21): A Middle Knowledge Perspective on Divine Inspiration." *Philosophia Christi* 1 (1999): 45–82.

———. "Middle Knowledge: A Calvinist-Arminian Rapprochement?" In *The Grace of God and the Will of Man*, edited by Clark H. Pinnock, 141–64. Grand Rapids: Zondervan, 1989.

———. "The Middle Knowledge View." In *Divine Foreknowledge: Four Views*, edited by James K. Beilby and Paul R. Eddy, 119–43. Downers Grove, IL: InterVarsity, 2001.

———. "No Other Name: A Middle Knowledge Perspective on the Exclusivity of Salvation through Christ." *Faith and Philosophy* 6 (1989): 172–88.

———. *On Guard*. Colorado Springs: David C. Cook, 2010.

———. *The Only Wise God: The Compatibility of Divine Foreknowledge and Human Freedom*. Eugene, OR: Wipf & Stock, 1999.

———. "Philosophical and Scientific Pointers to *Creation ex Nihilo*." In *Contemporary Perspectives on Religious Epistemology*, edited by R. Douglas Geivett and Brendan Sweetman, 185–200. New York: Oxford University Press, 1992.

———. *Reasonable Faith*. 3rd ed. Wheaton: Crossway, 2008.

Craig, William Lane, and James D. Sinclair. "The Kalam Cosmological Argument." In *The Blackwell Companion to Natural Theology*, edited by William Lane Craig and J. P. Moreland, 101–201. Malden, MA: Blackwell, 2012.

Cuneo, Terence, and Russ Shafer-Landau. "The Moral Fixed Points: New Directions for Moral Nonnaturalism." *Philosophical Studies* 17, no. 1 (2014): 399–443.

Cushman, Philip. "Why the Self Is Empty." *American Psychologist* 45 (May 1990): 599–611.

Darwin, Charles. *On the Origin of Species*. Cambridge, MA: Harvard University Press, 1964.

Davis, Stephen. *God, Reason and Theistic Proofs*. Edinburgh: Edinburgh University Press, 1997.

Dawkins, Richard. *The Blind Watchmaker: Why the Evidence of Evolution Reveals a Universe without Design*. New York: Norton, 1996.

———. *The God Delusion*. Boston: Houghton Mifflin, 2006.

Dembski, William. *Intelligent Design*. Downers Grove, IL: InterVarsity, 1999.

Dennett, Daniel C. *Breaking the Spell: Religion as a Natural Phenomenon*. New York: Viking, 2006.

Denton, Michael. *Evolution: A Theory in Crisis*. Bethesda, MD: Adler & Adler, 1985.

Descartes, René. *Discourse on Method*. Translated by Desmond M. Clarke. London: Penguin, 1999.

———. *Meditations on First Philosophy*. Translated by Donald A. Cress. 4th ed. Indianapolis: Hackett, 1993.

Devitt, Michael. "'Ostrich Nominalism' or 'Mirage Realism'?" *Pacific Philosophical Quarterly* 61 (1980): 433–39.

DeWeese, Garrett. *God and the Nature of Time*. Burlington, VT: Ashgate, 2004.

Diogenes Laertius. *Life of Pyrrho*. In *Hellenistic Philosophy*, translated by Brad Inwood and L. P. Gerson, 285–97. Indianapolis: Hackett, 1997.

Draper, John William. *History of the Conflict between Religion and Science*. London: Pioneer, 1874.

Eklund, Matti. "Metaontology." *Philosophy Compass* 1, no. 3 (2006): 317–34.

Elisabeth of Bohemia. "Elisabeth to Descartes—10 June 1643." In *The Correspondence between Princess Elisabeth of Bohemia and René Descartes*, edited and translated by Lisa Shapiro, 67–69. Chicago: University of Chicago Press, 2007.

Evans, C. Stephen. "Apologetics in a New Key: Relieving Protestant Anxieties over Natural Theology." In *The Logic of Rational Theism*, edited by William Lane Craig and Mark S. McLeod, 65–75. Lewiston, NY: Edwin Mellen, 1990.

———. *Natural Signs and the Knowledge of God*. Oxford: Oxford University Press, 2010.

———. *Why Christian Faith Still Makes Sense*. Grand Rapids: Baker Academic, 2015.

Farris, Joshua R., and S. Mark Hamilton. *Idealism and Christian Theology*. Idealism and Christianity 1. New York: Bloomsbury, 2016.

Feinberg, John S. *No One Like Him*. Wheaton: Crossway, 2001.

Ferry, Luc. *A Brief History of Thought: A Philosophical Guide to Living*. New York: HarperCollins, 2011.

Field, Hartry. *Science without Numbers*. Princeton: Princeton University Press, 1980.

Fischer, John Martin. "Frankfurt-type Examples and Semi-Compatibilism." In *The Oxford Handbook of Free Will*, edited by Robert Kane, 281–308. Oxford: Oxford University Press, 2002.

Fischer, John Martin, and Patrick Todd, eds. *Freedom, Fatalism, and Foreknowledge*. Oxford: Oxford University Press, 2015.

Fisher, Andrew. *Metaethics: An Introduction*. New York: Routledge, 2014.

Flew, Antony, and Gary R. Habermas. "My Pilgrimage from Atheism to Theism: A Discussion between Antony Flew and Gary R. Habermas." *Philosophia Christi* 6, no. 2 (2004): 197–211.

Flew, Antony, and Roy Abraham Varghese. *There Is a God: How the World's Most Notorious Atheist Changed His Mind*. New York: HarperOne, 2007.

Flint, Thomas P. *Divine Providence: The Molinist Account*. Ithaca, NY: Cornell University Press, 1998.

Frame, John M. *The Doctrine of the Christian Life*. Phillipsburg, NJ: P&R, 2008.

Frankfurt, Harry. "Alternative Possibilities and Moral Responsibility." *Journal of Philosophy* 66 (1969): 829–39.

Gale, Richard. "Evil as Evidence against God." In *Debating Christian Theism*, edited by J. P. Moreland, Chad V. Meister, and Khaldoun A. Sweis, 197–207. Oxford: Oxford University Press, 2013.

Garcia, Robert K. "Bundle Theory's Black Box: Gap Challenges for the Bundle Theory of Substance." *Philosophia* 42, no. 1 (2014): 115–26.

———. "Platonism and the Haunted Universe." In *Loving God with Your Mind: Essays in Honor of J. P. Moreland*, edited by Paul M. Gould and Richard Brian Davis, 25–50. Chicago: Moody, 2014.

———. "Two Ways to Particularize a Property." *Journal of the American Philosophical Association* 1, no. 4 (2015): 635–52.

Gaunilo. "In Behalf of the Fool." In Anselm, *Basic Writings*, edited by Thomas Williams, 99–103. Indianapolis: Hackett, 2007.

Geivett, R. Douglas. "Augustine and the Problem of Evil." In *God and Evil: The Case for God in a World Filled with Pain*, edited by Chad Meister and James K. Dew Jr., 65–79. Downers Grove, IL: IVP Books, 2013.

Gettier, Edmund L. "Is Justified True Belief [the Same as] Knowledge?" *Analysis* 23, no. 6 (June 1963): 121–23.

Giberson, Karl W. *Saving Darwin*. New York: HarperOne, 2008.

Gillespie, Neal. *Charles Darwin and the Problem of Creation*. Chicago: University of Chicago Press, 1979.

Ginet, Carl. *On Action*. Cambridge: Cambridge University Press, 1990.

Goetz, Stewart. "Substance Dualism." In *In Search of the Soul: Four Views of the Mind-Body Problem*, edited by Joel B. Green and Stuart L. Palmer, 33–60. Downers Grove, IL: IVP, 2005.

Goldman, Alvin. "A Causal Theory of Knowing." In *Knowledge: Readings in Contemporary Epistemology*, edited by Sven Bernecker and Fred Dretske, 18–30. Oxford: Blackwell, 2000.

Goodman, Nelson. *The Structure of Appearance*. Cambridge, MA: Harvard University Press, 1951.

Gould, Paul M., ed. *Beyond the Control of God? Six Views on the Problem of God and Abstract Objects*. New York: Bloomsbury, 2014.

———. "How Does an Aristotelian Substance Have Its Platonic Properties? Issues and Options." *Axiomathes* 23, no. 2 (2013): 343–64.

———. "The Problem of Universals, Realism, and God." *Metaphysica* 13, no. 2 (2012): 183–94.

———. "Three Reasons Why I Teach Philosophy at a Seminary." *Theological Matters* (blog). November 8, 2016. https://theologicalmatters.com/2016/11/08/three-reasons-why-i-teach-philosophy-at-a-seminary/.

Gould, Paul M., and Richard Brian Davis, eds. *Four Views on Christianity and Philosophy*. Grand Rapids: Zondervan, 2016.

———. "Where the Bootstrapping Really Lies: A Neo-Aristotelian Reply to Panchuk." *International Philosophical Quarterly* 57, no. 4 (2017): 415–28.

Gould, Paul M., and Stan Wallace. "On What There Is: Theism, Platonism, and Explanation." In *Loving God with Your Mind: Essays in Honor of J. P. Moreland*, edited by Paul M. Gould and Richard Brian Davis, 21–34. Chicago: Moody, 2014.

Greco, John. "A (Different) Virtue Epistemology." *Philosophy and Phenomenological Research* 85, no. 1 (2012): 1–26.

———. "The Nature of Ability and Purpose of Knowledge." *Philosophical Issues* 17, *The Metaphysics of Epistemology*, special issue of *Nous* (2007): 57–69.

Griffith, Meghan. *Free Will: The Basics*. New York: Routledge, 2013.

Groothuis, Douglas. "Truth Defined and Defended." In *Reclaiming the Center*, edited by Millard J. Erickson, Paul Kjoss Helseth, and Justin Taylor, 59–79. Wheaton: Crossway, 2004.

Grossmann, Reinhardt. *The Existence of the World: An Introduction to Ontology*. New York: Routledge, 1992.

Groza, Adam. "Idealism and the Nature of God." In *Idealism and Christian Philosophy*, edited by Steven B. Cowan and James S. Spiegel, 107–25. Idealism and Christianity 2. New York: Bloomsbury, 2016.

Hasker, William. "A Philosophical Perspective." In *The Openness of God: A Biblical Challenge to the Traditional Understanding of God*, by Clark Pinnock, Richard Rice, John Sanders, William Hasker, and David Basinger, 126–54. Downers Grove, IL: InterVarsity, 1994.

Heil, John. *Philosophy of Mind: A Contemporary Introduction*. 3rd ed. London: Routledge, 2012.

Hick, John. "Soul-Making Theodicy." In *God and the Problem of Evil*, edited by William L. Rowe, 265–81. Malden, MA: Blackwell, 2001.

Hitchens, Christopher. *God Is Not Great: How Religion Poisons Everything*. New York: Hachette, 2007.

Holmes, Arthur F. *Ethics: Approaching Moral Decisions*. Downers Grove, IL: IVP Academic, 2007.

Hopkins, Gerard Manley. "God's Grandeur." In *The Poems of Gerard Manley Hopkins*, edited by W. H. Gardner and N. H. MacKenzie, 66. 4th ed. New York: Oxford University Press, 1967.

Horwich, Paul. "Theories of Truth." In *A Companion to Metaphysics*, edited by Jaegwon Kim and Ernest Sosa, 596–601. Oxford: Blackwell Reference, 1995.

Howard-Snyder, Daniel. "God, Evil, and Suffering." In *Reason for the Hope Within*, edited by Michael Murray, 76–115. Grand Rapids: Eerdmans, 1999.

Howard-Snyder, Daniel, Michael Bergmann, and William L. Rowe. "An Exchange on the Problem of Evil." In *God and the Problem of Evil*, edited by William L. Rowe, 124–58. Malden, MA: Blackwell, 2001.

Howard-Snyder, Daniel, and Paul K. Moser, eds. *Divine Hiddenness: New Essays*. Cambridge: Cambridge University Press, 2002.

Hoyle, Fred. "The Universe: Past and Present Reflections." *Annual Review of Astronomy* 20, no. 16 (1982): 1–35.

Huemer, Michael. *Approaching Infinity*. New York: Palgrave, 2016.

Hume, David. *Dialogues Concerning Natural Religion*. London: Penguin, 1990.

———. *An Inquiry concerning Human Understanding*. New York: Oxford University Press, 2007.

———. *A Treatise of Human Nature*. Oxford: Oxford University Press, 1987.

Inman, Ross. "Gratuitous Evil Unmotivated: A Reply to Kirk R. MacGregor." *Philosophia Christi* 15 (2013): 435–45.

———. *Substance and the Fundamentality of the Familiar: A Neo-Aristotelian Mereology*. New York: Routledge, 2018.

Irenaeus. "Against Heresies." In *Ante-Nicene Fathers*, vol. 1, edited by Alexander Roberts and James Donaldson, 309–567. Peabody, MA: Hendrickson, 1994.

Jacobsen, Douglas, and Rhonda Hustedt Jacobsen. "Postsecular America: A New Context for Higher Education." In *The American University in a Postsecular Age*, edited by Douglas Jacobsen and Rhonda Hustedt Jacobsen, 3–15. Oxford: Oxford University Press, 2008.

James, William. *Pragmatism*. New York: Longmans, Green, 1907.

———. *Pragmatism*. Amherst, NY: Prometheus Books, 1991.

Kane, Robert. *A Contemporary Introduction to Free Will*. Oxford: Oxford University Press, 2005.

Kant, Immanuel. *Critique of Pure Reason*. Translated by Werner S. Pluhar. Indianapolis: Hackett, 1996.

———. *Grounding for the Metaphysics of Morals*. Translated by James W. Ellington. Indianapolis: Hackett, 1993.

———. *What Is Enlightenment?* In *Basic Writings of Kant*, edited by Allen W. Wood, 133–41. New York: Modern Library, 2001.

Kapitan, Tomis. "A Master Argument for Incompatibilism?" In *The Oxford Handbook of Free Will*, edited by Robert Kane, 127–57. Oxford: Oxford University Press, 2002.

Keating, James F. "The Natural Sciences as an *Ancilla Theologiae Nova*: Alister E. McGrath's *A Scientific Theology*." *The Thomist* 69 (2005): 127–52.

Kelly, Stewart. *Truth Considered and Applied: Examining Postmodernism, History, and Christian Faith*. Nashville: B&H, 2011.

Kelly, Stewart, and James K. Dew Jr. *Understanding Postmodernism: A Christian Perspective*. Downers Grove, IL: IVP Academic, 2017.

Kierkegaard, Søren. *Concluding Unscientific Postscript*. Translated by Howard Hong and Edna Hong. Princeton: Princeton University Press, 1992.

Kim, Jaegwon. *Mind in a Physical World: An Essay on the Mind-Body Problem and Mental Causation*. Cambridge, MA: MIT Press, 2001.

Kim, Joseph. *Reformed Epistemology and the Problem of Religious Diversity*. Eugene, OR: Wipf & Stock, 2011.

Koons, Robert C. "Staunch vs. Faint-Hearted Hylomorphism: Toward an Aristotelian Account of Composition." *Res Philosophica* 91, no. 2 (2014): 151–77.

Koons, Robert C., and George Bealer. Introduction to *The Waning of Materialism*, edited by Robert C. Koons and George Bealer, ix–xxxi. Oxford: Oxford University Press, 2010.

Koons, Robert C., and Timothy H. Pickavance. *Metaphysics: The Fundamentals*. Malden, MA: Wiley Blackwell, 2015.

Koukl, Greg. "The New Atheists: Old Arguments, New Attitudes." Apologetics Canada. August 28, 2012. https://www.youtube.com/watch?v=DWBPTuZq2xU.

Krauss, Lawrence M. *A Universe from Nothing: Why There Is Something Rather than Nothing*. New York: Atria, 2012.

Kreeft, Peter. *Making Sense out of Suffering*. Ann Arbor, MI: Servant Books, 1986.

Leftow, Brian. "God and the Problem of Universals." In *Oxford Studies in Metaphysics*, edited by Dean Zimmerman, 2:325–56. Oxford: Clarendon, 2006.

Lehrer, Keith, and Thomas Paxson Jr. "Knowledge: Undefeated Justified True Belief." *Journal of Philosophy* 66, no. 8 (1969): 227–35.

Lemos, Noah. *An Introduction to the Theory of Knowledge*. New York: Cambridge University Press, 2007.

Levering, Matthew. *Proofs of God: Classical Arguments from Tertullian to Barth*. Grand Rapids: Baker Academic, 2016.

Lewis, C. S. *Mere Christianity*. San Francisco: HarperOne, 2001.

———. *Miracles*. New York: Touchstone, 1975.

———. *The Pilgrim's Regress*. Grand Rapids: Eerdmans, 2002.

———. *The Screwtape Letters*. Westwood, NJ: Barbour Books, 1990.

Lewis, David. *On the Plurality of Worlds*. Oxford: Blackwell, 1986.

Linville, Mark D. "The Moral Argument." In *The Blackwell Companion to Natural Theology*, edited by William Lane Craig and J. P. Moreland, 392–448. West Sussex: Wiley-Blackwell, 2009.

Locke, John. *An Essay Concerning Human Understanding*. Oxford: Clarendon, 1975.

Loux, Michael J. "Aristotle's Constituent Ontology." In *Oxford Studies in Metaphysics*, edited by Dean Zimmerman, 2:207–50. Oxford: Clarendon, 2006.

———. *Metaphysics: A Contemporary Introduction*. 3rd ed. New York: Routledge, 2006.

Loux, Michael J., and Thomas M. Crisp. *Metaphysics: A Contemporary Introduction*. 4th ed. New York: Routledge, 2017.

Lowe, E. J. *The Possibility of Metaphysics: Substance, Identity, and Time*. Oxford: Clarendon, 1998.

MacGregor, Kirk R. "The Existence and Irrelevance of Gratuitous Evil." *Philosophia Christi* 14 (2012): 165–82.

Machen, J. Gresham. *What Is Christianity?* Grand Rapids: Eerdmans, 1951.

MacIntyre, Alasdair. *After Virtue*. 3rd ed. Notre Dame, IN: University of Notre Dame Press, 2007.

———. *Whose Justice? Which Rationality?* Notre Dame, IN: University of Notre Dame Press, 1988.

Mackie, J. L. "Evil and Omnipotence." *Mind* 64, no. 254 (1955): 200–212.

Madden, James D. "Giving the Devil His Due: Teleological Arguments after Hume." In *In Defense of Natural Theology: A Post-Humean Assessment*, edited by James F. Sennett and Douglas Groothuis, 150–74. Downers Grove, IL: InterVarsity, 2005.

———. *Mind, Matter, and Nature*. Washington, DC: Catholic University of America Press, 2013.

Mandik, Pete. *This Is Philosophy of Mind*. Malden, MA: Wiley-Blackwell, 2014.

Manley, David. "Properties and Resemblance Classes." *Nous* 36, no. 1 (2002): 75–96.

Maudlin, Tim. "Distilling Metaphysics from Quantum Physics." In *The Oxford Handbook of Metaphysics*, edited by Michael J. Loux and Dean W. Zimmerman, 461–87. Oxford: Oxford University Press, 2003.

McCall, Thomas H. *An Invitation to Analytic Christian Theology*. Downers Grove, IL: IVP Academic, 2015.

McGrath, Alister E. *A Fine-Tuned Universe: The Quest for God in Science and Theology*. Louisville: Westminster John Knox, 2009.

———. *The Open Secret: A New Vision for Natural Theology*. Oxford: Blackwell, 2008.

———. *The Science of God*. Grand Rapids: Eerdmans, 2004.

———. *A Scientific Theology*. Vols. 1–3. Grand Rapids: Eerdmans, 2001–3.

McNaughton, David. *Moral Vision*. Cambridge, MA: Blackwell, 1988.

Meister, Chad. "Evil and the Hiddenness of God." In *God and Evil: The Case for God in a World Filled with Pain*, edited by Chad Meister and James K. Dew Jr., 138–51. Downers Grove, IL: IVP Books, 2013.

———. *Introducing Philosophy of Religion*. New York: Routledge, 2009.

Meister, Chad, and James K. Dew Jr., eds. *God and Evil: The Case for God in a World Filled with Pain*. Downers Grove, IL: IVP Books, 2013.

———, eds. *God and the Problem of Evil: Five Views*. Downers Grove, IL: IVP Academic, 2017.

Merricks, Trenton. "How to Live Forever without Saving Your Soul: Physicalism and Immortality." In *Soul, Body, and Survival: Essays on the Metaphysics of Human Persons*, edited by Kevin Corcoran, 183–200. Ithaca, NY: Cornell University Press, 2001.

Meyer, Stephen C. *Signature in the Cell*. New York: HarperOne, 2009.

Mill, John Stuart. *Utilitarianism*. 2nd ed. Malden, MA: Wiley-Blackwell, 2003.

Miller, Ed. L. *God and Reason*. New York: Macmillan, 1972.

Miller, Kenneth R. *Finding Darwin's God*. New York: Harper Perennial, 1999.

Molina, Luis de. *On Divine Foreknowledge: Part IV of the "Concordia."* Translated by Alfred J. Freddoso. Ithaca, NY: Cornell University Press, 1988.

Moon, Andrew. "Recent Work on Reformed Epistemology." *Philosophy Compass* 11 (2016): 879–91.

Moore, G. E. "Proof of an External World." In *Philosophical Papers*, 127–50. New York: Macmillan, 1959.

Moreland, J. P. "Exemplification and Constituent Realism: A Clarification and Modest Defense." *Axiomathes* 23, no. 2 (2013): 247–59.

———. *Love Your God with All Your Mind*. 2nd ed. Colorado Springs: NavPress, 2012.

———. "Naturalism and the Ontological Status of Properties." In *Naturalism: A Critical Analysis*, edited by William Lane Craig and J. P. Moreland, 67–109. New York: Routledge, 2000.

———. *The Recalcitrant* Imago Dei*: Human Persons and the Failure of Naturalism*. Norwich, UK: SCM, 2009.

———. *Scaling the Secular City: A Defense of Christianity*. Grand Rapids: Baker, 1987.

———. *Universals*. Montreal: McGill-Queen's University Press, 2001.

Moreland, J. P., and William Lane Craig. *Philosophical Foundations for a Christian Worldview*. Downers Grove, IL: InterVarsity, 2003.

———. *Philosophical Foundations for a Christian Worldview*. 2nd ed. Downers Grove, IL: IVP Academic, 2017.

Moreland, J. P., and Garrett DeWeese. "The Premature Report of Foundationalism's Demise." In *Reclaiming the Center*, edited by Millard J. Erickson, Paul Kjoss Helseth, and Justin Taylor, 81–107. Wheaton: Crossway, 2004.

Moreland, J. P., and Timothy Pickavance. "Bare Particulars and Individuation: Reply to Mertz." *Australasian Journal of Philosophy* 81, no. 1 (2003): 1–13.

Moreland, J. P., and Scott Rae. *Body and Soul: Human Nature and the Crisis in Ethics*. Downers Grove, IL: InterVarsity, 2000.

Morris, Thomas V. *Our Idea of God*. Vancouver: Regent College Publishing, 1991.

Moser, Paul. "Cognitive Idolatry and Divine Hiding." In *Divine Hiddenness: New Essays*, edited by Daniel Howard-Snyder and Paul K. Moser, 120–48. Cambridge: Cambridge University Press, 2002.

———. *Evidence for God: Religious Knowledge Reexamined*. New York: Cambridge University Press, 2010.

Murphy, Nancey. *Bodies and Souls, or Spirited Bodies?* New York: Cambridge University Press, 2006.

———. "Nonreductive Physicalism: Philosophical Issues." In *Whatever Happened to the Soul?*, edited by Warren S. Brown, Nancey Murphy, and H. Newton Malony, 127–48. Minneapolis: Fortress, 1998.

Murphy, Nancey, and Warren S. Brown. *Did My Neurons Make Me Do It?* New York: Oxford University Press, 2007.

Nagasawa, Yujin. *Miracles: A Very Short Introduction*. New York: Oxford University Press, 2017.

Nagel, Thomas. *The Last Word*. New York: Oxford University Press, 1997.

———. *Mind and Cosmos: Why the Materialist Neo-Darwinian Conception of Nature Is Almost Certainly False*. New York: Oxford University Press, 2012.

Nash, Ronald. *Faith and Reason*. Grand Rapids: Zondervan, 1988.

Niekerk, Kees van Kooten. "A Critical Realist Perspective on the Dialogue between Theology and Science." In *Rethinking Theology and Science*, edited by Niels Henrik Gregersen and J. Wentzel van Huyssteen, 51–86. Grand Rapids: Eerdmans, 1998.

O'Brien, Dan. *An Introduction to the Theory of Knowledge*. Malden, MA: Polity Press, 2016.

O'Connor, Timothy. "Agent Causation." In *Agents, Causes, and Events: Essays on Indeterminism and Free Will*, edited by Timothy O'Connor, 173–200. Oxford: Oxford University Press, 1995.

———. "Indeterminism and Free Agency: Three Recent Views." *Philosophy and Phenomenological Research* 53 (1993): 499–526.

Paley, William. *Natural Theology: Or Evidence of the Existence and Attributes of the Deity, Collected from the Appearances of Nature*. London: C. Knight, 1845.

Pascal, Blaise. *Pensées*. New York: E. P. Dutton, 1958.

Peacocke, Arthur. *Theology for a Scientific Age*. Oxford: Basil Blackwell, 1990.

Pearcy, Nancy, and Charles B. Thaxton. *The Soul of Science: Christian Faith and Natural Philosophy*. Wheaton: Crossway, 1994.

Pickel, Bryan, and Nicholas Mantegani. "A Quinean Critique of Ostrich Nominalism." *Philosophers' Imprint* 12, no. 6 (2012): 1–21.

Plantinga, Alvin. "Afterword." In *The Analytic Theist: An Alvin Plantinga Reader*, edited by James Sennett, 353–58. Grand Rapids: Eerdmans, 1998.

———. *Does God Have a Nature?* Milwaukee: Marquette University Press, 2007.

———. *God and Other Minds: A Study of the Rational Justification of Belief in God*. Ithaca, NY: Cornell University Press, 1990.

———. *God, Freedom, and Evil*. Grand Rapids: Eerdmans, 1977.

———. *Knowledge and Christian Belief*. Grand Rapids: Eerdmans, 2015.

———. *The Nature of Necessity*. Oxford: Clarendon, 1974.

———. "On Ockham's Way Out." *Faith and Philosophy* 3, no. 3 (1986): 235–69.

———. "Reason and Belief in God." In *Faith and Rationality: Reason and Belief in God*, edited by Alvin Plantinga and Nicholas Wolterstorff, 16–94. Notre Dame, IN: University of Notre Dame Press, 1983.

———. "Self-Profile." In *Alvin Plantinga*, edited by James E. Tomberlin and Peter van Inwagen, 3–97. Dordrecht: D. Reidel, 1985.

———. "Supralapsarianism, or 'O Felix Culpa.'" In *Christian Faith and the Problem of Evil*, edited by Peter van Inwagen, 1–25. Grand Rapids: Eerdmans, 2004.

———. "Two Dozen (or so) Theistic Arguments." In *Alvin Plantinga*, edited by Deane-Peter Baker, 203–27. Cambridge: Cambridge University Press, 2007.

———. *Warrant and Proper Function*. New York: Oxford University Press, 1993.

———. *Warranted Christian Belief*. New York: Oxford University Press, 2000.

———. *Warrant: The Current Debate*. New York: Oxford University Press, 1993.

———. *Where the Conflict Really Lies*. Oxford: Oxford University Press, 2011.

Plato. *Plato: Complete Works*. Edited by John M. Cooper. Indianapolis: Hackett, 1997.

Polkinghorne, John. *Science and Creation: The Search for Understanding*. Philadelphia: Templeton Foundation, 2006.

———. *Science and Theology*. London: SPCK, 1998.

Pritchard, Duncan. *What Is This Thing Called Knowledge?* New York: Routledge, 2006.

———. *What Is This Thing Called Knowledge?* 2nd ed. New York: Routledge, 2010.

Quine, Willard V. O. *From a Logical Point of View*. Cambridge, MA: Harvard University Press, 1953.

Rachels, James. *The Elements of Moral Philosophy*. New York: McGraw-Hill, 1999.

———. *The Elements of Moral Philosophy*. 6th ed., with Stuart Rachels. New York: McGraw-Hill, 2010.

Rae, Scott B. *Moral Choices: An Introduction to Ethics*. Grand Rapids: Zondervan, 2009.

Rand, Ayn. *The Virtue of Selfishness*. 50th anniv. ed. New York: Signet, 2014.

Rea, Michael. "Divine Hiddenness, Divine Silence." In *Philosophy of Religion: An Anthology*, edited by Louis Pojman and Michael Rea, 266–75. 6th ed. Boston: Wadsworth/Cengage, 2012.

———. "Hylomorphism Reconditioned." *Philosophical Perspectives* 25 (2011): 341–58.

Reid, Thomas. "An Inquiry into the Human Mind on the Principles of Common Sense." In *Inquiry and Essays*, edited by Ronald E. Beanblossom and Keith Lehrer, 1–126. Indianapolis: Hackett, 1983.

Rice, Richard. *Suffering and the Search for Meaning: Contemporary Responses to the Problem of Pain*. Downers Grove, IL: InterVarsity, 2014.

Richards, Jay Wesley. "Proud Obstacles and a Reasonable Hope: The Apologetic Value of Intelligent Design." In *Signs of Intelligence*, edited by William A. Dembski and James M. Kushner, 51–59. Grand Rapids: Brazos, 2001.

Robb, David. "Substances." In *The Routledge Companion to Metaphysics*, edited by Robin le Poidevin, Peter Simons, Andrew McGonigal, and Ross P. Cameron, 256–64. New York: Routledge, 2012.

Roberts, Robert C., and W. Jay Woods. *Intellectual Virtues: An Essay in Regulative Epistemology*. New York: Oxford University Press, 2007.

Robinson, Howard. "Idealism and Perception: Why Berkeleyan Idealism Is Not as Counterintuitive as It Seems." In *Idealism and Christian Philosophy*, edited by Steven B. Cowan and James S. Spiegel, 2:71–89. New York: Bloomsbury, 2016.

———. "Modern Hylomorphism and the Reality and Causal Power of Structure: A Skeptical Investigation." *Res Philosophica* 91, no. 2 (2014): 203–14.

Rodriguez-Pereyra, Gonzalo. "Nominalism in Metaphysics." In *The Stanford Encyclopedia of Philosophy*, edited by Edward N. Zalta. Last modified April 1, 2015. http://plato.stanford.edu/entries/nominalism-metaphysics.

Rosenberg, Alex. *The Atheist's Guide to Reality: Enjoying Life without Illusions*. New York: Norton, 2011.

Russell, Bertrand. *Human Knowledge: Its Scope and Limits*. New York: Routledge, 2009.

———. *The Problems of Philosophy*. 1912. Reprint, New York: Oxford University Press, 1997.

———. *Why I Am Not a Christian*. New York: Touchstone, 1957.

Russell, Colin A. "The Conflict of Science and Religion." In *Science and Religion*, edited by Gary B. Ferngren, 3–12. Baltimore: Johns Hopkins University Press, 2002.

Schellenberg, John L. *Divine Hiddenness and Human Reason*. Ithaca, NY: Cornell University Press, 1993.

Scruton, Roger. *The Soul of the World*. Princeton: Princeton University Press, 2014.

Searle, John. *Mind, Language, and Society*. New York: Basic Books, 1998.

———. "Minds, Brains, and Programs." *Behavioral and Brain Sciences* 3 (1980): 417–57.

———. *The Mystery of Consciousness*. New York: New York Review of Books, 1997.

Sellars, Wilfrid. *Science, Perception, and Reality*. London: Routledge & Kegan Paul, 1963.

Sennett, James F., and Douglas Groothuis. "Introduction." In *Defense of Natural Theology: A Post-Humean Assessment*, edited by James F. Sennett and Douglas Groothuis, 9–20. Downers Grove, IL: InterVarsity, 2005.

Sextus Empiricus. *General Principles* [*Outlines of Pyrrhonism*]. In *Hellenistic Philosophy*, translated by Brad Inwood and L. P. Gerson, 302–25. 2nd ed. Indianapolis: Hackett, 1997.

Shafer-Landau, Russ. *Moral Realism: A Defense*. Oxford: Clarendon, 2003.

Simons, Peter. "Particulars in Particular Clothing: Three Trope Theories of Substance." *Philosophy and Phenomenological Research* 54, no. 3 (1994): 553–75.

Simpson, William M. R., Robert C. Koons, and Nicholas J. The. *Neo-Aristotelian Perspectives on Contemporary Science*. New York: Routledge, 2017.

Smart, J. J. C. "Free Will, Praise and Blame." In *Free Will*, edited by Gary Watson, 58–71. 2nd ed. Oxford: Oxford University Press, 2003.

Smith, Barry. "On Substance, Accidents and Universals: In Defense of Constituent Ontology." *Philosophical Papers* 26, no. 1 (1997): 105–27.

Sosa, Ernest. *A Virtue Epistemology: Apt Belief and Reflective Knowledge*. Vol. 1. New York: Oxford University Press, 2009.

Spiegel, James. "Idealism and the Reasonableness of Theistic Belief." In *Idealism and Christian Philosophy*, edited by Steven B. Cowan and James S. Spiegel, 2:11–28. New York: Bloomsbury, 2016.

———. "The Irenaean Soul-Making Theodicy." In *God and Evil: The Case for God in a World Filled with Pain*, edited by Chad Meister and James K. Dew Jr., 80–93. Downers Grove, IL: IVP Books, 2013.

Spykman, Gordon J. *Reformational Theology*. Grand Rapids: Eerdmans, 1992.

Stevenson, C. L. *Ethics and Language*. New Haven: Yale University Press, 1944.

Swinburne, Richard. *The Evolution of the Soul*. New York: Oxford University Press, 2007.

———. *The Existence of God*. Oxford: Oxford University Press, 2004.

———. *Mind, Brain, and Free Will*. Oxford: Oxford University Press, 2013.

Teresa, Mother. *Come Be My Light: The Private Writings of the Saint of Calcutta*. Edited by Brian Kolodiejchuck. New York: Doubleday, 2007.

Tertullian. *Prescription against Heretics*. In *Ante-Nicene Fathers*, edited by Alexander Roberts and James Donaldson, vol. 3. Peabody, MA: Hendrickson, 2004.

Thomas Aquinas. *Summa Theologiae*. In *The Treatise on the Divine Nature*, translated by Brian J. Shanley, OP. Indianapolis: Hackett, 2006.

———. *Summa Theologica*. Translated by the Fathers of the English Dominican Province. Notre Dame, IN: Christian Classics, 1947.

Tiessen, Terrance. *Providence and Prayer: How Does God Work in the World?* Downers Grove, IL: InterVarsity, 2000.

Timmons, Mark. *Moral Theory*. 2nd ed. Lanham, MD: Rowman & Littlefield, 2013.

Timpe, Kevin. *Free Will in Philosophical Theology*. New York: Bloomsbury, 2014.

Toner, Patrick. "Emergent Substance." *Philosophical Studies* 141 (2008): 281–97.

———. "On Substance." *American Catholic Philosophical Quarterly* 84, no. 1 (2010): 25–48.

Turner, Jason. "The Incompatibility of Free Will and Naturalism." *Australasian Journal of Philosophy* 87, no. 4 (2009): 565–87.

van Huyssteen, J. Wentzel. *The Shaping of Rationality*. Grand Rapids: Eerdmans, 1999.

van Inwagen, Peter. "Being, Existence, and Ontological Commitment." In *Metametaphysics: New Essays on the Foundation of Ontology*, edited by David J. Chalmers, David Manley, and Ryan Wasserman, 472–506. Oxford: Oxford University Press, 2009.

———. *An Essay on Free Will*. Oxford: Clarendon, 1983.

———. "Free Will Remains a Mystery." In *The Oxford Handbook of Free Will*, edited by Robert Kane, 158–80. Oxford: Oxford University Press, 2002.

———. "A Materialist Ontology of the Human Person." In *Persons: Human and Divine*, edited by Peter van Inwagen and Dean Zimmerman, 199–215. Oxford: Oxford University Press, 2007.

———. "The Place of Chance in a World Sustained by God." In *Divine and Human Action*, edited by Thomas V. Morris, 211–35. Ithaca, NY: Cornell University Press, 1988.

———. "The Possibility of Resurrection." *International Journal for Philosophy of Religion* 9, no. 2 (1978): 114–21.

van Roojen, Mark. *Metaethics*. New York: Routledge, 2015.

Walls, Jerry L. "Pharaoh's Magicians Foiled Again: Reply to Cowan and Welty." *Philosophia Christi* 17, no. 2 (2015): 411–26.

———. "Why No Classical Theist, Let Alone Orthodox Christian, Should Ever Be a Compatibilist." *Philosophia Christi* 13, no. 1 (2011): 75–104.

Ware, Bruce A. *God's Greater Glory*. Wheaton: Crossway, 2004.

Welty, Greg. "Theistic Conceptual Realism." In *Beyond the Control of God? Six Views on the Problem of God and Abstract Objects*, edited by Paul M. Gould, 81–111. New York: Bloomsbury, 2014.

Wesley, John. "An Address to Clergy." Delivered February 6, 1756. Reprinted in *The Works of John Wesley*, 6:217–31. 3rd ed. Grand Rapids: Baker, 1996.

White, Andrew Dickson. *A History of the Warfare of Science with Theology*. Vol. 1. 2nd ed. New York: Dover Publications, 1896.

Wielenberg, Erick J. "In Defense of Non-natural Non-theistic Moral Realism." *Faith and Philosophy* 26, no. 1 (2009): 23–41.

———. *Robust Ethics: The Metaphysics and Epistemology of Godless Normative Realism*. New York: Oxford University Press, 2014.

Willard, Dallas. *The Divine Conspiracy*. New York: HarperCollins, 1998.

———. "How Concepts Relate the Mind to Its Objects: The 'God's Eye View' Vindicated." *Philosophia Christi* 1, no. 2 (1999): 5–20.

———. "Knowledge and Naturalism." In *Naturalism: A Critical Analysis*, edited by William Lane Craig and J. P. Moreland, 24–48. New York: Routledge, 2000.

———. "The Three-Stage Argument for the Existence of God." In *Contemporary Perspectives on Religious Epistemology*, edited by R. Douglas Geivett and Brendan Sweetman, 212–24. Oxford: Oxford University Press, 1992.

Wisnefske, Ned. *Preparing to Hear the Gospel: A Proposal for Natural Theology*. Lanham, MD: University Press of America, 1998.

Wood, W. Jay. *Epistemology: Becoming Intellectually Virtuous*. Contours of Christian Philosophy. Downers Grove, IL: IVP Academic, 1998.

Yandell, Keith. "God and Propositions." In *Beyond the Control of God? Six Views on the Problem of God and Abstract Objects*, edited by Paul M. Gould, 21–50. New York: Bloomsbury, 2014.

———. "Moral Essentialism." In *God and Morality: Four Views*, edited by R. Keith Loftin, 97–134. Downers Grove, IL: IVP Academic, 2012.

Zagzebski, Linda. *On Epistemology*. Belmont, CA: Wadsworth, 2009.

———. *Virtues of the Mind: An Inquiry into the Nature of Virtue and the Ethical Foundations of Knowledge*. Cambridge: Cambridge University Press, 1996.

Zimmerman, Dean. "The Compatibility of Materialism and Survival: The 'Falling Elevator' Model." *Faith and Philosophy* 16, no. 2 (April 1999): 194–213.

———. "From Property Dualism to Substance Dualism." *Proceedings of the Aristotelian Society*. Supplementary vol. 84 (2010): 119–50.

# Scripture Index

# Author Index

# Subject Index